Language and Reality

Language and Reality

An Introduction to the Philosophy of Language

SECOND EDITION

Michael Devitt and Kim Sterelny

A Bradford Book
The MIT Press
Cambridge, Massachusetts

First MIT Press edition, 1999
© 1999 Michael Devitt and Kim Sterelny

This title is published outside the United States by
Blackwell Publishers Ltd, Oxford, UK.

Library of Congress Cataloging-in-Publication Data
Devitt, Michael, 1938–
   Language and reality: an introduction to the philosophy of
language / Michael Devitt and Kim Sterelny. — 2nd ed.
       p.   cm.
   "A Bradford book."
   Includes bibliographical references and index.
   ISBN 10: 0-262-04173-1 (hc : alk. paper)—0-262-54099-1 (pb : alk. paper)
   ISBN 13: 978-0-262-04173-7 (hc : alk. paper)—978-0-262-54099-5 (pb : alk. paper)
   1. Language and languages—Philosophy.   I. Sterelny, Kim.   II. Title.
P106.D458   1999
401—dc21

10 9 8 7 6 5 4 3 2   98-47178
                                                                   CIP

Contents

** indicates chapters and sections which are difficult and probably best ignored in an initial approach.

Preface to the Second Edition

The first edition of this book is now more than a decade old, and several years ago it became obvious even to the fond parental eye that it was fast approaching its use-by date. We had to commit to a massive rewrite or let the book die. For in the last ten years much has happened in philosophy of language and related areas of philosophy of mind; not just in its exotic and technical fringes of no concern to a book of this scope, but on more basic issues as well. These developments, both in our own work (particularly, Devitt 1996, *Coming to Our Senses*, and Sterelny 1990, *The Representational Theory of Mind*) and in that of others, would require a thorough rewrite of the first edition. The generally friendly reception of the first edition encouraged us to take that option, though we must confess that our first effort did not elicit unanimous delight. (A reviewer for *Mind*, incensed by our choice and treatment of topics, urged that students be advised *not* to consult it!)

Despite that rewriting, the most important ideas of the first edition have survived into the second. Most important of all, our philosophical approach remains realist and naturalist and that approach permeates the work. (Indeed, if either of us ever goes soft on these themes, it will be time to call the vet.) We are realist not just in thinking that the world of common sense — of sticks and stones; cats and trees — and of the mature sciences exists objectively, independently of us and our thoughts. We are realists as well in thinking that, methodologically, we should *start from realism*. It is, of course, *conceivable* that realism is false. But its epistemic security is vastly greater than any doctrine in philosophy of language or philosophy of mind. In our view, if a theory of meaning conflicts with realism, so much the worse for that theory. We are naturalists in two respects. Epistemologically, we are naturalists in rejecting the idea that philosophical knowledge (except, perhaps, that about logic) is *a priori*. To the contrary, we think that most, possibly all, philosophical theory is broadly empirical in character; such theories are continuous with those of science. Admittedly, philosophical theories are difficult to test experimentally, but that is because philosophical work tends to be on the most conceptually and theoretically obscure aspects of empirical theories, not because philosophical claims are inherently *a priori*. Metaphysically, we are naturalists in that we are physicalists: physical objects and physical process are all that exists. More specifically, this book continues to defend causal theories of reference and assume functionalist views of the mind. Much has happened on these issues in the last decade, and in many ways our views on the nature of mind and meaning have changed and developed. But the views set out in this book remain broadly similar to those of the first edition.

The basic structure and orientation of the first edition also survives into this one. After a brief introduction, Part II presents a truth-referential theory of meaning; Part III is focused on the relations between language and the mind; Part IV on the relation between theories of language and realism; and Part V on the role of philosophy of language within philosophy as a whole. As before, we hope this edition can be used both for a fairly elementary introduction to philosophy of language and for a somewhat more advanced and demanding course. So we have retained the use of asterisks (**) to mark off more difficult material that is probably best ignored except by more committed or more advanced students. But we have used it a bit more sparingly to avoid irritating intrusions into the text. The second edition is also at least as opinionated as the first. We said in the preface to the first edition that we saw no point in trying to produce a neutral inventory of views in the philosophy of language and on this at least the last ten years have given us no reason to change our mind.

So the overall organization of the second edition is the same as that of the first. Within the chapters, though, there has been much change and, for those familiar with the first edition, it may be worth our briefly indicating some of the most important of these. The material on causal theories of reference and their competitors has changed substantially. These changes include: a much fuller discussion of hybrids between causal and description theories (5.4; 5.5); a discussion of direct reference (4.4); a discussion of recent developments in description theories (3.5); a response to Gricean objections to the "ambiguity thesis" about definite and indefinite descriptions (5.8). It includes as well a discussion of other externalist approaches to meaning: indicator and teleological theories. Since these are normally seen as theories about the meaning of thoughts we discuss them in that connection (7.7).

In this edition (drawing on Devitt 1996), we explore more fully issues to do with a speaker's linguistic and conceptual competence. We are even more critical of the idea that this competence involves a sort of "Cartesian" access to meanings yielding propositional knowledge about them (8.6); rather, the competence is a skill, a piece of knowledge-how not knowledge-that (8.9). More important, we argue that the Cartesian idea plays an important, though mostly tacit, role in various crucial matters: in the view that an *informative* identity statement like 'Mark Twain is Samuel Clemens' must have names that differ in meaning (2.5); in the debate between description and causal theories of reference; in the view that we have *a priori* knowledge (5.6); in the "conceptual-analysis" view of philosophy (14.4); and perhaps even in the argument of Kripke's semantic skeptic (9.5).

Our views on the role of Chomsky's theory of grammar in a theory of mind and meaning have been completely reworked. Since that theory is in a state of permanent revolution, we have abandoned any attempt to track different versions. We have contented ourselves with providing some glimpses of the riches of the theory and relating these glimpses to the problem of explaining the meaning-relevant structure of sentences (ch. 6). Our discussion of the relation of theories of syntax to theories of the mind (ch. 8) has also undergone major overhaul, though our Chomskyan friends will still think that we have stubbornly clung to the errors of the first edition. For, we continue to argue, first, that developing a theory of the structure of sentences is a distinct project from that of explaining a speaker's ability to produce and understand those sentences; and, second, that a good theory of sentence structure is not thereby a good theory of linguistic competence. Our stand on this basic question, together with our general view that competence in using language need not involve propositional knowledge, frames and informs our treatment of the standard debates in philosophy of language on Chomsky's theory of language: those about the innateness of grammar; the psychological reality of a grammar; and the modularity of our linguistic competence.

We still endorse the "language-of-thought hypothesis" about the nature of mental representations (though Sterelny does so less confidently than he once did), but our view of the relationship between these representations and natural language has changed (7.3). Chapter 9, too, has been revised in major ways. The role and nature of a theory of meaning has been the focus of much discussion over the last decade. Deflationary theories of truth and reference, narrow theories of thought, and skeptical arguments about meaning have all found defenders. We are not amongst them, but the second edition reflects these issues.

In sum, and especially in Parts II and III, virtually every section of the first edition has been reworked; there is much new material, and some material of the first edition has been consigned to the infamous dustbin of history.

The first edition was a fully joint work. That is not true of this edition. Devitt produced the first draft of virtually all the new text. Sterelny's role has been largely to filter and revise Devitt's productions.

We struggled mightily once again with the "suggested readings" but this time we had some assistance from Amresh Kumar and Blaine Nelson, for which we are truly thankful. And we apologize again for errors and omissions.

Over the years we have received many helpful comments about the first edition from students and colleagues. We hope that we have taken appropriate notice of these. We are also indebted to the following for comments on parts of the second edition: Fiona Cowie, Peter Godfrey-Smith, Georges Rey, and Matthew Seaman.

Michael Devitt
Kim Sterelny
June, 1998

Preface to the First Edition

This book is an introduction to the philosophy of language. It is intended primarily, but not solely, as a textbook.

Our justification for writing a textbook is the usual one: dissatisfaction with the ones already available. We find some of these too discursive; some too long and encyclopedic; some too difficult; some too wrong. Most important of all, none have the particular purpose and orientation of this book.

Introducing the philosophy of language is undoubtedly difficult. It is a field in which a hundred flowers, and many weeds, bloom. There is amazingly little agreement, even about basics. It is often not clear what problems a theory is trying to solve. It is often not clear whether theories are in competition and, if not, how they relate to each other. As a result, attempts at achieving the neutrality usually regarded as desirable in a textbook tend to founder; the student is presented with a bewildering smorgasbord.

We make no pretense of neutrality. A definite theoretical perspective pervades this book. The work of others is organized and placed relative to this perspective. We hope that this mode of presentation will help even those who reject the perspective. Aside from that, we think the perspective is an important one that has been decidedly under-represented in the philosophy of language.

Because of the role of this theoretical perspective we hope that this book will be of interest not only to students embarking on the philosophy of language but also to advanced ones and to professionals.

We have written on the philosophy of language before. Naturally enough, many of our earlier thoughts reappear in this book. However, writing it forced us to break new ground. We have developed our causal theory of natural kind terms. We have made our first serious attempt at theories of reference for artifactual kind terms like 'pencil' and sociolegal kind terms like 'bachelor'. We have worked hard to place the work of the transformational grammarians within our perspective.

We think that the book should be suitable for two slightly different courses. One course would be a beginning- or intermediate-level course aimed at students with possibly no more than a passing interest in the philosophy of language. Aside from students majoring in philosophy, we have in mind: literature students who have come across, for example, structuralist thought; linguistics students interested in semantics; anthropology students interested in linguistic relativity; students in cognitive science interested in the problems of intentionality and linguistic competence.

The other course for which the book should be suitable would be a more traditional intermediate-level course for students with a committed interest in the philosophy of language. Passages in the book that are suitable for this course, but probably not for the other, appear between asterisks (**). These passages are difficult and are probably best ignored in an initial approach. ('**' before a chapter or section heading indicates that the whole chapter or section is in that category.)

We have followed the following convention with quotation marks. To name an expression we either put it between single quotation marks or put it on display. To quote a passage we either put it between double quotation marks or put it on display. We also use double quotation marks for "shudder" or "scare" quotes. All quotation marks within quotation marks are single.

**Our perspective has four aspects. First, and most important, we are committed to *naturalism*. (a) We give the theory of language no special status: it is an empirical and conjectural theory like any other. (b) Our approach is physicalistic: we see people as nothing but complex parts of the physical world.

Naturalism has been particularly under-represented in thinking about language. It leads directly to what may be the most controversial parts of the book: our deflationary view of the significance of the study of language. In this century, theories of language have led to surprising and mysterious views of reality. Many thinkers in several fields have been led to forms of neo-Kantian relativism: Benjamin Lee Whorf in anthropology; Thomas Kuhn and Paul Feyerabend in the philosophy of science; Hilary Putnam in philosophy; the structuralists in just about everything. Michael Dummett's verificationist theory of language leads him into a different, but equally mysterious, anti-realism. "Ordinary language" and "conceptual analysis" philosophers identify the very subject of philosophy with the study of language. For Wittgenstein, philosophy was grammatical therapy. We stand opposed to all these pretensions for the study of language.

Second, our philosophy of mind is *functionalist*. It draws on such philosophers as Jerry Fodor, Daniel Dennett, William Lycan, and Stephen Stich. We like to see our book as having a place in the exciting, and somewhat chaotic, interdisciplinary field that has become known as *cognitive science*.

Third, we help ourselves to the insights of *transformational generative grammar*, while remaining skeptical of its claims about psychological reality.

Finally, we embrace *causal theories of reference* of the sort introduced by Saul Kripke, Keith Donnellan, and Hilary Putnam. We are guided by Hartry Field in placing reference within the theory of language: reference is needed to explain truth.

Causal theories of reference have, of course, enjoyed quite a bit of attention and popularity in the philosophy of language. However, we do not think that the strength of the case for them has been fully appreciated, largely because they have not been placed firmly in a naturalistic setting.

Quine's influence on our thinking is apparent throughout, not least in our naturalism. However, the book contains no systematic discussion of his views on language. In particular, we do not discuss his arguments for the indeterminacy of translation (though we think that the skeptical view of truth considered in chapter 9 is derived from Quine). Our excuse is that the arguments are just too difficult to be discussed helpfully in a book of this sort. Certainly, they are too difficult for us to discuss helpfully.**

We think it prudent to offer a few preemptive apologies. First, though we are confident that the program we have endorsed *can* be carried out, certainly we have not demonstrated this. Still more certainly, we have not demonstrated it by doing it. These are early days for naturalistic philosophy in general and naturalistic philosophy of language in particular. So, though it is not surprising that its successes are fragmentary and partial, nonetheless those successes *are* fragmentary and partial. Second, the demands of clarity and our temperaments lead us to robust statements of our own views and their divergences from the views of other. Our responses to relativism and anti-realism are particularly vigorous. We do not mean to offend and hope we haven't. Finally, in the nature of things, reading guides cannot be comprehensive. We did our best to survey the literature in preparing the "suggested readings", but doubtless we have made many errors. All we can say to the disgruntled author of an omitted piece is that the omission may not have been deliberate.

The book was truly a joint production. In the beginning, there was the idea for a course along roughly the lines of the book. The idea was Sterelny's but it was for a course by Devitt. Reluctantly, Devitt adopted the idea. He gave the course in 1983, with the assistance of Sterelny. He wrote extensive notes. He was so pleased by this performance that he proposed a joint book to Sterelny. Sterelny wrote the first draft in 1984. Devitt used this for a repeat of the course in 1984 and began to write the second draft. He continued writing in 1985, and some version of the second draft was used for another repeat of the course. The final version of the book is the result of many amendments to the second draft by both of us, often, it seemed, far too many amendments.

The name proved difficult. We wanted *Language, Mind and Everything*, for we enjoy mocking the pretensions of recent philosophy of language. However, we gave in to the advice that jokey titles don't wear well and may not play in Peoria. We settled for something more sober.

We are grateful to the following for written comments on early versions of parts of the book: John Bigelow, Fiona Cowie, Stephen Gaukroger, Peter Godfrey-Smith, Richard Hall, William Lycan, Ruth Milliken, Connell O'Conoll, Philip Pettit, Stephen Stich, and David Stove. We are indebted to Elizabeth Gross for advice on structuralist literature. Finally we thank the following for their comments on the penultimate version: David Armstrong, David Braddon-Mitchell, John Bigelow, Fiona Cowie, and Peter Godfrey-Smith.

Michael Devitt
Kim Sterelny
June, 1986

Part I

Introduction

1

Introduction

1.1 The Philosophy of Language

The philosophy of language raises issues both important and difficult.

The importance of language to human life is obvious. All human societies are language using, as are all their more or less normal members.
Language acquisition is one of the few cognitive skills that is, near enough,
both common and peculiar to humans. This skill gives the human species
an enormous advantage over others: language is a quick and painless way
of passing on the discoveries of one generation to the next. Some theorists
see language as *the* most central characteristic of the human species.

The obvious importance of language makes its study worthwhile, but
does not prepare one for the ascendancy that this study has achieved in
philosophy. Over the last century or so the philosophy of language has
become the pivotal area of philosophy, particularly within the English-
speaking tradition. Opinions about language have been thought to settle
traditional philosophical problems in epistemology, metaphysics, and ethics. The very nature of philosophy itself has been linked by many to the
study of language. In our view, much of this goes too far: philosophy of
language has become too big for its boots. We shall return to this often
(Parts IV and V).

The philosophy of language is certainly difficult. In part this is because
of our closeness to language: we find it hard to get a proper perspective on
it. In any case, there is a vigorous, wide-ranging, and bewildering debate

on foundational and conceptual issues in the philosophy of language. Many competing theories are on offer, yet it is often hard to see what these are theories *of*. What problems are they trying to solve? What counts as *evidence* for or against a theory? Are different theories really concerned with the same problems, so that they are really in competition? If not – and it often seems not – how do they relate to one another? Finally, the status of philosophical theories of language is obscure and controversial, as we shall begin to see in section 1.3.

You may wonder why language is studied *in philosophy* at all. Why is the study not left to linguistics which is, after all, "the science of language"? The three main branches of linguistics are phonology, concerned with *sounds*; syntax, concerned with *grammatical structure*; and semantics, concerned with *meaning*. It is in semantics, or "the theory of meaning", that the theoretical and conceptual chaos mentioned above is most striking. There are also some similar problems in syntax. Philosophy is typically concerned with the most intractable and conceptually difficult parts of various disciplines. So it is not surprising that it is deeply concerned with semantics and has some concern with syntax. In contrast, it is not concerned with phonology at all.

Finally, a word of warning. What follows is not an auctioneer's catalogue of the theories and ideas in this controversial subject. It cannot therefore be either neutral or comprehensive. Our approach reflects our ideas of what is central and peripheral; of the main issues and of the blind and side alleys. The approach is not idiosyncratic, but it is not shared by all, or even most, philosophers.

1.2   What Is the Problem?

What is the main problem in the study of language? What are the phenomena that pose the problem? To get an appropriate distance from the phenomena, it helps to imagine that we are Martians visiting Earth for the first time. What linguistic phenomena strike us? We observe humans producing sounds and inscriptions: they are talking and writing to each other. We see that these activities play extraordinarily important roles in human life. We wonder what properties the sounds and inscriptions have that enable them to play these roles. We decide to call these properties "meanings". The problem then is to describe and explain these meanings: to say what they are and to say what makes it the case that something has one. In brief, the problem is to give a theory of meaning or a semantics.

This problem, in turn, gives rise to a second, psychological, problem. What features of the human mind make it possible for humans to produce, and react, to these sounds appropriately? How do we manage to use language? So, as we shall see, the problem of explaining meaning is linked to the problem of explaining linguistic competence and understanding.

We have identified the semantic problem by referring to the "important roles" of language in human life. What roles are these? We think that the folk saying, "language expresses thought", captures the central role: a human language is *a system for expressing or communicating thought*. Many thoughts are informational, being about the social or physical environment. But thoughts need not be informational, or purely so: language is used to greet, question, command, joke, offend, abuse, intimidate, and so on.

To say more about the importance of language we have to consider the roles of the thoughts that language expresses. There are two roles that are obviously of interest to us. First, thoughts cause people to do things: a person who believes that it is raining is likely to take her umbrella. So, knowing what others are thinking tells us *what they are likely to do*. We depend intimately on others, so this knowledge is important to us. Language is the main way we gain that knowledge. Second, many thoughts carry information or misinformation about the world. So, knowing what a person thinks often *tells us about the world*: if the person who believes that it is raining is reliable about such matters we can learn from her about the weather without looking outside. Much of our knowledge of the world comes from the linguistic expression of beliefs. This is why language gives us the great advantage over other species noted at the beginning of the chapter: it enables each of us to benefit richly from others' experience.

In sum, the central role of language is to express thoughts. Derivatively, it has at least these two roles: explaining behavior and informing us about the world. Meanings are the properties that enable it to play these roles.

We do not pretend that these brief remarks are sufficient to identify the semantic problem. Implicitly, the problem concerns the "natural" languages of humans; for example, English or Swahili. Such languages are not our only communication systems; think of flag signals or "body-language", for example. And many animals clearly have communication systems. Doubtless all of these systems can be used to explain behavior and learn about the world. So, what is special about our natural languages?

Consider also "animal language" experiments. Alex, an African grey parrot trained by Irene Pepperberg, produces intelligible and contextually appropriate English-like sounds. If one shows Alex a red plastic object and asks "what color?" Alex says "red". If one shows Alex a wooden peg, in response to a parallel question about composition, Alex says "wood". Dolphins can respond to sometimes quite complex and novel verbal commands. Most famously of all, a number of primate species have learned to interact with their trainers through gesture or the use of arbitrary plastic tokens. All these "utterances" could be used to explain behavior and inform us about reality. Yet controversy rages as to whether these animals are really speaking a human language. What might the animals be doing, or failing to do, that would settle the matter? What is it to use "red" as an English word rather than, say, just as a means of extracting reward from a trainer?

We think that progess with these questions, hence with identifying our problem, is chiefly to be made by looking more closely at the relation between human language and thought. We shall do so later (7.4). Meanwhile, we make some progress with identifying our problem by setting out some of the salient features that make human natural languages and their meanings so special:

a.   Stimulus independent

In most circumstances, as full a description as you like of a person's physical environment does not enable you to predict her next utterance. The contrast with animal communication systems, for example, is notable.

Briefly, animal communication systems seem to be of two sorts. First, birds (and apparently nonhuman primates) have a fixed and fairly small repertoire of distinct signals, each of which has a set function: flight call, alarm call, and the like. A particular environment elicits the appropriate response. Human language does not consist in such a small fixed repertoire of predictable responses. Second, consider bees. A bee returning from a distant food source dances a message. The positioning of the dance and its pattern indicate the direction and distance of the food source. This remarkably efficient system of communication differs from those of birds in having an unlimited number of signals: the length and the pattern are capable of indefinitely many variations. Nevertheless, the bee's system is not flexible in the way human language is. Each response is environmentally fixed: if you know where the bee has been, and if you know the coding system, you can predict the pattern of the dance. In contrast, if a person comes from a food source – a good restaurant, for example – you cannot predict her words. Her food description – indeed, whether she talks about food at all – is stimulus independent.

b.   Abstract

A sentence may abstract from many details of a situation, focusing on just one. Thus, 'Orson weighs 130 kg' tells you nothing about Orson other than his mass. Symbols in many other systems cannot be quite so abstract; a photograph or sketch of Orson will tell of many of his properties.

Even the bee's dance cannot be silent on the distance of the food source while revealing its direction.

c.   Arbitrary

In general, linguistic symbols have no intrinsic or necessary connection with their referents. The inscription, 'Ronald Reagan', happens to refer to a certain president of the USA, yet it is in an important sense arbitrary that it does so. That inscription could have been used to refer to Bob Hope; and Reagan could have been called 'Hopalong Cassidy'. This arbitrariness is nicely illustrated by the English logician, Charles Dodgson, better known as Lewis Carroll:

> " ... – and that shows that there are three hundred and sixty-four days when you might get un-birthday presents – "
> "Certainly," said Alice.
> "And only *one* for birthday presents you know. There's glory for you!"
> "I don't know what you mean by 'glory,'" Alice said.
> Humpty Dumpty smiled contemptuously. "Of course you don't – till I tell you. I meant 'there's a nice knock-down argument for you!'"
> "But 'glory' doesn't mean 'a nice knock-down argument,' " Alice objected.
> "When *I* use a word," Humpty Dumpty said, in rather a scornful tone, "it means just what I choose it to mean neither more nor less."
> "The question is," said Alice, "whether you *can* make words mean so many different things."
> "The question is," said Humpty Dumpty, "which is to be master – that's all." (Carroll 1962: 247)

What Humpty Dumpty is emphasizing is the arbitrariness of language: we can call anything anything. (This is not to say that Alice does not have a point too. This could be brought out using the distinction between speaker meaning and conventional meaning: section 7.4.)

d.   Learned

Many animal communications systems are complex mixes of the learned and the innate. The same is probably true of human language. Noam Chomksy has famously argued that the most important features of human syntax are innate (8.10). Yet it is uncontroversial that the large vocabulary of every human language must be learned. So the amount of learning involved in mastering any human language greatly exceeds the learning involved in nonhuman systems of communication.

e. Medium independent

Linguistic communication can be effected in speech, writing, braille, gesture, and so on. There seems to be no limit to the media we could use for, say, English. The birds and the bees are more limited.

f. Systematic

The matching of each signal with its meaning is not something that we learn signal by signal. We learn the elements of signals – words – together with a recipe for making complete signals – sentences – out of the elements. Thus your knowledge of a few words and the constructions of English enables you to understand 'Andropov liquidated the Hungarians' and 'The Hungarians liquidated Andropov' even though you may never have come across these sentences before. (The bee's system has *some* systematicity but note how simple its generating recipe is.)

g. Power

One very special thing about language is its power and versatility. It can serve the many purposes of communication. It enables us to deal with the past and the future, the present and the absent. We talk of an enormous range of topics: of "tables, people, molecules, light rays, retinas, air waves, prime numbers, infinite classes, joy and sorrow, good and evil" (Quine 1966: 215). Contrast this with the bee's monomania.

It is clear that language gets its power from many of the other special features we have mentioned.

We can use the arbitrary symbol 'Mandela' to convey information, or misinformation, about a politician who is thousands of miles away. We can use the arbitrary symbol 'Thales' to convey information, or misinformation, about a Greek philosopher who has been dead for two millennia. Linguistic symbols have properties, "meanings", that make these feats possible. These meanings enable the symbols to play extraordinarily important roles in human life, particularly roles in explaining and predicting behavior and informing us about the world. Symbols have their meanings in the context of language: a uniquely powerful communication system that is stimulus- and medium-independent, abstract, arbitrary, learned, and productive. We think philosophy of language is confronted with two related main problems. One is to describe and explain the properties of symbols in virtue of which they play the central role they do in our lives; we call this the problem of explaining meaning. The related problem is to describe and explain linguistic competence; the features of people's minds in virtue of which they can use and understand symbols and the symbol system we call language.

In Part II, our focus will be on meaning. We follow custom in identifying meanings with the properties that make linguistic symbols important to us, but that should not engender the idea that there is general agreement about the nature of the problems. The ordinary use of the term 'meaning' is loose, and theoretical uses are varied. Partly as a result of this, there is obscurity and controversy over the very problems in the philosophy of language. This is the first sign of the difficulties mentioned in the opening section. In Part II we will, so far as possible, set aside issues to do with the mind's relation to language. However, it will prove impossible to ignore the issue of competence. In Part III, the mind's relation to language is at centre stage.

1.3   What Is a Theory of Language?

There is obscurity and controversy not only over the problems for which we need theories of language but also over the status of the theories themselves. This issue of status is highly abstract: it requires a theory of theories of language, a "meta-theory". It would be nice to ignore the meta-theory and get on with the theory, but that is a luxury we cannot afford. We think that many mistakes in the theory of language arise from a mistaken meta-theory. Further, we think that these mistakes are often facilitated by a failure to be explicit about the meta-theory: once the implicit meta-theory is exposed, it can be seen to be implausible and unsupportable. So we shall start by laying our cards on the table, with little in the way of a defense. We shall offer some sort of defense in Part V. We shall return to meta-theoretical issues often in our criticism of other views.

Our approach to the problem of language is *naturalistic* in two respects. The first respect is *epistemological* (concerned with our way of knowing). A theory of linguistic phenomena has just the same status as a theory of any other phenomena: it is empirical and conjectural; it is known *a posteriori* ("justified by experience") not *a priori* ("justified independently of experience"). We are confronted with a mysterious and complex world and have developed theories to explain and render tractable these complexities: theories in physics, biology, the social sciences and the like. The theory of language is just another such theory; another part of our total theory of nature.

One can be misled into treating the theory of language differently by the fact that, at bottom, much of what it has to say at present is "common sense". People divide linguistic phenomena into sentences and words; they divide words into nouns, verbs, etc. They think that expressions are meaningful and have meanings. They think that words refer to parts of the world. They think that sentences express thoughts; that some are true and some false, but none are both; that some are questions and others commands; and so on. These gems of common sense, taken over by linguistics, may seem to have some special status. It is easy to succumb to the illusion that whereas science, especially its abstract and speculative branches like cosmology and particle physics, is conjectural, empirical, and fallible, common sense is not. So, it is thought to be a *theory* that the earth and moon are linked by gravitational force, but a *fact* that sentences have meanings. This illusion is engendered by the familiarity of common sense.

Common sense is best seen as a mix of *folk theories* or, if talk of theories seems too pretentious here, *folk opinions*. These, like scientific theories, help people better understand and explain the phenomena that confront them. So the above gems are best seen as articulations of folk linguistics' response to features of language of the kind discussed in the last section. Folk theories differ from scientific ones in being immature: they are less precise, systematic, and explicit; they lack a methodology for development. More seriously, they differ in being believed uncritically.

A glance at the past shows that folk theory has no special warrant. Early European folk geography, folk meteorology, and folk medicine have been comprehensively rejected. We no longer think that the Earth is flat, nor that the winds are under the direction of supernatural agents. We no longer explain health in terms of the humors of the blood. Nevertheless, where a folk theory is working well, just as where a scientific theory is working well, it is *unlikely* to be wholly wrong. So, it is reasonable to suppose, for instance, that folk psychology, with its long history of fairly successful use (we have *quite* a good understanding of one another), has a lot of truth in it. Similarly, perhaps, folk linguistics. Nonetheless, even the best folk theories stand in need of supplementation and revision.

The second respect in which our approach is naturalistic is *metaphysical* (concerned with what there is and with what it is like). How do facts about language relate to facts about people and to other facts about the world? The answer, in our view, is given by *physicalism*.

We think that people are best seen as part of the natural world. They are not special except in detail and complexity. (i) They are part of animate nature; part of the biological world. (ii) The biological differs from the inanimate only in complexity: no vital essence distinguishes the living from the nonliving. To be living is only to have a special, if complex, chemistry.

Physicalism is intrinsically plausible. It has excellent scientific support from evolutionary theory, biology, and biochemistry. These sciences underscore the biochemical and physiological continuities between humans and the rest of nature. There are, we believe, no good arguments *against* this perspective.

Our theory of language must, therefore, be physicalistic. Any linguistic facts there are must be, ultimately, physical. Semantic notions like meaning, truth, and reference can be used only if they can be explained in nonlinguistic terms; they are not primitive. Biologists were not satisfied to leave the notion of gene as primitive: they wanted to understand the mechanism by which inheritable characteristics are encoded in a cell. Their search led to the discovery of the structure of DNA. Similarly, we seek a deeper explanation of semantic notions. We might, for example, hope to explain them in psychological terms; then, hope to explain the psychological in neuro-anatomical and biochemical terms; then, explain those in physical and chemical terms.

Some think this hope is a vain one. In particular, the famous Harvard philosopher, W. V. Quine, doubts that we can explain a robust notion of meaning physicalistically. This leads him into semantic "eliminativism": the familiar notions of folk semantics have no place in a developed theory of humans and their languages. We are not eliminativist, but we accept his moral: if notions like meaning and truth cannot be explained in nonsemantic, naturalistic terms, we should do without them in our theory of language.

We return to the defense of naturalism in Part V.

**1.4   The Menu

(Passages and references between asterisks (**) are difficult and could well be ignored in an initial approach.)

We finish this chapter with a preview.

Part II is centered on the problem of meaning, on explaining those properties of linguistic symbols that enable them to play their distinctive role in our lives. In chapter 2 we propose a "representationalist" view of meaning. On this view, the core of a sentence's meaning is its truth condition; that is, the property of a sentence which, together with the world, make it true or false. We suggest that the truth condition of a sentence depends on the referential properties of its elements together with its syntactic structure. So, in chapters 3 to 5 we discuss reference and in chapter 6 we discuss structure.

Description theories of reference may work for some terms but we argue that they fail for proper names and natural kind terms. We initially favored pure-causal theories for these but think that we may have to settle for hybrid descriptive-causal theories. We explore other possible theories of reference for a variety of terms. In discussing structure, we draw on "transformational generative grammar".

In Part III, our focus changes from symbols and their meaning to an intimately related but nonetheless distinct arena, the mind.

In chapter 7 we suggest that the relation between thought and language is somewhat symbiotic. On the one hand, we argue for the "language-of-thought" hypothesis, the view that thought is typically language-like in character. Indeed, there is probably a close relationship between the language a person thinks in and her public language. On the other hand, the development of that public language and the system of conventions it embodies must depend on the achievement of cognitive pioneers in having thoughts not then expressible in their public language.

Chapter 8 is devoted to the vexed and difficult problem of linguistic competence. We develop, to some extent, a view of competence, but the basic thrust of the chapter is critical. We reject certain intellectualist theories favored by linguists and philosophers. We are dubious of the idea that grammatical rules play a significant role in language processing. We look critically at the view that some grammatical rules or principles are innate.

Chapter 9 briefly defends our sort of representationalism against rivals. One rival is the view that the meaning of an expression should be explained in terms of its "functional role" in the mind. Another is a "two-factor" theory that explains meaning partly in terms of functional role and partly in terms of representational properties. Finally, we consider the skeptical argument against representational meaning that Saul Kripke has found in the work of Wittgenstein.

In Chapter 10 we take a decidely critical view of linguistic relativism: the view that, (i) your general picture of the world is influenced and constrained by the language you speak; and that (ii) languages differ enough to produce incommensurable world views. We concede a little to this view but, in general, find it exciting only when false.

Part IV considers the relation between theories of language and the metaphysical doctrine of realism. Commonsense realism is the view that the ordinary furniture of our environment – cats, trees, stones, etc. – exist independently of us and our thoughts on the matter. Scientific realism takes a similar view of the objects of science. Many theorists have inferred anti-realist views from their favored theories of language. In some usually ill-specified sense, the world is said to depend for its existence or nature on us.

We consider several of these theorists, taking a mostly critical view of their theories of language, and a very critical view of the metaphysical views they derive from them. However, our main point is that a realist metaphysics has more secure epistemic foundations than *any* theory of language. So, the appropriate strategy is to construct theories of language from that perspective, not to construct metaphysical views from the perspective of one's favorite theory of language. If a theory of language contradicts our best overall picture of the world, so much the worse for the theory.

In chapter 11 we consider the verificationism of the logical positivists and Michael Dummett. In chapter 12 we consider "constructivism", the view that, one way or another, different groups make different worlds by imposing their views. We start with Benjamin Lee Whorf, who thinks that we construct realities with languages. We go on to the radical philosophers of science, who think that we do the job with scientific theories. Finally, we consider the former realist, Hilary Putnam. Chapter 13 is devoted to structuralism (or semiotics, as it is frequently known). This movement, centered in France, is an extreme form of constructivism.

The book ends, in Part V, with a discussion of philosophy itself. Considerations about language have dominated much of twentieth-century Anglo-American philosophy. In chapter 14 we recount that dominance, tentatively diagnose it, and reject it. Our stance is, as always, naturalistic. In chapter 15 we reject another challenge to naturalistic philosophy: rational psychology. That approach takes our ordinary views of people and their language – folk psychology and folk linguistics – to be outside science; they are thought to supply knowledge of a different sort altogether.**

Suggested Reading

1.1

On the centrality of language to the human species, and for its role in making us the creatures that we are, see: Bickerton 1991, *Language and Species*; Corballis 1991, *The Lopsided Ape*; Donald 1991, *Origins of the Modern Mind*; Lieberman 1991, *Uniquely Human*; Pinker 1994, *The Language Instinct*; Noble and Davidson 1996, *Human Evolution, Language and Mind*.

1.2

For a good survey of the animal communication literature from the standpoint of someone who thinks it shows a rich cognitive life, see: Griffin 1992, *Animal Minds*, especially chs. 8–11. For somewhat more measured views, see: Byrne 1995, *The Thinking Ape*, ch. 11; Roitblat and Meyer 1995, *Comparative Approaches to Cognitive Science*, Part V; and especially Hauser 1996, *The Evolution of Communication*. For a defense of the "language-likeness" of ape language, see: Savage-Rumbaugh 1986, *Ape Language*; Savage-Rumbaugh and Lewin 1994, *Kanzi* (1994). For a very skeptical view of the significance of these projects, see Pinker 1994, ch. 11.

For more on the nature of the semantic problem, see Devitt 1996, *Coming to Our Senses*, ch. 2.

1.3

In a series of works Patricia and Paul Churchland defend the possibility of massive revision of folk theory. They argue for eliminativism about the mind which, because of the links between mind and language to be explored later (Part III), is closely related to semantic eliminativism. See Paul Churchland 1993, "Evaluating Our Self Conception", for a nice summary of their position; also his excellent introductory text, *Matter and Consciousness* (1988). Part IV of Lycan 1990, *Mind and Cognition* has some classic papers on eliminativism.

Many philosophers argue that eliminativism is *incoherent*. See Hannan 1993, "Don't Stop Believing" for a sympathetic presentation of the argument. For criticisms see Sterelny 1993, "Refuting Eliminativism on the Cheap?", and Devitt 1996: 249–52.

Explanation of one set of facts in terms of another often involves quite complex relations between the two. See Fodor 1975, *The Language of Thought*, introduction. Boyd, Gasper, and Trout 1991, *The Philosophy of Science*, section III, is a good selection of papers on this issue.

Quine's classic assault on meaning and its relatives is "Two Dogmas of Empiricism", in *From a Logical Point of View* (1961). **This eliminativism was continued in *Word and Object* (1960) with his famous, but difficult, argument for the indeterminacy of translation: ch. 2.** When reading Quine it should be kept in mind that a behavioristic conception of language constrains his views. See Gibson 1982, *The Philosophy of W. V. O. Quine* for more on Quine's behaviorism. The most readable account of his position is in *Philosophy of Logic* (1970), ch. 1. A sympathetic and interesting examination of Quine's views is to be found in Romanos 1983, *Quine and Analytic Philosophy*. Antony 1987, "Naturalized Epistemology and the Study of Language", is a nice critical piece.

Just as linguistics should be naturalized so also should epistemology. The quotation from Quine in section 1.2 is from the opening paragraph of a marvellous essay arguing for a naturalized epistemology, "The Scope and Language of Science" in *The Ways of Paradox* (1966). Kornblith 1994, *Naturalizing Epistemology* is a very helpful collection.

1.4

There are a number of anthologies on philosophy of language, to which we shall often refer in "Suggested Reading". Two very helpful general ones are Martinich 1996, *The Philosophy of Language*, and Ludlow 1997, *Readings in the Philosophy of Language*.

Schwartz 1977, *Naming, Necessity, and Natural Kinds*, is a good collection focusing on the problems of reference. Davis 1991, *Pragmatics,* focuses on the pragmatic aspects of language. Searle 1971, *The Philosophy of Language*, attends to this too but its main focus is on the implications of contemporary linguistics.

Block 1981, *Readings in the Philosophy of Psychology, Volume 2*, is an excellent collection on issues raised in Part III. It is organized into parts, each of which has a helpful introduction. Stich and Warfield 1994, *Mental Representation*, is also helpful on Part III issues. It has a good selection of papers offering naturalistic theories of meaning. Lycan 1990 contains a number of papers that bear on Part III issues. So also do parts IV and V of Rosenthal 1991, *The Nature of Mind*.

Geirsson and Losonsky 1996, *Readings in Language and Mind*, brings out the close ties between theories of language and mind. It is an interdisciplinary collection, reflecting the rise of cognitive science.

Part II

Meaning

2

Truth and Reference

2.1 Meaning and Truth

Perhaps the favorite notion in folk linguistics is *meaning*. It is almost impossible to resist the temptation to start the explanation of language – such features as those listed in section 1.2 – by talking of the meaningfulness of language. We did not resist. We used 'meaning' as a blanket term to cover the special properties of linguistic symbols that enable them to play their striking roles in people's lives (1.2). Of course, this talk of meaning does not really explain anything; it is little more than a convenient label for what needs explaining. So, what we need is a *theory of meaning*.

However, first, a word of warning about the term 'meaning' (and cognates). Its popularity in linguistics is, in one respect, unfortunate. In its ordinary use the term is vague, perhaps even ambiguous. Certainly it has many applications that have nothing to do with language. Consider the following, for example: 'Aphrodite means to molest that Trojan'; 'Food must have no meaning for vegetarians'; 'Rich police mean corruption'; 'He means well, but he's not too bright'. So, we should be careful about relying on intuitions that we would express using 'mean': they may not concern our problem. (See section 2.7 for more terminological warnings.)

We start our theory of meaning, our semantics, with an hypothesis: that the core of a linguistic symbol's meaning lies in the fact that the symbol *represents* something; for example, the core of the meaning of 'Reagan' lies in the fact that it represents a well-known former president of the United States. This representational hypothesis may seem too obvious to mention; even the word "symbol" suggests it. Indeed, it is probably the oldest idea of all about meaning.

Let us apply the hypothesis to sentences, the basic unit of communication. What does a sentence represent? Think of an indicative sentence, the sort that is typically used in making an assertion (as opposed to asking a question, issuing a command, etc.). The sentence represents the situation that would *make it true*; it represents its *truth condition*. We cash this out as follows: the sentence is true if a certain situation in the world obtains and not true if the situation does not. So, the hypothesis is that this property of a sentence is the core of its meaning. Thus it is central to the meaning of 'Bulldogs are ugly' that it is true if and only if bulldogs really are ugly. The hypothesis is in the spirit of the popular philosophical slogan, "The meaning of a sentence is its truth condition".

This hypothesis is supported by folk semantics. Though, 'Max, he's a wimp' and 'Max is a weakling' have a marked difference in conversational flavor, in an important sense they "have the same meaning". Further, anyone would judge those two sentences more alike in meaning than either is to 'Max, he's an animal'. Why? Because the first two sentences have the same truth condition, whereas the third has a different one. This point can be illustrated in other ways. The main thing to preserve in translating one sentence into another is its truth condition. Moreover, two sentences that differ in truth value would not be found synonymous. If circumstances could make 'Many arrows didn't hit the target' true, while 'The target wasn't hit by many arrows' was false, the sentences cannot have the same meaning. (Test: do they have the same meaning?)

It is undoubtedly plausible to think that representing is the core of meaning in general, and hence that having a certain truth condition is the core of a sentence's meaning in particular. Nevertheless this "representationalism" *is* an hypothesis and it is not without controversy. Thus some people think that the core of a sentence's meaning is its property of being *verified* or *warrantedly asserted* if and only if a certain situation obtains. We shall consider this controversy briefly later (9.3, 11.4). Meanwhile, we shall simply adopt the hypothesis.

So, on this hypothesis, our main semantic task becomes that of explaining the representational properties of linguistic symbols. Applied to an indicative sentence, our task becomes that of explaining its property of being true if and only if a certain situation obtains. In virtue of what does a sentence have this property? In brief, the task is to give "a theory of truth conditions".

2.2   Explaining Truth Conditions

A theory of truth conditions must be *compositional*: the truth condition of a sentence must be a function of its elements. Only thus can we explain one of the important properties that make language special as a communication system: its systematicity (1.2). We do not learn sentences individually: we learn elements plus the procedures for constructing sentences out of elements. If you understand 'Semiotics is fashionable' and you understand 'punk', then you understand 'Punk is fashionable'. If you understand 'deconstruction', you understand *any* sentence containing it provided that you understand the structure of the sentence and the other words in it. An indefinitely large number of those sentences you have never come across; a likely example is, 'Deconstruction is as pretentious as it is worthless'.

So, a sentence has its truth condition, hence meaning, partly in virtue of its elements and partly in virtue of the way it is constructed from those elements. Its elements are *words* and its way of construction is its *syntactic structure*. We shall illustrate.

1. If we hold structure constant and vary the words, truth conditions vary. The following sentences share the simplest English sentence structure, "one-place" predication, but are made true by very different situations in the world:

Reagan is wrinkled
Thatcher is tough
Andropov is dead.

2. Less obviously, if we hold the words constant and vary structure, again truth conditions vary. This is illustrated most simply by changing word order in a "two-place" predication:

The USA nuked the USSR
The USSR nuked the USA.

However there is a lot more to syntactic structure than word order. This is vividly demonstrated by structurally ambiguous sentences: sentences that have two (or more) distinct truth conditions even though the meaning of each word is held constant. Some examples:

Cheap wine and cider encourage annoying drunks
Modern realist movies are made by insulting crooks and producers

Dad is cooking
Eighth Army push bottles up Germans

(the last is a famous Second World War headline).

What is it about a word that affects the truth conditions of sentences containing it? What part of its meaning plays this role? The obvious answer is: its *referent*. And this is what our representationalism directs us to. Just as the representational property of a sentence is its property of having a certain truth condition, the representational property of a word is having a certain referent.

In sum, the truth condition of a sentence depends on its syntactic structure and the referents of its words.

How does the dependence go? Consider a simple sentence, 'Reagan is wrinkled'. It has the property of being true if and only if Reagan is wrinkled; the property we are supposing to be at the core of its meaning. This property depends on the sentence having the simple structure of a one-place predication. It also depends on its containing 'Reagan', referring to Reagan, and 'wrinkled', referring to wrinkled things. Let us distinguish these two sorts of reference by calling the first one, which concerns a proper name, "designation", and the second one, which concerns a predicate, "application". Then we can be more precise about the dependence as follows. The sentence has its truth condition – is true if and only if Reagan is wrinkled – in virtue of the fact that it is true if and only if

i. there is some object that 'Reagan' designates and
ii. 'wrinkled' applies to that object.

The truth condition of any other one-place predication can be similarly explained; thus, 'Thatcher is tough' depends similarly on 'Thatcher' and 'tough'.

We saw truth conditions as the core of sentence meanings (2.1). Our strategy now is to explain truth conditions partly in terms of the referential relations of words – for example, designation and application – and partly in terms of the syntactic structure of sentences – for example, one-place predication – which determine how truth conditions depend on reference. Given reference and structure, truth conditions are determined. So we will need a theory of reference and a theory of structure. In virtue of what does 'Reagan' designate Reagan and 'wrinkled' apply to wrinkled things? In virtue of what does 'Reagan is wrinkled' have the structure of a one-place predication? We have moved from sentence meaning to truth condition; and from truth condition to reference and structure.

The approach to meaning that we have been outlining in this section and the last was started in the nineteenth century by the logician Gottlob

Frege (1952). At the same time, another very influential approach to meaning began as a result of the work of the linguist Ferdinand de Saussure (1916 [1966]): "structuralism". This approach differs most strikingly from Frege's in rejecting reference. We shall consider structuralism in chapter 13.

We shall begin our discussion of theories of reference in the next chapter. Before that, we must consider some questions. What does the presence of non-indicative sentences in language show about our truth-conditional approach? How can we explain the structure of the many sentences that are much more complicated than the simple predication used as our example? Is there more to word meaning than referential role? We shall take these in turn.

**2.3   Non-indicatives

So far, our attention has been on indicative sentences, the sort that are typically used to make assertions. But there are also non-indicative sentences, typically serving other communicative purposes. This fact has been illuminated by the work of J. L. Austin (1962a) and J. R. Searle (1969). They drew attention to such other "speech acts" as questions, requests, and promises. The notion of truth condition does not apply comfortably to these other uses of language involving non-indicatives.

Non-indicatives raise two questions about our truth-conditional approach to sentence meaning. Can that approach work for non-indicatives at all? Even if it can, does the truth condition of a sentence, or some condition analogous to truth condition, *exhaust* the sentence's meaning? In applying our representationalism to sentences, we were careful to claim only that a sentence's truth condition was *the core* of its meaning. Answering the second question may show that this care was appropriate: that there is more to a sentence's meaning than its property of representing a certain situation.

In answer to the first question, two ways have been suggested in which a theory of meaning for non-indicatives might be *modeled* on a theory of truth conditions.

First, it has been thought that while non-indicatives do not have truth conditions, at least some have analogous conditions. The view is that a theory of the *compliance conditions* of imperatives, sentences that are typically used to make requests, would capture the core of their meanings. J. J. C. Smart is one who has argued this (1984). Many of our earlier remarks about indicatives can then be transposed into remarks about imperatives. Thus, the view is another application of our hypothesis that the core of a linguistic symbol's meaning lies in the fact that the symbol represents something: an imperative represents the situation in which it would be complied with. People would say that two imperatives have the same meaning, in an important sense, if they have the same compliance condition; i.e. if the same situation in the world has to be brought about to comply with them. Compliance conditions must be explained in terms of the syntactic structures of imperatives and the referential properties of words that fill those structures.

According to this suggestion, then, the core of a sentence's meaning is not, strictly, its property of representing some situation that would make it *true*, but rather its property of representing some situation that would make it *true, complied with, or whatever*. Its meaning is largely its truth condition *or other analogous* condition. And these conditions are all to be explained in terms of structure and reference along the lines we have sketched for indicatives.

Consider the bearing of this suggestion on our second question. The meaning of a sentence consists not only in its representing some situation that would make it true, complied with, or whatever, but also in its asserting that the situation obtains, requesting that the situation be brought about, or whatever. Being an assertion or a request is part of the meaning of the sentence. There is indeed more to a sentence's meaning than its property of representing a certain situation.

Second, it has been thought that, despite appearances, non-indicatives can be true or false. This view has been defended in a number of different ways. One is through the technique of paraphrase. For example, some Scandinavian logicians have suggested that questions can be paraphrased as demands for knowledge (Aqvist 1965). Thus, 'Did Oswald kill Kennedy?' means 'Let it be the case that either I know that Oswald killed Kennedy or I know that Oswald did not kill Kennedy'. In turn, demands can be given a truth-conditional analysis in so-called "deontic" logic. The idea is to identify a demand with a statement about what *ought* to be the case, that is to say, with an indicative.

A less direct approach to questions has been proposed by the American logicians Belnap and Steel. Their proposal is to explain each question in terms of its possible answers. Thus the meaning of the question, 'Who is the ugliest president of the USA?' would be given by the disjunction of its possible answers. Since these answers are indicatives, the semantics of questions is given by atoms which are true or false. Derivatively, then, a *question* is true if it has a true answer, false otherwise ('When did you stop drinking your bathwater?', for most of us).

It seems that this second suggestion would allow us to retain the idea that truth conditions, alone, exhaust sentence meaning. However, the suggestion does this by linking a sentence to the truth condition of a paraphrase that is often intuitively very distant from the original sentence.

We find Smart's approach more natural and think that something like it must play some role in the theory of meaning. However, we have no need to adjudicate between the two suggestions. They are, after all, not incompatible: there are many different non-indicatives. So long as one of the suggestions is along the right lines, our interest in developing a theory of truth conditions is not parochial.

Some theorists have gone far down the path of the first suggestion, urging that a theory of meaning must find room for a theory of the *pragmatics* of language use, a theory of the deployment of symbols in a social context.

J. L. Austin (1962) distinguishes between the *locutionary* and *illocutionary* aspects of an utterance. The locutionary force of an utterence is, intuitively, its representational content: the condition that makes it true if an indicative, complied with if an imperative, and so on. The illocutionary force is what is done in making the utterance. It captures the "attitude" taken to the content in the utterance. The structure of an utterance may indicate its illocutionary force – as an imperative indicates a request – but it does not fully determine it. Thus, a given indicative sentence could be an assertion, an assumption, or a postulation. It could even be a threat: "Unless there is a million dollars in the briefcase, the bomb will explode."

One of the aims of pragmatics is to give a general account of illocutionary force; of the distinctions between requests, commands, and beggings; of the distinction between threats and warnings; and so on. These distinctions are, likely enough, in the beliefs and goals of the speaker. Someone who threatens believes that the content of the threat is undesired by its recipient. Similarly, with an assertion but not an hypothesis, the speaker intends the audience to see the utterence as an expression of his beliefs. We shall return to pragmatics briefly in Part III, when our focus is on the mind's relation to language (7.4, 7.5, 8.9).

We have already accepted that some of the distinctions attended to in pragmatics clearly have a place in the theory of meaning. They are the ones captured in structure; for example, that between assertions and questions. Perhaps all the pragmatic distinctions have a place in a theory of meaning, but this need not be the case. The theory of meaning is concerned with the properties of symbols that enable them to play their special roles in people's lives, roles that we have roughly indicated. We can expect that some properties of symbols, though important enough for some purposes, will not be essential enough to these special roles to warrant a place in the theory of meaning. A trivial example would be the length of a symbol. A non-trivial example might be the distinction in illocutionary force between an assertion and a threat.

The rest of our discussion of the theory of meaning will mostly ignore the possibility that the meaning of a sentence includes a force as well as a representational property. And we will let the property of representing a truth condition stand in for representing any analogous condition that might be appropriate.**

2.4   Explaining Structure

In section 2.2 we illustrated how truth conditions can be explained in terms of reference and structure. However, the example 'Reagan is wrinkled' has such a simple structure that it could give a grossly misleading impression of the difficulties of our task. In particular, many sentences contain words that are quite unlike 'Reagan' and 'wrinkled' and yet which play crucial roles in determining truth conditions. Consider the following passage:

> " . . . And I haven't sent the two Messengers, either. They're both gone to the town. Just look along the road, and tell me if you can see either of them."
> "I see nobody on the road," said Alice.
> "I only wish I had such eyes," the King remarked in a fretful tone. "To be able to see Nobody! And at that distance too! Why, it's as much as I can do to see real people, by this light!"
> . . .
> "Who did you pass on the road?" the King went on, holding out his hand to the Messenger for some hay.
> "Nobody," said the Messenger.
> "Quite right," said the King: "this young lady saw him too. So of course Nobody walks slower than you."
> "I do my best," the Messenger said in a sullen tone. "I'm sure nobody walks much faster than I do!"
> "He can't do that," said the King, "or else he'd have been here first . . . "
> (Carroll 1962: 258–61)

'Nobody' is not a name nor any other kind of definite singular term (=, roughly, a term that purports to refer to just one object), it is a "quantifier". Its important effect on truth conditions cannot be captured by treating it, as the King does, as if it had a referent.

Many other examples make the same point. The following one is beloved by writers of logic books:

Every man loves some woman.

This sentence is ambiguous between every man loving some woman or other, and some woman being universally loved by men. There is no parallel ambiguity in the following sentence:

Max loves Alphonse.

The moral is that the ambiguity of the first sentence cannot be understood by treating 'every man' and 'some woman' as if they were names. They are also quantifiers.

Our language contains many quantifiers, including 'all', 'each', 'some', 'many', 'most', 'few', 'a few', 'at least one'.

Since the work of Frege, and especially since Alfred Tarski's pioneering paper in 1931, "The Concept of Truth in Formalized Languages" (in Tarski 1956), generations of logicians have been beavering away, attempting to construct compositional theories of truth conditions for a range of different types of sentences, including those with quantifiers. Some have attempted to give truth conditions for sentences like 'It's possible to be an honest politician'. These are *modal* sentences, employing the concepts of necessity or possibility. Some have tried to handle tensed sentences. Much of this work is complex, difficult, and technical. All of it depends to some extent on modern logic. We shall, therefore, spare you an exposition of these results.

Despite the many advances that have been made in laying bare the structure of natural language sentences, and thus in showing how their truth conditions depend on reference, the task is far from finished. We shall note just two ways in which it is seriously incomplete.

**First, many apparently successful explanations make use of the notion of "possible worlds". Saul Kripke (1959) was an early and influential deployer of this notion to explain modal sentences. Necessity was seen as truth in all possible worlds; possibility, as truth in some possible world. Subsequently, the notion has been used for other kinds of sentences. For example, it has been used for subjunctive conditionals like 'If today had not been pension day, Granny would have been sober'. (This sort of conditional is often called a "counterfactual" because it implies the falsity of the indicative form of its antecedent; in this case, implying that it *is* pension day.) It has also been used on epistemic ascriptions like 'Thatcher believes that God is an Englishwoman'. The objection to all these explanations is that they leave us with a notion in our semantic theory that badly needs explaining: the notion of possible worlds.

Many possible-worlds semanticists seem surprisingly unconcerned by this problem. Some acknowledge it, but shuffle their feet in response. Some others offer reductions: possible worlds are really sets of sentences, or whatever. We do not find any of these reductions satisfactory. For one thing, the reductions are often to entities no more acceptable than possible worlds themselves: nonphysical objects of various kinds. Other suggestions look circular, from our point of view at least. One cannot *both* invoke possible worlds to explain the semantic properties of sentences *and* explain a possible world as a set of semantically interpreted sentences.

Finally, the various attempts to "explain away" possible worlds suffer from a variety of technical problems.

David Lewis confronts the problem of possible worlds squarely (1973, 1985). He scorns any shame-faced attempt to identify these worlds with entities usually found more acceptable. He thinks that they are perfectly respectable entities as they stand. He is committed to the genuine existence of a countless infinity of parallel universes among which ours is picked out as special only in being the one that is actual-for-us. This is some elephant to swallow without blinking. We shall return to it in section 2.6.**

Second, these theories of quantified sentences, modal sentences, and the like, typically do not, in the first instance, apply to the sentences of natural languages. They apply rather to formulae in the formal languages of logic. These languages have been specially invented to represent what seem to be the underlying structures or "logical forms" of the sentences of natural languages. They are, therefore, simpler than natural ones. They are also much better behaved than natural ones: they are explicit rather than elliptical; they are unambiguous; they bar monsters like 'This sentence is false'; and so on. So, the theories of formal languages must somehow be brought to bear on their true targets by linking the logical formulae to the sentences that are their natural language counterparts. For instance, the quantified formulae,

$$(x)(\text{Man } x \rightarrow (Ey)(\text{Woman } y \ \& \ \text{Loves } xy))$$

(read: For any x, if x is a man then there is a y such that y is a woman and x loves y) and

$$(Ey)(\text{Woman } y \ \& \ (x)(\text{Man } x \rightarrow \text{Loves } xy))$$

(read: There is a y such that y is a woman and, for any x, if x is a man then x loves y) are mapped onto the earlier

Every man loves some woman,

each capturing one of its meanings.

('x' and 'y' in the above formulae function like cross-referential, or "anaphoric", pronouns. Logicians call such symbols "variables". The variables are said to be "bound" by their respective quantifiers. So 'x' is bound by the "universal" quantifier '(x)', reading "for any x", and 'y' is bound by the "existential" quantifier '(Ey)', reading "there is a y". The difference between the two formulae is described as a difference in the "scope" of the quantifiers: in the first, the existential quantifier is inside the scope of the "universal" quantifier; in the second, the reverse is the case.)

This further task of relating all natural language sentences to logical formulae is necessary if those sentences are to be made amenable to truth-theoretic semantics. The task is very difficult. The great hope for solving it lies with the movement in linguistics started by Noam Chomsky in the 1950s, "transformational generative grammar". The generative approach has made great advances in understanding the syntactic structures of natural languages, and in time we can reasonably expect it to link the logicians' formulae to natural language sentences. We shall consider these matters in chapter 6.

In sum, it is certainly true that a vast amount of work remains to be done to explain the bearing of syntactic structure on truth conditions.

2.5   Are Referential Roles Enough?

According to our representational hypothesis, a word's property of referring to something is the core of its meaning. Is there more to its meaning than this referential role? Are the meanings of 'Thatcher' and 'snow' the simple "coarse-grained" properties of referring to Thatcher and snow, respectively, or are they more "fine-grained"? 'Thatcher' and 'The Baroness of Grantham' refer to the same individual and hence are importantly alike in meaning, but perhaps they do not have the same meaning. Perhaps having the same reference is necessary but not sufficient for identity of meaning.

The discussion of non-indicatives has already raised the possibility that there may be more to a sentence's meaning than its property of representing some situation; perhaps its meaning includes its "force", its property of being an assertion, a request, or whatever (2.3). Set that aside. The question we are considering about word meaning raises the possibility again. For, if there is more to a word's meaning than its property of representing something, so too must there be more to the meaning of a sentence that contains the word. We remarked that our approach is in the *spirit* of the slogan, "The meaning of a sentence is its truth condition" (2.1), but how close are we to the *letter* of the slogan?

We shall start with a simple case, proper names. Have we told the full story of a name's meaning when we specify its bearer? That seemed to be the view of Mill:

> proper names are not connotative: they denote the individuals who are called by them; but they do not indicate or imply any attributes as belonging to those individuals. (1961: 20)

We shall call the view that the meaning of a name is exhausted by its role of designating its bearer, the "Millian View" (though it is not obvious that Mill himself subscribed to it). The view is plausible and simple. Nonetheless, until recently, it has been almost unanimously rejected. Why? What has driven us out of the Millian paradise?

Identity statements

On a Millian view, it is easy to explain the difference in meaning between the following:

> Mark Twain is an author
> Ernest Hemingway is an author.

The meaning of a name is its role of designating a certain object. 'Mark Twain' and 'Ernest Hemingway' designate different objects and so differ in meaning. But now consider:

> Mark Twain is an author
> Samuel Clemens is an author

'Mark Twain' and 'Samuel Clemens' designate the same person. So the Millian must say that these two sentences have the same meaning.

Any plausibility this may have seems to evaporate when we consider identity statements; for example:

> (1) Mark Twain is Mark Twain
> (2) Mark Twain is Samuel Clemens.

Intuitively, (1) and (2) differ strikingly in meaning. Suppose that they really do differ. Then 'Mark Twain' and 'Samuel Clemens' must differ in meaning because the only difference between the statements is in those names. Then the meaning of each name cannot be simply its role of designating a certain object because each of them designates the same object. So the Millian view is wrong. (The traditional example compares 'Hesperus is Hesperus' with 'Hesperus is Phosphorus'. The ancient Greeks used 'Hesperus' for what they took to be a star rising in the evening and 'Phosphorus' for one rising in the morning. In fact these "two stars" are the planet Venus.)

This argument depends, of course, on the claim that the two identity statements *do* differ in meaning. The claim could do with more than intuitive support. Traditionally, philosophers have attempted to give this further support in various ways. But these attempts are dubious, as we shall briefly indicate.

Some have claimed that the two statements differ in meaning because (1) is necessary while (2) is only contingent. But Kripke has argued (1980) – we think plausibly – that both statements are necessary. Some have claimed that (1) is "analytic" (truth dependent only on meaning) while (2) is "synthetic" (truth dependent partly on the world). But Quine has influenced many to reject the analytic–synthetic distinction (1960, 1961). And we think that, insofar as the notion can be made good, both statements are analytic (5.6). Some have claimed that (1) is known *a priori* while (2) is known empirically. But a satisfactory account of *a priori* knowledge has yet to be produced. Finally, the received view is that the two statements differ in meaning because (1) is uninformative, a mere instance of "the law of identity" – for any x, x is x – whereas (2) is informative, an interesting discovery. But why suppose that a difference in informativeness – an *epistemic* difference – reflects a difference in meanings – a *semantic* difference?

We think that this supposition is based on two underlying assumptions:

If (1) and (2) meant the same then the competent speaker would (tacitly) know that they meant the same.
If she knew this then (1) and (2) would be equally informative to her.

Since (1) and (2) are not equally informative, it follows that they do not mean the same. Our problem is with the first of these assumptions. It is an application of the following quite general assumption about linguistic competence: for a speaker to be able to use an expression with a certain meaning is for her to (tacitly) *know that* it has that meaning. Linguistic competence is a mental state of the speaker. The general assumption stems from the idea that the speaker, simply in virtue of having this mental state, is in a position to discover the facts about it. These facts include facts about the meanings of expressions with which the speaker is competent. So, simply in virtue of her competence, the speaker has some sort of "privileged access" to facts about those meanings. To get knowledge of the meanings she does not have to carry out the sort of empirical investigation of the world that knowledge usually requires, she can simply "look inwards". Since this line of thinking is in the tradition of René Descartes, according to whom the contents of a person's mind were in some way "transparent" to her, we shall call this general assumption about competence "the Cartesian assumption". There is no doubt that the Cartesian assumption is appealing; indeed, it is almost universally believed in the philosophy of language. However, we are dubious of it for reasons that will start emerging soon (4.1). We think that competence may well be simply a skill or ability that does not require any knowledge, even tacit knowledge, *about* meanings.

How then *are* we to support the intuition that (1) and (2) have different meanings? We should go back to the account of the semantic problem

(1.2). Meanings are the properties of linguistic symbols that enable them to play their important roles in human lives. One of these roles is the explanation and prediction of behavior. Suppose we are interested in predicting the behavior of Alice. Might it make a difference to us whether she would be prepared to assert (2) as well as (1)? It clearly might. Thus, suppose that Alice wants to meet the famous author known as Mark Twain. She is aware that she has a nearby neighbor known as Samuel Clemens. If she is prepared to assert (2), then we predict that she will head off to introduce herself to her neighbor. If not, not. So the difference between (2) and (1) makes a behavioral difference of just the sort that meanings are supposed to explain. So the difference is a difference of meaning. In order to explain behavior, names must have meanings finer-grained than the property of referring to the author.

Existence statements

Consider next the following statements:

James Bond does not exist
Reagan exists.

These singular existence statements pose a further problem for the Millian view of names. How could a negative existence statement like the first one be meaningful? It would not be meaningful if it had nonsense syllables where a term should be. Yet, since it is *true*, there is nothing for 'James Bond' to designate, and hence, on the Millian view, that name should be just nonsense syllables. The view leads to the paradoxical conclusion that if a negative existence statement is true then it is meaningless. The positive statements pose a problem too. They become tautologous: if they are meaningful then they are true, for their contained name must have a bearer to be meaningful. Once again we see that the meaning of a name must involve something other than its referent.

Empty names

A closely related problem is posed by "empty" names. An empty name is one without a referent; 'James Bond' is an example. Empty names occur in many perfectly meaningful statements (other than existence ones); for example:

James Bond is handsome
James Bond is disgustingly successful.

How could such a statement be meaningful on a view that can give no meaning to a name that does not designate?

Experience suggests that many will be tempted to reply that while "'James Bond' may not designate a flesh and blood man it does designate something: an idea, perhaps, or a concept". Now whatever the merits of this response – and we think they are few – it is beside the present point. Think back to the simple example that introduced our talk of reference (2.2): 'Reagan is wrinkled'. This sentence is made true by a wrinkled Reagan, which is a situation in the external world not in the world of ideas. And the referential relation which we are using to help explain this truth condition, and which we called 'designation', is a relation between 'Reagan' and Reagan, a flesh and blood part of that external world not an idea in someone's mind. Whatever relation there may be between 'Reagan' and a Reagan-idea is not, in this sense, designation. For notice that the idea of James Bond is not handsome; people and horses are handsome; ideas are not. On the Millian view, designation exhausts a name's meaning. And the problem for that view is that 'James Bond' does not designate anything.

In saying this, we are not claiming that you *could not* designate an idea if you wanted to. Of course you could, and we just did with 'Reagan-idea'. We could even designate the idea of James Bond:

The idea of James Bond is disgustingly successful: it made Fleming millions.

The point is simply that, on our usage, neither 'Reagan' nor 'James Bond' *does* designate an idea.

The relationship between words and ideas may be important in a theory of meaning. But that is to move away from a Millian view. Moreover, a consideration of the word/idea relationship certainly should not be at the expense of a focus on designation, on the relationship between language and the world. Our task is to explain the special role of language in our lives. A cursory glance at our earlier description of this role (1.2) shows how much it involves the world of bread, wine, shelter, other people, etc. An explanation of meaning that ignores this world in favor of ideas is very implausible. Note, for example, that the earlier existence statements are not concerned with the existence of ideas but with that of people. *An explanation of meaning must somehow relate language to the external world.* (We return to this when discussing the structuralists in chapter 13.)

There is a second response employing the idea of possible worlds that we introduced in section 2.4. 'James Bond' does not designate anyone in this world, but it does in some other possible worlds. James Bond exists in those worlds and claims made about him, like ours above, may be true in virtue of the way things are in those worlds. We return to the idea of possible worlds, and explain our deep skepticism about them, in section 2.6.

Opacity

From the sentences

Falwell persecutes Bob Dylan
Bob Dylan is Robert Zimmerman

we may infer

Falwell persecutes Robert Zimmerman.

In true sentences like the first one we can substitute for any singular term a codesignational term and be sure of preserving truth; the rule of "substitutivity of identity" applies; the sentences are "extensional" or "transparent". In contrast, from the sentences

Falwell believes Bob Dylan destroyed the moral fiber of America
Bob Dylan is Robert Zimmerman

we may not always infer

Falwell believes Robert Zimmerman destroyed the moral fiber of America.

Falwell may be unaware that Robert Zimmerman is none other than the dreaded Bob Dylan, with the result that the latter sentence is false. The rule of substitutivity may not apply to names in contexts like this. The sentences are then "non-extensional" ("intensional", spelled, notice, with an 's') or "opaque".

Opaque contexts are troublesome and intriguing. Attempts to deal with them have built a small industry within the philosophy of language. They are too hard for more than a passing mention in this book. They get such a mention here because they pose another problem for the Millian view of names. If all there were to the meaning of 'Bob Dylan' was its role of designating Dylan, then we could *always* substitute for it the codesignational name 'Robert Zimmerman' without change of meaning. Yet we have just seen that this substitution into an opaque context does change meaning, for it may change a true sentence into a false one. Once again, there must be something other than reference to the meaning of a name.

Our discussion in this section has all been about names. Names seem more connotation-free than most words. So it is not surprising that the meaning of words other than names also goes beyond reference.

Consider cases of identities only. First, take two statements involving another sort of singular term, definite descriptions. (A definite description is usually formed in English by placing the definite article, 'the', in front of a general term. In contrast, an indefinite description has an indefinite article, 'a' or 'an', before a general term. A general term is one that usually admits a plural ending and can apply to each severally of any number of objects; e.g. 'cat'.)

> The morning star is the morning star
> The morning star is the evening star.

What we said of identity statements involving names applies equally here. The difference between being prepared to assert the second sentence and being merely prepared to assert the first is behaviorally significant. The definite descriptions 'the morning star' and 'the evening star' cannot have the same meaning even though they have the same referent, the planet Venus. Their meanings are finer-grained than their referential role.

Next, take two statements involving general terms:

> Cordates are cordates
> Cordates are renates.

These statements are both true and yet intuitively they differ in meaning; we want to say that "'cordate' means *creature with a heart*" whereas "'renate' means *creature with a kidney*". This inclination is supported by the behavioral significance of the difference between the two statements. So, the meanings of the general terms 'cordate' and 'renate' are different and hence not to be identified with their referential roles.

2.6   Enter Senses

Faced with the phenomena described above, semanticists have devised three strategies. The first is to hold to the view that referential roles exhaust meaning by attempting to explain away the phenomena. This is the strategy of "direct-reference" philosophers in handling names, at least. They argue that, despite the phenomena, there really is no more to the meaning of a name than its property of referring to its bearer: they refuse to leave the Millian paradise. We shall discuss it later (4.4).

The second strategy abandons the paradise: theory is enriched by accepting that there is indeed more to the meaning of a word than its referential role. This was the strategy of Frege and of many who have followed him. The usual idea is to supplement reference (sometimes called "extension") with "sense" (sometimes called "intension"): each word has a sense and, normally, a referent. Coreferential words may differ in meaning because they differ in sense; sense provides the needed finer grain. Empty words are abnormal in lacking a referent, but differ from nonsense syllables in still having a sense. This will be our strategy.

The third strategy is to enrich not theory but ontology. This is the strategy of the earlier-mentioned possible-worlds semanticists, in particular of David Lewis (2.4). Much earlier it was the strategy of Meinong. The strategy accepts an ontology of possible worlds. As well as this universe, there is a countless infinity of alternative universes. Somewhere in this thicket, anything that could exist does exist; anything that could happen does happen. That is what it means to say that something is possible, on this view. This vast ontology enables Lewis to say that apparently coreferential words are not really coreferential. Though 'the first female Prime Minister of Great Britain' and 'the person who led Great Britain into the Falklands War' both designate the same entity *around here*, they do not do so in all possible worlds. Though 'James Bond' designates nothing in this world, there are many other possible worlds where it does designate something. On this view, many uses of 'exist' are rather like 'here'. To say that 'James Bond' does not exist is just to say that he is not local; from the perspective of people elsewhere he does exist. It is not that a notion of reference is insufficient to capture the meaning of names and other words. It is rather that the notion of reference we have employed is too parochial. A more cosmopolitan notion is called for.

This strategy has an internal problem. Kripke (1980) has argued that a proper name designates the same object in each possible world; it is a "rigid" designator. (We shall discuss this view in section 3.2.) If so, the strategy fails to explain the differences we have noted in the meanings of identity statements. If Kripke is right, 'Mark Twain' and 'Samuel Clemens' designate the same object not just in this world but in every possible world in which they designate at all. So we still cannot explain the differences noted in terms of the referential roles of the names: they have the same referential roles. We are left with one of the main problems of the last section.

We find Kripke's modal intuitions plausible, but doubt that they can bear much epistemic weight. Our objection to the possible-worlds strategy is more global. It has already been indicated: we find the claim that there literally exist non-actual possible worlds *simply incredible*. Resting our case with this remark would place us among the philosophers who respond to Lewis's views with an "incredulous stare", with which he claims, reasonably enough, it is hard to argue (1973: 86).

**Lewis concedes that his ontology does violence to common sense, but he thinks that its virtues outweigh this drawback. For it has explanatory value outside the theory of reference; most famously, in the explanation of modality. Some things that did not happen could have happened. Germany might have won the Second World War. America might have lost the War of Independence. These are grand-scale unactualized possibilities. There are myriad small-scale ones: you might not have read this book; Rebecca might not have popped the question; and so on. Lewis takes this talk to be all about possible worlds. To say that such and such is possible – to say that it might have happened – is to say that it *did* happen somewhere else: it happened in some other possible world. It is true that Germany might have won because there is some unfortunate world where it did win.

Modality is perhaps the most appealing place to make use of possible worlds, but Lewis uses them elsewhere as well: to explain causation and counterfactuals ('If today had not been pension day, Granny would have been sober').

What are we to say to this list of virtues? Can we do better than our stare? We think so, though the details of our response depend on just how we take the commitment to possible worlds. We might take the commitment to be essentially semantic: possible worlds are entities that function only to provide truth conditions for troublesome sentences; sentences containing modal notions, causality, and the like. We cannot accept possible worlds for this role, because doing so would violate the naturalistic approach we endorsed in section 1.3. We would be committed to entities with no nonsemantic justification. We would also be committed to nonnatural relations: someone using the name 'Reagan' would be in a relation not just to our Reagan, but also to entities in other possible worlds. These are entities to which we stand in no causal relation: possible worlds are segregated one from another. Indeed, there would be no naturalistic relation between us and denizens in this soup of possibilia; no relation employed outside semantics. So on this construal of the commitment to possible worlds, semantic theory would be *sui generis*. The idea that language is special is to be resisted; it is just another natural phenomenon, albeit one especially characteristic of us.

We do not think Lewis understands his proposal in this way. He takes himself to be explaining features of a reality we should believe in for reasons that are quite independent of language. Among these are modal features: the many ways that things could have been. True, the apparatus of possible worlds does yield a neat account of the semantics of various sentences, but only because it provides a plausible explanation of the facts the sentences report.

To deal with this view of possible worlds, we need to deploy our naturalistic predilections in a different way. We think that *explanations* must be given in naturalistic, typically causal, terms. We explain events and processes by appeal to the causal order of the world. We explain some features of that order – say the characteristic chemical property of valency, a property partially determining the way elements combine – by appeal to deeper features of that order: the structure of the electron shells of the atoms of those elements. Explanation appeals to the order and structure of our world. Lewis's possible-world explanations do not have this characteristic. Facts about our world are explained in terms of the goings on in worlds that cannot affect our world at all. There are *no* transworld causal relations. The point is not just that these explanations are too high-priced. We do not think that they are explanations at all.**

We endorse the second strategy: we think that in order to explain the important roles of words we should suppose that words have senses. So the sense of a word is at least part of its meaning. And we now need to say what these senses are: we need a theory of sense.

According to our earlier representational hypothesis, the property of referring to something is the core of a word's meaning. How are we to reconcile this with our present acceptance of senses? One idea is to take the sense of a word as a factor of its meaning that is *independent* of its reference. This "two-factor" view has been embraced by some. We will discuss it briefly later (9.4). We prefer a more classical idea that relates sense closely to reference.

The classical idea is that sense *determines* reference; in Frege's terminology, the sense contains "the mode of presentation" of the object (1952: 57). It is in virtue of its sense, together perhaps with some features of its environmental context, that a term has its reference, if any. On this view, then, the sense of a word, together perhaps with some contextual features, *exhaust* its meaning.

A theory of meaning must encompass both a theory of sense and a theory of reference. On the classical idea, the latter two theories come together. For, a theory of sense will say how a word's sense determines its reference and so will explain its reference (something, it is worth noting, that is left unexplained by the Millian theory). And a theory of reference will say how a word's reference is determined and so explain its sense.

In the next chapter we examine a theory of reference for one of the simplest categories of terms, proper names. The theory is, briefly, that names abbreviate descriptions.

We have accepted that words have senses. What consequences does this have for our view of sentence meaning? In particular, how close do we stay to the slogan, "The meaning of a sentence is its truth condition"? Strictly interpreted, this slogan claims that a sentence's meaning is its property of representing a certain situation. We must reject this. With our acceptance of senses goes the view that there is more to the meaning of a word than its property of representing something. We must have a corresponding view of the meaning of any sentence that contains the word. So we must reinterpret the slogan as follows: a sentence's meaning is its property of representing a certain situation *in a certain way*, its meaning is its *mode of representing* its truth condition. We have departed from the letter of the slogan but remain in the spirit.

With this change must go a change in our view of the semantic task for sentences (2.2). It becomes the task of explaining their modes of presenting truth conditions. This explanation will be in terms of modes of reference – senses – and syntactic structures. We moved from sentence meaning to mode of presenting a truth condition; and from that to structure and mode of reference.

Our concern so far has been with meaning, a property of linguistic symbols. Our other main problem concerns the human capacity to *understand* these symbols (1.2). Understanding a language – being *competent* in it – is a property of human minds (and perhaps of some other minds), and so will be mostly discussed in Part III (ch. 8). However, it is appropriate to introduce it now because the positing of senses has led philosophers into a certain theory of understanding. Intuitively, understanding a term is grasping its meaning or sense. Now add the classical idea that sense determines reference. So to understand a term is to grasp something that determines its reference. It is then tempting to go further: to understand the term is to have possession of knowledge sufficient to identify the referent. Indeed, Frege took this as definitive of sense. So, for example, someone who understands 'Spiderfingers Lonergan' must know identifying facts about the infamous mobster. Most who subscribe to the classical idea have succumbed to this temptation, as we shall see in the next chapter.

2.7   Terminological Warnings; Use and Mention

We have adopted a range of terminology: 'meaning', 'truth', 'refer', 'designate', 'sense', and so on. There is more to come. These terms are taken over from ordinary language; they are part of folk linguistics (1.3). It is important not to presume that our technical uses of these terms are the same as their ordinary uses. Indeed, it is most unlikely that they will be the same. We have already sounded a warning by pointing to the vagueness of the ordinary term 'meaning' (2.1) and to the limitations on our use of 'designate' (2.5). Much the same goes for many other terms. When we take one into our theory, we usually give it a meaning that is related to its ordinary one, but different from that meaning in being more precise. There is nothing peculiar about this practice. Many technical scientific terms started out in life as ordinary ones; think of the physical term 'mass', for example.

This warning has a corollary. One should be on the watch for different technical usages among semanticists. Sometimes these variations are relatively systematic within cultures or subcultures. For example, British philosophers tend to use 'refer' for something close to the relation between proper names and their bearers, whereas American philosophers tend to use it more generally for relations *all* terms have to the world. We follow the latter practice; thus designation and application are both modes of reference for us. Though sometimes one usage of a semantic term is more common than another, or more felicitous than another, there is no question of one being *right*. Sensitivity to variations of usage is important to avoid disagreements that are not substantive but merely verbal.

These points may seem straightforward enough, but they are not without controversy. The "ordinary language" school of philosophy takes the philosophy of language to *be* the study of the ordinary use of semantic terms. So sensitivity to ordinary usage is all that is required. The test of a theory is whether it accords with "what we would ordinarily say". There is no place for technical terms (except perhaps ones that are *defined* in ordinary terms). Our discussion in section 1.3 implies the rejection of this "ordinary language" view. We shall criticize it directly in chapter 14.

Throughout our discussion, we have been careful to put a name inside single quotation marks when we want to talk about it – to *mention* it – rather than *use* it to talk about its bearer. This care about "the distinction between use and mention" may seem rather pedantic, yet it is very important in the philosophy of language. Elsewhere, it is hardly worth the fuss because the difference between the referent of a name when used and when mentioned is so obvious; nobody would confuse the person Thatcher with the name 'Thatcher' (or so one would think, yet many myths, religions, superstitions, and sayings are riddled with such confusions). As a result people are ordinarily rather casual about putting quotation marks around a name when they mean to mention it. However, in the philosophy of language we are talking *about names* (and other expressions). To do this we have to use the names of names. The difference between the referent of such a name when used and when mentioned is not obvious at all. Indeed, many philosophical works have been vitiated by a failure to distinguish use and mention.

No philosopher has done more to emphasize the importance of care with this distinction than W. V. O. Quine. The following example of care is taken from him and should be studied as an exercise.

'Boston is populous' is about Boston and contains 'Boston'; "'Boston' is disyllabic" is about 'Boston' and contains "'Boston'". "'Boston'" designates

'Boston', which in turn designates Boston. To mention Boston we use 'Boston' or a synonym, and to mention 'Boston' we use "Boston" or a synonym. "Boston" contains six letters and just one pair of quotation marks; 'Boston' contains six letters and no quotation marks; and Boston contains some 800,000 people. (1940: 24)

Putting an expression between quotation marks is not the only device that can be used to mention it: the expression can be put on display. We have made extensive use of this device. A few pages back, for example, we concluded section 2.5 with a discussion of the identity statements 'Cordates are cordates' and 'Cordates are renates', both of which were put on display.

Putting an expression on display or between quotation marks does not always indicate that it is being mentioned not used. It is often the sign, not surprisingly, that the expression is being taken from someone else and quoted. Quotation marks also have the role of "shudder" or "scare" quotes. This indicates that the author, while using the expression, is distancing himself from its full meaning. In this book, our use of single quotation marks will always indicate that an expression is being mentioned. We shall reserve double quotation marks for quotation and scare quotes.

Suggested Reading

2.2

For Frege's approach to language, see several essays reprinted in *The Philosophical Writings of Gottlob Frege* (1952), particularly the first seven or so pages of his 1892 paper "On Sense and Reference", also reprinted in Martinich 1996, *The Philosophy of Language*, (under the name "On Sense and Nominatum"), and Ludlow, *Readings in the Philosophy of Language*. For a nice introduction, see Currie 1982, *Frege, an Introduction to his Philosophy*.

The view that a truth-conditional approach to language requires a substantive theory of reference is not uncontroversial. In a classic article that guides our approach, "Tarski's Theory of Truth" (1972), Hartry Field pointed out that Tarski himself was content with a trivial theory of reference. Both Donald Davidson in "Reality without Reference", first published in 1977 and reprinted in Davidson 1984, and John McDowell in "Physicalism and Primitive Denotation: Field on Tarski" (1978), argue that a theory of reference is not needed. We find these arguments obscure and unconvincing: see chapter 15 below; also, Devitt 1981a, *Designation*: secs. 4.8–4.9; 1997, *Realism and Truth*: secs. 10.1–10.5. The articles by Field, Davidson, and McDowell are all reprinted in Platts 1980,

Reference, Truth and Reality. Soames 1984b, "What is a Theory of Truth?" is an interesting criticism of Field.

The view that truth consists in "correspondence to the facts" has been known as the *correspondence theory* of truth. In attempting to explain truth in terms of reference and structure, we are offering a correspondence theory. For more on this, see Devitt 1997: 27–9.

For a careful and systematic exposition of the view that a theory of meaning is a theory of truth, see Lycan 1984, *Logical Form in Natural Language*. He is more sympathetic than we are to Davidson's formulation of these issues.

**2.3

Smart outlines his theory of compliance conditions simply and readably in *Ethics, Persuasion and Truth* (1984). The Scandinavian line on non-indicatives was first presented in Aqvist 1965, *A New Approach to the Logical Theory of Interrogatives*, Part I. The more general Scandinavian line is summarized in Follesdal and Hilpinen 1970, "Deontic Logic: An Introduction". Belnap has defended his views on questions in a number of places, for example in Belnap and Steel 1976, *The Logic of Questions and Answers*. All these works except Smart's are technical and difficult.

Two classic, nontechnical, works in pragmatics, emphasizing the importance of non-indicative uses of language, are Austin 1962a, *How to do Things with Words*, and Searle 1969, *Speech Acts*. See also the the first three papers in Searle 1971, *The Philosophy of Language*, Part IV of Davis 1991, *Pragmatics*, and Part II of Martinich 1996.**

2.4

Tarski's famous definition of truth was in "The Concept of Truth in Formalized Languages", reprinted in Tarski 1956. This is a long and difficult article. Tarski 1944, "The Semantic Conception of Truth", reprinted in Martinich 1996 and Geirsson and Losonsky 1996, is a more accessible discussion. A good exposition of Tarski's main ideas can be found in Quine 1970, *Philosophy of Logic*: ch. 3; see also Field 1972.

**More complex languages – including adverbs, tenses, pronouns and the like – are treated in Lewis 1972, "General Semantics", in Davidson and Harman 1972, *Semantics of Natural Language*, and reprinted in Lewis 1983, *Philosophical Papers: Volume I*. See also Montague 1974, *Formal Philosophy*, and Dowty, Wall and Peters 1981, *Introduction to Montague Semantics*.

Frege and Tarski treated quantifiers like 'all' and 'some' as "unary" in their logics. Barwise and Cooper 1981, "Generalized Quantifiers and Natural Language", focuses on quantifiers like 'most' and 'few' in arguing that natural language quantifiers are "binary". See Larson and Segal 1995, *Knowledge of Meaning*, chs. 7 and 8 for an interesting development of this idea; also Neale 1990, *Descriptions*, sec. 2.5 for a very readable account.

The most accessible of Kripke's works on modal logic is, "Semantical Considerations on Modal Logic" (1962), reprinted in Linsky 1971, *Reference and Modality*. For Lewis' views on counterfactuals and possible worlds, see *Counterfactuals* (1973). Jaakko Hintikka pioneered the application of possible worlds semantics to epistemic contexts: *Knowledge and Belief* (1962). A clear introduction to the utility of talk of possible worlds in semantic theory and logic is provided by Bradley and Swartz 1979, *Possible Worlds*. They illustrate the metaphysical coyness that is endemic among those who talk about possible worlds: they do not come clean on the status of possible worlds. The technical problems alluded to in our text are pointed out by Lewis and Lycan (see suggestions for section 2.6).

Quine is a famous skeptic not only about possible worlds but about modal notions in general: see "Reference and Modality" in *From a Logical Point of View* (1961), reprinted in Linsky 1971; "Necessary Truth" and "Three Grades of Modal Involvement" in *Ways of Paradox* (1966).**

Donald Davidson was the first to take an optimistic view of the task of applying Tarski to natural language in his 1967 essay, "Truth and Meaning", reprinted in Davidson 1984, Martinich 1996, and Ludlow 1997.

2.5

The classical account of the problem posed by identity statements is in the first two pages of Frege's, "On Sense and Reference" (see 2.2 above). The problem has seemed intractable to many and has developed a vast literature. Kripke's argument for the necessity of identity statements involving names is in *Naming and Necessity* (1980), pp. 97–116, excerpts of which are in Martinich 1996 and Ludlow 1997. This very influential work plays an important role in our book.

The problem of existence statements for the Millian view is nicely brought out by Russell in his 1918 paper, "The Philosophy of Logical Atomism", reprinted in *Logic and Knowledge* (1956): 233, 241. Quine considers and rejects the view that an empty name refers to an idea in his classic paper, "On What There Is", in *From a Logical Point of View* (1961).

**The difficult matter of opaque contexts is discussed by Frege in the above-mentioned article. Two classics on the topic are Quine's "Quantifiers and Propositional Attitudes", reprinted in Quine 1966, and Kaplan 1969, "Quantifying In", in Davidson and Hintikka 1969, *Words and Objections*. Both papers are reprinted in Linsky 1971 and Martinich 1996.

See also Quine 1960, *Word and Object*, secs. 30–2, reprinted in Ludlow 1997.**

2.6

The strategy of introducing senses is also to be found in Frege's article.

**For the possible-worlds strategy, see the suggestions for sections 2.4 above. Plantinga 1974, *The Nature of Necessity*, chs. VI to VIII, provide an interesting defense of commitment to possible worlds. Max Cresswell has pursued the strategy very systematically: see *Structured Meanings* (1985); *Semantical Essays* (1988); *Language in the Worlds* (1994); *Semantical Indexicality* (1996). Lycan 1994, *Modality and Meaning*, critiques the major positions on possible worlds and discusses their relations to semantics. Loux 1979, *The Possible and the Actual* is a helpful collection. Miller 1991, "Reply of a Mad Dog", is a response to our criticisms.

A comparison of Kripke's writings on modal logic with *Naming and Necessity* suggests that even he is coy about possible worlds.

Lewis defends his position in *On the Plurality of Worlds*. He argues that his position is coherent and plausible, and that attempts to purchase the advantages of possible worlds at a smaller ontological price cannot succeed.**

2.7

The quotation from Quine is drawn from sec. 4 of *Mathematical Logic* (1940); the section is called "Use versus Mention" and is a very nice discussion of the issue.

3

Description Theories of Reference: Names

3.1   The Classical Description Theory

According to the classical description theory derived from the works of Gottlob Frege and Bertrand Russell, the sense of a name is given by a definite description associated with the name; its sense is the sense of that description. So names can be treated as abbreviated descriptions. Consider the following example taken from Frege (1952: 58n.). Given what is commonly believed about Aristotle, we might suppose that the definite description associated with 'Aristotle' is 'the pupil of Plato and teacher of Alexander the Great'. If so, that description expresses the sense of 'Aristotle'.

Sense is supposed to determine reference, so this theory of sense should supply a theory of reference (2.6). And so it does. (And this is a decided advantage of the theory over the Millian theory, which left the reference of a name unexplained.) Consider a name a which has a sense expressed by the description 'the F' and which *designates x*. The theory says that

'a' designates x in virtue of 'the F' denoting x.

This reduces our original problem of explaining reference for names to that of explaining reference for definite descriptions. In virtue of what does a definite description *denote x*? Nevertheless, we have made progress because we had that problem anyway; two problems have been reduced to one. Further, thanks to Russell's famous "theory of descriptions", we have an answer to the problem for descriptions:

'The F' denotes x if and only if 'F' applies to x and to nothing else;

for example, 'the author of *Word and Object*' denotes Quine because 'author of *Word and Object*' applies only to Quine. Once again we solve one problem by raising another: that of explaining reference for the general terms that fill the place of 'F'. In virtue of what does a general term *apply* to an object? But once again we have made progress, because this is also a problem we had anyway. (Interestingly enough, this other problem did not strike enthusiasts for the description theory of names. We shall return to this in sections 3.5 and 4.2.) In sum, the description theory of names, together with Russell's theory of descriptions, reduces three problems of reference to one: the problems of designation for names, denotation for definite descriptions and application for general terms are reduced to the problem of application for general terms.

The description theory supplies a theory of sense and thereby a theory of reference. There seems to be nothing else to the meaning of a name than its sense and reference (2.6). So the description theory is a complete theory of meaning for names.

We have an interest not only in meaning, but also in understanding. What is it to be in a position to use 'a' properly – to be competent with the name? It is to "grasp its sense". What is that? The description theory has a simple answer: to grasp 'a's sense is to associate 'a' with 'the F'. But what is it to *associate* a name with a description? There is a plausible answer available to description theorists, one that appeals to the inferential dispositions of the speaker. Max associates 'the teacher of Alexander' with 'Aristotle' in virtue of his standing disposition to infer from claims using the name 'Aristotle' to claims using the description 'the teacher of Alexander' and back again. The description has a "conceptual role" or "functional role" that links it tightly in inference to the name, and vice versa.

Combine this view of competence with the theory of reference and we can conclude that the competent speaker associates the name with a description that uniquely applies to, hence identifies, its bearer. This association will result in a a belief that she would express, "a is the F". Given that, according to the theory, 'a' designates what 'the F' denotes, this belief must be true. Classical description theorists go further: the belief is *knowledge*. So, someone who understands 'Spiderfingers Lonergan' not only must believe something that as a matter of fact identifies the mobster, she must *know* that it identifies him. Thus the classical description theory gives in to the temptation mentioned in section 2.6.

The move from true belief to knowledge needs a license. A true belief counts as knowledge only if it is *justified*. For example, your belief that a certain horse will win the race may turn out to be true but it is not knowledge unless it is well- based rather than, say, a fortunate guess. Why do description theorists suppose that the reference-determining belief about *a* of a speaker competent with '*a*' must be justified and hence be knowledge? After all, it is rather likely that many of the beliefs that the speaker has about *a* will be unjustified. Perhaps the reference-determining one is among those. We conjecture that description theorists count the reference-determining belief as knowledge because of an implicit assumption that permeates their thinking about semantics, "the Cartesian assumption" that a speaker's competence in using an expression amounts to (tacit) knowledge about its meaning; the competence involves a non-empirical "privileged" access to its meaning (2.5). This access provides the needed justification: since her association of 'the *F*' with '*a*' determines the reference of '*a*', then her competence puts her in the position to *tell* that it does; she must tacitly *know* that it does. So she doesn't simply *believe* that *a* is the *F*, she *knows* it. (In effect, this is the argument that analytic truths are knowable *a priori*; 5.6.)

Consider next how the classical description theory handles the various issues that led us to introduce senses (2.5).

We saw that the identity statements

Mark Twain is Mark Twain
Mark Twain is Samuel Clemens

differ in meaning. How does the theory account for that? The two names have different senses in virtue of being associated with different descriptions: 'Mark Twain' is associated with, say, 'the author of *Hucklebury Finn*'; 'Samuel Clemens' with, say, 'the man living at 12 Elm Street'. These descriptions have different senses and so the statements differ in meaning. The theory yields the finer-grained meanings we want.

The theory is equally successful with singular existence statements containing names. These are seen as equivalent to statements containing definite descriptions; that is, like 'The *F* exists' if positive, and like 'The *F* does not exist' if negative. The former is true if and only if the definite description denotes; the latter, if and only if it does not denote. With the help of Russell's theory of descriptions, once again, we can give the necessary further explanation: 'the *F*' denotes if and only if there exists one and only one thing that '*F*' applies to. So, the negative statement is true if the general term fails to apply uniquely. Such failure does not render the statement meaningless and thus does not lead to paradox. Similarly, there is nothing tautological about a true positive statement: even if it were false, it would be meaningful.

Appearances of empty names in other contexts are also treated readily. A name is empty because its associated description fails to denote. But the description, and hence the name, still has a sense. Its sense depends partly on its structure – that of a definite description – and partly on the sense of its contained general term. Neither of these are affected by its failure to denote.

The problem of opacity is not so easy. The description theory explains why substituting one name for another with the same referent changes the *meaning* of a sentence: see above on identity statements. However, it does not explain why the substitution can change the *truth value*. There is no obvious reason why the two sentences,

> Monique believes that the author of *Syntactic Structures* is a great linguist
> The author of *Syntactic Structures* is the most influential contemporary anarchist writer,

fail to entail

> Monique believes that the most influential contemporary anarchist writer is a great linguist.

The failure of the rule of substitutivity of identity is just as puzzling for definite descriptions as for names, and so treating names as abbreviated descriptions does not help with it. Differences in sense that do not lead to differences in reference should be irrelevant to truth conditions.

Most of those who have worked on the opacity problem suggest that the truth conditions of belief sentences like these depend not just on the reference of (say) 'the author of *Syntactic Structures*' but also on its *mode* of reference. Description theories give a clear account of a name's mode of reference and so are well-placed to exploit this approach. We shall say no more on the matter in accordance with our policy of treating opacity lightly (2.5).

Despite these virtues, the classical description theory seemed to have serious problems from the beginning.

1. *Principled Basis*. People often associate many definite descriptions with a name. We do with 'Aristotle'; apart from that mentioned, we associate 'the systematizer of syllogistic logic', 'the author of *The Nichomachean Ethics*', and so on. Which of these gives the sense of the name? If the classical description theory is right, one of these descriptions trumps all the others. If it fails to denote, the name is empty, even if all the other associated descriptions pick out the one object. The theory must supply a "principled basis" for giving one association that special importance.

2. *Unwanted Ambiguity.* Suppose that we had such a principled basis and that we applied it to one user of a name. It would select a certain definite description that has this important role for that person. It seems most unlikely that it will select the same description for all users of the name. With a name like 'Aristotle' we would expect to find many different descriptions playing that role in the speech community. So 'Aristotle', even when used to refer to that famous Greek philosopher, would be many-ways ambiguous. (Frege accepted this consequence of his theory, regarding the ambiguity as an imperfection of ordinary language; 1952: 58n.).

Think back to the Millian theory's problem with identity statements. If the Cartesian assumption about meanings is accepted, then the Millian theory is refuted by the informativeness of 'Mark Twain is Samuel Clemens' (2.5). Why then is the description theory, which accepts the Cartesian assumption, not similarly refuted by the *un*informativeness of 'Aristotle is Aristotle'? Given the many senses of 'Aristotle', why is that statement not usually as informative as 'Mark Twain is Samuel Clemens'? The description theory was partially motivated by an apparent contrast between 'Mark Twain is Samuel Clemens' and 'Aristotle is Aristotle'. But if the classical description theory is right, there is no such contrast.

3. *Unwanted Necessity.* Suppose that we had removed this problem of ambiguity, perhaps by restricting ourselves to a speech community in which the one description expresses the sense of 'Aristotle' for all. And suppose that the description which gives the sense of 'Aristotle' is the one we took from Frege. Now consider:

(a) Aristotle taught Alexander the Great.

According to the description theory it abbreviates

(b) The pupil of Plato and teacher of Alexander the Great taught Alexander the Great.

Yet (b) seems to be *necessary* whereas (a) does not. *Of course* the teacher of Alexander taught Alexander but it is an entirely contingent fact about Aristotle that he taught Alexander. Indeed, Aristotle might have died young and never taught anyone. The description theory yields unwanted necessities.

This problem for the classical theory rests on intuitions about modality. So too does one recently posed by Kripke which we shall consider in the next section.

In sum, it seems that names do not abbreviate descriptions in the simple way specified by the classical description theory. In the next two sections we will raise two further problems for the classical theory.

3.2   The Modern Description Theory

The implausibilities of the classical theory led to the modern theory, often called the "cluster" theory. The earliest sign of this theory seems to have been in a typically enigmatic remark by Ludwig Wittgenstein (1953: sec. 79). However, the most influential exponents of the theory were Peter Strawson and John Searle. Instead of tying a name tightly to one definite description, as the classical theory does, the modern theory ties it loosely to many. This cluster of descriptions expresses the sense of the name and determines its reference; the name refers to the object, if any, that *most*, but not necessarily all, of those descriptions denote. The theory can be made more sophisticated still by allowing some descriptions to have greater weight in the vote than others. Thus, in the cluster associated with 'Aristotle', doubtless 'the systematizer of syllogistic logic' weighs more heavily than 'the son of the court physician to Amyntas II'.

Where does the modern theory stand on understanding? The straightforward view, taking understanding as "grasping the sense", requires the speaker to make a functional-role association of the name with the appropriate cluster of descriptions. Adopting the Cartesian assumption once again, the speaker (tacitly) *knows* that the name refers to the object that most of those description denote. So the competent speaker of 'Spiderfingers Lonergan' knows facts sufficient to *identify* the mobster.

However, the modern theory's view of understanding is unclear. Sometimes the suggestion seems to be that it is sufficient for the speaker to associate at least one of the cluster with the name, thus combining a classical theory of understanding with a modern theory of sense. Sometimes even it seems that the speaker may associate some identifying description that is not in the cluster, thus divorcing understanding from sense altogether. Either way, the connection between understanding and sense (and hence reference) is left unexplained and mysterious. For this reason, we shall ignore these possibilities.

The modern theory may seem to handle the problems for the classical theory (3.1) as follows. It avoids 1 by not requiring that we pick one of the many descriptions a person associates with a name to bear the burden of reference; the cluster of descriptions bears the burden. So we don't need a principled basis for picking one. The problem of unwanted ambiguities posed by 2 is removed because the many descriptions associated with the name by the speech community can all be accommodated in the cluster. The problem of unwanted necessities posed by 3 is solved because the theory does not require that *all* the descriptions in the cluster denote the bearer of the name. Even though, say, the description 'the pupil of Plato and teacher of Alexander the Great' is in the cluster that expresses the sense of 'Aristotle', it might have been one of the minority that did not denote Aristotle. So the theory leaves open the possibility that (a) is not true, that Aristotle did not teach Alexander.

However, the success of the modern theory in handling these problems is far from complete, for it faces an analogous set of problems.

1. *Principled Basis.* Presumably, not every description associated with a name, however incidental, is to be included in the cluster. So the modern theory is committed to selecting some descriptions that *define* the name. What is the principled basis of this selection? The modern theories will either be pushed backwards towards the classical theory, or forwards to an implausible holism in which every associated description is included in the defining cluster (so every change in belief about the bearer changes the meaning of the name).

2. *Unwanted Ambiguity.* It seems most unlikely that a principled basis will select the same cluster for all users of a name: people vary so much in their beliefs about an object. So the name 'Aristotle' would still be many-ways ambiguous.

3. *Unwanted Necessity.* According to the modern theory, it is contingent that Aristotle has any one property – so the theory handles (a) well – but it is not contingent that Aristotle has *most of the group* of properties picked out by the cluster of descriptions associated with his name. A sentence like

(c) Aristotle had most of the following properties: born in Stagira, pupil of Plato, author of the *Nichomachean Ethics*, systematizer of syllogistic logic, teacher of Alexander the Great . . .

should be necessary. Yet, as Kripke emphasizes (1980), it does not seem so: Aristotle might not have had *any* of these properties. The modern theory, like the classical one, yields unwanted necessities.

We find Kripke's point persuasive, but many do not. For example, John Searle, one of the founders of the modern theory, had this to say:

it is a necessary fact that Aristotle has the logical sum, inclusive disjunction, of properties commonly attributed to him: any individual not having some of these properties could not be Aristotle. (1958: 160)

In this passage Searle grasped the nettle of necessity long before Kripke presented it to cluster theorists. Kripke's point rests on modal intuitions that many do not share.

In recent times, two further problems for description theories have come to light. They are problems for both the classical and the modern theories.

4. *Lost Rigidity.* The first, posed by Kripke, also rests on modal

intuitions. The problem deploys his famous notion of *rigid designation*, explained as follows: for a term '*a*' to be a rigid designator is for it to designate the same object in every possible world where it designates at all; or, less picturesquely, for it to be such that '*a* is *F*' would truly characterize some counterfactual situation if and only if the object that the term *actually* designates is *F* in that situation. Kripke argues that names are rigid designators whereas the descriptions that names are supposed to abbreviate are not. So description theories are wrong.

We shall illustrate the problem on the classical theory because doing so is more simple and vivid. Compare:

(d) Aristotle was fond of dogs.
(e) The pupil of Plato and teacher of Alexander the Great was fond of dogs.

Suppose that Aristotle had died young, long before his philosophical fulfillment, and that some other pupil of Plato had gone on to teach Alexander. In those circumstances the truth of (e) would depend on whether that other person was fond of dogs. But the truth of (d) would still depend, just as it does depend in the actual world, on whether Aristotle was fond of dogs. The name 'Aristotle' designates Aristotle in a counterfactual situation just as it does in the actual situation, whereas the description 'The pupil of Plato and teacher of Alexander the Great' denotes whoever is the pupil of Plato who taught Alexander in that situation, whether Aristotle or not. So the name does not abbreviate that description. Similarly, it does not abbreviate any other description that is a candidate to express its sense. (Note that what we are evaluating in a counterfactual situation are expressions *with the meanings that they actually have as a result of our usage*. Clearly any expression could have a different meaning as a result of different usage in a counterfactual situation – language is arbitrary (1.2) – but that is beside the point.)

Evidence for this difference in rigidity between names and descriptions is also to be found in modal contexts. Consider the following:

(f) Aristotle might not have been Aristotle
(g) Aristotle might not have been the pupil of Plato and teacher of Alexander the Great.

Whereas (g) is true, (f) is surely not. Who else would Aristotle have been if he had not been Aristotle, i.e., himself?! (Of course, Aristotle might not have been *called* "Aristotle", but that is a different matter.)

**Kripke points out a way of avoiding problems 3 and 4. We have been taking the description theory as a theory of sense, and hence of meaning: a description expresses the sense of a name; the name abbreviates the description and so is synonymous with it. It is because of this that the theory is committed to the unwanted necessity of statements like (a) or (c) and to names being no more rigid than descriptions. But suppose we took the theory not as a theory of sense, a sense that determines reference, but *only* as a theory of reference: the name refers to whatever is picked out by the associated descriptions, but no claim is made about its meaning. Then neither problem would arise. For each depend on the idea that the description is semantically equivalent to the name.

However, this maneuver is no help with problems 1 and 2, the problems of a principled basis and unwanted ambiguity. And it creates two others.

First, the typical description theorist accepts the Cartesian assumption that if a description, or cluster of descriptions, determines the reference of a name then the competent speaker must (tacitly) know that it does. Furthermore, she thinks that this sort of knowledge is *a priori*. So mere understanding of the name 'Aristotle' would suffice for knowledge of (a) or (c). The typical description theorist will see no problem in this *provided she thinks that (a) or (c) are necessary*: necessary truths are precisely the ones that she thinks can be known *a priori*. But, as we have noted, (a) and (c) are not necessary. Indeed, the whole point of the maneuver was to avoid commitment to the necessity of the likes of (a) or (c). Yet the maneuver leaves intact the commitment to *a priori* knowledge of the likes of (a) or (c). Mere understanding of a name suffices for *contingent* knowledge about its bearer. In brief, for the typical description theorist, the maneuver results in that strange beast, the contingent *a priori*.

Second, the maneuver leaves us with a seriously incomplete theory. If a reference-determining cluster of descriptions does not give the sense of a name, what does? Senses were introduced to solve various problems – for example that of identity statements – which showed there was more to the meaning of a name than its role of designating its bearer (2.6). We still need senses for those purposes and so we still need a theory of sense. We would need to break with the Fregean idea that sense determines reference; sense would have to be a factor of meaning that is independent of reference. In brief, we would be committed to a "two-factor" theory (2.6). We discuss two-factor theories in section 9.4.

A better way to avoid problems 3 and 4 is to revise the description theory, claiming that a name is synonymous with a *rigidified* description. Our language seems to have descriptions that contain 'rigidity operators'; for example, the italicized part of 'the person who, *in the actual world*, was the pupil and teacher of Alexander the Great' seems to make this description denote Aristotle in every possible world. If descriptions of this sort are indeed rigid, the revised theory can claim that a name is synonymous with such a description.

Finally, note that though the cluster theory does well with the fact that language is arbitrary, learned, stimulus- and medium-independent (1.3), it does not do so with the fact that language is abstract. 'Orson weighs 130kg' seems to be concerned with only one thing about Orson. According to the cluster theory, it is concerned with all the high points of his nature and history.

The four problems we have raised so far for the description theory of names, whether classical or modern, are serious but not catastrophic. They should shake one's faith in the theory but, in the absence of an alternative, perhaps not lead one to abandon it. However, Kripke has raised a further problem which, in our view, *is* catastrophic for description theories:

5. *Ignorance and error*. This problem will be the concern of the next section. It does not rest on modal intuitions. A similar argument was offered by Keith Donnellan (1972).

3.3   Ignorance and Error

Kripke's argument is aimed at the central idea of all description theories (even those that are only theories of reference) that the reference of a name is determined by the descriptions the speaker associates with the name. More precisely, the argument is aimed at:

For any name token 'a' and object x, 'a' designates x if and only if x is denoted by a weighted most of the definite descriptions associated with 'a' by the speaker.

This is general enough to cover all description theories. Classical theories assign a weight other than zero to only one description. Holistic modern theories assign such weights to all the associated descriptions. More plausible localistic ones assign them to a few descriptions.

In opposition to this central idea, Kripke showed that, for a name to designate an object, it is *neither necessary nor sufficient* for the speaker to associate with the name descriptions that denote the object. Given that the association of a description with a name yields a belief, and that a description that denotes an object identifies it, we can say that Kripke showed that it is neither necessary nor sufficient for the speaker to have beliefs that identify the object. He concluded that the associated descriptions do not determine reference. So they do not express the sense which determines reference. Description theories place too heavy an epistemic burden on competent users of a name.

We have already shown that when the central idea is enhanced by the Cartesian assumption it places an even heavier epistemic burden on the competent: they must not merely have identifying beliefs about the name's bearer, those beliefs must be *knowledge*, they must be *justified* (3.1, 3.2). Until recently this view was regarded as a truism in the philosophy of language. ("*How else* could a speaker's act of reference pick out a particular object?"). Kripke's argument against the central idea must count against the enhanced one. He showed that the "truism" is false.

Identifying beliefs are not necessary

Consider the name 'Cicero'. Many people have heard of Cicero and can refer to him by that name. Do they associate the descriptions required by description theories? Our situation is probably typical. We associate with 'Cicero' the descriptions 'is Tully' and 'the denouncer of Catiline'. That near enough exhausts our beliefs about Cicero. The problem for description theories is that though these associated descriptions do indeed identify Cicero they are not *appropriate*: for they contain names. Descriptions must then be found for these names. We can do no better for 'Tully' than 'is Cicero' and, of course, 'the denouncer of Catiline', and no better for 'Catiline' than 'the person denounced by Cicero'. We can supply descriptions that identify the referent of each name in terms of the others but have no independent way of identifying the referent of any. Our efforts to comply with the demands of description theories lead us in an obvious circle. Nor is the problem one of our special ignorance. Even those with a good deal of classical knowledge will find it difficult to produce a *name-free* identifying description of Cicero.

'Einstein' is a name on everyone's lips. How many associate descriptions that identify its bearer? It is common to associate 'the discoverer of the Theory of Relativity' with 'Einstein'. But that will do the job only if the Theory of Relativity is identified independently of Einstein. Few of us could manage that.

What these two examples show is that description theories require people who appear to refer successfully with names to have beliefs that they do not in fact have: they are too *ignorant*. The theories also face a problem of *error*: they seriously underestimate the number of *false* beliefs people have.

Public opinion polls and the like show that people are often quite mistaken about famous and historical figures. They think, for example, that Einstein invented the atomic bomb, or that Columbus was the first person to think that the world was round. Often the only nontrivial belief that they hold about someone is false. Yet when they use the names for such people they still succeed in referring to them; their assertion, "A city in Ohio was named after Columbus" is a truth about Columbus not a falsehood about some ancient Greek.

These are examples of *actual* error. Using examples of Wittgenstein and Kripke we can see how the mere *possibility* of error shows that it is not necessary to have identifying beliefs of a name's bearer. Wittgenstein's example concerns Moses. Suppose that we discovered that nobody satisfied the descriptions normally associated with 'Moses': 'the man who led the Israelites out of Egypt', 'the man who as a child was taken out of the Nile by Pharaoh's daughter', etc.. We would probably conclude that there was no Moses; that 'Moses' was an empty name designating nothing. And so we should conclude according to description theories. These theories miss an alternative possibility, as Kripke's speculations about Jonah demonstrate.

It is unlikely that the biblical story of Jonah is true of any actual man; unlikely even that substantial parts of it, particularly the parts about the big fish, are. Does it follow that 'Jonah' is an empty name? It does not: Jonah *might have been a real person about whom a legend has grown.* Imagine we discover that the facts were as follows. There was a person called 'Jonah' who lived a fairly ordinary life. The only unusual thing about his life was the superstitious regard his fellows held him in: they tended to tell peculiar stories about him. After his death these stories blossomed into the biblical story of Jonah; all the truths about Jonah (except trivial ones like being a man) were forgotten.

In the situation imagined, our uses of 'Jonah' designate the man around whom the legend grew. Earlier predications using the name, such as those in the Bible, are mostly false because that man lacked the ascribed properties. Present predications, reflecting the deflation of the legend, will be true.

Description theories cannot accommodate these claims. These theories must conclude that the imagined discovery shows that 'Jonah', in its earlier uses, was an empty name: our beliefs involving the name did not identify anyone. None of the earlier predications, not even the trivial ones like being a man, can be true. We have not replaced a false theory about Jonah with a true one about him: until the discovery, we had no theory *about him* at all. Note that it is *not possible*, on the description theory, for an earlier scholar to speculate, or find evidence, that Jonah was a certain ordinary man that he, the scholar, has tracked down. Such speculations, such evidence, cannot be *about Jonah* because they deny the descriptions on which our use of the name depends. These consequences of description theories are not plausible.

The possibility that the Jonah case raises is not fanciful. For instance, it precisely parallels scholarly speculation about King Arthur: that the Arthurian legends grew around a real, though less colorful, figure.

We conclude that it is not necessary to have the identifying beliefs required by description theories. We can use a name to designate an object even when we are ignorant of the object. We can do it even when our error about the object is massive. The epistemic burden placed on us by description theories is far too heavy.

Identifying beliefs are not sufficient

Suppose that a person intent on misleading his audience launches on a narrative without making it clear that he is story-telling. Alternatively, to avoid deliberate deception, suppose the person tells something that is in fact a vivid dream but which he, deluded as he is, thinks is true. The audience believes the narrative and later passes it on to others. It turns out that there are people, not known to the narrator, who fit the descriptions of his characters. *Must* we say that the narrator (and thence his audience) was talking about those people? We *might*, especially if the parallels were both striking and unexpected: some might even see it as a case of extrasensory perception. There is an alternative: we might dismiss the parallelism as a matter of chance. Despite the fact that the narrator's descriptions fit those people, he did not refer to them.

Examples of error also illustrate the insufficiency of identifying beliefs. The person who associates with 'Einstein' the description, 'the inventor of the atomic bomb', does not designate Oppenheimer; the person who associates 'Columbus' with the description, 'the first person to think that the world was round', does not designate some ancient Greek.

The point can be made also with examples of possible, though not actual, error. Consider Kripke's famous example of Godel. Most people with some knowledge of logic know that Godel first proved the incompleteness of arithmetic. Suppose that this proof had really been discovered by Schmidt, a student of Godel, and had been stolen by Godel. Schmidt, naturally depressed and disillusioned by this turn of events, dies. Godel goes on to undeserved fame and Princeton. Now consider the many who associate with 'Godel' only the description 'the discoverer of the incompleteness of arithmetic'. In this counterfactual situation the description they associate with 'Godel' denotes Schmidt. Does their use of 'Godel' then designate Schmidt? Surely not. If Kripke's slander were correct, their assertion of 'Godel discovered the incompleteness of arithmetic' would be a false statement about Godel not a true one about Schmidt.

These examples show that even where a speaker's beliefs involving a name succeed in identifying an individual, the name may not refer to that individual. Identifying beliefs are no more sufficient for reference than they are necessary.

3.4 Reference Borrowing

We have written so far as if everyone has to stand on his own in determining reference for a name: each person has to provide identifying descriptions that signal the bearer's famous achievements, or most distinctive personal or physical characteristics. But perhaps we can borrow our reference from others. There are some who could provide descriptions that identify Cicero and Einstein. Maybe they can carry the rest of us. This is an important suggestion, which we shall later adopt, but it does not save description theories.

Strawson explicitly adopts reference borrowing (1959: 182n.). The form it takes for Strawson is the form it must take for a description theory: the association of a definite description that refers to another person's reference. (John Bigelow has ingeniously suggested to us a fall-back position for the description theorist on reference borrowing: borrowing from one's former self. We shall leave it to the reader to adapt the argument to this position.) Suppose that yesterday Alice heard George talking with enthusiasm of someone called 'Joshua'. She does not know Joshua from Adam, but she rightly thinks that George is very much better off. So Alice's gossip today can meet the requirements of description theories: she associates with 'Joshua' the identifying description, 'the person George was referring to yesterday by 'Joshua''. This is only satisfactory, of course, because Alice can support her use of 'George' with an appropriate description, and because George can identify Joshua. Borrowing can go further: Alice talks to Ruth, Ruth to Sebastian, and so on. Each person designates Joshua in virtue of associating with his name a description that refers to the previous person in the chain.

The idea of a reference chain is well taken and does help with our present problem. But, we note first, it does so at the expense of worsening the problems of a principled basis and unwanted ambiguity, problems 1 and 2. We now need a principled basis for choosing among what will often be a much larger set of associated descriptions, a set including *many* reference-borrowing descriptions, reflecting conversations with many people about a name's bearer. Which of these, or which cluster of these, expresses the name's sense for a speaker and determines her reference? Suppose that we had a principled basis for answering this question. Then if reference borrowing is to help the many people who are ignorant or wrong about the bearer, the principled basis must select reference-borrowing descriptions; descriptions like 'the person George called' Joshua yesterday. But these people have different borrowing histories with the name and so the basis will yield many different senses for the name. And all of these senses will differ from those of the few knowledgeable users of the name who do not rely on reference-borrowing descriptions.

Next, although, reference borrowing does help with our present problem of ignorance and error, it does not help *enough*. This version of the description theory still requires identifying beliefs where there may be none. First, the borrower must remember at least one other user of the name, and remember that user not merely by name: an identifying description must be provided. This may, of course, send the borrower off on further reference borrowing which in turn requires further beliefs. Second, the reference *lender* must be able either to supply descriptions that directly identify the referent, or remember where she borrowed the name from. And so on. There is a danger of circularity here: Sebastian depends on Ruth, Ruth depends on Alice, and Alice, forgetting all about George, comes to depend on Sebastian. Someone in the chain must be able to go it alone. Aside from this problem of circularity, it is unlikely that the required beliefs are present for most uses of a name; we naturally *forget* most of this information. We forget where we got a name from. Or we remember but can't supply descriptions that identify the person satisfactorily or supply ones that identify the wrong person. Or we identify the right person, but she is no better off than we are: she cannot identify the bearer, perhaps identifying something else. The epistemic burden of the description theory is still too heavy.

So far, the case against description theories of names has depended on our intuitive judgments about particular cases. These theories are also difficult to reconcile with one quite general feature of language: its stimulus independence (1.2). Language does not constrain a speaker to speak of his and her immediate environment: she can speak of the elsewhere and elsewhen; of entities and events arbitrarily distant in space and time. This fact about human language, together with a suitably modest view of our epistemic grip on the distant, undercuts description theories. On those theories, our names can refer only to those objects that we can accurately describe. Yet as the objects we talk about become increasingly distant in space and time, our relations to them become increasing indirect. Typically, the informational channels that link us to these objects are thus increasingly interrupted and less reliable, leading to both ignorance and error.

3.5   Rejecting Description Theories

We think that description theories of names are wrong not merely in details but in fundamentals. The whole program is mistaken. Of course, we do not claim to have *demonstrated* this: there are few knock-down arguments in philosophy. So, moves can still be made to continue the program; for example, by denying the evidence ("The ignorant do *not* designate

Einstein"); or by proposing description theories that seem to avoid the arguments from ignorance and error. We shall briefly consider some proposals in a moment. But, after that, we will not follow these lines of thought further. Instead, we aim to undermine description theories in two further respects. First, in the rest of this chapter, we shall emphasize their *essential* limitations. Second, in the next few chapters, we shall develop an alternative.

Even were we to set aside Kripke's objections and accept the epistemic burden, a description theory would be essentially incomplete. A description theory of names explains the referential properties of one category of term, names, by appeal to those of another, definite descriptions: on the classical theory, '*a*' designates *x* in virtue of being associated with 'the *F*' which denotes *x*; designation is explained in terms of denotation. The referential properties of descriptions are explained, in turn, by appeal to those of general terms: 'the *F*' denotes *x* in virtue of the fact that '*F*' applies to *x* and to nothing else; denotation is explained in terms of application (3.1). What account of general terms is on offer? In virtue of what does '*F*' apply to *F*s? Perhaps a description theory of *some* general terms would be satisfactory: words like 'bachelor', 'judge' and 'murderer' may seem definable. This process cannot, however, go on for ever: there must be some terms whose referential properties are not dependent on others. Otherwise, language as a whole is cut loose from the world. Description theories, which explain one part of language in terms of another, can give no clue as to how, ultimately, language is referentially linked to reality. These theories pass the referential buck. But the buck must stop somewhere.

Of course, this alone does not show that any particular description theory – even a description theory of names – is wrong. But it does show that we will need nondescription theories in the end and so we should be receptive to the idea that we may need one in a particular case. And it should lead us to look skeptically at apparently desperate attempts to come up with description theories that avoid the problems of ignorance and error. So we should be skeptical of the following two sorts of description theories that have attracted some attention.

The first sort, which we might call "circular descriptivism", builds the required description around a term for the very semantic relation that we are seeking to explain. We face the question: In virtue of what does 'Einstein' designate Einstein? The theory answers: because speakers associate with 'Einstein' the description, 'the object designated by (or called, named, etc.) 'Einstein'' and because that description denotes Einstein. Our main objection to this is indicated by our calling it "circular". For, the theory passes the referential buck to a description which raises the following question: In virtue of what does 'the object designated by 'Einstein'' *denote* Einstein? This in turn raises the question: In virtue of what does the term 'designate' *apply to* a relation holding between 'Einstein' and Einstein? Now if this description theory were the *right* theory of reference for names, that relation would have to be the very relation between a name and its bearer that we sought to explain in the first place. The theory's buck passing is degenerate.

The second sort, which is called "causal descriptivism", is best approached by considering what form a *non*description theory of designation must take. Such a theory will claim that 'Einstein' designates Einstein in virtue of 'Einstein' standing in some relation R to Einstein. For example, in the next chapter, we shall propose that R is a certain sort of causal relation. Causal descriptivism adapts this claim to its own purposes by building the description it needs around *the term for* this relation. So the nondescription theory claims that 'Einstein' designates Einstein in virtue of standing in relation R to him. This sort of description theory claims that 'Einstein' designates Einstein in virtue of 'the object that 'Einstein' stands in relation R to' denoting him. Thus, some philosophers, impressed by causal theories like the one we shall be proposing, but still intent on saving description theories, claim that people associate with 'Einstein' a description along the lines of, 'the cause of my 'Einstein'-talk', and that this description determines the reference of 'Einstein'.

This is ingenious. If a description theorist really does build her description around the term 'R' drawn from the theory of her nondescriptionist rival, then the rival *must* accept that the description does denote the referent on pain of giving up his own theory! Ingenious, but "fishy". The first problem is that the requirement that speaker associate this "'R'-description" with 'Einstein' seems to be theoretically redundant. In claiming that the 'R'-description denotes the referent of 'Einstein', the causal descriptivist accepts the fact that 'Einstein' stands in the distinctive relation R to that referent. This fact alone is sufficient to explain reference. Requiring the speaker to associate the 'R'-description with 'Einstein' does no theoretical work.

The second problem with causal descriptivism is that although designed to avoid problems of ignorance and error it raises new ones; with a vengeance. It requires that everyone who designates – i.e., everyone – has a *theory of* designation, *and that the theory is right.* Everyone who uses a name has to be able to provide a description that *correctly explains* the reference of the name; everyone must "know the right 'R'". So causal descriptivism requires that the folk have already managed what, we shall soon suggest, no semantic theorist has yet managed! ('The cause of my 'Einstein'-talk' is only the very vague and inadequate beginning of what is required.) Once again, far too heavy an epistemic burden is being placed on speakers.

The need for nondescription theories is implicitly acknowledged in the theory that some have taken from Frege's discussion of names. This theory has a broader view than the description theory of the ways in which speakers can identify those to whom they refer by name. The theory allows that a speaker may not be able to *describe* the bearer provided that he is able to *recognize* her: the name will refer if the speaker can pick the bearer out in a lineup by saying, for example, "that person". This more general theory – we shall call it "the identification theory" – increases the value of reference borrowing: the lenders are often people we could recognize but not describe. Despite these advantages, the identification theory is still too demanding. There are limitations on the number of objects most of us could successfully point out. We could manage it for our friends, many of our acquaintances, and some of our famous contemporaries. However, we can but dimly call to mind many we can name. We certainly cannot identify historical figures like Cicero this way. And we would often pick out the wrong person in the lineup. The identification theory suffers less than the description theory from problems of ignorance and error, but it still suffers.

Our present interest in the identification theory is in its departure from the guiding idea of description theories: the idea that a name designates what its associated description denotes. 'That person' is a *demonstrative* not a definite description, and its reference does not seem to be determined by denotation. We need a different sort of theory altogether to explain its reference. Indeed, the information the speaker associates with a name on this development may not be linguistic at all but rather a perceptual or discriminative capacity of some kind. In thus appealing to nondescriptive mechanisms to explain reference, the identification theory implicitly acknowledges the incompleteness of the description theory.

Strangely enough, theorists of reference give little explicit attention to the essential incompleteness of description theories.

Finally, we must consider a famous science-fiction fantasy invented by Hilary Putnam (1975: 223–7). The fantasy concerned natural kind terms but we shall adapt it for proper names. Imagine that somewhere in the universe there is a planet, Twin Earth. Twin Earth, as its name suggests, is just like Earth. In particular, each Earthling has a *doppelgänger* on Twin Earth who is molecule for molecule the same as the Earthling. Consequently, many Twin Earthlings speak a language that seems like English. Indeed it is phonologically and syntactically the same as English. Is it semantically the same too? It cannot be if we deem it to include the proper names that Twin Earthlings use, because it is not referentially the same. When an Earthling uses a name in English, he refers to an object on Earth. When his *doppelgänger* uses what is apparently the same name, he refers to an object on Twin Earth. Friend Oscar declares his voting intentions: "I'll vote for Reagan; we need a dangerous president for a dangerous world". He is talking about our local Earthly Reagan. Twin Oscar produces an utterance that sounds the same, but he is not referring to Reagan;

he has never heard of Reagan nor of any other Earthling. He has his own problems with Twin Reagan in Twin USA.

What does this show? First of all, it shows that nothing internal and intrinsic to Oscar or Twin Oscar – no mental images, associations, feelings, or whatever – is sufficient to determine the reference of 'Reagan'. For Oscar and Twin Oscar are internally alike and yet their references are different. We must look for some relation that Oscar and Twin Oscar have to things outside themselves for the ultimate explanation of meaning and reference. As Putnam puts it, "meanings just ain't in the *head*" (1975: 227).

Indeed, *how could* meanings be in the head? Meaning depends on reference and reference relates a person and his word to one particular external object and not others. An internal state of a donkey might be an excellent symptom, even a perfectly reliable symptom, of that donkey's having been kicked by its owner. But that internal state alone cannot make it true that the donkey has been thus kicked. Equally, no internal state of a man can make him the father of Wayne. And internal facts about salt cannot alone make it soluble in water, for salt's solubility derives as well from features of water. No more could internal facts be sufficient to determine reference. To suppose otherwise is to suppose that an internal state has a truly magical power.

Second, the fact that reference partly depends on external facts confirms our finding that description theories are essentially incomplete. Even if a description theory is true for some word, the theory explains meaning in terms of associations that are entirely in the head of a speaker and so could not be a *complete* explanation.

Third, and most pertinent to this chapter, the fantasy provides another argument against description theories of names of the sort that we have been discussing. For Oscar and Twin Oscar are internally alike and so must associate exactly the same descriptions with 'Reagan'. Yet they refer to different people. So the association of a description with a name is not sufficient to secure reference.

(Twin-Earth fantasies appeal to philosophers, but not to many others, as Stephen Stich has emphasized; 1983: 62n. If you are one of the others, try to invent a less outlandish example that makes the same point.)

For all this, there are some important truths in the description theory. Indeed, the theory we propose, tentatively, is a hybrid that includes many elements from the description theory. The idea that we must have some true beliefs about an entity in order to refer to it by name is appealing. We shall return to it (4.5). The idea of reference borrowing is especially important. It highlights what Hilary Putnam calls "the linguistic division of labour" (1975: 227–8). Our ability to use our language is, in part, a social capacity. It depends on our interactions with others in a community of varying interests, capacities, and expertise. Putnam made the point about general terms: our capacity to talk about chromosomes, microchips and, curved spacetime, despite our ignorance of these things, is a result of our social links to others whose acquaintance with them is more intimate. The same is true of names: a person often succeeds in designating an object only in virtue of being at the end of reference chains running through her linguistic community to the object. However, our view of the nature of those links is very different from that of the description theorist.

Suggested Reading

3.1

Frege's theory of names is briefly introduced in the 1892 paper, "On Sense and Reference" (1952: 57–8), reprinted in Martinich 1996, and Ludlow 1997. For more on his view of names, see his much later (1918), "The Thought", reprinted in Ludlow 1997.

Russell's theory of names appears in several works first published between 1910 and 1920. The simplest statement is probably *The Problems of Philosophy* (1967), ch. 5. See also "Knowledge by Acquaintance and Knowledge by Description", in *Mysticism and Logic* (1957); and "The Philosophy of Logical Atomism", in Logic and Knowledge (1956). Russell distinguished ordinary proper names from "logically proper names". His description theory applies to the ordinary ones. He had a Millian theory of the logically proper ones. They behave the way he thought names *ought* to behave. They stand in a relationship of the utmost intimacy to their bearers. They immediately and directly focus attention on an object and that is all they do. Only 'this', which we would not normally call a proper name at all, seems to qualify as a logically proper name. The reader must avoid being misled by the fact that Russell often writes as if ordinary names were logically proper. He does this to get familiar examples.

Russell's theory of descriptions first appeared in his famous 1905 paper, "On Denoting", reprinted in Russell 1956, Martinich 1996, and Ostertag 1998, *Definite Descriptions*. See also his *Introduction to Mathematical Philosophy* (1919), ch. 16, reprinted in Martinich 1996, Ludlow 1997, and Ostertag 1998.

3.2

For Searle's theory of names, see "Proper Names" (1958), reprinted in Martinich 1996, and Ludlow 1997. See also his *Speech Acts* (1969), pp. 162–74. For Strawson's theory, see *Individuals* (1959): 180–3, 190–4. A cluster theory is also to be found in Wilson 1959, "Substances without Substrata".

The suggestion that the understander need not know the whole cluster seems to be present in Strawson. Evans 1973, "The Causal Theory of Names", pp. 193–4, reprinted in Schwartz 1977, *Naming, Necessity, and Natural Kinds*, Martinich 1996, and Ludlow 1997, takes Strawson in this way.

For Kripke's discussion of the modal consequences of description theories, rigid designation, and the distinction between theories of meaning and theories of reference, see *Naming and Necessity* (1980), particularly pp. 3–15, 48–78, excerpts of which are in Martinich 1996 and Ludlow 1997; also, "Identity and Necessity" (1971), reprinted in Schwartz 1977. Dummett 1973, *Frege*, pp. 111–35, is a vigorous response to Kripke. See also Linsky 1977, *Names and Descriptions*, chs. 3 and 4. The ramifications of Kripke's lines of argument are thoroughly explored in Salmon 1981, *Reference and Essence*.

3.3–3.4

For Kripke's nonmodal argument against description theories see his 1980: 79–91, reprinted in Ludlow 1997 and excerpted in Martinich 1996. A similar line of argument is to be found in Donnellan 1972, "Proper Names and Identifying Descriptions", which appeared with the original version of Kripke's work in Davidson and Harman 1972, *Semantics of Natural Language*. See Kroon 1982, "The Problem of 'Jonah': How *not* to Argue for the Causal Theory of Reference", for a criticism of one Kripkean argument.

3.5

The following defenses of description theories in the face of Kripke's argument seem to threaten circularity: Loar 1976, "The Semantics of Singular Terms"; McDowell 1977, "On the Sense and Reference of a Proper Name"; Schiffer 1978, "The Basis of Reference". On the problems of circularity, see Kripke 1980: 160–2; also Devitt 1981a, *Designation*: 21–3. Kroon 1989, "Circles and Fixed Points in Description Theories of Reference", is a critique of Kripke's noncircularity condition.

The term 'causal descriptivism' comes from Lewis 1984, "Putnam's Paradox". The idea is mentioned by Kripke (1980: 88n.) crediting Nozick. Kroon 1987, "Causal Descriptivism", is a helpful defence of the view. The view forms part of Frank Jackson's ingenious defense of description theories, "Reference and Description Revisited" (1998).

Dummett 1973, *Frege*, ch. 4, takes Frege to have urged the more general identification theory of names, not the description theory.

See the suggested readings for section 5.1 for discussions of Putnam's "meanings just ain't in the head".

4

A Causal Theory of Reference: Names

4.1 A Causal Theory

The basic idea of causal, or historical, theories of reference, due to Kripke (1980) and Donnellan (1972), is that a term refers to whatever it is causally linked to in a certain way. These links do not require speakers to have identifying beliefs about the referent. The causal links relate speakers to the world and to each other.

We start with the simplest case, proper names. How is a person able to use 'Einstein' to designate a physicist he has never met and whose theories he does not grasp? This problem divides in two.

1. How do we explain the introduction into our language of 'Einstein' as a name for Einstein? We need to explain how people were first able to use that noise to designate a certain individual. This requires a theory of *reference fixing*. Our theory of reference fixing looks to the causal *grounding* of a name in an object.

2. How do we account for the social transmission of the name 'Einstein' within the linguistic community? None of us had anything to do with the introduction of the name but can use it to designate Einstein because we have gained the name from others. To explain this we need a theory of *reference borrowing*. We shall offer a causal theory of this also.

The basic idea of the causal theory of grounding is as follows. The name is introduced at a formal or informal dubbing. This dubbing is in the presence of the object that will from then on be the bearer of the name. The event is perceived by the dubber and probably others. To perceive something is to be causally affected by it. As a result of this causal action, a witness to the dubbing, if of suitable linguistic sophistication, will gain an ability to use the name to designate the object. Any use of the name exercising that ability designates the object in virtue of the use's causal link to the object: perception of the object prompted the thoughts which led to the use of the name. In short, those present at the dubbing acquire a semantic ability that is causally grounded in the object.

The basic idea of the causal theory of reference borrowing is as follows. People not at the dubbing acquire the semantic ability from those at the dubbing. This acquisition is also a causal, indeed perceptual, process. The name is used in conversation. Hearers of the conversation, if of suitable linguistic sophistication, can gain the ability to use the name to designate the object. The exercise of that ability will designate the object in virtue of a causal chain linking the object, those at its dubbing, and the user through the conversation.

A name not only has reference (usually), it has sense (2.6). If the causal theory is to emulate the description theory in accounting for both (3.1), we must give a theory of sense. According to our theory, the sense of a name is a particular property of the name, the property of designating its bearer by a certain type of causal link between name and bearer. (More exactly, as the name may be empty, the sense is the property of purporting to designate an object by such a link.) The aspects of reality we have to call on to explain reference are all we need for sense. The reference of a name is determined by the appropriate causal chains and, in virtue of that, by its sense. The chains yield what Frege would call "the mode of presentation" of the object (2.6). So Frege was right in thinking that there was more to a name's meaning than its referent, but wrong in thinking that the extra was expressed by a definite description.

With the description theory of reference went a theory of understanding, a theory of what it is to be competent with a name (3.1). Such a theory is also implicit in the above causal theory. When we talk of an ability to use a name gained at a dubbing or in conversation, we are talking of competence. So competence with the name is simply an ability with it that is gained in a grounding or reference borrowing. Underlying the ability will be causal chains of a certain type that link the name to its bearer. Since the name's sense is its property of designating by that type of chain, we could say that, in a psychologically austere way, competence with a name involves "grasping its sense". But competence does not require any *knowledge about* the sense, any *knowledge that* the sense is the property of designating the bearer by a certain type of causal chain. This sense is largely external to the mind and beyond the ken of the ordinary speaker. In thus abandoning the Cartesian assumption for names, the causal theory departs further from a Fregean notion of sense and from description theories as they have been standardly understood (3.1, 3.2). Many would reject our theory simply *because* it posits a sense that ordinary speakers are unlikely to know about. We shall later argue that the Cartesian assumption should be abandoned for all terms (8.6). And we shall say more about competence later (8.9), after we have discussed thoughts (ch. 7).

So the picture is this. At a dubbing, a name is introduced by grounding it in an object. There is a causal chain linking the ability gained at the dubbing to the object. In virtue of that link, the reference of the name is fixed as the object. Exercising the ability by using the name adds new links to the causal chain: it leads to others having abilities dependent on the original ability. Thus, we can use 'Einstein' to designate Einstein because we are causally linked to him by a chain running through our linguistic community to someone present at his dubbing.

Let us illustrate this picture. The typical name is of a humble object and so we take as our example the name of Devitt's late cat: 'Nana'. Two people were present at her dubbing. There was no elaborate ceremony: one said, "Let's call her 'Nana' after Zola's courtesan", and the other agreed. This simple suggestion, agreed to, was enough. Each person saw and felt the cat, saw the other person, and heard his or her words. Each person was sophisticated enough to know what was going on. The cat occupied a unique place in this complex causal interaction. In virtue of that place she was named 'Nana'. In virtue of that place the abilities the two gained were ones to designate Nana.

A few minutes later, the name was used for the first time: "Nana is hungry". That first use designated Nana. It did so because that name token was produced by an ability created by the dubbing in which Nana played that unique role. Underlying the token is a causal chain grounded in Nana.

The two dubbers did not keep the name to themselves. They introduced others to the cat: "This is Nana". They told others of her name: "Our cat is called 'Nana'". They used the name in conversation: "I must get home to feed Nana". Those who heard and understood these utterances gained abilities to designate Nana by her name; they borrowed their reference from the dubbers. When they went on to use the name there were causal chains underlying those uses that stretched back to Nana via the ability of the reference lender. From those uses still others gained abilities; abilities depending on similar chains. Such chains are "designating chains" or, briefly, "d-chains". So, underlying a name is a network of d-chains.

Note that reference borrowing is not simply a matter of learning a word from another person. Clearly any word can be thus learned. In a case of reference borrowing, it is (partly) *in virtue of* the referential abilities of another person, that the speaker's use of the term has its reference. Not only was the other person causally responsible for the speaker's reference, but that reference is still dependent on a d-chain that runs through that other person.

4.2   Virtues of the Causal Theory

The theory developed so far is oversimplified in various ways, but we can see already that it has many attractive features. First, it shares with description theories the capacity to account for the following special features of natural language (1.2): that it is stimulus independent; arbitrary; medium independent; learned. A name is stimulus independent in that the causal chain on which its use depends does not require the presence of the object. It is arbitrary and medium independent in that any symbol in any medium can be placed in the appropriate causal relation to the object. And because of this, it has to be learned. However, unlike description theories (3.2), it can also account for the apparent abstractness of proper names: as Mill observed, names do not "imply any attributes as belonging to" the object (2.5).

Second, the causal theory avoids the five problems of description theories. Since a name does not abbreviate a cluster of definite descriptions, there is no problem finding a principled basis for selecting which descriptions are in the cluster for a person (cf. 1 in 3.1–3.2); nor, avoiding unwanted ambiguities arising from cluster differences between people (cf. 2); nor, coping with unwanted necessities (cf. 3); nor, losing the rigidity of names (cf. 4). Indeed, the theory explains this rigidity: a name refers in all possible worlds to the object it is causally related to in the actual world. The connection between names and identifying beliefs is cut, thus avoiding the problem of ignorance and error (cf. 5 in 3.3–3.4). We do not require that name users associate descriptions with a name that identify its bearer; we offer a very different view of competence with a name. People designate Catiline despite their ignorance of him; they designate Jonah despite their errors about him. They do this by borrowing their reference from others who in turn borrowed theirs, and so on, right back to those who named the objects. None of these borrowers needs to be able to identify his lender. No lender needs to be an expert about the object. Ignorance and error are no bar to reference. The epistemic burden is lightened.

Third, the theory can solve the problem of identity statements. This was one of the problems that led to the introduction of senses (2.5–2.6) and thus encouraged description theories in the first place (3.1). That our theory can solve this problem may seem surprising, for our theory is rather similar in spirit to the Millian view, as our agreement with the above Millian observation indicates. However, we disagree with the Millian view in a way that is important to the problem of identity statements. There is more to the meaning of a name than its role of designating a particular object. A name has a finer-grained meaning because it has a sense involving a *mode* of designation. (In this we differ from "direct reference"; 4.4.) We identify this sense with the property of designating by a certain type of d-chain, the type that makes up the network for the name.

The problem is to explain the difference in meanings of the identity statements:

(1) Mark Twain is Mark Twain
(2) Mark Twain is Samuel Clemens.

The explanation is that (1) and (2) differ because the names 'Mark Twain' and 'Samuel Clemens' have different senses in that they have underlying them d-chains of different types. The d-chains differ in that the groundings and reference borrowings that created them involve, in one case, the sounds, inscriptions, etc. of the name 'Mark Twain', and in the other case, the sounds, inscriptions, etc. of the name 'Samuel Clemens'. And they differ in that those for one name are linked together by speakers to form one network, those for the other, another.

(1) and (2) differ not only in meaning but also in informativeness. Indeed, under the influence of the Cartesian assumption – that the competent speaker (tacitly) knows about the meanings of her terms – many take the difference in informativeness to be the main reason for thinking that there is a difference in meaning. We are dubious of the Cartesian assumption and so this is not our reasoning (2.5). Still, the two statements *do* differ in informativeness. How is that to be explained if the causal theory is right?

Very easily, and the explanation does not depend on the causal theory. We focus on why (1) is uninformative. To understand 'is (the same as)' is to master "the law of identity": for any x, x is x. Any instance of the law will be an uninformative consequence of that understanding. An instance of the law contains two occurrences of the same name for the same object. Since (1) is obviously an instance, it will seem uninformative. In contrast, (2) is not an instance and will not seem to be an instance because 'Mark Twain' and 'Samuel Clemens' *sound*, *look*, etc. different. So (2) will seem to be informative. So, we have explained the difference in informativeness without mention of the causal theory. Indeed, this easy explanation does not appeal to any theory of the meaning of a name and so can be adopted by *any* theory of that meaning, provided only that the theory does not make the Cartesian assumption.

On the Cartesian assumption a theory of meaning must explain the informativeness of (2), 'Mark Twain is Samuel Clemens'. For, on that assumption, (2) must be informative *because* 'Mark Twain' and 'Samuel Clemens' differ in meaning; (2) could not be informative unless the names differed in meaning. If the names were synonyms, and you knew it, then *of course* you would find (2) uninformative. The Cartesian assumption requires that if the names were synonyms, you would indeed know that they were (assuming that you are competent with the names). And, since (2) is clearly informative, the names must differ in meaning and you must know that they do. So, the informativeness of (2) depends on the difference in meaning. So, it is the job of the theory of meaning to explain how it does. But now drop the Cartesian assumption: just because the names differ in meaning it does *not* follow that you know that they do. The informativeness of (2) no longer depends on that difference of meaning: indeed, for all we have argued, (2) could be informative even if the names had the same meaning. It is no longer the job of the theory of meaning to explain anything about informativeness.

What about the other problems that led to senses? Existence statements and empty names require further developments, which we will give briefly in the next section. Opacity is hard and cannot be handled here. However, we can indicate the lines of our solution. The sentence

Falwell believes Bob Dylan destroyed the moral fiber of America

depends for its truth not simply on the referent of 'Bob Dylan' but also on the mode of presentation of the referent. In this respect our solution follows Frege. However, our view of that mode differs from Frege's, as we have noted (4.1). The above sentence can be true only if Falwell's belief involves the appropriate causal network.

Fourth, consider a problem that we have so far ignored: that posed by the *ambiguity* of names. Proper names typically have more than one bearer. What determines which bearer is designated by a particular use of such a name? This problem can be put clearly in terms of a helpful distinction between *types* and *tokens*.

Tokens are datable, placeable parts of the physical world. Thus, Nana and her successor, Lulu, are cat tokens. The obvious examples of word tokens are inscriptions on a page or sounds in the air. Types, on the other hand, are kinds of tokens. Any token can be grouped into many different types. Thus, Nana and Lulu are tokens of the type *cat, female, pet of Devitt*, and so on. And, prior to this sentence, this paragraph contains two tokens of the inscription type 'Nana' and twelve of the inscription type *four-lettered*. Inscription types and sound types are identifiable by their overt physical characteristics and so we might call them "physical" types. Word tokens are also grouped semantically. Suppose that an inscription type 'Liebknecht' is used in a book on German history to refer to two different people, father and son; the type is *ambiguous*. Sometimes we will group the tokens that refer to the father in one type and those that refer to the son in another. We thus get "semantic" types. Tokens that are in different media cannot be of the same physical type but may be of the same semantic type; for natural languages are medium-independent. A spoken and written token of 'Liebknecht' might supply an example of tokens of the same semantic type from different media.

We can now put the problem of ambiguity as follows. What settles which semantic type a given token of an ambiguous physical type belongs to? In virtue of what does a token of 'Liebknecht' have one referent rather than the other?

Intuitively, the semantic type is determined by *what the speaker had in mind* in producing the token. So the matter is settled by some facts about the speaker's psychology. What facts precisely? Description theories say that it is the descriptions the speaker associates with the name token that counts. So, a token of 'Liebknecht' designated the father not the son because the speaker associated descriptions with it that denote the father not the son. We have seen that this kite will not fly. Our causal theory gives a different answer: it is the ability exercised in producing the token that counts. So 'Liebknecht' designated the father because it was caused by an ability which is grounded in the father.

Our solution to the problem of ambiguity, like that of description theories, is speaker-based. We do not overlook the importance of the linguistic and nonlinguistic *context* of an utterance but see all aspects of it, aside from the relevant parts of the causal history, as having only evidential significance. The context guides an audience in removing ambiguity; it supplies evidence of what the speaker has in mind and hence evidence of the semantic reality, but it is not that reality.

Some philosophers have thought differently: they have given a context-based solution according to which the context determines the semantic type of a token. We can see that this solution is wrong by considering an example that is most favorable to it: the sound type, 'Newton', which is used to designate both a famous physicist and an Australian golfer who lost an arm. These bearers of the name are as different as could be. If context disambiguates, it will do so unequivocally here. Suppose someone says, "The unit of force, a newton, is named after Newton". Suppose this takes place in a science classroom. Indeed, let every contextual feature point towards Isaac. According to the context-based view, these features are not merely very good evidence that 'Newton' here designates Isaac but determine that it does so. Yet it may still designate Jack. The speaker may be joking; or he may think the golfer moonlights in physics;

or whatever. No piling up of contextual detail makes it impossible for 'Newton' to designate the golfer.

Fifth, and perhaps most important of all, the causal theory promises an explanation of the *ultimate* links between language and the world. Furthermore, the explanation in terms of causation seems agreeably naturalistic (1.3). In rejecting description theories, we pointed out that they cannot explain the ultimate links (3.5): they make the reference of some words dependent on that of others, and thus leave reference *internal* to the language. We need an explanation of the *external* relation that the whole system of words bears to the world. We emphasized this with the help of Putnam's Twin-Earth fantasy. The causal theory we have offered in this chapter makes the reference of names dependent on an external relation. When Oscar declares, "I'll vote for Reagan; we need a dangerous president for a dangerous world", he refers to our Earthly Reagan not Twin Reagan. Why? Because his words stand in a certain causal relation to the Earthly Reagan. If Oscar has any causal relation to Twin Reagan, it is a very different one that is irrelevant to reference.

Return to our solution to the problem of ambiguity. The reference of a speaker's token of 'Liebknecht', who he "has in mind", is determined by his psychological states *together with* the way those states are causally embedded in the environment. For, the token refers to the object which grounds the ability exercised in producing the token.

4.3   Developing the Theory

It is scarcely possible to exaggerate the extent to which the theory proposed so far is in need of supplementation. We have already mentioned the problems of existence statements, empty names, and opacity (4.2) and will say something about the first two in this section. We shall also discuss *multiple grounding*, an elaboration of the causal theory that is important for handling many problems. In the next section, we shall look critically at a different response to the collapse of the description theory of names: "direct reference". This influential movement responded by returning to Millianism, rejecting senses altogether. In the last section, we shall consider whether users of a name must have *some* true beliefs about its bearer to secure reference. Other matters must be set aside, most notably the following.

1. What are abilities to designate? What goes on when we borrow reference? What kind of perceptual link to an object is required for grounding? We need to discover the social and linguistic preconditions of learning and introducing names. We shall throw some light on these questions in Part III when considering the relation of mind to language. However, we

shall not throw much. Partly this is because this book is not the appropriate place to attempt to do so, but largely it is because we are unable to do so. We, and we think others, simply do not know enough about the cognitive areas of the mind to answer these questions.

2. Our theory so far is concerned only with names. What of other terms? We need a theory of reference for all terms. Are they all to be treated causally like names, or are some to be handled by a description theory or some other theory of reference? How far can the causal theory be extended? We shall consider these questions in the next chapter.

Empty names

The causal theory distinguishes empty names from nonsense syllables, for even an empty name has an underlying causal network. What makes it empty is that its network is not properly grounded in an object. This can come about in two different ways.

First, a name may be introduced as a result of a false posit: a person wrongly thinks that an entity exists. Suppose that Zappa, perhaps after indulgence in strange chemicals, hallucinates an extraterrestrial visitor. Zappa attempts to name this visitor 'Tilda'. Since there is nothing there, he does not really name anything of course; his attempt at grounding fails. But he tells people about his experience, believing it real, and a network grows in just the way it would have had 'Tilda' named a real visitor. Names for various monsters may well have histories of this kind.

Second, and much more common, a name may be introduced in what is explicitly or implicitly a work of fiction: a story, novel, film, etc. Suppose that Zappa is not hallucinating but rather is bent on cashing in on the general fascination with science fiction. He writes a novel about an extraterrestrial named 'Tilda'. Out of his imaginative act a network for the name grows up that is not grounded in an object. How does it do so? Why does it do so? These are interesting questions which must be left to another time.

Existence statements

Our account of singular existence statements follows straightforwardly from this. The skeptical who respond to Zappa's alleged encounter with an extraterrestrial by claiming,

Tilda does not exist,

will be saying something which is both meaningful and true. It is meaningful because the name has an underlying causal network. It is true because its network is not grounded in an object. On the other hand, the gullible who claim

Tilda exists,

will be saying something which is both meaningful and false.

Reference change and multiple grounding

The theory sketched so far makes reference change impossible, for the reference of a name is immutably fixed at a dubbing. So the theory's account of language change is deficient. We have shown how additions to the language occur through dubbings. It is clear how a name dies out: people cease to add new links to its network by using the name. However, there is no explanation of how the reference of a name can change.

Gareth Evans (1973) has emphasized the importance of such an explanation with a number of nice examples. Here is an adaptation of one of them. Twins A and B are born and dubbed 'Shane' and 'Dawn' respectively. After the ceremony, the twins are somehow mixed up: everyone calls A 'Dawn' and B 'Shane'. The mistake is never discovered: the twins grow up, and grow apart, with each invariably "misnamed". Twin A turns out to be fiery, aggressive and physical, quite unlike twin B, who is mild, self-effacing and intellectual. What do we say of the boringly many utterances, 'Dawn is fierce' and 'Shane is mild'? Our simple version of the causal theory gives the wrong result: twin B was dubbed 'Dawn' and B is not fierce. Hence all those 'Dawn is fierce' tokens should be false. Yet they are surely not false. We want to say that all the years of calling A 'Dawn' and B 'Shane' have resulted in these *being* their names. The names have changed their references since the dubbings.

A more sophisticated causal theory is called for. Its central idea is that a name is typically *multiply* grounded in its bearer. In our original sketch, the reference of a name was fixed at a dubbing. All subsequent uses of the name were parasitic on that dubbing; all d-chains trace back to that one grounding. What this account misses is that many uses of a name are relevantly similar to a dubbing. They are similar in that they involve the application of the name to the object in a direct perceptual confrontation with it. The social ceremony of introduction provides the most obvious examples: someone says, "This is Nana", pointing to the beast in question. Remarks prompted by observation of an object may provide others: observing Nana's behavior, someone says, "Nana is skittish tonight". Such uses of a name ground it in its bearer just as effectively as does a dubbing. As a result it becomes multiply grounded. The dubbing does not bear all the burden of linking a name to the world.

Return to the twins and the problem of reference change. The name 'Dawn' was grounded in B at the dubbing, but from then on always grounded in A. The initial grounding in B pales into insignificance when compared with these thousands of groundings in A. So 'Dawn' now designates A.

There are actual instances of reference change. "Aotearoa" is now widely used in New Zealand as an alternative name for New Zealand, but it was originally the Maori name for only the north island. Evans gives another example: the name 'Madagascar'. For us it is the name of a large African island. However, it (or something like it) was originally the name of a portion of the African mainland. The change took place because of a misunderstanding by Marco Polo. Our account of the change is as follows. Before Marco Polo all groundings of 'Madagascar' were in the portion of the mainland and so that was what the name designated. For some time after his mistake there was doubtless a good deal of confusion, with those influenced by him grounding the name in the island and those influenced by the locals grounding it in the mainland. However, Marco Polo's mistake led finally to a systematic pattern of groundings in the island. The d-chains underlying our uses go back to those groundings. So those uses designate the island.

What about the period of confusion? What did the name refer to then? There would have been no serious problem if those influenced by Marco Polo and those influenced by the locals did not mingle. Marco Polo's mistake would then have quickly led to 'Madagascar' having a new meaning and reference while its old meaning and reference lived on with the locals. The name would have become ambiguous. However, it is more likely that the two groups did mingle. So, for a period, each use of the name would have underlying it some d-chains grounded in the mainland and some others grounded in the island. In these circumstances, there is no fact of the matter which object the name designated; reference is simply indeterminate. What we need is a new semantic notion: *partial* designation. We can then say that though the name did not designate either object, it partially designated both. Notions of partial reference are very useful in handling cases of confusion. However, this is not the place to discuss such refinements.

4.4   Direct Reference

The arguments of Kripke and Donnellan led us to a theory that, in its acceptance of senses, keeps us outside the Millian paradise (even though it is "similar in spirit" to the Millian view). These arguments have been one major influence in leading others back to that paradise. The other major influence has been David Kaplan's theory (1989) that demonstratives (like 'this' and 'he') and indexicals (like 'I' and 'now') are "directly referential": they refer without the mediation of a Fregean descriptive sense and are rigid designators (3.2). This theory is subtle and complicated. We are in broad agreement with it but will only discuss its bearing on names. The theory does not strictly entail the Millian view of names but it does strongly suggest the view. Kaplan himself embraces Millianism only tentatively but other direct-reference philosophers embrace it fervently.

This is *prima facie* puzzling. The traditional problems for Millianism (2.5) still stand. In the face of these problems, how *can* it be maintained that names have the coarse-grained meanings of the Millian view? There are two main themes to the answer. First, direct-reference theorists claim that the standard problems for the Millian view are not problems in semantic theory after all. So, for example, faced with the problem of identity statements, they claim that

(1) Mark Twain is Mark Twain
(2) Mark Twain is Samuel Clemens

do mean the same after all. And they have devoted much attention to the problem of opacity. They consider some well-known "puzzles" which they think lessen, if not remove, the threat to their view posed by apparent failures of substitutivity. We think that they are wrong, but this is not the place to go into these difficult matters.

Second, they do of course recognize that there *are* differences between (1) and (2), but they deny that these are *semantic* differences; they attempt to export the traditional problems from semantics either to the theory of mind or to pragmatics.

This strategy raises very difficult issues. It cannot be dismissed out of hand. We agree that some important differences between expressions are not semantic differences (2.3). We even agree with some direct-reference philosophers that one difference between (1) and (2) should be placed elsewhere: the cognitive difference in *informativeness* (4.2). Nonetheless, we are very skeptical of the direct-reference line here. First, we have defended a view of the role of meanings which makes the difference between (1) and (2) a difference in meaning. Second, direct-reference theorists offer no rival view of the role of meanings that supports their view that these differences are not meaning differences. Third, there is nothing problematic in taking non-Fregean senses to be semantic properties. That idea does not depend at all on the details of our causal theory of reference.

1. We began this book with a view of meanings that provides a basis for distinguishing meaning differences from other differences (1.2). Meanings

are the properties of symbols that enable them to play certain extraordinarily important roles in our lives, particularly roles in explaining and predicting behavior and informing us about the world. This is not very precise and so it will not always settle whether a difference is a difference in meanings. But it is precise enough to show that the difference between 'Mark Twain' and 'Samuel Clemens' is a difference in meanings. For, as we have already seen, the difference is central to the explanation of behavior (2.5). Alice is ready to assert, "Mark Twain is a famous author", but not, "Samuel Clemens is a famous author". As a result, on being told, "That is Mark Twain", she would rush over to meet the person indicated, but on being told, "That is Samuel Clemens", she would not.

2. Perhaps a different view from ours of the roles of meanings would support the Millian view that 'Mark Twain' and 'Samuel Clemens' have the same meaning despite their different modes of reference. Unfortunately, direct-reference philosophers do not provide such a view. They do not address the issue. What purposes do we serve in ascribing meanings to symbols? What is our interest in meanings? Without answers to these questions, direct reference provides no basis for exporting the difference in modes from semantics to pragmatics or the theory of mind. The exportation is theoretically *ad hoc*.

3. It is of course true that our talk of causal modes of reference needs more explanation than we have given it. But direct-reference philosophers do not use this objection as a reason for rejecting modes as meanings. This is as well because it would not be a good reason. Even on their view, there must be some non-descriptive-causal link between a name 'Mark Twain' and its bearer Mark Twain that explains the fact that 'Mark Twain' refers to Mark Twain. The link may not be as we have described it but its existence cannot be denied. So the property of referring by that link is a candidate for being the meaning of 'Mark Twain'. So direct-reference theorists must accept the link but deny that the property of referring by it is the meaning. For this they need some principled basis for counting something a meaning, a basis that does not beg the question in favor of their theory.

Why is direct reference so popular? We conjecture that these philosophers start from the insight that the referent of a word is central to its meaning. Next, they are very impressed by the refutation of description theories of names. Given that the meaning of a name is not descriptive they see no viable alternative to taking the meaning to be the referent. The possibility that the meaning might involve a nondescriptive causal mode of reference is either ignored, set aside, or dismissed as preposterous. We think this critical possibility is overlooked from inattention to our *interest* in meanings. This inattention explains the attempt to export semantic problems, and the dismissal of causal modes of reference.

4.5 The *Qua*-problem

In rejecting description theories of names and urging our causal theory, we have insisted that a person can use a name successfully without having beliefs that identify its bearer. The causal theory inclines us to go further: the person need not have any beliefs that are true of the bearer; none of the descriptions he associates with the name need apply to the bearer. Is this going too far?

Some philosophers have thought that the user of a name must at least associate with it a description of *the kind* of object that the bearer is; she must believe truly that it is of a certain kind (e.g. Geach 1962: ch. 2). Yet when we consider the way a person can borrow reference, this does not seem plausible. She can pick up a name on a very slender basis, wrongly inferring all sorts of things about its bearer. Perhaps it names a university yet she believes it to name a person, a cat or a river. She is linked into the causal network for the name and so there seems to be no good reason to deny that she uses the name to designate the university.

However, when we consider the way references are ultimately fixed in groundings, the total rejection of descriptive requirements on reference for names begins to seem too extreme. Two features of a grounding suggest this.

(1) Think once more of a grounding of 'Nana'. The name was grounded in Nana in virtue of perceptual contact with her. But that contact is not with *all* of Nana, either temporally or spatially. Temporally, the contact in any one grounding is only with her for a brief period of her life, with a "time-slice" of Nana. On the strength of such contacts, Nana, the sum of many time-slices sighted and unsighted, is the referent of 'Nana'. Spatially, the contact is only with an undetached part of her, perhaps a relatively small part like her face (she may be peering around a corner). In virtue of what was the grounding in the whole Nana not in a time-slice or undetached part of her?

The question is not to be airily dismissed on the assumption that names do, as a matter of fact, always designate "whole objects". Even if this were so, it would surely be possible to name temporal or spatial parts of objects. So there must be something about our practice which makes it the case that our names designate whole objects. In any case, we often do name parts. Sickeningly coy examples are to be found in *Lady Chatterley's Lover*. Think also of 'Sydney' which is the name of part of Australia. Temporal examples do not leap to mind so readily. Perhaps, 'The Crab Nebula' is an example: it names a star after it exploded. And we might name a tadpole without thereby naming the frog it turns into.

(2) Think next of a situation where the would-be grounder is very wrong

about what he is perceiving. It is not a cat but a mongoose, a robot, a bush, a shadow, or an illusion (like Zappa's extraterrestrial: 4.3). At some point in this sequence, the grounder's error becomes so great that the attempted grounding fails, and hence uses of the name arising out of the attempt fail of reference. Yet there will always be some cause of the perceptual experience. In virtue of what is the name not grounded in that cause?

Consideration of (1) shows that there must be something about the mental state of the grounder that makes it the case that the name is grounded in the cause of the perceptual experience *qua whole object*. It is unhelpful to say that it is the grounder's intention that makes it so. In virtue of what was the intention one to ground in the whole object? It seems that the grounder must, at some level, "think of" the cause of his experience under some general categorial term like 'animal' or 'material object'. It is because he does so that the grounding is in Nana and not in a temporal and spatial part of her.

This immediately yields an answer to our question in (2). The grounding will fail if the cause of the perceptual experience does not fit the general categorial term used to conceptualize it.

It seems then that our causal theory of names cannot be a "pure-causal" theory. It must be a "descriptive-causal" theory: a name is associated, consciously or unconsciously, with a description in a grounding. A descriptive element has entered into the characterization of a d-chain.

Clearly, we have moved some distance back toward the description theories rejected earlier (3.3–3.4). However, the extent of the move should not be exaggerated. First, the associated general categorial term does not *identify* the object; it does not distinguish the object from others of that sort. Second, our move is a modification of the causal theory of grounding, the ultimate fixing of a reference. The causal theory of reference borrowing remains unchanged and pure-causal; borrowers do not have to associate the correct categorial term.

The move away from a "total" pure-causal theory of names to a hybrid theory has a price, as we shall see (5.3).

This discussion, particularly the distinction between theories of reference fixing and borrowing, prompts a quick reconsideration of the case against description theories of names. That case, consisting of problems 1–5, is aimed primarily at description theories that do not contemplate reference borrowing (3.1–3.3); so they are theories of the reference fixing that any competent speaker must manage on her own. The case is aimed secondarily at description theories that are, in effect, a combination of a description theory of reference fixing with a description theory of reference borrowing (3.4). We have already indicated that we find the case against both these "total" description theories convincing. But what about a hybrid theory that combined a description theory of reference fixing with a pure-causal theory of reference borrowing? This hybrid would be no better off than the description theories on problems 3 and 4 – unwanted necessity and lost rigidity – but it would be on problems 1, 2, and 5. Concerning 1, the hybrid does not need to worry about the descriptions associated with the name by reference borrowers because those descriptions do not determine reference. So it only needs a principled basis for choosing among the descriptions of reference fixers. Concerning 2, since the reference fixers may be few in number and similar, it is less likely that a principled basis will generate unwanted ambiguity. Concerning 5, the reference fixers are likely to be much less ignorant and wrong than the reference borrowers. So, the problems for this hybrid theory of names are not as severe as for the description theories. Still, they are severe enough to make the theory unattractive for most names. However, we shall see later (5.5) that a similar hybrid theory of some other terms is quite attractive. And the theory does hold for a few "attributive" names (5.8).

In this chapter we have introduced our causal theory of names. This serves as a model for causal theories of reference. We must now turn to developing such theories for other terms. The plausibility of the Millian intuition that names lack connotation suggests that names are semantically unusual. So even if a causal theory is right for them, it may not be right for others.

Suggested Reading

4.1

Causal theories of names originated with Kripke 1980, *Naming and Necessity*, pp. 91–7, reprinted in Ludlow 1997 and excerpted in Martinich 1996; and with Donnellan 1972, "Proper Names and Identifying Descriptions". For a fuller development of the ideas in this section, see Devitt 1981a, *Designation*, secs. 2.1–2.3.

4.2

For more on this non-Cartesian approach to identity statements, see Devitt 1996, *Coming to Our Senses*, sec. 4.7.

**Our causal theory is applied to the problems of opacity in Devitt 1981a: chs. 8–10; 1996, ch. 4. These show that epistemic contexts can be handled without recourse to possible worlds.

See Lewis 1972, "General Semantics", in Davidson and Harman 1972, reprinted in Lewis 1983, for an example of a context-based approach to ambiguity.**

4.3

For more on empty names and existence statements, see Devitt 1981a: ch. 6. Donnellan 1974, "Speaking of Nothing", reprinted in Schwartz 1977, also discusses these topics from a causal perspective.

For some nice examples of reference change and confusion, see Evans 1973, "The Causal Theory of Names", reprinted in Schwartz 1977, Martinich 1996, and Ludlow 1997. For more on multiple grounding and the solution to these problems, see Devitt 1981a: secs. 2.8, 5.4. The notion of partial reference was introduced in Field 1973, "Theory Change and the Indeterminacy of Reference".

The following are critical of one or more versions of the causal theory of names: Loar 1976, "The Semantics of Singular Terms"; Erwin, Kleinman, and Zemach 1976, "The Historical Theory of Reference" ('the historical theory' is the name for the causal theory preferred by Donnellan); McKinsey 1976, "Divided Reference in Causal Theories of Names", and 1978, "Names and Intentionality", to which Bertolet 1979, "McKinsey, Causes and Intentions", is a response; Canfield 1977, "Donnellan's Theory of Names"; Linsky 1977, *Names and Descriptions*, ch. 5; Searle 1983a, *Intentionality*, ch. 9, reprinted in Martinich (Devitt 1990, "Meanings Just Ain't in the Head", is a response); McKay 1984, a critical study of Devitt 1981a; Rice 1989, "Why Devitt Can't Name His Cat"; McKay 1994, "Names, Causal Chains, and De Re Beliefs".

4.4

Kaplan's long paper, "Demonstratives" (1989a), which circulated for many years unpublished, is the main source of direct reference. For his view of names, see pp. 562–3, and "Afterthoughts" (1989b), pp. 574–6, 599. Nathan Salmon is a striking example of a direct-reference philosopher who exports the traditional problems for the Millian view to pragmatics, *Frege's Puzzle* (1986). He lists many others who have taken this path before (167n.). For examples of exportation to the theory of mind, see Almog 1985, "Form and Content"; Lycan 1985, "The Paradox of Naming"; Wettstein 1986, "Has Semantics Rested on a Mistake?". Kaplan seems to be tempted; 1989a: 529–40, 562–3. Recanati 1993, *Direct Reference*, proposes a comprehensive direct-reference semantics. For more criticism along the line of the text, see Devitt 1996: sec. 4.8. Katz 1990, "Has the Description Theory of Names Been Refuted", is an argument against direct reference.

5

Theories of Reference:
Other Terms

5.1 Description Theories of Natural Kind Terms

In this chapter we consider how far the causal approach to reference can be extended to terms other than names. Insofar as it cannot, other "mechanisms of reference" must be found. Perhaps description theories of reference will have a place with some other terms. Indeed, we shall argue that, for many terms, theories combining elements of causal and descriptive theories are quite plausible. Our coverage is not exhaustive; there are many terms – adjectives, adverbs, and verbs – whose referential mechanisms we do not discuss. While it is certainly no easier to explain these terms than the ones we do discuss, we may hope that doing so will not pose sharply different problems.

In the first five sections we shall consider general terms and mass terms. General terms, like 'tiger' and 'computer', are "count nouns": we can count what they refer to, tigers and computers. Notice though that an aggregation of tigers is not itself a tiger. This distinguishes general terms from mass terms like 'water'. We count glasses and drops of water but not water itself. Mass terms refer cumulatively: "any sum of parts which are water is water" (Quine 1960: 91). Note that some terms can function either way. In 'Mary had a little lamb', 'lamb' is a general term, but it is a mass term in 'Pass me some lamb'. In the last two sections we shall consider singular terms other than names.

General and mass terms come in many different varieties. We begin with terms for natural kinds. These are general terms like 'tiger', and mass terms like 'gold', referring to the members of observable natural kinds; of general terms like 'atom', and mass terms like 'oxygen', referring to the members of unobservable natural kinds. Just as there are description theories of names, so too there are description theories of natural kind terms. Speakers of the language associate various descriptions with each term. Using the terminology of Frege, we can capture these description theories as follows: one of these descriptions, or most of a cluster of them, expresses the sense of the term, which determines its reference. Using the terminology of the leading positivist Rudolf Carnap, we can capture the theories as follows: one of these descriptions, or most of a cluster of them, expresses the *intension* of the term, which determines its *extension*. If only one description counts, the view is analogous to the classical description theory of names (3.1). If a cluster of descriptions counts, the view is analogous to the modern description theory of names (3.2).

There are also description theories of understanding a natural kind term. Understanding a term consists in grasping its sense or intension; it consists in associating the right descriptions, the descriptions that determine the term's extension. Description theorists went further. Since they accepted the Cartesian assumption that speakers (tacitly) *know about* the meanings of their terms, they concluded that speakers have identifying knowledge of the kind.

We shall focus our discussion on general terms referring to the members of observable natural kinds and on simple rather than cluster theories. We draw on Kripke (1980) once again, and also on Putnam (1975).

The descriptions associated with our example, 'tiger', would be along the lines, 'large carnivorous quadrupedal feline, tawny yellow in color with blackish transverse stripes and white belly'. Another example is 'lemon', for which the descriptions would be along the lines, 'pale yellow, tart, oval, citrus fruit'. 'Tiger' or 'lemon' refers to the members of whatever kind its associated descriptions, or most of them, apply to.

Just like description theories of names, description theories of natural kind terms give a nice solution to the problem of identity statements (2.5, 3.1). The sentences

Cordates are cordates
Cordates are renates

differ in meaning because though 'cordates' and 'renates' are coreferential, they are associated with different descriptions (with 'having hearts' and 'having kidneys').

But just like description theories of names, these description theories have three immediate problems (3.1–3.2). 1) There is a *principled-basis* problem: the need for a basis for choosing which of the many descriptions a speaker associates with a term are the ones that express its sense and determine its reference. 2) There is a problem of *unwanted ambiguity* arising from variations in descriptions from person to person. 3) There is a problem of *unwanted necessity*. Suppose that the description that expresses the sense and determines the reference of 'tiger' is the one set out above. Now consider:

(a) Tigers are striped
(b) Large carnivorous quadrupedal felines that are tawny yellow in color with blackish transverse stripes and white belly are striped

According to the description theory these two sentences should be synonymous and (a) should be as necessary as (b). Yet this does not seem to be so.

Many philosopher were prepared to say that the sentences in pairs like this are indeed synonymous and necessary. Grasping this mettle for natural kind terms does seem easier than grasping the analogous one for names. But it is not very easy.

According to the description theorist's picture of language, the descriptions associated with a term like 'tiger' tend to be ones referring to gross observable characteristics; for example, being striped. These characteristics are the result partly of inner nature and partly of environment. Consequently, unusual environments can produce anomolous members of a natural kind: tigers may have only three legs, lack stripes, or be as tame as a domestic cat; lemons may not be yellow, oval, or tart. Yet, according to description theories, it should be impossible for such objects to be tigers and lemons respectively.

4) Next, these description theories seem to have a *lost rigidity* problem. Let us say that for a general term '*F*' to be a *rigid applier* is for it to be such that if it applies to an object in the actual world, and that object exists in another possible world, then it applies to that object in that world; or, for it to be such that '*F*s are *G*' would truly characterize some counterfactual situation only if any object that '*F*' *actually* applies to, and that exists in that situation, is *G* in that situation. Similarly for a mass term. (It is more common to try to define rigidity for these words in terms of designating abstract objects like kinds or properties. But these definitions raise difficult questions about the identity conditions of abstract objects.) The problem then seems to be that natural kind terms are rigid appliers whereas the descriptions alleged to be synonymous with them are not.

Compare:

(c) Tigers are reluctant to attack people
(d) Large carnivorous quadrupedal felines that are tawny yellow in color with blackish transverse stripes and white belly are reluctant to attack people.

Suppose that the Indian environment had been different enough to cause tigers to be yellow without black stripes and yet elsewhere, say in Africa, another species had evolved that was like our tigers, including being yellow with black stripes. In those circumstances, the truth of (d) would depend on whether that other species is reluctant to attack people. But the truth of (c) would still depend, just as it does in the actual world, on whether tigers are reluctant to attack people. (We have our doubts about this arising from the received scientific view of biological species; see 5.2.) So the description 'Large carnivorous quadrupedal . . . ' does not express the sense of 'tiger'.

5) These problems for description theories are serious but perhaps not catastrophic. What is catastrophic, once again (3.3), is the problem of *ignorance and error*; the theory places too heavy an epistemic burden on speakers. Putnam's example of 'elm' and 'beech' (1975: 226–7) is a vivid one of ignorance. He, like most of us, cannot describe the difference between elms and beeches. The meager descriptions he associates with these terms are inadequate to determine their extensions. Nor could he pick elms from beeches in a crowd of trees. Yet he is perfectly able to use 'elm' to refer to elms and 'beech' to refer to beeches. Whales provide a good example of error. Central to what most people used to associate with 'whale' was the description 'fish'. This description is false of whales. Yet all those people referred to whales by 'whale'.

The mere possibility of error counts against the description theories, as a fantasy due largely to Kripke (1980: 119–21) demonstrates. Imagine that we discovered that tigers do not have *any* of the properties we think them to have. They really have very different properties, including the unusual one of having an uncanny effect on humans: they cause humans to have illusions of large carnivorous quadrupedal felines . . . Perhaps they are extraterrestrials, pets left behind by von Daniken's extra-solar helpers. Yet, despite our universal error about tigers, our word 'tiger' would still have referred to them.

Reference to the members of a natural kind can occur despite the speaker's ignorance of, or error about, that kind. It is not necessary that the speaker associate descriptions that identify the objects referred to by a natural kind term. Neither is the association of identifying descriptions sufficient to make the term refer to the objects identified.

Suppose that in some hitherto unexplored place we discover some animals that fit all the descriptions usually associated with 'unicorn'. Does this likeness to unicorns establish that these animals are referred to by 'unicorn'? It does not. They *may* well be referred to, of course, if our unicorn myths had their origin in sightings of animals of that kind. However, it is much more likely that such animals have nothing to do with our term 'unicorn' and that their resemblance to unicorns is a mere matter of chance. If so then the term does not refer to them.

Reference borrowing helps description theories with problem 5, just as it did for names (although again at the price of worsening problems 1 and 2), particularly if the borrowing is from scientific experts. But all the problems of the description theory of reference borrowing must surface again. That theory requires beliefs where none may exist; in particular, a person may not have beliefs that identify the experts who are doing the lending (3.4).

Probably the most influential argument against description theories of natural kind terms is Putnam's Twin-Earth fantasy (1975: 223–7). We have given a version of this fantasy before (3.5). Putnam's argument concerns a mass term, 'water' and involves the following version of the fantasy. Suppose that Twin Earth is exactly like Earth except that, where on Earth there is H_2O on Twin Earth there is a water-like substance, XYZ. This substance is clear, drinkable, odorless, and so forth. The substance is called 'water'. When Oscar, on Earth, uses the term 'water' he refers to water (= H_2O). When his Twin-Earth *doppelgänger* uses 'water' he refers to XYZ. Yet Oscar and Twin Oscar are in exactly the same internal states. There can be nothing about their states, no capacity to describe or identify, that would pick out H_2O rather than XYZ, or vice versa. (If this seems a little implausible about a contemporary Earthling, who would probably believe that water is H_2O, place Oscar and his twin in 1750 when nobody knew the chemical composition of water.)

The obvious moral of this is that no intrinsic internal state can express a sense that is sufficient to determine the reference of 'water'. As Putnam says, "meanings just ain't in the head". Indeed to suppose that they could be in the head is to adopt a magical theory of reference, as we pointed out (3.5). A less obvious moral is the essential incompleteness of description theories. According to these theories, the reference of 'tiger' is determined by the reference of such words as 'carnivorous' and 'striped' with which 'tiger' is internally associated. What then determines *their* reference? If there is to be any reference at all, this buck passing must stop. Some terms must get their reference not in virtue of internal associations with other terms, but in virtue of external relations to things outside language and mind. Such external relations are, of course, the sort that causal theories appeal to.

Finally, the Twin-Earth fantasy shows that description theories for natural kind terms must be rejected. For Oscar and Twin Oscar associate exactly the same descriptions with 'water'. Yet they refer to different stuff. So the association of a description with the term is not sufficient to secure reference.

5.2   A Causal Theory of Natural Kind Terms

A causal theory of natural kind terms, like one for names, divides in two (4.1). First, there must be a theory of reference fixing, which explains how a term is linked to its referent in the first place. We shall offer, once again, a theory of the causal grounding of the term in its referent. Second, there must be a theory of reference borrowing, which explains the social transmission of a term to those having no contact with its referent.

As a first approximation, the grounding of a natural kind term includes both an ostensive component and a "nature" component. In a paradigm case, such a term is introduced into the language by ostensive contact with samples of the kind. Thus, 'tiger' is introduced by causal contact with sample tigers and 'gold' by causal contact with samples of gold. The extension of the term is then all those objects, or all those examples of stuff, that are of the same kind as the ostensively given samples, that share the underlying essential nature of the samples. Thus 'tiger' refers to all and only the objects that are of the same kind as the sample tigers – that is, to all tigers; similarly, 'gold' refers to all gold. In virtue of what is one thing of the same kind as another, sharing its underlying nature? This is discovered only by empirical scientific research. The received scientific view is that, in the case of a biological species like tiger, the shared nature is a certain evolutionary origin and, in the case of a chemical kind like gold, it is a certain internal structure. A competent user of a natural kind term need not, and normally does not, have true beliefs, let alone knowledge, about such scientific matters. So she is likely to have no true beliefs about what determines the reference of the term. Quite often, nobody has such beliefs.

The extent of ignorance is even greater than this. In many cases, most of those who use a natural kind term will not be acquainted even with samples of the kind: they borrow their reference from others by a procedure just like that for names. Such reference borrowers are unlikely to have true beliefs about the underlying nature of the relevant kind but are also unlikely to have beliefs sufficient to identify its members. Those of us who are as ignorant as Putnam about trees are in this situation with 'elm' and 'beech'. The causal theory lightens the epistemic burden once again.

Putnam brings out the significance of reference borrowing by talking of "the linguistic division of labour" (1975: 227–8), as we have mentioned before (3.5). Language is a social phenomenon. People are equally able (in principle) to use each term of language in their interactions with the world even though they are not equally able to relate that term to the world. How? Because they each gain the benefit of their linguistic involvement with others. Those on whom everyone ultimately depends are, of course, those who have grounded the term. These grounders may be experts, able to give identity conditions, but it is not essential that they be. What matters is that they have, as a matter of fact, linked the term to the world.

Consider the case of an apprentice jeweller learning the term 'platinum'. A sample of platinum is pointed out to him with the words, "That is platinum". He gains an ability to use the term to refer to platinum, an ability grounded in the metal by this introduction. His later uses of the term, exercising that ability, will refer to the metal in virtue of their causal link to it. He will come across further samples of platinum and so his use of the term will be multiply grounded. He will use the term 'platinum' to his friends in banking, building, and butchering, thus enabling them to borrow the reference from him. In such a way the causal network for a term grounded in a natural kind is established and grows in a linguistic community.

The causal theory of natural kind terms, like that of names, is not only a theory of reference but also a theory of sense and competence (4.1). We identify the sense of a term with the term's property of referring by a certain type of causal chain. Each such chain is grounded (unless there is reference failure). As a result the shared nature of members of the natural kind is involved in the sense of the term.

Competence with a natural kind term is simply an ability with it that is gained in a grounding or by reference borrowing. A person has the competence in virtue of being linked appropriately into the causal network for the term. Only in this psychologically austere way does she "grasp the sense". She need not have any true beliefs, let alone knowledge, about the sense. The sense is largely external to the mind and beyond the ken of the ordinary speaker. Once again, the Cartesian assumption is a casualty of the causal theory. We shall say more about competence later (8.9), after we have discussed thoughts (ch. 7).

Multiple grounding is important with natural kind terms, as it was with names (4.3), in handling certain mistakes and the phenomenon of reference change. If reference were fixed solely by the samples involved in the dubbing of a kind, reference would be immutable. However, a natural kind term is grounded just as effectively by subsequent groundings. A few of these may, by mistake, be in samples of a different kind. Intuitively, this should not affect reference. Theoretically, we can set these mistaken groundings aside as insignificant in number relative to those in the original kind. Should they not be relatively insignificant – should the mistakes be systematic, leading to a change in the pattern of groundings – then the reference of the term will change. Such a change can, of course, also be brought about deliberately: people decide to use an old term in a new way and so initiate a new pattern of groundings.

If the pattern of groundings changes by mistake not by decision, then there will be a period while the change is taking place when there will be no determinate matter of fact which of the two kinds the term refers to. The situation is analogous to one for names (4.3) and requires the same solution: the introducion of notions of *partial reference* into our theory. However, this is beyond the scope of this book.

Grounding, according to the above account, involves perception of a sample. This is possible when the natural kind term refers to observables but is clearly not if it refers to unobservables; for example, 'atom' and 'oxygen'. This is a difficult problem. What we must look for is some quasi-perceptual contact with unobservables through instruments.

There is another serious problem to be solved before the causal theory of natural kind terms could be regarded as complete. It is the "*qua*" problem, to be discussed in the next section. This is sufficiently serious to make us doubt that the causal theory alone has the resources to give an ultimate explanation of reference, to explain how language is ultimately linked to reality. We shall briefly consider some other possible explanations later (7.7).

****5.3 The *Qua*-problem**

Users of a natural kind term need not have true beliefs about the underlying nature of the relevant natural kind nor even have any beliefs sufficient to identify its members. Is it necessary to have any true beliefs about the members at all? Is there any descriptive requirement on reference? The rejection of description theories and acceptance of a causal theory may seem to suggest not. Would such a suggestion go too far?

A similar question arose for names (4.5). A consideration of reference borrowing did not then encourage any descriptive requirement, but a consideration of grounding did. We concluded that the grounder must associate a general categorial term with the name being grounded. This amounts to a move away from a total pure-causal theory to a hybrid, a descriptive-causal theory of grounding with a pure-causal theory of borrowing. Consideration of groundings again encourages a descriptive requirement and the departure from a total pure-causal theory.

Note first that a descriptive element seems implicit in our account already: the belief that the sample *is* a member of a natural kind. There are many kind terms other than natural kind ones; for example, there are terms like 'bachelor' referring to the members of sociolegal kinds and terms like 'pencil' referring to artifacts. People often use these other terms in ostensive contact with samples of the appropriate kind. We shall consider what relevance this has to the reference of these terms in the next section. Yet, clearly, whatever relevance ostensive contact does have for these other terms, it cannot have the same relevance as it does in the grounding of a natural kind term. There must be something about the grounding situation that makes it the case that it *is* a grounding of a natural kind term and not talk about, say, an artifact. Think of the grounding of 'human' in a sample who also happens to be a bachelor. Something must be going on that makes the nature-determining evolutionary origin of the sample relevant to the future reference of the term in a way that it is not relevant to the future reference of 'bachelor'. Something must pick the sample out *qua* member of a natural kind. Presumably, that something must be the mental state of the grounder. It seems that the grounder must, in effect and at some level, "think of" the sample as a member of a natural kind, and intend to apply the term to the sample as such a member.

The *qua-problem* is much more extensive than this. The term is applied to the sample not only *qua* member of a natural kind but also *qua* member of one particular natural kind. Any sample of a natural kind is likely to be a sample of many natural kinds; for example, the sample is not only an echidna, but also a monotreme, a mammal, a vertebrate, and so on. In virtue of what is the grounding in it *qua* member of one natural kind and not another? As a result of groundings, a term refers to all objects having the same underlying nature as the objects in the sample. But *which* underlying nature? The samples share many. What makes its nature as an echidna relevant to reference rather than its nature as a mammal (a nature it shares with kangeroos and elephants)?

In discussing names we pointed out that it had to be possible for a grounding to fail: nothing of the appropriate sort is present (4.5). This is true also of natural kind terms. The term 'witch' is empty – there are no witches and never have been – despite many purported groundings of the term in social outsiders of one sort or another. Those groundings all failed. The term 'phlogiston' is empty and yet there was certainly something present in the grounding situations causing the phenomena that led to the introduction of the term; sometimes it was oxygen. In virtue of what did these terms fail to be grounded in the social outsiders and oxygen, respectively?

It seems that something about the mental state of the grounder must determine which putative nature of the sample is the one relevant to the grounding, and should it have no such nature the grounding will fail. It is very difficult to say exactly what might determine the relevant nature, but presumably the answer would have to be along the following lines.

People group samples together into natural kinds on the basis of the samples' observed characteristics. They observe what the samples look like, feel like, and so on. They observe how they behave and infer that they have certain causal powers. At some level, then, people "think of" the samples under certain descriptions – perhaps, 'cause of O' where O are the observed characteristics and powers – and as a result apply the natural kind term to them. It is this mental activity that determines which underlying nature of the samples is the relevant one to a grounding. The relevant nature is the one that is, as a matter of fact, picked out by the descriptions associated with the term in the grounding. If the sample does not have the appropriate properties – if, for example, the alleged witch does not have the power to cast spells – then there will be no relevant nature and the grounding will fail.

In sum, the idea is that the grounder of a natural kind term associates, consciously or unconsciously, with that term first some description that in effect classifies the term as a natural kind term; second, some descriptions that determine which nature of the sample is relevant to the reference of the term.

We are under no illusion that these remarks are close to a complete solution to the *qua*-problem. One difficulty is that there are *individual* differences between members of a natural kind; think of the differences between dogs for a vivid example. These differences are often the result of nature not nurture. Suppose that a natural individual difference is among the properties picked out by the determining descriptions in a grounding. The underlying nature made relevant to reference by this grounding should then include that individual difference. So, the resulting reference should be not to all other members of the natural kind but only to objects, if any, that share the nature responsible for that difference. Something has gone wrong.

Differences between subgroups of a kind pose an even greater problem. Consider the term 'swan'. Before Australia made its great contribution to philosophy with the discovery of black swans, all observed swans had been white. It seems certain that among the descriptions playing a determining role in the grounding of 'swan' up to that time, 'white' played a central role. So the reference of the term should have been restricted to objects sharing the nature that made those swans white. Yet the reference was not so restricted. 'Swan' referred then, just as it does now, to swans which lack the nature making some of them white; viz. to black swans. Some change in the theory is called for.

A consideration of the *qua*-problem for names led us away from a pure-causal theory to a descriptive-causal theory of groundings (but not of reference borrowing; 4.5). So too has the *qua*-problem for natural kind terms. These moves have a price. First, they raise the possibility of refutation by arguments from ignorance and error (3.3, 5.1). Second, we have emphasized the essential incompleteness of description theories of reference: they explain the reference of some words in terms of the reference of other words, leaving the latter unexplained (3.5, 5.1). To the extent that a descriptive-causal theory is descriptive, it has the same incompleteness. The categorial term that plays a role for a name, the description that classifies a term as a natural kind term, and the descriptions that determine the relevant nature of the samples of a natural kind, all raise further problems of reference. In virtue of what do they refer?

We are torn two ways in explaining reference. The interest in an ultimate explanation pushes us away from description theories toward causal theories. But causal theories confront the *qua*-problem. Attempts to solve that push us back toward description theories, hence postponing the ultimate explanation. We must look for some very basic terms which do not give rise to *qua*-problems and so are amenable to treatment by a pure-causal theory. On this foundation we might then hope to explain other fairly basic terms – like names and natural kind terms – by descriptive-causal theories. We could then use the basic terms to explain the nonbasic ones by description theories.

We rather doubt that the sort of pure-causal theory we have presented so far can supply the ultimate explanation of reference that we need. We shall discuss some other possible theories later (7.7). We turn now to consider how the causal and description theories might handle some other terms.**

**5.4 Other Kind Terms

Putnam, who did so much to launch the causal theory of natural kind terms, saw the theory as having much wider application; it stretched even to kind terms like 'pencil' and 'pediatrician' (1975: 242–5). We are as enthusiastic for conquest as any causal theorist could be, but the wise imperialist knows his limitations. We think that Putnam goes way too far.

Putnam reaches his view of 'pencil' from a consideration of the description theory. If we apply that theory to 'pencil', certain sentences involving both the term and its associated descriptions should seem necessary (5.1). Putnam supposes that 'artifact' is one of the appropriate associated descriptions for 'pencil'. He again resorts to science fiction to reject the description theory.

> Imagine that we someday discover that *pencils are organisms*. We cut them
> open and examine them under the electron microscope, and we see the al-

most invisible tracery of nerves and other organs. We spy upon them, and we see them spawn, and we see the offspring grow into full-grown pencils – there are not and never were any pencils except these organisms. (1975: 242)

This shows that 'Pencils are artifacts' is not necessary; pencils might not be artifacts at all. So *being an artifact* is not part of the meaning of 'pencil'. This description theory yields an unwanted necessity; it has problem 3. Putnam moves straight from this conclusion to his view that 'pencil' is to be treated causally like 'water' or 'gold'; it refers to anything having the same underlying nature as our sample pencils (p. 243).

What is wrong with this refutation of the description theory, as Stephen Schwartz points out (1978), is that Putnam has picked the wrong description; 'artifact' is not a description that expresses, even partly, the meaning of 'pencil'. We can indeed imagine that pencils are organisms or that they grow on trees. Change the example and we do not have to use our imagination to make the point. A pencil is a tool to serve a human purpose. So too is a paperweight. Some paperweights are not artifacts but perfectly natural objects: stones or pieces of driftwood. Yet these objects are all part of the extension of 'paperweight'. So-called "artifactual" terms need not refer to artifacts! (Through lack of a suitable alternative, we shall also call these terms referring to tools and instruments, "artifactual", but we will always add scare quotes to distance ourselves from the usage; 2.7.)

A plausible description theory of 'pencil' will attend not to the accidental fact that pencils are artifacts, but to the function of pencils and how they must perform that function. A pencil is a *writing instrument*; the writing must be *by graphite* (note that pens are not pencils); and so on. Similarly, the appropriate description for 'chair' will be found by attending to the fact that chairs are things to sit on and to the fact that they have backs and legs (stools are not chairs). The necessities such a theory yields do not seem unwanted: chairs are indeed necessarily things to sit on.

Consider, next, a sociolegal term like 'pediatrician'. If the description theory applies to 'pediatrician' then the likely associated description is 'doctor specializing in the care of children'. Putnam doubts that the theory does apply because it could turn out that pediatricians are not doctors but Martian spies (p. 244). The theory has yielded an unwanted necessity again. In our view, Schwartz has once again responded correctly to Putnam's criticism (1980: 193–4). Certainly pediatricians could turn out to be Martian spies, but that is irrelevant to the theory: the above associated description does not entail that they are not Martian spies. The description does entail that they are doctors. So it *would* count against the description theory if they could turn out not to be doctors, but Putnam has given no good reason to suppose that they could so turn out.

So it is not hard to come up with description theories of "artifactual" and sociolegal terms that do not seem to yield unwanted necessities. How do such theories fare with the other four problems we have found for description theories of names and natural kind terms? The theories do not have problem 4, lost rigidity, because these sorts of terms are no more rigid than the descriptions associated with them: 'paperweight' may apply to a piece of driftwood in this world that never leaves the beach in another; 'pediatrician' may apply to a person in this world who is a plumber in another. And it is not obvious, at least, that they have problems 1 and 2, principled basis and unwanted ambiguity. However, they may have problem 5, ignorance and error.

An argument we adapt from Tyler Burge (1979) suggests that they do. The argument seems to count against description theories for a wide range of terms including "artifactual" and sociolegal ones. Consider the "artifactual" term 'sofa', for example. It is plausible to think that this is covered by a description theory, the relevant description being along the lines, 'couch with raised ends and back on which several people can sit'. But now imagine a person who seems to use the term properly to refer to sofas, saying truly for example that her neighbor "has a new sofa" and that "sofas are more comfortable than church pews". Then we discover that she fails to realize that a sofa must be multi-seated, being prepared to call a broad overstuffed armchair "a sofa" or being uncertain whether to do so. In the face of this, the description theory entails that she is not competent with the English term 'sofa': her term does not mean *sofa* and the beliefs she expresses with it are not simply about sofas. When she buys a leather armchair and proudly tells her neighbor, "I too have a new sofa", the description theory requires that this utterance be straighforwardly true: for, by 'sofa' she does not mean what it means in English but rather something like "large thing for sitting in with raised ends and back". But there is an alternative view of her utterance: it is strictly speaking false because she has no new sofa. Many take this line, arguing that there is nothing aberrant with the meaning of her term, just something wrong with her view of sofas. Consider next the sociolegal term, 'contract'. It is plausible to think that its meaning is given by the description 'legally binding agreement'. Yet many people think that a contract must be written. Must we say that these people do not mean *contract* by the term? Many are inclined to think not. Finally, Burge's most famous example is the medical term 'arthritis'. It is plausible to think that its meaning is given by 'inflammation of a joint'. Yet imagine a person who says a lot of apparently true things about arthritis but then adds, "I have arthritis in my thigh"; or is unsure whether to add this. Isn't this a mistake or ignorance about arthritis rather than about 'arthritis'?

Suppose that we follow these inclinations and say that these people are indeed using the terms with their normal meanings but are mistaken in various ways about the world. Burge contrasts what we thus say about these people in the above actual situations with what we would say about these same people – physically the same, with the same histories, and making the same utterances – were they living in situations where the community used the terms a bit differently: where 'sofa' applied to some single-seat armchairs, 'contract' was restricted to written agreements, and 'arthritis' applied to various rheumatoid ailments apart from those in the joints. In those situations, we would say that the people's utterances were not mistaken, they were true. What explains the difference in what we say? Not any intrinsic differences in the people doing the uttering, because the people are identical. The differences are to be explained by differences in the speech communities. There is a *social* dimension to meaning: the meaning of an individual's word depends not only on her but also on her community.

Burge-type arguments from ignorance and error are supposed to show the importance of what we have called "reference-borrowing": when such an argument works on a term, that term can be acquired by reference borrowing. Since we have already rejected the description theory of reference borrowing (3.4), we must then conclude that description theories alone cannot explain the term: any "total" description theory for the term must be false. It is clear that there is room for a good deal of debate about where Burge-type arguments *do* work. It is hardly obvious, after all, what we should say about 'sofa', 'contract', and 'arthritis'. Many will probably deny that the argument is effective on 'pediatrician'. These terms, many will insist, simply cannot be borrowed: everyone who is competent with them must associate the reference-fixing description with them. (Note that this is not the absurd claim that a person cannot *learn* a term from another. It is the claim that once a person has learned a term, her reference is not dependent on that of another; 4.1.)

Perhaps it should be obvious that rejecting a total description theory for a term is one thing, rejecting *any* role for descriptions in the explanation of the term's meaning and reference is another. But, as it happens, the possibility of hybrid theories combining descriptive and causal elements has been rather neglected. In the next section, we will consider the prospects of such theories for artifact terms and some others.**

**5.5 Hybrid Theories

Let us start by making explicit the two distinct ways in which a theory for a term might be a hybrid:

   (I) A theory of reference fixing, or a theory of reference borrowing, might not be merely causal – what we have called "a pure-causal theory"

– or merely descriptive – what we have called "a description theory" – it might be some combination of both – what we have called "a descriptive-causal theory". We have emphasized the possibility of this combination in discussing reference fixing for proper names (4.5) and natural kind terms (5.3). We shall soon contemplate the combination for reference borrowing.

(II) In discussing names and other terms, we have distinguished the process through which a term is introduced into a linguistic community from the process by which competence in its use spreads through that community. This opens the possibility of different accounts of those processes. So a theory of reference fixing of *one* sort, pure-causal, descriptive-causal, or descriptive, might be combined with a theory of reference borrowing of a *different* sort. We first raised this possibility in struggling with the *qua*-problem for names (4.5), and it has come up again in our discussion of kind terms (5.3, 5,4). It is contrasted with what we have called "a total theory" for a term. A total theory combines a theory of reference fixing of some sort – either pure-causal, descriptive-causal, or description – with a theory of reference borrowing *of the same sort* (or with the theory that the term cannot be borrowed). We shall soon contemplate some examples of theories that are hybrid in this way.

Before considering Burge, we suggested that a plausible description theory for 'pencil' and 'chair' will associate the terms with a description of function together with a description of certain physical characteristics; and that a plausible one for 'pediatrician' will associate it with something like 'doctor specializing in the care of children'. Now, even if we are inclined to think that these terms can be borrowed and so a total description theory will not work, the suggestion can be resurrected as a description theory simply of reference *fixing*: the "experts" who fix the reference must associate the appropriate description with the term even though the rest of us need not. This can then be combined with a causal theory of reference borrowing explaining how the rest of us depend on the experts. If the latter is a pure-causal theory, then we have a theory of the sort contemplated at the end of section 4.5. It is hybrid in way (II).

The pure-causal theory of reference borrowing does not require borrowers to associate with a term any description of its referent. This seemed appropriate for names and natural kind terms but much less so for these other terms we have been considering. The Burge-type argument does not incline us to think that a person could use 'pencil' to refer to pencils if he was *completely* mistaken: if he associated the term with a description of, say, a chair. So perhaps borrowers need to have *some* true beliefs about the referent. If so reference borrowing involves a causal chain of communication *together with* with some associated description. This is a descriptive-causal theory of reference borrowing, a hybrid in way (I). Combining it with a description theory of reference fixing yields a hybrid in way (II), hence a "doubly hybrid" theory of 'pencil'. This theory of 'pencil' is closer to the old total description theory than the one in the last paragraph.

The "artifactual" terms that we have considered so far seem to be *basic* ones. Many others like 'sloop' and 'dagger' do not, being defined in terms of other "artifactual" terms. For these nonbasic ones a description theory of reference fixing that does not mention function seems appropriate. Thus the meaning of 'sloop' may be given by 'boat having a single mast with a mainsail and jib'; that of 'dagger', by 'short two-edged weapon with a sharp point'. These descriptions contain the basic, or at least more basic, "artifactual" terms, 'boat' and 'weapon'. And the theory of reference borrowing that we need here again seems to be descriptive-causal: perhaps you cannot refer to sloops by 'sloop', even as a borrower, unless you realize that they are boats; to daggers by 'dagger', unless you realize that they are edged weapons.

These doubly hybrid theories, combining a description theory of reference fixing with a descriptive-causal theory of borrowing have a problem (reminiscent of problem 1 – the principled basis problem – for total description theories): What determines who the "experts" are? There must be some objective fact about the community that determines that the descriptions certain people associate with a term fix the reference and those others associate do not.

Perhaps this problem can be solved. If so, the description theory of reference fixing for the nonbasic "artifactual" terms may well be correct. Perhaps the description theory of the basic ones is, too, but we shall briefly explore a causal alternative. The alternative is not pure-causal but descriptive-causal, and so hybrid in way (I). The pure-causal theory faces a massive *qua*-problem, as we shall soon see.

The descriptive-causal theory of reference fixing for the basic "artifactual" terms is analogous to that for natural kind terms (5.3). The descriptive element is taken over from the description theory. It is the description of physical characteristics ('graphite' for 'pencil', 'back' for 'chair'). The causal element arises from groundings in samples. Whereas on the description theory, the reference-determining function is fixed by an associated description of the function, on the descriptive-causal theory it is fixed by the objects in the sample used to ground the term. The term refers to any object (with the physical characteristics) that has the same function as the objects in the sample.

A key difference between the description and descriptive-causal theory of reference fixing for basic "artifactual" terms is that the former requires, but the latter does not, that there be some "experts" who believe truly that samples of the kind have a certain function; indeed, if the description theory is Cartesian, as it usually is, the experts must *know* that the samples have a certain function. If a person on whom reference borrowers depend could use one of these terms successfully even though ignorant of, or wrong about, the function of the objects to which it refers then the description theory is wrong.

It would be much harder to find the counter-examples to show that the description theory is wrong about "artifactual" terms than it was to show that it was wrong about natural kind terms. The difficulty is that whereas experts often do not know the underlying natures of natural kinds, they do seem to know the functions of tools and instruments. The best places to look for counter-examples to the theory are to cases where religious or social beliefs mystify the function of certain artifacts; or to archaelogy, where the interpretation of the uses of various implements is often conjectural. We shall not go into the matter any further.

We noted at the beginning of the last section that a person grounding a natural kind term must associate with it something that makes it a term for a natural kind rather than an "artifactual kind"; that something must make the underlying nature of the sample relevant to reference. Our discussion here reinforces that remark. If a description theory of reference fixing for "artifactual" terms is correct, then ostensive contact with samples is irrelevant to their reference. So there must be something associated with natural kind terms that distinguishes them from "artifactual" terms by making the ostensive contact relevant to reference. On the other hand, if a descriptive-causal theory of "artifactual" terms is correct, then the function of the samples is relevant to reference. So there must be something associated with those terms, and something *else* associated with natural kind terms, that makes the function of the samples relevant to the reference of the "artifactual" terms, and the underlying nature of the samples relevant to that of the natural kind terms.

This discussion of the initial *qua*-problem brings out the failings of Putnams's (apparently) pure-causal theory of "artifactual" terms. This theory "leaves it to the world to decide" what a term refers to: it refers to whatever kind the samples exemplify. But a sample may exemplify many kinds; for example, the one object can be a cat, a pet, and a paperweight. There must be something going on in the ostensive contact with an "artifact" that makes its function, not its nature or sociolegal status, relevant to reference. This is a further descriptive element in the grounding (further to the description of physical characteristics.)

The pure-causal theory of reference fixing for natural kind terms faced a more extensive *qua*-problem than this: a sample exemplifies not just many kinds but many *natural* kinds. Our descriptive-causal theory for "artifactual" terms faces a similar problem: a sample may exemplify more than one basic "artifactual kind" – for example, it may be both a paperweight and a doorstop. So another descriptive element is required.

Let us sum up the often rather tentative discussion in this chapter so far. We have identified three sorts of theory of reference fixing: description, descriptive-causal, and pure-causal. There are these three sorts of theory of reference borrowing too, but there is also a fourth theory: the theory that a term cannot be borrowed. The theory of any term must combine one of the three for fixing with one of the four for borrowing.

At one extreme is a total description theory for a term. There are two alternatives here. The first is a description theory of fixing with no borrowing allowed. This is implicit in standard presentations of description theories. Such theories always face problem 5, ignorance and error. In the case of natural kind terms, the problem is severe. In the case of other terms – for example, "artifactual" terms – it is often troubling. And in the case of natural kind terms, the first four problems are also severe: principled basis, unwanted ambiguity, unwanted necessity, and lost rigidity. The second alternative is a theory that allows reference borrowing, combining a description theory of borrowing and of fixing (as Strawson's theory of names did). But problem 5 is still bad for such a theory and problems 1 and 2 are worse (3.4). And any description theory has the disadvantage of being essentially incomplete.

At the other extreme is the total pure-causal theory for a term: a pure-causal theory of fixing and borrowing. This theory of fixing has a severe *qua*-problem, whatever the term, which prompts a move to a descriptive-causal theory of fixing, a hybrid in way (I). Combining this theory of fixing with a pure-causal theory of borrowing yields a theory that is hybrid in way (II). It has plausibility for natural kind terms. The further move to a descriptive-causal theory of borrowing, yielding a total descriptive-causal theory that is hybrid only in way (I), has some plausibility for basic "artifactual" terms and perhaps some other terms. But we rather doubt that the details of a descriptive-causal theory of fixing can be satisfactorily worked out. And the descriptive part of any descriptive-causal theory makes it partly incomplete.

A doubly hybrid theory combining a description theory of fixing with a descriptive-causal theory of borrowing may be as plausible for basic "artifactual" terms as the total descriptive-causal one just mentioned. And it seems quite plausible for nonbasic ones and various other terms. But such theories face a problem determing the experts in a principled way. And they have the familiar disadvantage of incompleteness.

Other combinations are possible, of course, but they seem unpromising. One of these is the combination of a causal theory of reference fixing with the no-borrowing view. For, many of the arguments that led us to a causal theory pointed to the importance of reference borrowing. Yet it is interesting to note that the theories we shall discuss briefly later, which are causal theories of a different type, pay little attention to reference borrowing.

What we have been calling a "causal" theory so far appeals only to the idea of the *historical* cause of a particular token to explain reference. So it might be better be called an "*historical*-causal" theory. Other theories appeal to the idea of the *reliable* cause of tokens of that type. Still others appeal to the *teleological* cause or *function* of tokens of that type. And others appeal to some combination of these three ideas. These theories are essentially about the relations between thoughts and the world and so we shall discuss them in them in the next part of the book (in 7.7). The *qua*-problem for our historical-causal theory gives ample motivation for us to look elsewhere for an explanation of how reference is ultimately fixed.**

5.6   Analyticity, *Apriority*, and Necessity

Many philosophers hold that there are two sorts of true statements, *analytic* ones that are true simply in virtue of their meaning, and *synthetic* ones that depend for their truth not only on their meaning but also on the world. A favorite example of an analytic one is

(A) All bachelors are unmarried.

For, it is plausible to think that 'bachelor' is covered by a description theory according to which its meaning is partly constituted by its association with 'unmarried'; this association is part of its very *definition*. So, it is claimed, (A) must be true. In contrast, the truth of the synthetic statement, 'All men are mortal', depends not only on its meaning but also on the worldly fact that men are mortal. Where do we stand on this line of thought?

We have just suggested that description, or descriptive-causal, theories may be true for many terms. So it may seem as if we would endorse the line. To an extent we do, but we have an important qualification. According to the description theory, the meaning of 'unmarried' is part of the meaning of 'bachelor'. But, as has often been pointed out, this makes the truth of (A) dependent on the truth of

(L) All unmarrieds are unmarried.

If (L) were not true, the meaning relation between 'bachelor' and 'unmarried' would not be enough to make (A) true. So (A) is true *solely* in virtue of meaning only if (L) is. Some have claimed that (L) is indeed. Certainly, (L) is *obviously* true; it is a "logical truth" in that it would remain true whatever we substituted for 'umarried'. But we can see no basis for the claim that (L) is true solely in virtue of meaning. We follow Quine in thinking that (L) is true partly in virtue of what it means *and partly in virtue of the way the world is*, in virtue of the "logical" fact that all unmarrieds are indeed unmarried. So neither (A) nor (L) are analytic in the above sense. Still, they are analytic in another, weaker, sense: in this sense a sentence is analytic if it is either a logical truth (like (L)) or "reducible by definition" to a logical truth; ie. can be turned into a logical truth by substituting synonyms for synonyms (like (A)). In this weaker sense, note, the claim that logical truths are analytic is trivial: it amounts to the claim that logical truths are logical truths.

It is worth noting that true identity statements involving terms covered by a *causal* theory also turn out to be analytic in this weaker sense (as we foreshadowed in section 2.5). Consider 'Mark Twain is Samuel Clemens', for example. According to the causal theory, the meaning of 'Mark Twain' is its role of designating a certain person by a certain type of causal chain, and the meaning of 'Samuel Clemens' is its role of designating that same person by a different sort of causal chain. So, it is a consequence of the meanings of these names that they designate the same person. Given this fact about meaning, 'Mark Twain is Samuel Clemens' reduces to 'Mark Twain is Mark Twain' which is a logical truth, an instance of the law of identity.

Philosophers who think that some statements are analytic in either of the two senses, usually go further: *because* these statements are analytic, they can be known *a priori*, they can be justified without any appeal to experience. Indeed, analyticity's role in explaining *apriority* is thought to be one of its main attractions. The idea is that knowledge of analytic statements is available to us *simply in virtue of our competence in the language*. Thus, assuming that (A) really is analytic, someone who understands 'bachelor' tacitly knows that its meaning is partly constituted by its association with 'unmarried' and can bring this knowledge to consciousness by reflecting on these meanings. So, simply on the basis of this competence, the person is in a position to know that (A) is true: she just has to reflect upon the meaning of 'bachelor'. She can discover the truth of (A) by "conceptual analysis" without paying any attention to her experiences of the world. (This is important to the conceptual-analysis view of philosophy to be discussed later; 14.4.)

There are two problems with this argument. The first is that it requires the Cartesian assumption (as we have, in effect, pointed out in discussing description theories; 3.1, 5.1): to be competent with a term is to have tacit knowledge about its meaning. We have already abandoned this popular assumption for terms covered by causal theories (4.1, 5.2). Indeed, reflection on our discussion of Twin Earth and the incompleteness of description theories (3.5, 5.1) suggests that the assumption *has* to be abandoned for such meanings constituted "outside the head", the meanings on which all meanings ultimately depend. We shall later argue that the assumption should be abandoned even for aspects of meaning constituted "in the head" (8.6). Still, for such aspects, there might seem to be some hope of explaining how a speaker's competence can amount to knowledge about the meaning. Thus, assuming the description theory for 'bachelor', we might hope to explain how someone competent with 'bachelor' must know that it applies to whatever 'adult unmarried male' applies to. For, the association of 'bachelor' with 'adult unmarried male' is at least in the head. But insofar as the meaning of a term is not in the head, the Cartesian view of it seems hopeless. Thus, suppose that 'Mark Twain' and 'Samuel Clemens' do indeed both designate the famous author in virtue of standing in certain sorts of causal relations to him. It is hard to see how we *could* explain the Cartesian view that every competent speaker must know this, must know what seems to be a highly theoretical matter about the external world. In particular, *how could* any amount of reflection on what competence with the names puts inside the head establish the fact that is crucial to the analyticity of 'Mark Twain is Samuel Clemens', the fact that the two names designate the same object? This fact seems obviously empirical.

In sum, the argument that analytic truths are knowable *a priori* does not work when it depends on Cartesian access to meanings that are outside the head. The argument seems more promising when it depends on Cartesian access to meanings inside the head, meanings covered by description theories. But we shall later argue against even that much Cartesianism.

The second problem with the argument is that knowledge about the meaning of 'bachelor' is *not sufficient* for knowledge of (A): one also has to have knowledge that (L), 'All unmarrieds are unmarried' is true. It has been common to claim that such knowledge of logic is *a priori*. But no satisfactory account of how logic can be known *a priori* has ever been given. One of us (Devitt) thinks that we should follow Quine in thinking that logic – indeed, all knowledge – is empirical.

Analyticity is usually thought to have another attraction: it explains the *necessity* of statements like (A). And we think that it does, but the explanation is limited. It explains how (A) is necessary *given that (L) is*, but it does nothing to explain the necessity of (L).

In essence, we think that some statements are analytic in the weak sense of being logical truths or reducible to logical truths by definition. We are dubious that any of these are known *a priori*. Analyticity has only a limited role in explaining their necessity.

Finally, it should be noted that a notion of analyticity that has been thus weakened, that does not yield *a priori* knowledge, and that has only this limited role in explaining necessity, is of little, if any, theoretical interest.

**5.7   Donnellan's Distinction

In this section and the next we shall return to the discussion of singular terms. Our focus will be on ones other than names.

We start with definite descriptions, the basic form of which is, 'the F'. Our discussion so far suggests that the mechanisms of reference for these terms are certainly not open to our causal approach. For, we have followed Russell's theory which treats definite descriptions like existential quantifiers with a uniqueness requirement: 'the F is G' is equivalent to 'there is something that is alone in being F and it is G'. And we say that 'the F' denotes x if and only if 'F' applies to x and to nothing else (3.1). So reference to x does not depend on a causal link to it, but rather on the unique application of a general term to it. We think that a distinction made by Keith Donnellan (1966, 1968) shows that the right story for definite descriptions is more complicated than this. Definite descriptions are ambiguous. Russell's theory does fit one meaning, but the other is to be treated causally.

Donnellan distinguishes two uses of definite descriptions – an "attributive" use and a "referential" use:

> A speaker who uses a definite description attributively in an assertion states something about whoever or whatever is the so-and-so. A speaker who uses a definite description referentially in an assertion, on the other hand, uses the description to enable his audience to pick out whom or what he is talking about and states something about that person or thing. (1966: 285)

Donnellan illustrates the two uses with a number of examples, including the following pair:

> *Attributive use.* A group of people happen on the savagely mutilated body of the harmless and lovable Smith. One says, "The murderer of Smith is insane".
> *Referential use.* A group of people are present in court where Jones is being tried for the murder of Smith. Throughout the trial, Jones behaves very strangely. One of the group says, "The murderer of Smith is insane".

Donnellan points out how different are these two uses of 'the murderer of Smith'.

In the first case, if Smith was *not* murdered but, say, attacked by wild dogs or hit by a meteor, the description is empty; it refers to nobody. As a result, the utterance containing it fails to predicate insanity of anyone and so cannot be true. This is just what Russell's theory implies.

In the second case, however, things are different. Even if Smith was not murdered, the description is not straightforwardly empty. In using the description, the speaker has Jones in mind and seems to have succeeded in referring to him. Suppose that Jones, despite his innocence, is insane. Then there seems to be a respect in which the speaker has said something true. So, apparently, despite the fact that 'murderer of Smith' does not uniquely apply to Jones (indeed it does not apply to him at all), the speaker used the definite description to predicate a truth of Jones.

Consider a different situation. Suppose that Jones is both innocent and feigning insanity because he fears a conviction. Further, Smith really was murdered by a madman. Yet the utterance in the second case does not seem to be straightforwardly true. The problem is that the speaker had Jones in mind in using 'the murderer of Smith' and Jones is not insane. The speaker does not seem to be referring to the real killer, who does of course uniquely satisfy 'murderer of Smith'. Russell's theory does not seem to apply to this use.

We think that what examples of confusion and mistake like this indicate is that definite descriptions are ambiguous. The truth conditions of statements containing them vary according as the description is referential or attributive. (Donnellan himself is rather eqivocal about the significance of his distinction.) We do not think that examples like this alone *establish* this ambiguity; other explanations of the examples are possible. However, when the examples are joined by the considerations to follow, we think that the ambiguity is established.**

**5.8   Designational Terms

Suppose that definite descriptions are indeed ambiguous. What then are the mechanisms of reference for each meaning? Those for an attributive description are clear already. They are the Russellian ones set out earlier; reference depends on unique application of a general term. But what are the mechanisms for a referential description? In virtue of what does it refer to its object?

When using a description referentially, the speaker has a particular object in mind. In discussing names we pointed out that the reference of an ambiguous name depends on which object the speaker has in mind. We went on to give a mostly causal account of this (4.2, 4.5): the speaker had a particular object in mind in using a name because a d-chain grounded in that object was causally active in producing the use of the name. This indicates a possible answer to our question. Perhaps we should say that the mechanism of reference for a referential description is (mostly) a causal one like that for names. So the person had Jones in mind, and referred to him, because it was his experiences of Jones during the trial that prompted his use of 'the murderer of Smith'. We might extend our usage: the person referred to Jones in virtue of a d-chain.

This possible answer is encouraging for the view that definite descriptions are ambiguous. It shows how there could be a use of descriptions that does not depend on Russellian mechanisms of reference; the use depends instead on causal d-chains. However, we should like more than Donnellan's examples of confusion and mistake to convince us that there actually is this other referential use. More is to be found by considering demonstratives and personal pronouns, and comparing them with "incomplete" definite descriptions.

Demonstratives like 'this' and 'that', and personal pronouns like 'he', 'she', and 'it' are often "deictic": they are used out of the blue to "point to" something present (or recently so), rather than being used "anaphorically" to cross-refer to something previously mentioned. Graham observes Nana and says, "She is hungry". In virtue of what did he designate Nana? An appealing idea is that he designated her because he *demonstrated* her; he *pointed*. One problem with this idea is that a demonstration is often so vague that it alone would not distinguish one object from many others in the environment. A more serious problem is that demonstratives and pronouns are not always accompanied by a demonstration. Thus Graham may not bother to point if Nana is sufficiently salient in the environment. And reference is often to an object that is not around to be demonstrated. The appealing idea must be abandoned. A better one is that Graham designated Nana because his perception of her led to the utterance; he designated her in virtue of a d-chain grounded in her.

The *qua*-problem for names led to a move from a pure-causal to a descriptive-causal theory of reference; a descriptive element entered into the characterization of a d-chain (4.5). Just the same *qua*-problem faces the simple demonstratives 'this' and 'that', and the pronoun 'it'. Suppose someone points at Nana and says "I'd like to paint that". In virtue of what was 'that' grounded in Nana rather than in a part of Nana? And how wrong could he be about what he was pointing at and yet still succeed in referring? What if what he took to be a cat was a mere shadow? This problem pushes us once again to a descriptive-causal theory.

Consideration of other demonstratives and pronouns gives another reason for introducing a descriptive element into our theory. 'He' and 'she', unlike 'this', 'that', and 'it', seem to have *explicit* descriptive content: they indicate the gender of the referent. It is plausible to think that the reference of 'she', for example, is partly determined by what 'feminine' applies to: in a successful deictic use, its d-chain is grounded in whatever feminine object is playing the appropriate causal role. So, we explain its reference (in its deictic use) by a descriptive-causal theory.

Complex demonstatives like 'that man' have still more explicit descriptive content. It is plausible to think that the mechanisms of reference for deictic uses of them are also partly causal, partly descriptive. So, if a person at the trial is prompted by Jones's behavior to say, "That man is insane", he designates Jones partly in virtue of the fact that 'man' applies to Jones, and partly in virtue of the fact that 'that' is causally grounded in Jones.

Consider, now, "*incomplete*" descriptions. These are definite descriptions like 'the book' and 'the table' which are very often deictic and yet which do not come close to denoting anything. They do not come close because general terms like 'book' and 'table' apply to millions of things not to just one. If these descriptions were treated as they stand in the Russellian way, they would all fail to refer. The way to save the Russellian view of them is to see them as *elliptical*: speakers have in mind a longer description which, if asked, they would produce to complete the brief description uttered. But this suggestion, like the description theory of names, has the problems of principled basis and ignorance and error (3.1–3.2). Which of the many completions that may be possible for a speaker is "the one he has in mind" and hence the one that carries the burden of determining reference? There may be no basis for a determinate answer. And it will often be the case that the speaker's beliefs about the referent are too impoverished to yield the required completions, or so wrong that they would yield a completion that identify an object that is not the referent. Despite these problems, there are surely *some* incomplete descriptions that can be handled in the Russellian way: they are elliptical attributive descriptions. But it is not plausible to think that *all* incomplete descriptions can be handled in this way. Many are much more plausibly seen as like complex demonstratives and hence as referential. 'The book' is usually like 'that book' in depending for reference partly on the application of 'book' but largely on a d-chain grounded in the book in question.

Return to the scene of the trial. The person who said, "That man is insane", might have been prompted by the same experience to say, "The man is insane". That sentence would have served his communicative purposes as well as the one he uttered; it would have meant very much the same. So, if it is plausible to claim that reference for the complex demonstrative, 'that man', is determined by d-chains, it is plausible to claim the same for the incomplete description, 'the man'. And it is very plausible to claim this for the complex demonstrative. Denotation usually has no more to do with the reference of 'the man' than it has to do with that of 'that man'.

The moral of this is that there are deictic uses of demonstratives, pronouns, and definite descriptions, which share a mode of reference depending on d-chains. These singular terms differ in the amount of their descriptive content: at one extreme, 'this', has no such content; 'she' has a little content; 'that book' and 'the book' have quite a lot. There is no reason to stop at this point. Even definite descriptions that are very rich in content have a use depending on d-chains. These are the descriptions like 'the murderer of Smith' which featured in Donnellan's examples.

We conclude that definite descriptions really are ambiguous: aside from the attributive use explained by Russell, there is a use to be explained partly causally. Donnellan called this use "referential". However, we use 'refer' as a generic term for all modes of reference and so this name is not appropriate for us. Since this use of a description depends on d-chains for reference, it is appropriate to call it "designational".

A description used designationally yields a designational token. So also does a deictic use of a demonstrative or personal pronoun. All of these tokens are designational terms.

Just as a person can borrow the reference of a name from another, he can also borrow the reference of a designational description. The person at the trial can tell a friend all about Jones using, say, 'the man on trial'. On the strength of this, the friend is in a position to use that description designationally. When he does so use it he will have Jones in mind in virtue of a d-chain stretching back from his use through the reference lender to Jones himself.

'This', 'that', and 'it' have little or no explicit descriptive content but we have supposed that on each deictic use they have some implicit descriptive content. Clearly this content is important to reference: it was proposed to solve the *qua*-problem. According to our descriptive-causal theory of the pronouns and demonstratives with explicit descriptive content, that content is also important to reference. If we are right about this when the person says, with Jones in mind, "The murderer of Smith is insane", he will not have succeeded in designating Jones if Jones is innocent. His description token is designational and so it will not matter to reference that Jones is not the *unique* murderer of Smith, but it will matter that he is not a murderer of Smith at all. In this we seem to depart from Donnellan (though he is rather equivocal, as we have remarked; 5.7): the description is not *straightforwardly* empty, because of the causal link to Jones, but it is empty nonetheless.

In the previous chapter, we wrote about names as if they were all introduced in a face-to-face dubbing (4.1). This is certainly the common form of introduction, but it is not universal. Names for an object can be introduced in its absence using a definite description. If that description is designational, then there will still be a d-chain underlying the name. However, the description may be attributive. Thus, it seems that the name 'Jack the Ripper' was once introduced in London by an attributive description along the lines of, 'the murderer of those prostitutes'. The description, and hence the name that depends on it, refer to whoever committed those murders; people had nobody particular in mind; the terms were not grounded in anyone. A name of this sort is attributive. Names of the normal sort, discussed in the last chapter, are designational names.

An attributive name is covered by a hybrid theory of reference, a description theory of fixing, and a causal theory of borrowing. Description theories of names seem so false in general because, first, so few names are like 'Jack the Ripper' in being attributive; second, because the description theory of reference borrowing is false for all names.

Finally, it has been argued by Charles Chastain that *in*definite descriptions – those of the form 'an F' – are also ambiguous, having a use analogous to designational definite descriptions (1975).

The standard interpretation of the sentence, 'A mosquito is in this room', takes it as equivalent to the existentially quantified sentence, 'There is something that is both a mosquito and in this room'. So the sentence is true if somewhere or other in the room there is a mosquito, whether noticed or not. Interpreted in this way an indefinite description is an attributive definite description without the uniqueness requirement.

However, there seems to be another use of an indefinite description where the speaker has a particular object in mind. Suppose that the above sentence was uttered by Fiona after hearing a particular mosquito, x. She gets some insecticide, sprays the room, and withdraws saying, "That will kill it". The spraying does kill a mosquito, y, previously unnoticed, but x survives. Now 'it' in Fiona's second sentence is clearly anaphoric, referring to whatever 'a mosquito' in the first sentence refers to. On the standard quantificational interpretation, 'a mosquito' refers not to any particular mosquito but to any mosquito at all; to x or y or any one of the billions of mosquitoes in the world. So, on that interpretation, Fiona's second sentence is true: y is indeed a mosquito killed by the spraying. However, the sentence seems false because Fiona had x in mind and x is still alive. It seems then that 'it' in the second sentence refers to x. So 'a mosquito' on which 'it' depends for reference must also refer to x. Indefinite descriptions have a designational meaning as well as the familiar attributive one.

The idea that descriptions are ambiguous has been quite widely resisted. This resistance exploits a distinction due to Grice that we will discuss in some detail later (7.4). It is a distinction between what an expression means – its "conventional" or "literal" meaning – and what a speaker means by it – its "speaker" meaning. So these philosophers accept that a description can be *used* with a particular object in mind but deny that this exemplifies a distinct meaning. Thus, in their view, when the speaker utters "The murderer of Smith is insane" with Jones in mind, the truth of the utterance depends on the sanity of whoever murdered Smith, whether Jones or not. Stephen Neale has argued the case persuasively:

> Suppose it is common knowledge that Smith is the only person taking Jones' seminar. One evening, Jones throws a party and Smith is the only person who turns up. A despondent Jones, when asked the next morning whether his party was well attended, says,
>
> > Well, everyone taking my seminar turned up
>
> fully intending to inform me that only Smith attended. The possibility of such a scenario, would not lead us to complicate the semantics of 'every' with an ambiguity; i.e., it would not lead us to posit semantically distinct quantificational and referential interpretations of 'everyone taking my seminar'. (1990: 87–8)

No more, Neale argues, should the possibililty of Donnellan's scenarios lead us to complicate the semantics of 'the *F*'. Those scenarios merely illustrate the general point made by Grice and illustrated above: what an expression means may not be what a speaker intends to convey in using that expression.

This is a nice point. The mere fact that a quantified sentence can be used to convey a thought with a particular object in mind – a "designational" thought – does not show that its quantifier literally has a designational meaning. For Grice has drawn our attention to the way sentences can convey meanings that they do not literally have. 'Every' has only one meaning even though it can be used to express a designational thought about Smith. Why should we not say the same about 'the *F*' and 'an *F*'?

The answer is that not only *can* we use a description to express a designational thought, we *regularly* do so. When one has a thought with a particular *F* object in mind, one regularly uses 'the *F*' or 'an *F* to express it. We standardly use 'the book' to designate a particular book, 'a man' to designate a particular man, and so on. There is no such standard use of 'every': its designational use demands a special stage setting. The regular standard use of descriptions to express designational thoughts is strong evidence that there is a *convention* of so using them. These conventions are semantic, as semantic as the ones for an attributive use. In each case, there are conventions of using the 'the *F*' and 'an *F*' to express thoughts with a certain sort of meaning.

This completes our discussion of word meaning. We shall now move on to consider syntactic structure.**

Suggested Reading

5.1

Classical versions of the description theory for general terms in general, and natural kind terms in particular, are to be found in Mill 1961, *A System of Logic*: bk. I, ch. 2, sec. 5; and in Carnap 1956, *Meaning and Necessity*: sec. 4.

A more recent manifestation of the theory is the "componential analysis" movement in generative grammar. The founding document in the movement is Katz and Fodor 1963, "The Structure of Semantic Theory", reprinted in Fodor and Katz 1964, *The Structure of Language*. This theory was further developed in Katz 1972, *Semantic Theory*. Fodor has since abandoned it, but Katz gives a lengthy defense of it in "Logic and Language" (1975), in Gunderson 1975, *Language, Mind, and Knowledge*.

In effect, positivist philosophers of science developed and defended a description theory of theoretical terms. Clear introductions to their views are to be found in Hempel 1966, *Philosophy of Natural Science*: ch. 7; and in 1954, "A Logical Appraisal of Operationism". Lewis's paper, "How to Define Theoretical Terms", reprinted in Lewis 1983, is a sophisticated version of such theories, minus the positivist prejudice in favor of observational descriptions.

For Kripke's refutation of the description theories of natural kind terms, see *Naming and Necessity* (1980), pp. 116–35, 156–7. For Putnam's, see "Is Semantics Possible?" in *Mind, Language and Reality* (1975), reprinted in Schwartz 1977, and "Meaning and Reference" (1973), reprinted in Schwartz 1977 and Martinich 1996. An expanded version of the latter forms the early part of "The Meaning of 'Meaning'" also in Putnam 1975 (and in Gunderson 1975 and Geirsson and Losonsky 1996).

Searle's *Intentionality* (1983a) is a vigorous rejection of Putnam's view that meanings are not in the head (particularly in ch. 8). Devitt 1990, "Meanings Just Ain't in the Head", is a response. For another criticism of Putnam (and Burge), see Crane 1991, "All the Difference in the World", which contains helpful references to the literature. Pessin and Goldberg 1996, *The Twin Earth Chronicles*, is a helpful collection.

The difficulty of giving description theories for most terms arises from the difficulty of finding definitions for them. This is brought out nicely by Fodor in "The Present Status of the Innateness Controversy", particularly pp. 283–92, in his *Representations* (1981a).

5.2

Kripke's causal theory of natural kind terms is set out briefly in his 1980, pp. 135–9. Putnam's theory is set out in some detail in the above papers, together with "Explanation and Reference" and "Language and Reality" in Putnam 1975.

**5.3

David Papineau points to the *qua*-problem in *Theory and Meaning* (1979): ch. 5, sec. 7. See Miller 1992, "A Purely Causal Solution to One of the Qua Problems", for an interesting discussion. For some other criticisms of the views of Putnam and Kripke, see Fine 1975, "How to Compare Theories"; Zemach 1976, "Putnam's Theory on the Reference of Substance Terms"; Mellor 1977, "Natural Kinds"; Dupre 1981, "Natural Kinds and Biological Taxa"; Unger 1983, "The Causal Theory of Reference"; Donnellan 1983, "Kripke and Putnam on Natural Kinds"; Kroon 1985, "Theoretical Terms and the Causal View of Reference".

Our own earlier discussions of these problems are: Devitt 1981a, *Designation*, ch. 7; Sterelny 1983, "Natural Kind Terms".**

**5.4–5.5

Putnam's discussion of other kind terms is in "The Meaning of 'Meaning'", Putnam 1975, pp. 242–5. Schwartz responds in "Putnam on Artifacts" (1978) and "Natural Kinds and Nominal Kinds" (1980). Kornblith 1980, "Referring to Artifacts", is a defense of Putnam. Burge presents his view in "Individualism and the Mental" (1979). Donnellan 1993, "There is a Word for That Kind of Thing", is an interesting discussion of the thought experiments of Burge and Putnam. See Davies 1991, "Individualism and Perceptual Content", for a discussion of Burge.**

5.6

Quine is the most famous skeptic about analyticity and *apriority*. This goes with his skepticism about meaning in general; see the suggested readings to 1.3. For more along the lines of the text, and some references to the literature, see Devitt 1996, *Coming to Our Senses*, 1.5–1.13 and 2.2, and 1998b "Naturalism and the A Priori".

**5.7

Ostertag 1998, *Definite Descriptions*, is a very helpful collection. For Russell's theory, see suggested readings for 3.1. Donnellan's classic paper, "Reference and Definite Descriptions" (1966), is very readable. It has been reprinted in many places, including Schwartz 1977, Davis 1991, Martinich 1996, Ludlow 1997, and Ostertag 1998. Donnellan's response to a critic, "Putting Humpty Dumpty Together Again" (1968), is also helpful. Donnellan is critical not only of Russell's theory but also of Strawson's criticism of Russell in "On Referring" (1950). That paper has also been reprinted many times, including in Martinich 1996, Ludlow 1997, and Ostertag 1998. Bertolet 1980, "The Semantic Significance of Donnellan's Distinction", brings out nicely the problems in interpreting exactly what Donnellan is claiming.**

**5.8

For more details on this approach to demonstratives, pronouns, and definite descriptions, see Devitt 1981a: sections 2.5–2.7. A similar view is urged in Wettstein 1981, "Demonstrative Reference and Definite Descriptions", reprinted in Ostertag 1998. See also two papers by Wilson, "On Definite and Indefinite Descriptions" (1978) and "Reference and Definite Descriptions" (1991). For further discussion, see Salmon 1982, "Assertion and Incomplete Descriptions", Soames 1986, "Incomplete Definite Descriptions" (reprinted in Ostertag 1998), and Reimer 1992, "Incomplete Descriptions".

Kaplan 1989a, "Demonstratives", and 1989b, "Afterthoughts", are influential works on demonstratives. Two of his earlier and shorter works are "Dthat" (1978a), reprinted in Yorgau 1990, *Demonstratives*, Martinich 1996, and Ludlow 1997; and "On the Logic of Demonstratives" (1978b), reprinted in Davis 1991. Also influential is Perry 1977, "Frege on Demonstratives", reprinted in Yourgau 1990, Davis 1991 and Ludlow 1997. For helpful discussions, see Reimer 1991, "Do Demonstratives Have Semantic Significance", and Bach 1992, "Paving the Road to Reference".

Chastain 1975, "Reference and Context", in Gunderson 1975, is an extensive and interesting discussion of singular terms along lines similar to those urged here; see particularly pp. 201–15 for the source of our views on indefinite descriptions.

Kripke takes a Gricean line against the view that descriptions are ambiguous in "Speaker's Reference and Semantic Reference" (1979), reprinted, along with other papers on the topic, in Part II of Davis 1991. It is also in Ludlow 1997 and Ostertag 1998. For a response, see Devitt 1981b, "Donnellan's Distinction". Neale 1990, *Descriptions*, is an excellent defense of the Russellian view of definite descriptions; see ch. 3 particularly, reprinted in Ludlow 1997 and Ostertag 1998. Ludlow and Neale 1991, "Indefinite Descriptions", is a similar defense of the Russellian view of indefinites, reprinted in Ludlow 1997.**

6

Syntactic Structure

6.1 Introduction

Our hypothesis is that the meaning of a sentence is its property of representing a certain situation in a certain way; its meaning is its mode of presenting its truth condition (2.1, 2.6). This mode is to be explained in terms of modes of reference and syntactic structures (2.2). We have devoted several chapters to explaining reference. We have said little about syntactic structure beyond bringing out its obvious relevance to truth conditions (2.2) and mentioning the problems of explaining it (2.4).

The bearing of syntactic structure on the truth conditions of simple sentences, such as 'Reagan is wrinkled', was easy enough to explain. However, most sentences are much more difficult to deal with. The problems can be roughly divided into two sorts, one which has particularly occupied logicians, and the other, linguists. The logicians have concentrated on what are intuitively "basic" structures of a natural language. The logicians capture each structure in the symbols of formal logic and seek a theory explaining that structure's role in determining truth conditions. Some of these underlying structures – for example, those involving quantifiers – have proved very difficult to explain. The linguists, on the other hand, have been concerned with the much more complicated structures of actual sentences in a natural language. The hope must be that the explanations offered by logicians for basic structures can be developed to handle the complicated structures described by linguists.

We have already ruled that the findings of the logicians are beyond the scope of this book (2.4). For the most part, we must do likewise with the findings of the linguists. The understanding of syntactic structures has increased dramatically in the last forty years under the influence particularly of the revolutionary ideas of Noam Chomsky. This is not the place to explore the details of the many rich theories that have resulted. We shall simply give a glimpse of these riches, drawing attention to their relevance to the explanation of meaning.

There are reasons for an interest in structure independent of an interest in truth conditions. Many strings of English words would sound queer if ever uttered. Why? In many cases the strings do not form proper sentences. Consider, for example, 'the Opera House likes was' and 'who did John believe the rumour that came'. These strings are simply *ungrammatical*. They are, in that respect, meaning*less*. What makes a string of words ungrammatical and hence not a sentence? We need a theory that tells us which structures are to be found in English (and other natural languages). Any string that is not of an acceptable structure will sound queer.

A cautionary word is appropriate here. Seeming queer is neither necessary nor sufficient for being ungrammatical. It is not sufficient because strings of words may seem queer for other reasons: they may be too long and complicated to be quickly understood; they may be irrelevant; they may be too boring to be worth stating; they may be absurdly false. Ungrammaticality is just one possible explanation for queerness. It is the most plausible one in some cases – for example, those in the last paragraph – but not at all plausible in others; for example, 'It was while kicking heads on Mars that Thatcher first ran into Reagan'. In some cases it is not immediately obvious what is a plausible explanation of the queerness; consider, 'Mount Everest plays good ping pong' and 'Colorless green ideas sleep furiously' (a favorite example of the linguists). In fact, initial judgments of plausibility simply reflect our folk theory (1.3). What we need before making a final decision on which strings are or are not grammatical is a theory of grammaticality.

Seeming queer is not necessary for being ungrammatical because some grammatical failures are so common as to pass almost unnoticed. This is particularly true of failures in speech. Our ordinary speech is liberally sprinkled with false starts, 'um's and 'ah's, slips of tongue, and so on. Such speech is strictly ungrammatical but does not strike us as queer.

Our two interests in structure converge. When we seek to explain meaning and truth conditions, which items are we concerned with? We are concerned only with the possible sentences of the language; ungrammatical strings of words have no truth conditions (but see the qualification in 7.4). All (indicative) sentences have truth conditions; further, those conditions depend in part on the syntactic structure that makes a string grammatical and hence a sentence.

We should emphasize that the notion of grammaticality that concerns us is a *descriptive* one, not a *normative* one. We are not concerned with how a person ought to speak, according to the approved standards of her society. We are concerned with a notion that applies to the language she does, as a matter of fact, speak; a notion that applies to her idiolect, however much that may depart from the approved standards.

Chomsky's approach to explaining grammaticality is called "generative grammar" because it seeks a theory of a language, a "grammar", that provides an *explicit* statement of the rules for generating all and only the possible sentences of the language from the words (or morphemes) of the language. In showing how a sentence can be thus formally generated by applying certain rules, the approach provides a syntactic description of the sentence. (The approach is sometimes also called "transformational grammar" because key steps in the generation, particularly prominent in early versions of the approach, transform one sentence-like structure into another.) The approach clearly addresses both of our interests in structure. Nevertheless, we cannot take over its findings *en bloc*. Chomsky and his followers have formulated the question they seek to answer in a different way. Whereas we see a grammar as explaining some of the properties of linguistic symbols, these linguists see it as *primarily* explaining linguistic competence, a property of people (on which we have often commented; for example, 5.1–5.2). More accurately, since their concern is really only with structure, they see the grammar as primarily explaining *syntactic* competence.

At the beginning we remarked on the bewildering nature of the study of language (1.1). It is often hard to see what question a theory is trying to answer and whether different theories are concerned with the the same question. This problem is acute in studying the generative linguists. One would think that explaining structure is one thing, explaining syntactic competence, a different though related thing. Yet the linguists run them together, as we shall demonstrate later (8.2). And there are other puzzles. Why suppose that a grammar explains competence at all? The generative linguists think that the grammar does so because competence consists in *tacit knowledge* of the grammar. Further, some of this knowledge is said to be innate. Why suppose that speakers know any more about grammar than the little they learn at school?

These puzzles are appropriately dealt with in our Part III discussion, "Language and Mind". They are the main concern of chapter 8. However, our discussion has already indicated where we think the main trouble lies: in the failure to distinguish sharply between the linguistic competence of speakers and the syntactic structure of linguistic symbols.

Competence, together with various other aspects of the speaker's psychology, produce linguistic symbols, but a theory of the one is not a theory of the other.

The distinction we are insisting on should not be confused with the linguists' one between competence and performance. A theory of performance is concerned with those factors which, together with competence, bear on the production (and understanding) of linguistic symbols; such factors as memory, attention, and interest. So a theory of performance is like a theory of competence in being psychological. It is a theory of the production (and understanding) of linguistic symbols, not a theory of the products, the symbols themselves. It is the latter theory that we are anxious to distinguish from the theory of competence.

A major motivation for the linguists' distinction between competence and performance is their observation that much of a person's linguistic performance is a poor reflection of her competence: it is full of the grammatical failures (relative to her idiolect) that we have already mentioned. The competence which concerns the linguists is an *idealization*: it is those aspects of the speaker's psychology that, were it not for the other factors, would lead the speaker to produce only grammatical sentences. Similarly, we are concerned not with the actual linguistic symbols produced by speakers but with an idealization of them (except when considering speaker meaning; 7.4).

Without more ado, we shall return to the task of examining the properties of linguistic symbols.

6.2   Some Reasons for Structure

It is of course obvious that the order of a string of words affects whether that string is a grammatical and meaningful sentence. And we are used to thinking that a sentence must have a structure in a much more serious respect: its words must all belong to grammatical or syntactic *categories* like *noun, verb, preposition,* and so on. We think that words from these categories are combined in quite complicated ways to form phrases and sentences. But why should we think this? Our aim in this section is to give some basic reasons. In the next, we shall consider some evidence in favor of particular categories of words and phrases.

1. We have already alluded to one reason for thinking that sentences have structures. Some strings of words sound queer because they are ungrammatical (6.1). What is it for a something to be grammatical? In the case of some simple languages – for example, the sign language divers use for underwater communication – there is nothing more to being grammatical than being on a list of conventional signals. But no such explanation is

possible for any natural language, for the list would have to be indefinitely long. There are, for example, indefinitely many good English sentences. Clearly, a natural language is a *system* (1.2, 2.2). It must consist of a finite number of rules specifying the ways in which words can be combined. How could this work? One very plausible way for it to work has all words collected into syntactic categories. The rules will then specify how these categories fit together; they will describe the general patterns of grammatical sentences. So, to take an over-simple example, one such pattern in English might be: Name – Transitive Verb – Name. Plugging in words of the appropriate category yields a sentence. Thus the rules specify the ways in which words of a finite number of syntactic categories can be legitimately combined to form an infinite number of sentences. These rules reveal the structure of sentences. A sentence is grammatical in the language in virtue of having one of those structures (and being made up of words in the language: "the slithy toves did gyre and gimble in the wabe" is not English).

2. Many sentences in a language are *structurally ambiguous*. They have ambiguities that are additional to any lexical ambiguities that they may contain. For example:

Tex likes exciting sheep
Spanish money lenders are more avaricious than cautious.

Even if the meaning and reference of all the words in these sentences are held constant, their truth conditions can vary. Thus, is it being said that Tex enjoys causing sheep to become excited? Or is it that he enjoys the company of interesting and stimulating sheep? Either way Tex has a problem, of course, but they are very different problems.

How can these ambiguities be explained? Consider 'Spanish money lenders are more avaricious than cautious'. As a first approximation, we can say that it has two distinct structures. It may be about the lenders of Spanish money, in which case 'Spanish' and 'money' will be grouped together as a *constituent* of the sentence but 'money' and 'lenders' will not be. Or it may be about the Spanish lenders of money, in which case 'money' and 'lenders' will be grouped together as a constituent but 'Spanish' and 'money' will not be. This shows that sometimes there is more than one way of assembling words into subsentential constituents of a sentence. There is more to the structure of a sentence than simply the order of the words out of which the sentence is built. There are *intermediate layers* of sentence organization between the level of words and the level of the sentence itself. The ambiguity of the sentence about Tex illustrates a different sort of complexity. On both readings 'exciting sheep' is a constituent but the constituents seem different, in one case standing for an activity and in the other for a sort of sheep.

It is common to capture the internal structure of sentences using *trees* which display the *hierarchical organization* of sentences. If the sentence is structurally ambiguous, it gets more than one tree. These "phrase-structure" trees, or "phrase-markers", organize the sentence elements into successively larger constituents, or phrases, of the sentence.

Take as an example the two trees for 'Tex likes exciting sheep' (figure 6.1).

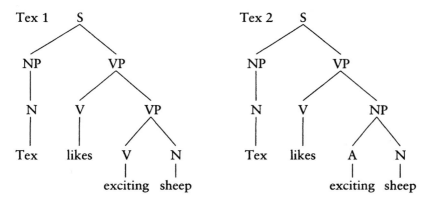

Figure 6.1

Both Tex 1 and Tex 2 are oversimplified: the details should not be taken too literally. But they are right in dividing S (the sentence) into two basic units, NP (noun phrase) and VP (verb phrase). This basic, or "matrix", VP is what we would ordinarily called a predicate. Tex 1 differs from Tex 2 only in the structure of its matrix VP. In Tex 1 this VP is composed of a V (verb) and a complex *VP* made up of a V and an N (noun); in Tex 2 it is composed of a V and a complex *NP* made up of an A (adjective) and an N. As a result of these different underlying structures, the sentence has two sets of truth conditions and two meanings.

Instead of displaying the structures of sentences using trees, we can display it using brackets. Thus, instead of Tex 1 and Tex 2, we have:

$[_S[_{NP}[_N Tex]] [_{VP}[_V likes] [_{VP}[_V exciting] [_N sheep]]]]$
$[_S[_{NP}[_N Tex]] [_{VP}[_V likes] [_{NP}[_A exciting] [_N sheep]]]]$.

In our other example, the source of the ambiguity is in the first major constituent of the sentence (its *subject*). Thus, when the sentence concerns the lenders of Spanish money, it is displayed as in figure 6.2 (ignoring the structure of the VP).

Note that 'Spanish money' is a constituent of this tree: there is a single

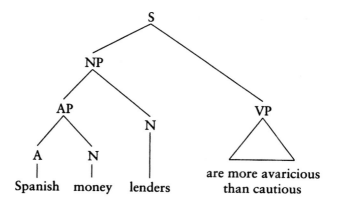

Figure 6.2

node – AP (adjectival phrase) – that dominates the elements 'Spanish' and 'money' and nothing else. That is not true of the alternative interpretation, where the sentence concerns Spanish nationals (figure 6.3). In this tree, 'money lenders' is a constituent, being dominated by an NP. Note that in both trees 'Spanish money lenders' is a constituent.

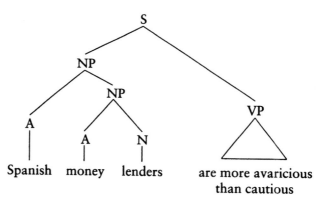

Figure 6.3

3. Consider the following pairs of sentences:

Alex can lift Natasha
Can Alex lift Natasha?

Chess is generally played by obsessives
Is chess generally played by obsessives?

They will want to buy two children
Will they want to buy two children?

The first sentence of each pair is a statement; the second, the correlative "yes–no" question. Clearly the form of the one is related to the form of the other. This relation is an example of the systematicity of language that we have often mentioned (for example, in 1.2). How can we capture this relation in our theory of English sentencehood? Were we to restrict ourselves to examples like these, nothing could be easier: the question has the same form as the statement except that the first two words occur in reverse order. But it is easy to see that this will not work in general:

Chess generally is played by obsessives
Generally chess is played by obsessives
Is chess generally played by obsessives?

The third sentence, not the second, is the question that corresponds to the first.

Perhaps we should amend our generalization: the question has the same form as the statement except that *the first verb* of the statement appears at the front of the question. This generalization covers our examples to date. And it commits us to more internal structure than word order because it requires us to classify words into groups, in particular, to classify some as verbs. But it won't do. The regularity that links questions to statements is dependent on a more complex structure.

Consider the following:

Chess players who get to be grandmasters are generally obsessive
*Get chess players who to be grandmasters are generally obsessive?

Our revised generalization predicts that the string marked '*' is the correlative question. But that string is no sentence at all. The correlative question is:

Are chess players who get to be grandmasters generally obsessive?

The verb that needs to be moved in this case is the second one.
Examples of this kind can be made indefinitely complex. Thus:

Chess players who get to be grandmasters who can hold their own in tournaments in Zambia in which candidates for the world championship play are generally obsessive

Are chess players who get to be grandmasters who can hold their own in tournaments in Zambia in which candidates for the world championship play generally obsessive?

The relationship between this statement and question is essentially the same as in our other examples, but in this case it is the fourth verb that needs to be moved. Clearly, no simple numerical story will capture the relationship. Instead, we need to appeal to a structural fact about sentences: they are organized into two major constituents. Conventionally, these are called the subject, which is an NP, and the predicate, which is a VP. So, taking one of the simpler examples, we can illustrate the basic organization of the indicative sentence as in figure 6.4.

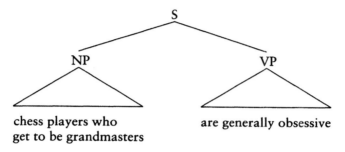

chess players who   are generally obsessive
get to be grandmasters

Figure 6.4

In terms of this fact of sentence structure, we can now say (roughly) how a yes–no question is related to its correlative statement: the question has the same form as the statement except that the *auxiliary verb of the statement's matrix VP* appears at the front of the question. Linguists have usually expressed this relation along the following lines: the different "surface structures" ("S-structures") of the statement and question are "derived" from a common "deep structure" ("D-structure"); the question is formed by a "transformation" that moves the auxiliary to the front.

This discussion confirms an important grammatical principle emphasized by Chomsky:

The Structure-Dependence Principle: All grammatical rules are structure-dependent.

The rules are structure-dependent in that they advert to syntactic categories and not to something superficial like word order.

So far, we have argued that sentences have structures consisting not just of words in sequence, but of words organized into successively larger constituents or phrases. We have placed all these words and phrases into categories. The structures of sentences, and the categories of their constituents, can be conveniently displayed by trees. These structures are the sort that must go into the explanation of the meanings and truth conditions of sentences.

6.3   Linguistic Categories

Our argument supports the fact that there are syntactic categories. Let us now look more closely at the evidence for particular categories. We shall first consider categories of words, then categories of phrases, and then categories that come in between.

There is *morphological* evidence for word categories (morphology is concerned with the *forms of words*): categories differ in the sorts of endings (or "inflections") they can take. We have already noted (2.5) that count nouns like 'cat' usually admit a plural ending. In contrast, mass nouns like 'gold' do not. This is just the tip of the iceberg. Verbs in English usually have a base form and various endings; for example, the base 'show' yields 'shown' (participle), 'showed' (past), 'shows' (present), and 'showing' (gerund). Many adjectives are like 'quick' in taking the comparative ending '-er', and adverbs generally are like 'quickly' in having the '-ly' ending. Finally, prepositions like 'at' differ from all these in not taking any of these endings.

A problem with this evidence is indicated by our qualifications "usually", "generally", etc. "Rules" like these tend to be subject to exceptions. Most famously, many verbs in English, including those most frequently used, are *irregular*; the verb 'to be' has eight distinct forms.

We also noted earlier (2.5) that count nouns accept the indefinite article. The contrast, once again, is with mass nouns; we can say 'a cat' but not 'a gold'. This illustrates the very important fact that words of different categories appear in different positions in sentences; they "distribute" differently. Thus, consider what words can be placed in the following position:

—— can be injurious to your health.

Nouns are fine; for example, 'smoking', 'Alice', 'cockroaches', 'postmodernism'. But verbs, adjectives, adverbs, prepositions, and the articles are not. Only a verb can be inserted into:

They can ——.

Only an adjective or an adverb can occur after 'very'. And so on.

Using these sorts of morphological and distributional evidence, we can group words into the familiar categories.

Turn now to phrases. Once again we find a range of distributional and related evidence bringing out the surprising subtlety of phrasal constituents. The contrast between phrases involving 'easy' and 'eager' provides favorite examples of this subtlety. Consider:

Noam is easy to please
Noam is eager to please.

These two sentences seem to have exactly the same structure, apparently differing only in a single adjective. Appearances are deceptive. The constituents 'easy to please' and 'eager to please' are members of very different families as the following pairs show:

It is easy to please Noam
*It is eager to please Noam

*Noam is easy to please Lyndon
Noam is eager to please Lyndon.

The strings marked '*' are not acceptable sentences. The first pair exemplifies a construction, apparently related to those of the original sentences, which permits 'easy to please' but not 'eager to please'. The second pair exemplifies one which permits 'eager to please' but not 'easy to please'. Despite the apparent similarity of the original sentences, this contrast shows that these sentences are made up of phrasal constituents with very different structures; their S-structures are derived from very different D-structures. These different structures will yield different ways in which the meanings of the sentences depend on the meanings of their parts.

Let us now look more closely at an example based on one of Andrew Radford's (1988: 90–101) to illustrate the sort of evidence that bears on the constituent structure of sentences. Consider

(a) Drunks would get off the bus
(b) Drunks would put off the customers

Again we have two apparently similar sentences which are really quite different in phrasal structure. The difference is that in (a) the preposition 'off' goes with the noun phrase 'the bus' to form the prepositional phrase ("PP") 'off the bus' – see figure 6.5. ("TP" stands for *tensed phrase*, a category we have previously ignored. "AUX" stands for *auxiliary*, "P" for *preposition*, and "D" for *determiner*, a category that covers not only the articles but also quantifiers like 'all' and 'few'.)

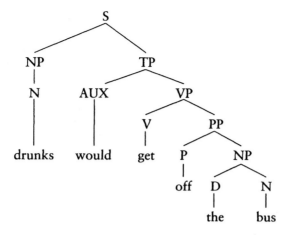

Figure 6.5

In contrast, in (b) the preposition 'off' goes with the verb 'put' to form the phrasal verb 'put off' (figure 6.6).

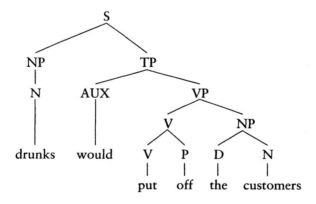

Figure 6.6

What is the evidence that the two sentences do differ in this way? Here are three pieces.

1. If 'off the bus' in (a) is indeed a prepositional phrase then we would expect to be able to *replace it by other such phrases*; for example, by 'on the bus'. And so we can:

Drunks would get on the bus

is fine. Similarly, if 'off the customers' in (b) were a prepositional phrase, then we would expect

Drunks would put on the customers

to be in order. But it is not (at least, it is not if the meaning of 'put' is held constant). This confirms that 'off the customers' is not a prepositional phrase and suggests that it is not a constituent at all. The constituent is the phrasal verb 'put off'.

2. Phrases can *undergo "movement"*. Thus in the interests of emphasis we might prefer the second of these sentences to the first:

Jane beat Tarzan with a dead snake
With a dead snake, Jane beat Tarzan

The second is derived from a D-structure like the S-structure of the first by a transformation that "preposes" the prepositional phrase 'with a dead snake'. But we cannot prepose part of the phrase:

*Dead snake, Jane beat Tarzan with a

Return now to Radford's example. The following sentence shows that 'off the bus' can be preposed, thus meeting the movement test for phrasehood:

At the driver's order, off the bus drunks would get.

But 'off the customers' fails this test:

*Despite the driver's best efforts, off the customers drunks would put.

'Off the customers' is not a phrase.

3. Finally, if 'off the bus' is a prepositional phrase, we should be able to *conjoin it with another*. And so we can:

Drunks would get off the bus and on the train

'Off the customers' fails this test of phrasehood too:

*Drunks would put off the customers and off the waitresses

We have considered some evidence for word categories and for phrasal categories. There is also evidence for categories between words and phrases.

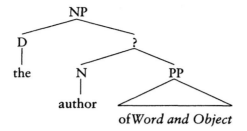

Figure 6.7

Consider the noun phrase 'the author of *Word and Object*' (what we earlier called a "definite description"; 2.5). Its constituents obviously include the determiner 'the', the noun 'author', and the prepositional phrase 'of *Word and Object*'. The total structure of the noun phrase then seems to be that in figure 6.7.

The "?" in figure 6.7 raises the question: What sort of category is 'author of *Word and Object*'? At first sight it may seem to be just another noun phrase. But distributional and other reasons have been adduced for thinking that this is not so: for thinking that 'author of *Word and Object*' is an intermediate nominal category. For instance, 'the author of *Word and Object*' and 'author of *Word and Object*' cannot replace one another. Where you have one in a sentence you cannot replace it with the other without moving from grammaticality to ungrammaticality. In contrast, 'author of *Word and Object*' and 'assassin of Martin Luther King' can replace one another. Two notations have been introduced to capture this intermediate category (and are often both used in the same discussion!). In one notation the "head" noun, 'author', is an N, the single phrasal expansion of this, 'author of *Word and Object*', is an N', and the double phrasal expansion, 'the author of *Word and Object*', is an N". In another notation, an N' constituent is an $\bar{N}$ ("N-bar") and an N" is an $\bar{\bar{N}}$ ("N-double-bar").

We have been discussing the constitution of noun phrases. Similar remarks apply to the constitution of verb, adjectival, adverbial, and prepositional phrases. Thus, the adjectival head 'angry' is an A, 'angry with her government' is an A' or A-bar, and 'very angry with her government' is an A" or A-double-bar. It is common to use 'X' as a variable for the various head categories (noun, verb, adjective, etc.) and to call the general theory of the structure of phrases "X-bar theory".

The sorts of empirical considerations we have briefly discussed in this section have led to general agreement among linguists that sentences have a heirarchical structure of constituents, each of which is in some category. However there is still disagreement over precisely which categories there are.

**6.4 Anaphora

We have mentioned anaphora very briefly in earlier sections. We noted that a bound variable in logic is like an anaphoric, or cross-referential, pronoun, depending for its interpretation on the quantifier that binds it (2.4). And we distinguished anaphoric pronouns from deictic pronouns, the latter being ones used "out of the blue" without any dependence for their reference on any other part of the discourse. We suggested that the reference of a deictic pronoun is to be explained by a causal d-chain grounded in the referent (5.8). It is time to say a little more about anaphora, a syntactically rich matter on which both linguists and philosophers have made contributions. We shall distinguish four sorts of anaphora.

Our discussion will be about anaphoric pronouns but it should be noted that definite descriptions like 'the man' and complex demonstratives like 'that dog' can play anaphoric roles very similar to those of pronouns.

1. *Bound*: The anaphoric pronoun 'him' in the following sentence is probably an example of a pronoun functioning like a bound variable of logic:

(1) Every man believes that Monica loves him.

If so, the pronoun is bound by the quantifier 'every man'; the quantifier is its "antecedent".

2. *Designational*: Anaphoric pronouns can also be anaphorically linked to designational terms: to proper names, deictic pronouns, and designational descriptions. This is probably the case with 'him' in

(2) Bill believes that Monica loves him.

If so, 'him' is dependent for its reference on the antecedent 'Bill' and so designates what 'Bill' designates.

These interpretations of (1) and (2) are probable but not certain because 'him' might be used deictically in these sentences to designate, say, Al. If so the beliefs are that Monica loves Al. So (1) and (2) are examples where the pronoun may be either anaphoric or deictic. In some other sentences, the anaphoric option is not available. Thus in the following sentence 'him' cannot be anaphoric on 'Bill':

(3) Bill loves him.

'Him' must be deictic, having its reference determined independently of 'Bill'. As the linguists say, it cannot be "coindexed" with 'Bill'. (The linguists also tend to say that it cannot be coreferential with 'Bill'. This is a mistake. The speaker of (3) might designate Bill with 'him' without realizing it; perhaps the light is bad, or Bill is in disguise, or reference is via a poor photograph; or the speaker might be striving for rhetorical effect. The point about (3) is that it cannot be interpreted so that coreference is *demanded by the syntax*. But there may be "accidental" coreference.)

Linguists have discovered that pronouns are interestingly different from "reflexives" like 'himself'. The most obvious difference is that reflexives *have to be* anaphoric in order to be grammatical: there is no deictic option for them. But there is a more interesting difference. We have just noted that the pronoun in (3) cannot be anaphoric on 'Bill'. Yet the reflexive in

(4) Bill loves himself

has to be anaphoric on 'Bill'. In contrast, whereas the pronoun in (2) can be anaphoric on 'Bill', the reflexive in

(5) *Bill believes that Monica loved himself

cannot be, and so (5) is not grammatical. In general, it turns out that reflexives and pronouns are complementary: the domains in which pronouns must be free are the domains in which reflexives must be bound. The task of specifying that domain has proved tricky.

As a first stab we note that the pronoun 'him' seems "too close" to 'Bill' to be bound by it in (3) but not in (2), whereas the reflexive 'himself' seems to be "close enough" to 'Bill' to be bound by it in (4) but not in (5). Indeed, it seems that a pronoun and its antecedent cannot be in the same clause, "clause mates", whereas a reflexive and its antecedent must be. But this condition proves to be too simple.

Consider

(6) Bill's friend loves himself
(7) Bill's friend loves him.

'Bill's friend' is a clause mate of both the reflexive in (6) and the pronoun in (7). So the clause-mate condition seems to explain why 'Bill's friend' is the antecedent of the reflexive but not the pronoun. But the condition fails to explain why 'Bill' cannot be the antecendent of the reflexive in (6) but is that of the pronoun in (7) (unless the pronoun is deictic). For 'Bill' is also a clause mate of both the reflexive and the pronoun. Clearly, something more needs to be said. What accounts for these differences between 'Bill's friend' and 'Bill' in anaphoric situations?

The answer is to be found using the important notion of *c-command*, defined over nodes in a phrase-structure tree:

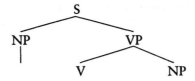

Figure 6.8

A node, A, c-commands a node, B, if and only if the first branching node dominating A also dominates B and neither A nor B dominates the other.

Consider this simple tree in figure 6.8. The subject NP (on the left) c-commands the object NP (on the right) because the first node dominating the subject is S which also dominates the object. But the object NP does not c-command the subject because the first node dominating the object is VP which does not dominate the subject. And the rule we need is that a reflexive must have an antecedent that c-commands it within its clause; a pronoun cannot have such an antecedent within its clause. (Linguists define a notion of *binding* that applies to designational terms in order to state the rule.)

Return to our examples. Figure 6.9 is the tree for (6). 'Bill's friend' c-commands 'himself' because the node that first dominates it is S which also dominates 'himself'. But 'Bill' does not c-command 'himself' because the node that first dominates it is the NP 'Bill's friend' which does not dominate 'himself'. So 'Bill's friend' can be the antecedent of 'himself' but 'Bill' cannot. When considering the antecedent of 'him' in (7), just the reverse is the case.

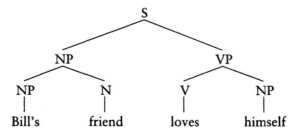

Figure 6.9

Despite this success our rule is still needs further refinement to handle other examples. But we will leave the matter here.

"Reciprocals" – for example, 'each other' in 'Bill and Monica love each other' – are governed by the same rule as reflexives. Somewhat confusingly, the term 'anaphor' is usually reserved in linguistics for reflexives and reciprocals; i.e. it does not cover anaphoric pronouns.

In discussing anaphoric pronouns of type 2, we have restricted ourselves so far to anaphoric links *within a sentence*. Indeed, these are the only anaphoric links that linguists think are the concern of a grammar. Yet, pronouns can have apparently identical links to designational terms in an earlier sentence, even to a sentence uttered by someone else. Thus, in the dialogue,

Al: Monica loves Bill
Betty: Yes, but does she trust him?

'him' seems to be anaphorically dependent on 'Bill' in just the same way as it is in (2): it designates whatever 'Bill' designates.

3. *Unbound*: Cross-sentential anaphoric links are not only to designational terms but also to quantifiers. Thus, in the dialogue,

Al: Surely some woman trusts Bill
Betty: She would have to be very gullible

'she' is anaphorically dependent on the quantifier 'some woman'. What are we to say about this? It seems strange to say that one person's quantifier binds another person's utterance. The discussion may go on for hours, involving many people and dozens of pronouns anaphoric on that quantifier. Can we really think of these as all within the scope of the one quantifier, as if they had the form of one long conjunctive utterance? Or should we rather suppose that there is a third type of pronoun, one anaphoric on a quantifier but not bound by it?

This supposition has been confirmed by Gareth Evans (1985). Consider,

(8) Few women trust Bill and they are very gullible.

If the pronoun 'they' were bound by the quantifier 'few women' then (8) should be equivalent to

(9) Few women are such that they both trust Bill and are very gullible.

But it is not: (8) entails that few women trust Bill, period; and that *all* of those are very gullible. Many examples such as this have led to general agreement that Evans has identified a distinct type of unbound pronoun.

And with the help of the notion of *c-command* we can distinguish it from a bound pronoun: a pronoun anaphoric on a quantifier is bound by it if and only if the quantifier c-commands it. 'Few women' does not c-command 'they' in (8) but 'every man' does c-command 'him' in (1). Since no quantifier in one sentence can c-command a pronoun in another, there can be no cross-sentential binding.

How are we to interpret these unbound pronouns? An appealing theory, close to Evans' own, is that such a pronoun goes proxy for a definite description that is recoverable from its quantified antecedent clause. So (8) is equivalent to

(10) Few women trust Bill and *the few women who trust Bill* are very gullible

(the recovered description is in italics). This has the desired consequence that *all* the Bill trusters are very gullible. But there is a problem: when applied to some other examples it has consequences that seem undesired. A famous case is

(11) Socrates owned a dog and it bit him.

According to the theory, this is equivalent to

(12) Socrates owned a dog and *the dog he owned* bit him.

The problem is that (12) entails that Socrates owned only one dog and yet (11) seems quite consistent with Socrates owning *another* dog which did not bite him.

The theory also faces a severe difficulty with the notorious "donkey" sentences:

(13) Every man that owns a donkey beats it
(14) If John owns a donkey, he beats it.

The difficulty arises because, on one reading, (13) and (14) concern not simply the unique donkey of each donkey owner but *all* the owner's donkeys. Donkey sentences are formidably hard for any theory to handle and we shall say no more about them.

4. *Laziness*: There is one final sort of anaphoric pronoun, what Peter Geach (1962) calls a "pronoun of laziness". These are pronouns that simply go proxy for a noun phrase that is formally identical to some earlier one. Rather than repeat the earlier phrase one uses a pronoun out of "laziness". Thus, consider

(15) A person who mocks postmodernism has more sense than one who takes it seriously.

Here 'one' simply stands in for the words 'a person' and has the meaning that 'a person' would have had in that spot.

This concludes our discussion of syntax. We have barely scratched the surface of this very fertile subject. To do more we would need to go deeply into linguistics.* *

Suggested Reading

Chomsky's two early classics are *Syntactic Structures* (1957) and * **Aspects of the Theory of Syntax* (1965).* * A more readable early work is *Topics in the Theory of Generative Grammar* (1966), parts of which are reprinted under the same title in Searle 1971, *The Philosophy of Language*. * *Lectures on Government and Binding* (1981) led to a fairly radical change in approach among generative linguists. More recently, so did *The Minimalist Program* (1995a), chs. 3 and 4.* *

Introductory texts in generative grammar include the following: Radford 1988, *Transformational Grammar*; Lasnik and Uriagereka 1988, *A Course in GB Syntax*; Haegeman 1994, *Introduction to Government and Binding Theory*; Baker 1995, *English Syntax*; Newson and Cook 1996, *Chomsky's Universal Grammar*. * *Webelhuth 1995, *Government and Binding Theory and the Minimalist Program* is a more advanced work.* *

Searle 1972, "Chomsky's Revolution in Linguistics", reprinted in Harman 1974, a collection of papers *On Noam Chomsky*, gives a good overview of generative linguistics emphasizing its differences from its predecessors. Other collections include George 1989a, *Reflections on Chomsky*, and Kasher 1991, *The Chomskyan Turn*.

Geach 1962, Reference and Generality, a classic philosophical work on anaphora, argues that all anaphoric pronouns are either like bound variables or are pronouns of laziness. Evans 1985, Collected Papers, chs. 4, 5, and 8, are influential papers arguing against Geach and for pronouns of type 3, which he calls "E-type". Neale 1990, Descriptions, chs. 5 and 6 is

Part III

Language and Mind

7

Thought and Meaning

7.1 Thoughts as Inner Representations

Our focus so far has been on meaning, a property of linguistic items. This focus has frequently led to remarks about the mental states of language users, the people who produce the linguistic items. For meaning clearly depends in various ways on those states. In particular, it has proved impossible to discuss meaning without discussing linguistic competence or understanding. In this part of the book, the focus will be on those areas of the mind that are relevant to language. We start with thoughts. The relevance of thoughts to language is captured in the folk idea that "language expresses thought".

Thoughts – or, as they are sometimes called, "propositional attitudes" – are inner states: beliefs, desires, hopes, fears, etc. Why suppose that there are such inner states? Because we need to in order to explain behavior. Why does Oscar vote for Reagan? We answer in terms of beliefs and desires: he believes that Reagan is dangerous; he believes that a dangerous president is more likely to stop the Russians; he desires that the Russians be stopped; and so on. Thoughts are behavior-controlling states.

Our starting hypothesis about language was that it is *representational* (2.1). So also is our starting hypothesis about thoughts. Thoughts are inner representations (and misrepresentations) of the external world; they have *contents*. The desire to meet Jane Fonda is different from the desire to meet the prettiest CIA agent simply because these two thoughts have different representational contents. (Note that this would be so even if Jane Fonda were the prettiest CIA agent: the problem of opacity again; 2.5.) Further, the content of a thought is causally relevant. It is because a person desired *to meet Jane Fonda* that he lined up at a certain stage door. If he had desired *to meet the prettiest CIA agent*, he would have done something else. Similarly, if Oscar had believed that *a dangerous president was the last thing he wanted*, he would have voted for somebody else.

Thoughts differ not only in their representational content: the same content can be involved in a belief, a desire, and so on. Each of these is a behavior-controlling states but each feeds into behavior in a different way. What then is it to have a thought? It is to have a certain relation or "attitude" – for example, that of believing – to a certain content.

In sum, thoughts are inner states of people (and possibly other things) that have their causal powers partly in virtue of their representational contents and partly in virtue of the relation people have to these contents.

The standard way to ascribe a thought to a person, x, is to use a sentence of the form 'x V that p' where 'that p' specifies the content and 'V', the relation that x must stand it to this content; for example, 'Oscar believes that Reagan is dangerous'.

There is an ambiguity in the ordinary term 'thought'. It can be used, as we have above, to refer to a mental state: the having of an attitude to a content. It can also be used to refer simply to the content. In this use it is rather like 'proposition'. We shall use it both ways.

7.2   The Language-of-Thought Hypothesis

What kind of inner representation are thoughts? We go along with "the language-of-thought hypothesis", attributable largely to Jerry Fodor (1975) and Gilbert Harman (1973), according to which thoughts are like the sentences of human languages (English, etc.) and hence linguistic in character. Thoughts are *mental* sentences; and their parts, concepts, are *mental* words.

1. Thoughts seem to have the same semantic properties as sentences of human languages. (a) Thoughts have referential relations with the world, just as sentences do. Oscar's belief that Reagan is dangerous refers to Reagan ("is about" Reagan) in just the same way as the utterance 'Reagan is dangerous' does. (b) Beliefs, like assertions, are true or false. Desires and hopes are not, but they are like requests in having compliance or satisfaction conditions (2.3). (c) Thoughts, like sentences, can stand in inferential relations. Oscar might have arrived at his belief by inferring it from his beliefs that all Christians are dangerous and that Reagan is a

Christian. In brief, the representational "content" of a thought seems to differ only in name from the representational "meaning" of the sentence used to express or communicate that thought.

This alone does not show that a thought is *syntactically* like a sentence because it does not show that a thought has its sentential meaning partly *in virtue of having a sentential syntax*. There are other ways of having that meaning. Thus, part of a map can mean *Canberra is closer to Sydney than to Melbourne* and yet the "syntax" of that part – the way its meaning depends on the meanings of its simpler constituents – is very different from that of a sentence. And a certain naval flag, having no syntax at all, once meant *this ship has yellow fever*.

2. We think that a thought is like a sentence not only in having the meaning of a sentence but also in having the syntax of a sentence. One reason for thinking this comes from the explanation of (c) above. How could Oscar infer his belief from the other two mentioned? How can we explain Oscar's thought *process*, his *thinking*? One of the rules governing Oscar's thinking licenses all inferences of the form:

All *F*s are *G*
a is *F*
So, *a* is *G*.

Oscar's inference is an instance of this form. So in explaining Oscar's thinking, we attribute certain forms to his beliefs. These forms are syntactic structures that the beliefs can share with sentences.

3. Another reason for attributing a syntax to thoughts is that thought, like language, is systematic. People do not learn to produce and understand sentences one by one: they learn the elements of sentences and recipes for putting those elements together (1.2). This requires, as we pointed out (2.2), that sentences have syntactic structure. Similar remarks are true of thoughts. People have the capacity to think indefinitely many thoughts that they never have, and never will, think. For they have gained the concepts contained in those thoughts and have acquired the recipe for putting those concepts together. This capacity requires that thoughts have syntactic structure.

These reasons are decisive against the view that thoughts are structurally simple like the naval flag, but not so decisive against the view that thoughts are like maps, images, or diagrams. Still, we do think that the reasons are very persuasive against that view. Perhaps that view could account for the systematicity of thought, but it is difficult to see how it could account for thinking. Formal logic gives us a very good idea of how an inference like Oscar's might proceed if the steps are represented linguistically. From its very beginning, computer science has used this idea to build machines that do process linguistic representations. In recent years, computer science has attempted to develop "connectionist" machines that use representations of a very different sort. Despite the striking success of these machines with some forms of problem solving, connectionist processes seem rather far from capturing anything like human inference.

4. We have two further reasons in favor of the language-of-thought hypothesis. First, thoughts are like sentences in being abstract. The sentence 'Orson weighs 130kg' tells you nothing about Orson other than his mass (1.2). Similarly, the thought that Orson weighs 130kg. Images, maps and diagrams are too rich and ambiguous to capture the content of thought; a picture of Reagan is no more a repesentation of the belief that Reagan is wrinkled, than it is of the belief that he is caucasian, or of the belief that he is surprisingly hairy for an old man. Thought and talk are abstract, and abstract in the same way. (Of course, pictures may be *associated with* thoughts, particularly with perceptually-based ones, but they are not themselves thoughts.)

5. Finally, we need to *explain* the contents of thoughts. We take it as established that the thought that Reagan is dangerous, like the sentence 'Reagan is dangerous', has a part that means *Reagan*. How are we to explain the contribution that a part like this makes to the meaning of the whole? When we are concerned with sentences, we have seen how to proceed. We look largely to linguists for information about syntactic structures and largely to logicians for information about how truth conditions depend on structure (6.1). We are a long way from having all the details, of course, but the approach seems promising. If the language-of-thought hypothesis is correct then the same approach is just as promising for thoughts; for, on that view, the contents of thoughts are the meanings of *mental* sentences. And, once again, we have very little idea of any alternative explanation. Consider maps, for example. We see clearly how a map represents *Sydney being north of Melbourne* but we wonder how it would represent nonspacial relations; for example, *Sydney being more lively than Melbourne*. And we have no idea how it could represent nonrelational situations; for example, *Felix being a tiger* and *Reagan being dangerous*. And what about *turtles making poor lovers* and *high interest rates possibly causing a banking collapse*? And how could it capture quantification, counterfactual conditionals, and other complex thoughts?

We conclude that the language-of-thought hypothesis is correct: thought is in a language.

7.3   A Public Language of Thought or "Mentalese"?

This raises the question: Which language is thought in? It seems clear that a person's language of thought is similar in various ways to the public language in which she expresses her thought. In the light of this, it is tempting to suppose that two are *the same*. According to this "public language-of-thought hypothesis", her language of thought is her language of talk. That was the line *we* took in the first edition. An alternative hypothesis is that a person's thought is in a special mental language, "Mentalese". So, if the person speaks English, then the Mentalese hypothesis is that she talks by *translating* Mentalese into English and that she understands English by doing the reverse. Famously, Jerry Fodor has defended an extreme version of the Mentalese hypothesis, according to which Mentalese is both universal *and largely innate*. We remain very skeptical indeed about this version of the hypothesis and will discuss the moderate version: Is the language of thought a public language (for those who speak one) or some sort of Mentalese?

Note that this question is distinct further question from the one we discussed in the last section. It is one thing to conclude that we think in a language, a further thing to conclude that we think in one language and not another.

One objection to the public language-of-thought hypothesis can be dismissed quickly. When the living brain of an English speaker is examined, we find no cerebral blackboard on which English sentences are written. Nothing inside the head *looks like* a sentence. This objection is confused. What *does* a sentence look like? Sentences, unlike pictures, are medium-independent (1.2). Whereas the relation between picture and pictured is, in some vague sense, natural or intrinsic, that between name and named is arbitrary. Practical problems aside, anything could be used to refer to anything. Indeed we are familiar with a range of very different physical types being used for the one semantic type (4.2); a sentence may be physically realized as a sequence of acoustic vibrations, as gestures in a sign language, as marks on paper, as a sequence of flags, as electric pulses of various kinds, and so on. So there is nothing incoherent in the idea that sentences could be realized in a neural medium as well. Perhaps tokens of thought, just like tokens of speech or braille, are sentences of a public language.

It is generally agreed that this hypothesis must at least be qualified: *all* thinking could not be in a public language. The higher animals and pre-linguistic children think, but obviously not in a public language. And some mature human thought is surely not in such a language either: consider our thought about music or chess, for example. So the thesis must be that *most* mature human thought consists in having attitudes of believing, desiring, hoping, etc., to mental sentences in a public language.

This hypothesis has intuitive appeal because our cognitive capacities seem closely correlated with our linguistic capacities. The general development of the two capacities goes hand in hand. Further, it is very plausible to suppose that our ability to think certain thoughts depends on language. Could we have had beliefs about aircraft, or desires about nuclear bombs before we had words for aircrafts and bombs? (We return to this matter of the dependency of thought on language in chapter 10.)

The hypothesis also has some introspective support. Speech often *seems* to be thinking out loud; thought often *seems* to be talking to oneself. Moreover, consider a familiar barrier a person must break through in learning a foreign language: learning to "think in the language". Until she crashes through this barrier, she uses the foreign language by translating back and forth to the familiar home language. Or, so it seems to introspection.

These considerations are far from decisive in support of the public language-of-thought hypothesis, for the alternative Mentalese hypothesis may well be able to accommodate them. Perhaps the simultaneous development of language and thought can be accounted for by taking the one environmental cause to be responsible for both developments. And it seems fairly straightforward for the Mentalese hypothesis to account for the introspective data about thinking in a language. The claim might be that, before breaking through the barrier, the person's translation of Mentalese into the foreign language takes two steps: she first translates into her native language and then translates that language into the foreign one. Whereas the translation into the foreign language is laboured and conscious, the translation into the native language is practiced and unconscious. Hence her initial sense of translating the foreign language but not her native one. She breaks through the barrier when she collapses the two steps into the one unconscious one. Hence her later sense of thinking in the foreign language.

Furthermore, there is introspective and experimental evidence that seems to count against the public hypothesis. We often seem to have a thought and yet have trouble expressing it: "the words are on the tip of my tongue". Yet if the thought were in the very words that express it why would we have the trouble? The phenomenon suggests, rather, that we are struggling to translate our thought from Mentalese into English. But perhaps not. Perhaps we are struggling to form the thought, a thought which once formed is in English and can be easily expressed.

Experiments show that when we read a passage, we tend to remember "the message" rather than the precise wording. Thus, take some English sentence that did *not* appear in the passage we read. If we are asked whether that sentence appeared, we are likely to say that it did if it has much the same meaning as one that did. This suggests that we have stored a representation in Mentalese and do not remember which of several English translations of it appeared in the passage. But, again, perhaps not. Perhaps we stored a representation in English but, given our primary interest in the message not the particular form of words that presented it, we were not concerned to store it in the form that presented it: we chose a form that is most "natural" for us, perhaps the one most suitable for retrieval. When asked the question we do not remember whether that sentence or an equivalent one appeared in the passage.

It is common to object to the public hypotheses by pointing out that public languages are often inexplicit but the language of thought cannot be. Thus, a public sentence "looks like"

(1) John hit the boy.

But a mental sentence must "look more like"

(2) $[_s[_{NP}[_N John]]\ [_{VP}[_V hit]\ [_{NP}[_{DET} the]\ [_N boy]]]]$.

This difference is brought out by the fact that public languages are *ambiguous* whereas the language of thought cannot be. Thus, the English sentence 'Visiting relatives can be boring' is notoriously ambiguous. In contrast, whenever a person has a thought that this sentence expresses, that thought cannot be ambiguous if the person's thinking is to proceed in the appropriate rational manner: the central processor can only operate on a thought sentence that makes explicit whether it means that the visiting of relatives can be boring or that relatives who visit can be boring.

The objection is confused about ambiguity and the significance of explicitness. Ambiguity is a property of representation *types*. A certain type in a physical medium – for example, a sound type – is ambiguous if some of its tokens have one meaning and others another (4.2). The objection rightly points out that the thought expressed on a particular occasion, a mental *token*, is not ambiguous. But then neither is the utterance token that expresses it: any token of 'Visiting relatives can be boring' will have one meaning or the other (ignoring confusions and deliberate puns). Ambiguity is no more a property of utterance tokens than it is of mental tokens. What about explicitness? The objection rightly points to a difference here: whereas the utterance token has some syntactic properties that are not explicit, all the syntactic properties of the underlying Mentalese token must be explicit. This points to differences in the brute physical form of the tokens but does not alone show that they differ in syntactic properties; written tokens of 'Cheap food and wine can be interesting' and 'Cheap (food and wine) can be interesting' differ in form too but can be syntactically identical; so too, (1) and (2). Whether or not a token has a syntactic property is one thing, whether or not its form makes the property explicit is another. Thoughts differ from utterances in that they must be syntactically explicit not in that they must be syntactically different.

Perhaps the strongest influence against the public hypothesis has come from the views of Noam Chomsky. He has argued for a highly cognitivist account of linguistic competence. He thinks that human language use is rule-governed in a very strong way. Linguistic behavior is controlled by rules explicitly represented in the mind of the speaker, rules of which the speaker is cognizant. Knowledge of these rules tells the speaker which strings of words are sentences and what sentences mean. Finally, many of the rules governing linguistic behavior are *innate*. We are born pre-programmed with information about the kinds of rules we will need to learn in learning a language. We have innate knowledge of "universal grammar".

Now if a speaker understands English in virtue of knowing rules for its employment, these rules cannot be in English. If you do not already understand Japanese, a Japanese–Japanese dictionary is no help to you. Similarly, if you do not already understand English, a system of rules in English, telling you how to construct sentences, and what they mean, is no help. It follows that the speaker must represent those rules in a language of thought that is not English; and, of course, it cannot be any other public language either. It must be in Mentalese. How rich must Mentalese be? Jerry Fodor has appealed to learning theory in arguing that Mentalese has to be at least as rich as any public language whose rules it represents (1975). He goes further, in his inimitable way: Mentalese, in its rich entirety, is innate.

The public hypothesis concedes some place for Mentalese but the place is much more limited than this. The hypothesis sees Mentalese as the impoverished system of representation of the higher animals and pre-linguistic children; and as a supplement to the public language representations of the adult human. The above rich view of Mentalese arises from the assumption that linguistic competence consists in *knowledge*, an assumption we shall argue against in the next chapter (8.4–8.7), and from assumptions about the nature of learning. Further, though we shall find some merit in the idea that the *syntax* of the language of thought is partly innate, our earlier discussion (chs. 4 and 5) already casts doubt on the idea that the vocabulary is. We shall add to these doubts in what follows.

So far we have found nothing decisive one way or the other on whether the language of thought is largely a public language or Mentalese. However, we rather doubt that this is a theoretically interesting issue. What precisely would be required for a mental sentence to be a sentence of, say, English? Clearly it must consist of English words in an English structure. We think that sense can be made of it having an English structure. But what sense can be made of it consisting of English words? What would make a mental word English? We doubt that there is a theoretically interesting answer. So we propose to set aside the public vs. Mentalese issue. We shall treat the language of thought as if it were a distinct Mentalese and focus instead on what seems a more theoretically productive issue: How closely related is a person's Mentalese to her public language?

Here is a powerful argument for thinking that the syntax of an English speaker's Mentalese cannot be very different from English. (1) The translation process of producing and understanding English must preserve meanings, in some sense: when a thought is expressed by an utterance, the utterance must mean the same as the Mentalese sentence involved in the thought; when an utterance is understood, it must be assigned to a Mentalese sentence that means the same. (2) The meaning of a sentence is a function of its syntax. So, the syntax of the speaker's Mentalese sentence has to be close enough to that of its English expression to make them mean the same.

Of course, in the absence of an account of the sense in which a thought has to match its expression in meaning, this conclusion leaves room for quite a lot of difference in the syntax of the two tokens. After all, there is a sense in which an active English sentence means the same as its passive, despite their syntactic differences; and there is a sense in which an English sentence means the same as its Japanese translation, despite their syntactic differences.

Fodor has given another reason for thinking that the syntax of a person's Mentalese is like that of her language: we have to account for the great *speed* of language processing: "the more structural similarity there is between what gets uttered and its internal representation, the less computing the sentence understander will have to do" (1975: 152). And the less the computing the less the time needed to compute. We can explain the speedy process from an English utterance to the mental sentence that is its interpretation by supposing that they are syntactically alike.

In the light of this discussion, it is appropriate to return to our earlier problem with identifying the semantic task (1.2). The task is to explain "meanings", which we characterized as the properties of utterances that enable them to play their roles in explaining behavior and informing us about the world. But then how do these utterances differ from bird signals and bee dances which play similar roles and so might also be thought to have "meanings"? More importantly, what should settle the controversy over whether Alex, an African Grey Parrot, and several nonhuman primates have been successfully taught English? How might their "utterances" fail to be English? We think that the crux of the answer is this. For utterances to be English, they have to be expressions of thoughts with the rich syntactic structure of our thoughts. It is because English is the expression of such thoughts that it has the salient features we noted (1.2). It is because Alex's language does not express such thoughts (we presume) that it is not English. The controversy over the primates is over whether their "utterances" arise from anything like our thoughts.

We shall find further support for a close relationship between the mental and public syntax in the *explanation* of their syntax. Similarly, the explanation of the meanings of mental and public words will indicate a close relationship between these words (7.5). But first we must take account of Paul Grice's view of meaning.

7.4   Grice's Theory of Meaning

At the beginning of chapter 2, we mentioned the vagueness and ambiguity of the term 'meaning'. Grice starts from an awareness of this. This leads him to distinguish a number of species of meaning. He first pares off what he calls "natural meaning". In 'fetid breath means tooth decay', 'means' is roughly synonymous with 'is a reliable sign of'; it identifies a species of meaning that Grice (writing before the development of indicator theory; 7.7) assumed was not semantic. Grice goes on to identify two important species of "nonnatural meaning" or "meaning$_{NN}$", which are semantic: on the one hand there is the *standard*, *literal*, or *conventional* meaning of a sign; on the other, there is *what a speaker means by* the sign on some given occasion.

Mostly conventional meaning and speaker meaning coincide, but sometimes they do not. Thus, in *The Old Dick* the protagonist describes a thug as 'so primitive that he could regenerate missing limbs'. The literal or conventional meaning of this utterance is of course a falsehood; even the dimmest tough cannot sprout new arms and legs. But what speaker means by the utterance is true, for what he means is that the thug is exceptionally stupid.

Metaphors like this one about the thug provide support for the distinction between speaker meaning and conventional meaning. In any such nonliteral use of language, a speaker means something that is different from, and to a degree independent of, the words' conventionally meaning. The speaker's meaning is derived from the conventional meaning, but transcends it.

Further support for the distinction can be found from situations where there seems to be speaker meaning without conventional meaning. Consider the original development of language. Presumably this development was replete with examples of noises and gestures being used with communicative intent – with speaker meaning – before there existed a settled system of conventions for so using them. Communicative effort that was at least partly successful must have been a precondition for the development of linguistic conventions. The conventions came from regularities in speaker meanings. Even now, there is speaker meaning without conventional meaning when people without a common language are thrown together: they attempt to communicate by gestures, mime, and the like.

In a metaphor a speaker deliberately brings about a divergence of speaker meaning from conventional meaning. Divergence can also be accidental. When we say to someone, "You didn't say what you meant", we are usually indicating just such a divergence. Accidental divergences, like metaphors, are very common. In any case of divergence, there are two distinct meanings of a sign to assess. So, for example, we can talk of both the speaker reference and the conventional reference of a term. And, a slip of the tongue may be conventionally ungrammatical, and hence lack conventional truth conditions, and yet have a speaker syntax and truth conditions. (This bears on the qualifications mentioned in 6.1.)

(We have written as if the conventional meaning of an expression is the same as its literal meaning. Mostly this is so, but not always. A person may have an eccentric idiolect: the literal meaning of her expression may not be a meaning it has according to any linguisitic convention. Donald Davidson (1986) brings this out nicely in his discussion of Mrs Malaprop's "a nice derangement of epitaphs": what she literally means is "a nice arrangement of epithets" and yet her words do not mean this according to any convention. We shall continue to overlook this subtlety.)

**A distinction like that between speaker and conventional meaning also applies to pragmatic features of sentences, and in particular to illocutionary force (2.3). Consider, for example:

I promise that if you butt your cigarette on my rook again, I'll call the tournament director
Is it within your capacities to pass that jug of water? My wooden leg has caught fire.

The first of these is likely to be intended as a threat, perhaps a warning. The second is unlikely to be a question about the hearer's qualifications as a waiter. Yet these sentences have the conventional forms, respectively, of a promise and a question. Adapting Grice's terminology to these cases (known in the literature as *indirect* speech acts), we might say that their conventional force is different from their speaker force. These differences are, at least, analogous to those between conventional and speaker meaning. To the extent that illocutionary force is part of meaning – and we think that it is to some extent (2.3) – the differences are further examples of those between conventional and speaker meaning.**

We shall suppose then that the distinction is real. Which sort of meaning is more basic or prior? Grice thinks that speaker meaning is prior to conventional meaning. The discussion above suggests that he is right. It reveals cases of speaker meaning without, or independent of, conventional meaning. Yet conventional meaning cannot be similarly detached from speaker meaning.

At first sight it may seem that a sentence can have conventional meaning without a speaker meaning anything by it: a monkey might randomly type out – or, to be more modern, a computer might randomly print out – the works of Shakespeare; the wind may carve out the words 'Reagan is dangerous' in the Mojave desert. But does such a chance occurrence really have meaning? Notice that there is no fact of the matter *which* Reagan the desert sentence refers to and, therefore, no fact of the matter *which* conventional meaning it has. Wherever a token is of a type that is ambiguous within a language, or between languages, it is impossible to assign it a conventional meaning in the absence of a speaker meaning; for its conventional meaning depends on which convention the speaker had in mind (4.2). Even if the token is of an unambiguous type, it is doubtful if there is any point to assigning it a conventional meaning. And even if there is a point, these examples do not cast any doubt on the fundamental Gricean view: a sentence could not have a conventional meaning which is not derived from *past* regularities in speaker meanings.

We conclude that speaker meaning is indeed prior to conventional meaning.

What account can we give of speaker meaning? A communicative intention, Grice thinks, is in some way reflexive. You intend to communicate by means of your audience's recognition of *that very intention*. He is led to this view by a certain contrast. Suppose Tom wishes to induce in Dick the belief that Dick's lover is having an affair with Harry. He might use one of the following two procedures:

1. Tom arranges for Dick to see a photograph of his lover and Harry in compromising circumstances
2. Tom draws a picture of Dick's lover and Harry in such circumstances and shows it to Dick.

Grice makes the following claims in this connection. First, he suggests that the photograph has natural meaning but no meaning$_{NN}$; only the drawing has speaker meaning. Second, there is a crucial difference in the role intentions play in the two cases. Dick may come to the target belief from the photograph without any view of Tom's intentions. He might, for example, think that his discovery of the photograph is an accident. Contrast this with the case of the drawing. Unless Dick takes Tom to be drawing a picture of his lover and Harry, and drawing it with the point of inducing the target belief, Dick will not come to that belief. If he takes Tom to have a different purpose, say of producing an interesting drawing, Tom will not achieve his aim. Dick must recognize Tom's intentions and Tom knows this.

Grice's remarks on this case are plausible enough. They lead him to the following account of speaker meaning:

> 'A meant something by x' is (roughly) equivalent to 'A intended the utterance of x to produce some effect in an audience by means of the recognition of this intention'; and we may add that to ask what a meant is to ask for a specification of the intended effect . . . (Grice 1957: 442)

Later work by Grice and others led to many revisions and complications. The results were elaborate and baroque structures of nested intentions. We shall not concern ourselves with these complications. Nevertheless, to give their flavor, we reproduce one of Grice's later tries:

> 'U meant something by x' is true iff U uttered x intending thereby: (1) that A should produce response r (2) that A should, at least partly on the basis of x, think that U intended (1) (3) that A should think that U intended (2) (4) that A's production of r should be based (at least in part) on A's thought that U intended (1) [that is, on A's fulfillment of (2)] (5) that A should think U intended (4). (Grice 1969: 156)

Even this definition proves insufficiently complex to rule out all the suggested counter-examples. What should we think of such an account of speaker meaning? Is it supposed to be psychologically real? If so, it is not very plausible; we do not seem to have this complex of nested intentions when we speak. Grice's response to this worry is rather vague. He disclaims "any intention of peopling all our talking life with armies of complicated psychological occurrences" (1957: 443). What then are we to make of his talk of intentions? His answer is not clear but seems behavioristic: to have these intentions is simply to behave in a certain sort of way.

> Explicitly formulated linguistic . . . intentions are no doubt rare. In their absence we would seem to rely on very much the same kinds of criteria as we do in the case of nonlinguistic intentions where there is a general usage. An utterer is held to convey what is normally conveyed . . . we require a good reason for accepting that a particular usage diverges from general usage . . . (1957: 443)

This line of thought will not do. Behaviorist accounts of most mental states are hopeless (8.5). If the Griceans are right about speaker meaning, then the complex structure of intentions that they talk about must be part of the unconscious mental life of speakers.

Why are Grice's definitions so exceptionally complex? The answer, we suggest, is to be found in his view of his task. He sees himself as doing "conceptual analysis" or the "analysis of ordinary language": his definitions are attempts to analyze an ordinary concept of meaning. We shall discuss conceptual analysis in some detail later (14.4). Meanwhile, we note two features of it that help with our current question. First, an analysis must be constructed out of elements familiar to all: commonsense concepts. As a result the weight of Grice's analysis of meaning is born by only two notions: intention and belief. Second, an analysis must be both necessarily true and knowable *a priori*. So, Grice's analysis has to be inviolable to our intuitions about *any* situation that can be *imagined* in a "thought experiment". The complexity of Grice's definitions reflects the difficulty, perhaps even the impossibility, of covering such an enormous range of possible counter-examples using such a thin stock of basic elements.

We have a different view of the task in the philosophy of language (1.3, 14.1; see also 2.7). From our naturalistic perspective, the most that an analysis could reveal is our implicit folk theory of language. The discovery of that theory is only the beginning of the task. It is an open empirical question just how good that theory is. How well does it explain the phenomena? It may be wrong. It will almost certainly be incomplete.

In the light of this, if conceptual analysis reveals a distinction between speaker meaning and conventional meaning, then it reveals that folk make that distinction. What matters to us, primarily, is not whether folk do make it but whether it is theoretically profitable to make it. We have indicated that we think it is. Next, if analysis shows that it is difficult to explain speaker meaning in terms of familiar notions, this may indicate that folk intuitions about some alleged counter-examples are mistaken: folk theory is wrong here. Or it may indicate that folk have no explanation of speaker meaning; folk theory is incomplete here. We may have to seek an explanation that involves unfamiliar notions. This explanation may appeal to aspects of our psychological organization that differ from intentions and beliefs in being undreamt of in folk psychology.

We have a deeper objection to Grice's approach to speaker meaning. At best it will help to distinguish communicative acts from other human behavior (and, perhaps, distinguish the illocutionary force of communicative acts). It tells us nothing about the *content* of such acts; *nothing about what distinguishes one speaker meaning from another* (beyond, perhaps, their illocutionary force). In virtue of what does a speaker mean by 'Armadillos are dangerous' that armadillos are dangerous and not, say, that turkeys gobble? The Gricean answer is that the former not the latter was the content of the belief that the speaker intended to convey. This answer accords with the folk idea that an utterance expresses the thought that underlies it, an idea we have endorsed. But it raises a crucial question: In virtue of what was *that* the content of the underlying thought?

What makes it the case that the content was *armadillos are dangerous* not *turkeys gobble?* The Griceans provided no answer.

The failure to answer this question is a serious weakness of the Gricean program. How do we answer it? We have a *prima facie* problem here. If we were to explain a thought's content simply in terms of its direct causal relation to the world it concerns and/or its relation to other thoughts we would have no problem. But we have one because our theory of reference borrowing implicitly gives the conventions of the public language a role in explaining thought content. Given our qualified approval of the Gricean program, this threatens an explanatory circle.

7.5   Avoiding the Explanatory Circle

The threatened circle is generated as follows. Suppose that a person has a certain thought. (a) We have endorsed the language-of-thought hypothesis and so identify the content of this thought with the meaning of the sentence involved in the thought (7.2). Suppose now that the person expresses the thought in her public language. (b) We agree with the Gricean view, and the folk view, that the content of the thought determines what the person means by the sentence she utters. (c) Furthermore, we accept the Gricean view that the conventional meaning of her sentence in the public language is to be explained in terms of regularities in speaker meanings. That conventional meaning must depend in some way on what people have commonly meant by words of the physical type exemplified in the sentence; and on what they have commonly meant by sentences of that structure (7.4). We have illustrated this dependence, in effect, in our theory of the introduction of names (4.1, 4.3) and natural kind terms (5.2). (d) Yet, finally, our theory of reference borrowing implicitly appeals to the conventions of the public language to explain the meanings of mental sentences. This step, completely at odds with the Gricean insistence on the priority of speaker meaning, may seem to close the explanatory circle.

In brief, the threatened circle is as follows: (a) the meanings of mental sentences explain thought contents; (b) thought contents explain speaker meanings; (c) speaker meanings explain conventional meanings; (d) conventional meanings explain the meanings of mental sentences.

To break out of this circle we must examine (d) closely. The meaning of a mental sentence, like the meaning of a public sentence, is explained in terms of its syntactic structure and the referential properties of the mental words that fill that structure (7.2). Insofar as the meaning of a mental word depends on reference *borrowing* it does indeed depend on a convention of the public language, but insofar as that meaning depends on an independent reference *fixing*, it does not depend on a convention. And nobody can borrow until someone has fixed; fixings explain conventions. And the syntax of the mental sentence does not depend on convention. Ultimately, the meaning of a mental sentence is determined by causal relations to the world and to other sentences. There is truth in (d), but nowhere near enough to close the explanatory circle.

In developing this point we shall, for the sake of argument, presuppose an historical-causal theory of how reference is ultimately fixed. We have seen that such theories have a deep problem, the *qua*-problem (4.5, 5.3), and will soon contemplate some alternative theories (7.7). But the choice between these theories, or indeed any ultimate explanation of reference, is beside the point of this section.

Consider the mental words underlying the fairly basic words – names and natural kind terms – covered by descriptive-causal theories of reference fixing and pure-causal theories of borrowing (4.1, 5.2–5.3). Someone of our century can have thoughts including the mental word SOCRATES (we use capital letters to represent mental words), thoughts that she would express using the English word 'Socrates', only by being plugged into a causal network grounded in a certain ancient philosopher. This network was established and maintained by the convention of using the sound and inscription types for 'Socrates' to refer to the philosopher. Such uses participate in the convention. Thus the meaning of SOCRATES, its property of designating Socrates by causal chains of the type that constitute this network, is partly explained in terms of the convention. Similarly, most of us have thoughts about protons in virtue of being linked to them by the network for 'proton', a network established by the conventional linguistic practices of physicists.

The respect in which these mental words do not have their meanings in virtue of conventions is indicated by the qualifications that must accompany such accounts of the dependence of mental meaning on convention. (1) *Some* people *once* thought about Socrates without depending on the convention: the people who named him 'Socrates', thus *fixing* the reference. Similarly, 'proton'. Furthermore, all those involved in *subsequent* groundings of a word have thoughts that are, to that extent, dependent for their meaning not on convention but on direct confrontation with the appropriate object(s) (4.3, 5.2). (2) Indeed, it is the regularities of speaker meanings arising out of these convention-independent thoughts that establish the convention. It is in this way that speaker meaning is prior to conventional meaning. So even the thoughts of those who have made no groundings, thoughts which are therefore totally dependent on the convention – for example, *our* thoughts including SOCRATES – have meanings that are ultimately explained in terms of groundings. For, the convention itself is explained in terms of groundings.

Consider, next, the mental words underlying the least basic words, ones that are covered by a description theory of reference fixing and cannot be borrowed at all; PEDIATRICIAN, BACHELOR, and HUNTER are likely examples. The meaning of such a mental word is determined first by its association with other words. This is a matter of the word's "functional role" – its function in the cognitive processes of the thinker – not a matter of convention at all. The meaning is determined second by whatever explains the meanings of these other mental words. Convention may play a role in explaining those meanings, but they must rest ultimately on the causal reference fixing of the fairly basic words, hence not on convention.

We have aired the possibility of many other sorts of words in our language, ones lying between the fairly basic and the least basic (5.5). These terms depend more for their reference on associated descriptions than do the fairly basic ones but less than do the least basic ones. Our theory of the mental words underlying these "in-between" words combines elements of the theories for the fairly basic and the least basic. As a result, the dependence of these mental words on convention will be *at most* equal to the limited dependence of the fairly basic words.

What about the syntactic structure of a mental sentence? In virtue of what does it have the structure of a predication, a quantification, or whatever? This is a matter of functional role, including particularly the sentence's possible inferential interactions with other sentences. Thus, the sentences REAGAN IS WRINKLED and THATCHER IS TOUGH share a syntactic structure in virtue of a similarity in their roles in our cognitive lives. Similarly, ALL POLITICIANS ARE RICH and ALL POLICE ARE CORRUPT, which share a different structure and role.

It is difficult to say more about what determines the syntax of thought and we shall not attempt to. The main point is that it is not determined by the conventions of language. Indeed the conventional syntax of an utterance is explained in terms of regularities in the way in which thoughts with a certain syntax have produced utterances of that form.

Finally, such aspects of illocutionary force as enter into the meaning of a thought are explained, in the first instance at least, by functional role. What gives a thought the force of a question, statement, threat, or promise, we suppose, is its interactions with various beliefs, desires, intentions, and the like (2.3). The regular use of a certain spoken form to express a certain illocutionary force may lead to that form being the conventional one for that force.

In our rejection of description theories and adoption of causal theories of reference, we have enthusiastically adopted Putnam's slogan, "meanings just ain't in the head" (3.5, 5.1). Like all slogans, this one can mislead. It is aimed at the view, derived from description theories, that meanings are determined *entirely* by what is in the head. The point of the slogan is to emphasize that extra-cranial links to reality are also important. However, the slogan should not mislead one into supposing that no aspect of meaning is determined by what is in the head. We have just seen some that are.

Our task was to explain the meanings of mental sentences without getting caught in an explanatory circle because of the role we give to reference borrowing. This we have done. Even words that can be borrowed ultimately depend for their meanings on convention-independent reference fixing by grounding thoughts. Words that cannot be borrowed, and syntax, introduce no additional dependence of mental meanings on conventions.

We earlier (7.3) set aside the question of whether the language of thought *is* the public language of the thinker but we suggested that the languages are, at least, *closely related*. Our discussion in this section supports this suggestion. We have seen that explanations of the meanings of words and of syntax relate mental sentences very closely to the public sentences that express them.

We shall now fill out our solution to the apparent circle with some speculations about the origins of language. These speculations will bring out the way conventions *facilitate* thought. This is a very different matter from the one we have been examining: conventions *partly explaining the content* of thought.

7.6   The Origins of Language

We had thoughts before we were able to say anything, and before we learned any linguistic conventions. This is true of us as a species, and of us all individually. The higher animals can think but not talk. Perhaps these preconventional thoughts – primeval, babyish, or nonhuman – are very primitive, so primitive as to be unlike the thoughts of language-using adults. (If so, they may be thoughts only in a more liberal sense than is employed in our earlier discussion.) These early thoughts preceded the learning of conventions, but we need not suppose that they are innate. Presumably we have innate dispositions to respond in different ways to different stimuli. These predispositions, together with the stimuli we receive, lead us and our biological kin to represent the world in thought. It is because of the causal relations amongst these representations, and between the representations and the world, that the representations refer as they do. Though these early thoughts are primitive, we need not suppose that they are structureless: presumably the nonhuman ones have crude structures; perhaps the human ones have structures like ours.

Mental representations of the world come with theorizing about it. We feel a pressing need to understand our environment in order to manipulate and control it. This drive led our early ancestors, in time, to express a primitive thought or two. They grunted or gestured, *meaning something by* such actions. There was speaker meaning without conventional meaning. Over time the grunts and gestures caught on: linguistic conventions were born. As a result of this trail blazing it is much easier for others to have those primitive thoughts, for they can learn to have them from the conventional ways of expressing them. Further, they have available an easy way of representing the world, a way based on those conventional gestures and grunts. They can borrow their capacity to think about things from those who created the conventions. With primitive thought made easy, the drive to understand leads to more complicated thoughts, hence more complicated speaker meanings, hence more complicated conventions. If this sketch is right we have, as individuals and as a species, engaged in a prodigious feat of lifting ourselves up by our own semantic bootstraps.

The picture is of a language of thought expanding with the learning of a public language to which it is related. The language is public in having a conventional form, the regular association of sounds with speaker meanings. Feedback goes both ways. No conventions can be established without the existence of the appropriate speaker meanings. But the existence of conventions facilitates speaker meaning. And conventions introduce into the language of thought mental representations that are causally based on, and have the same meaning as, the sounds that figure in the conventions. The language of thought becomes more and more tied to the public language, but always remains a little ahead of it. We still have the capacity to think beyond the conventional established public language, as is shown by our ability to express new thoughts in new words. We can now think thoughts which a century ago were unthinkable.

We suppose that the development in humanoid society of a complex and rich public language was very slow. (But perhaps not: see the brief discussion of creolization in 8.10.) In contrast its development in a contemporary child is very quick. This is to be expected, for the child gets the benefits of past struggles. The stimuli he receives include many linguistic ones: sentences conventionally related to thoughts that are rich in content. These stimuli make it much easier to have these rich thoughts. Moreover, it may be that current human brains are in part designed for this job, whereas the brains of the trailblazers were not.

We could state the primacy of speaker meaning as follows. Speaker meanings create the conventional written and spoken forms of the language. But it is because we have learned those conventions that we are able to have the rich variety of thoughts, and hence produce the rich variety of speaker meanings, that we do. The *creation* of a convention requires some people to have thoughts the contents of which are not fully dependent on conventions. Once created each convention encourages other people to have new thoughts. Often the contents of many of those thoughts are to be explained partly in terms of that convention. Thought contents explain the conventions that explain *other* thought contents. There is no circle in the explanation.

**7.7   Indicator and Teleological Semantics

In this chapter so far we have worked with pure-historical-causal theories of how reference is ultimately fixed. These are the theories we did our best to motivate and explain earlier in discussing the proper names and natural kind terms of a natural language (chs. 3–5). We have recently been applying the theories to the mental analogues of those terms (7.5). Yet, the theories have a deep problem, the *qua*-problem (4.5, 5.3), which provides ample motivation for us to look elsewhere for an ultimate explanation. So in this section we shall consider pure-causal proposals of two other sorts, indicator and teleological theories.

These theories have been developed as theories of the relationship between thought and the world and that is why we have left them until this chapter. However, on our Gricean approach, the reference fixing of a linguistic word depends on the reference fixing of the mental word that it expresses. So, a theory of the one carries over to the other, as we have seen with our historical-causal theory.

In saying that historical-causal theories of reference attempt explanations of how reference is "ultimately" fixed we have had in mind that they will be combined with other theories explaining aspects of reference that rest on ultimate links. An ultimate link is a direct one between a word and reality. We have suggested that there are also two sorts of indirect links. First, a person's word may depend for its reference on other words that she associates with it: it is covered by a description theory (or a descriptive-causal theory) of reference fixing, not a pure-causal one. The link of such a word to its referent is indirect in that it is via the direct links of other words to the world. Second, we have argued that the words allegedly covered by historical-causal theories of reference fixing can be borrowed. So, typically, a person's reference with such a word will depend on other people's reference with it. If it does then its link to its referent is indirect in that it is via the links of the other people to the referent.

Where do indicator and teleological theories stand on this matter? Interestingly enough, those who propose these theories do not normally seem to contemplate the possibility of these two sorts of indirect referential links: they do not seem to contemplate supplementing their pure-causal theories with description theories or theories of reference borrowing. Implicitly, at least, they seem to hold that each person's thought stands in some direct causal relation to its referent not an indirect one via other words or other people. Still, the rejection of indirect links does not seem to be an *essential* feature of indicator and teleological theories. Clearly we think that the theories would be wise not to make the rejection, given the strong case for reference borrowing and the plausibility of description theories for some terms. So, we think that the theories are best construed as simply theories of ultimate reference fixing to which other theories of reference could be added.

We begin with "indicator semantics". These theories were first proposed by Dennis Stampe (1979) and Fred Dretske (1981). The idea is that a token represents what tokens of that type are *reliably correlated with*. Our token HORSE refers to horses, because there is a horse about whenever we have a token of that type in our mind. We think HORSE only when (but not necessarily when and only when) there is a horse in the immediate vicinity. The token "carries the information" that a certain situation holds in much the same way that tree rings carry information about the age of a tree. Tokens of that type are "reliably correlated" with the situation and hence "indicate" that situation.

From our perspective, interested in the meanings of linguistic and mental sentences, this picture suffers from four important problems. First, it seems to be a theory of meaning for perceptual states. Our thought is no more stimulus dependent than our language (1.2). Nobody could suppose that all thoughts about horses – including, for example, I'D RATHER HAVE A HORSE THAN A PORSCHE – are reliably correlated with horses. So thoughts about horses can be tokened veridically without there being any horse about. So indicator theories need some internal psychological analogue of reference borrowing. The meaning of stimulus independent thoughts about horses derives it reference from the meaning of perceptual thoughts about horses. Horse musings borrow their reference from horse recognitions.

Second, indicator theories would need to be developed to take into account the compositionality of language. According to these theories, representations are said to get their content, in one way or another, from causal interactions with reality. This interaction is always between a state of affairs and a representation of that state of affairs. In humans, at least, this representation is a complex syntactic structure, a mental sentence, not simply a mental word. Thus, in the example we have been using, the representation would not be HORSE, but something like THAT IS A HORSE. Indicator theories need to be developed so that the referential properties of the words can be abstracted from these interactions. Other complex symbols can then derive their truth conditions from the referential properties of the words they contain.

Third, what should we say about Twin Earth? There is an important difference between historical-causal theories and indicator theories over Twin Earth. According to historical-causal theories, reference is determined by an actual interaction with the referent. This enables them to handle the Twin-Earth problem: WATER refers to H_2O not XYZ because it was actually grounded in H_2O not XYZ. According to indicator theories, reference does not depend on any actual causal interaction with the referent: it depends on a disposition to interact in a certain way. This poses a problem for the indicator theory, since WATER is as reliably correlated with XYZ as with H_2O and so should refer to H_2O-or-XYZ. Perhaps this problem can be solved by taking a word to refer to what it is correlated with "in normal conditions". Environments filled with H_2O but no XYZ are normal for us, and thus in our case there is a correlation between WATER tokens and H_2O. Our Twins live in environments in which there is plenty of XYZ but no H_2OO, hence their WATER tokens correlate with XYZ. This idea is important in connection with the next problem too, but it is not without its own problems. For what sets the boundaries of a normal environment?

Finally, we come to a problem on which most effort has been expended. How can indicator theories allow *error*? Occasionally we see a muddy zebra but *mis*represent it by thinking HORSE. So, some zebras are among the things that would cause tokens of HORSE. What HORSE is reliably correlated with is really the presence of horses or muddy zebras or the odd cow or . . . So according to indicator theories, it should refer to horses, muddy zebras, the odd cow . . . , with the result that the representation is *not* in error. The problem is that many things that a token of a certain type does not refer to, including some denizens of Twin Earth, *would* cause a token of that type.

One response to this problem deploys the idea of normal conditions that we have just introduced. The circumstances in which muddy zebras cause HORSE are not appropriate for fixing its reference. For a token of HORSE represents what such tokens are caused by in "normal" circumstances. The problem then is to give a naturalistic account of "normality", and that has led to hybrid theories in which indicator semantics are grafted together with the idea of a biological function. This "teleological" idea – concerned with the design or purpose of a perceptual and psychological mechanism – has been made naturalistically respectable by Darwin. Indicator theorists appeal to Darwin to show that certain circumstances – the circumstances in which mechanisms evolved – are the "normal" ones for the functioning of that mechanism. States represent what they indicate in those circumstances. So errors we make about colors and shapes under sodium lights or strobe lights do not count, for our visual mechanisms did not evolve to cope with such lighting conditions. Nor did they evolve for detecting XYZ on Twin Earth.

However, the problems for this attempt to graft together teleology with reliability appear overwhelming. First, we are likely to be error-free at best in *optimal* conditions and yet our perceptual mechanisms have certainly evolved to help us in suboptimal ones. By the standards of many mammals we have good night vision, and our eyes are adapted for seeing at night and not just the day. So nightime is a "normal" condition for our vision. Even so, we make many visual mistakes at night. "Normal" conditions – the conditions under which our perceptual mechanisms are adapted to operate – are not optimal conditions.

Second, Peter Godfrey-Smith has pointed out an even more fundamental problem, a problem not only for the hybrid theory but for any indicator theory. It is the problem of harmless "false positives". An organism in nature commonly seems to represent a situation as one in which there is a predator, or food, or whatever, and to be *more often wrong than right*. So what it indicates is mostly not what it represents. This situation is common because it has an evolutionary pay-off; so the circumstances of error are as "normal" as could be. Consider the typical bird that is the prey of hawks. A high proportion of the time that it registers the presence of a predator it is wrong; it has responded to a harmless bird, a shadow, or whatever. These false positives do not matter to its survival; they have no *significant* cost. What matters is that the bird avoid *false negatives*; what matters is that it tokens HAWK when there is a hawk. The price the bird has to pay for that is frequently tokening HAWK when there isn't one. What nature has selected is a safe mechanism not a certain one. So what the bird's mental states are about – hawks – are not what they indicate.

Jerry Fodor (1987, 1990a) has responded to the error problem in a quite different way, proposing a more complicated indicator theory without any appeal to teleology. He thinks that its a law that horses cause HORSE tokens; that is, the correlation between HORSE tokens and horses is no accident. The problem then is that it is also a law that the odd cow causes HORSE tokens. Fodor's solution is that HORSE nevertheless refers only to horses because the latter causal relation holds *because* the former does, but not vice versa: the relation to the odd cow is *asymmetrically dependent* on the relation to horses.

We think that there is a compelling objection to Fodor's theory. Fodor is in need of some paradigm cases of A referring to *a*s where the following is the case: *a*s cause A, *b*s cause A, and *it is obvious that the latter causal relation is asymmetrically dependent on the former*. The asymmetric dependency that Fodor claims in the case of HORSE, for example, is far from obvious. At first sight, the basic law seems to be that horses, muddy zebras, the odd cow, . . . cause HORSE. That is, the basic law seems to be that creatures which typically or occasionally have a certain appearance, a "horsey look", cause HORSE tokens. That is why horses cause them, and also why muddy zebras, the odd cow, the occasional billboard, and so on all cause them. So HORSE refers to things that look horsey. And someone who thinks HORSE at the sight of a muddy zebra does not misrepresent after all. So Fodor seems to be stipulating, or hoping for, the existence of some very complex causal dependencies, without ruling out an alternative view of these relationships that fits just as well, or better, with the empirical facts.

In view of these problems, the prospects for indicator theory seem depressing. An alternative, developed in the last decade or so by Ruth Millikan (1984), David Papineau (1984, 1987), and Karen Neander (1995), goes totally teological, explaining representation by biological function alone. The earlier hybrid theory appealed to function simply to identify the circumstances that fixed reference. WATER means water, because in those "normal" circumstances the agent thinks "WATER!" only when there is water about. The appeal to function is to say what those circumstances are: they are circumstances like those which caused the ability to token WATER to evolve in our species. But on this hybrid view, meaning still depends on indication. A full-blown teleological theory appeals to function to explain the very content of the representational states. Thus the mental state of the chicken that hides when it sees the shadow is about hawks because its function is to adapt the chicken's behavior to the presence of hawks in its environment. Biological function, in turn, is explained in terms of the history of selection. Chickens that hide when they see shadows of a certain kind are around because their ancestors that behaved that way were fitter than those who did not, and fitter because they had a better chance of avoiding hawk predation.

Teleological theories of representation, like indicator theories, face the problem of compositionality. In this respect they are no advance on indicator theories. But in two other respects they are. Because thinking that all's well when there is a hawk about is so much more costly than mistakenly thinking there is danger, teleological theories of representation do not have the error problem that plagued indicator theories (although they may have others). Second, since the biological function of any structure or system depends on past selective history, these theories, like historical-causal theories, have no problem with Twin-Earth examples. Since XYZ has played no part in the selection of any mental structures on earth, none of them are adaptations to XYZ. If any animals have a WATER concept built into them by selection, its about H_2O not H_2O-or-XYZ.

However, on the face of it, this theory seems to face an enormous problem as a theory of the representations involved in thought. For, surely, most human thoughts have no biological function. The chicken's capacity to represent hawks is part of the chicken's basic biological heritage, built by selection and now near enough built into all chickens. Perhaps we have a few concepts and thoughts built into us this way; it is very easy to teach children to be afraid of snakes and spiders; much harder to teach them to be afraid of apples. So perhaps a few thoughts have biological functions which specify their meaning. Perhaps those meanings, in turn, explain the meaning of sentences which express those thoughts. Even this much is not obviously the case. The size and complexity of the human brain are good evidence for taking it to be an adaptation of some kind shaped by selection as a behavior control system. But very little is known of the specific selective forces responsible for the evolution of our psychology. However, even setting aside worries about our ignorance of the details of human evolutionary history, at most only a tiny fraction of our thoughts could be part of our biological heritage in the way that HAWK thoughts are part of the biological heritage of chickens. So, surely, most thoughts and sentences have no biological function.

This is a very powerful objection but it is perhaps not quite decisive. There are at least two possible responses. The simplest idea (and one that has been defended by Papineau) is to argue that the learning process is a selection process, and one similar enough to natural selection to give beliefs and desires biological functions. Of course, this is an ambitious claim. For not only would learning have to be a selection process that conferred functions on beliefs and desires, the functions would have to explain their meaning. Does our passionate desire that Australia always beat England at cricket really have a function? Even if it does – perhaps social solidarity of some kind – how would this function explain its meaning?

A second option draws on the distinction between mental states and the mechanisms that produce them. A chameleon and some species of octopus can camouflage themselves by matching their skin color to their background. Consider an octopus sitting on a polka-dotted face mask and adjusting its body colors so it is disguised against its background. Millikan argues that, in such a case, its skin color pattern has the biological function of matching that polka-dot pattern (and hence camouflaging the octopus) even though in all probability no previous octopus has ever had such a skin pattern. A unique state can have a biological function because that state is produced by more general mechanisms, mechanisms which have been selected to produce particular states of that general type. So perhaps a particular belief or desire might have a biological function after all, one derived from the function of the mechanism that formed it. This is an ingenious idea. But even if we accept that thoughts do have functions of this sort, it remains to be shown that those functions explain the content of thoughts. We need to be shown that the function of a desire is to represent the particular state that would satisfy it, and that the function of a belief is to represent the particular state that would make it true. Millikan has attempted to argue this case with great ingenuity but it remains an extremely ambitious and difficult program to carry out.

We are attracted by a less ambitious use of teleology to explain meaning. Instead of taking biological functions to determine the contents of *thoughts* we take them to determine the contents of more basic representational states, *perceptions*. Perceiving a rabbit as a rabbit is a matter of being in a state with the biological function of representing a rabbit. An interesting thing about this idea is that it does not *replace* the historical-causal theory of reference fixing, it *supplements* it. That theory, it will be remembered, suffered from the *qua*-problem: In virtue of what is a particular grounding of 'rabbit' a grounding in rabbits rather than mammals, vertebrates, or whatever? The present idea offers a teleological answer: the grounding is in rabbits because it involves a perceptual state that has the function of representing rabbits. The teleological theory of perception becomes an essential part of the theory of groundings.

We suggested earlier that indicator and teleological theories are best construed as simply theories of ultimate reference fixing to which other theories of reference could be added. Our present idea goes further, incorporating teleology into the historical-causal theory of reference fixing.**

Suggested Reading

7.2 and 7.3

For arguments for the language-of-thought hypothesis. see Harman 1973, *Thought*, particularly pp. 54–9, 84–92, Harman 1975, "Language, Thought, and Communication", Fodor 1975, *The Language of Thought*, particularly pp. 27–33, and "Why There Still Has to Be a Language of Thought" in Fodor 1987, *Psychosemantics*, and Lycan 1990, *Mind and Cognition*. Rey 1997, *Contemporary Philosophy of Mind*, ch. 8, is a nice presentation of the case for the hypothesis. Aizawa 1997, "Explaining Systematicity", is an interesting criticism of the argument from systematicity.

Loar 1983, "Must Beliefs be Sentences?", Churchland and Churchland 1983, "Stalking the Wild Epistemic Engine", reprinted in Lycan 1990, Dennett's "The Language of Thought Reconsidered" in Dennett 1987, *The Intentional Stance*, Braddon-Mitchell and Fitzpatrick 1990, "Explanation and the Language of Thought", and Lewis 1994, "Reduction of Mind", are skeptical of the language-of-thought hypothesis. **So too is Andy Clark, who offers some informed speculation about how alternative connectionist models might be developed: *Associative Engines*

(1993) and *Being There* (1997). On connectionism, see Fodor and Pylyshyn 1988, "Connectionism and Cognitive Architecture: A Critical Analysis"; Smolensky 1988a, "On the Proper Treatment of Connectionism", and 1988b, "Putting Together Connectionism – Again"; Fodor and McLaughlin 1991, "Connectionism and the Problem of Systematicity".**

Harman thinks that the language of thought is mostly the public language of the thinker. Fodor argues against this view. Pinker 1994, *The Language Instinct*, pp. 78–82, has an argument against the public hypothesis of the sort that we criticize. Kaye 1995, "The Languages of Thought", argues that some of our thoughts are in the language we speak.

Block 1981, *Readings in Philosophy of Psychology, Volume 2*, Part I, "Mental Representation" and Stich and Warfield 1994, *Mental Representation*, are useful collections of readings.

For powerful critiques of the view that thoughts could be images, see Pylyshyn 1973, "What the Mind's Eye Tells the Mind's Brain", and Fodor 1975, ch. 4. See also Block 1981, Part II, "Imagery" and Lycan 1990, sec. 19, "The Imagery Issue".

7.4

Grice first put forward his theory in "Meaning" (1957). This, together with many later developments, are to be found in his *Studies in the Way of Words* (1989). It is also in Martinich 1996 and Geirsson and Losonsky 1996. For a short, readable, development of Grice's ideas, see Armstrong 1971, "Meaning and Communication". For longer developments, see Bennett 1976, *Linguistic Behaviour*, **and Schiffer 1972, *Meaning***. Neale 1992, "Paul Grice and the Philosophy of Language", is a helpful review of Grice's work.

For an interestingly different view from Grice's see Searle 1983a, *Intentionality*, ch. 6. Davidson 1985, "A Nice Derangement of Epitaphs", reprinted in Martinich 1996, is a nice discussion of literal meaning. For discussions of metaphor, see Davis 1991, Part VII, and Martinich 1996, Part VI.

The phenomenon of ellipsis also demonstrates the distinction between speaker and literal meaning: we mean more than we say. On this see Bach 1987, *Thought and Reference*.

Any attempt to explain conventional meaning must consider David Lewis' famous work, *Convention: A Philosophical Study* (1969). See also his follow-up essay, "Languages and Language" (1975) in Gunderson 1975, reprinted in Lewis 1983, Martinich 1996, and Geirsson and Losonsky 1996. ("Languages, Language, and Grammar" in Harman 1974 is made up of short excerpts from both.)

7.5

Causal theories of thought about an object, like that in the text, are rejected in an interesting but difficult book, Evans 1982, *The Varieties of Reference*. He defends "Russell's Principle", according to which thought about an object requires discriminating knowledge of the object. This view is criticized in Devitt 1985, a critical notice of the book.

7.6

Our account of the origins of language is, of course, no more than an outline. For still speculative but more detailed and empirically informed hypotheses, see: Corballis 1991, *The Lopsided Ape*; Donald 1991. *Origins of the Modern Mind*; Noble and Davidson 1996, *Human Evolution, Language and Mind*.

7.7

Stampe 1979, "Toward a Causal Theory of Linguistic Representation", was the first proposal of indicator semantics. Dretske 1981, *Knowledge and the Flow of Information*, is the classic development of view. Dretske 1986, "Misrepresentation", and 1988, *Explaining Behavior* (ch. 3 is reprinted in Geirsson and Losonsky 1996) are modifications and further developments. Godfrey-Smith 1989, "Misinformation" and 1992, "Indication and Adaptation", are critical of indicator theories. So too is Millikan 1990, "Seismograph Readings for Explaining Behavior". McLaughlin 1991, *Dretske and His Critics*, contains some helpful discussions.

Fodor proposed a teleological view in "Psychosemantics or: Where Do Truth Conditions Come From?" (1990b) but vigorously rejected that whole approach long before that paper was published in Lycan 1990. His rejection is to be found in his 1987 and in *A Theory of Content and other Essays* (1990a), along with the proposal of his version of reliablism, the asymmetric dependency theory. Loewer and Rey 1991, *Meaning in Mind: Fodor and his Critics* has a helpful introduction. It also includes Millikan's "Speaking Up for Darwin", a response to Fodor's rejection, and the following papers critical of Fodor's theory: Antony and Levine, "The Nomic and the Robust"; Baker, "Has Content Been Naturalized?"; and Boghossian, "Naturalizing Content". It also includes Fodor's "Replies".

Millikan 1984, *Language, Thought, and Other Biological Categories* is the most detailed teleological semantics but it is very difficult. The most accessible introduction to her ideas is "Biosemantics" in *White Queen Psychology* (1993). The critical distinction between the functions of general mechanisms and the states they produce is found in her "In

Defense of Proper Functions" in the same collection. Neander 1995, "Misrepresenting and Malfunctioning" is a clear presentation of a similar teleological view. More support for teleosemantics can be found in Papineau 1984, "Representation and Explanation", and 1987, *Reality and Representation*. Godfrey-Smith 1991, "Signal, Detection, Action", is a sophisticated attempt to think through teleosemantic ideas for primitive representation. Pietroski 1992, "Intentionality and Teleological Error" is a nice criticism of the teleosemantic approach. Akins 1996, "Of Sensory Systems and the 'Aboutness' of Mental States", argues against both indicator and teleological theories.

Stich and Warfield 1994 has helpful sections on all these theories for naturalizing content. Sterelny 1990, *The Representational Theory of Mind*, ch. 6, discusses the theories, concluding with the teleological view of perception mentioned in the text.

8

Linguistic Competence

8.1 Introduction

In the previous chapter we have related language to beliefs, desires, and other thoughts. Another mental state that is relevant to language is *linguistic competence*. This is the state that enables a native speaker to use her language successfully. Describing and explaining competence is one of the main tasks in the philosophy of language. We have already started the task. We have often talked skeptically of the Cartesian assumption that competence involves "privileged access" to meanings (e.g. in 5.6). We have discussed description theories of competence with names (3.1–3.2) and natural kind terms (5.1). We have discussed causal theories of competence with names (4.1–4.2) and natural kind terms (5.2). This chapter will say a lot more about competence.

We have seen that sentence meaning is complex, being partly a matter of word meaning and partly a matter of syntactic structure. Competence in a language is similarly complex, being partly a matter of being able to produce and understand the words of the language – lexical competence – and partly a matter of being able to combine them into the sentences of the language – syntactic competence. Our earlier discussions of competence have all been about lexical competence. In this section our discussion will be largely, although not entirely, about syntactic competence. We shall focus on generative grammar, the movement in linguistics begun by Chomsky, just as we did in our discussion of syntactic structure (ch.

6). In this discussion, we have two aims. First, we want to show that the theory of syntactic competence developed by Chomsky himself, and some other, somewhat similar, contemporary philosophical ideas about full linguistic competence, are *prima facie* both puzzling and implausible. Second, we want to outline at least the beginings of an alternative view.

We begin by listing a number of puzzling features of these contemporary discussions of competence.

1) Generative grammar is not offered primarily as a theory of the syntactic properties of linguistic symbols, but as a theory of competence, a property of people. (We noted this in 6.1.) In fact, generative linguists run the two sorts of theory together. Similarly, many philosophers run the theory of the meaning of symbols together with a theory of full linguistic competence. This conflation of symbol and competence is the first and perhaps the most important problem about current views of competence (8.2).

2) Generative linguists attempt to construct grammars of languages in which they are interested. As we shall see, they take these grammars to do double duty. At one and the same time, they give an account of the structure of sentences in that language, and an account of the cognitive state that enables speakers to produce and understand (parse) sentences. In other words, the generative linguists think that the syntactic rules (or principles) described by the grammar are "internalized" by the native speaker and are thus "psychologically real". But why suppose that? Why suppose that a grammar explains competence at all (8.8)?

3) The linguists' most common expression of their views suggest that syntactic rules are psychologically real in a special way: they are *represented* in the speaker. For, the linguists identify competence with *knowledge* of those rules: each truth about English, hard won by the linguist, is said to be "tacitly known" by English speakers already. The rules are psychologically real in that the grammar itself – the *theory* of those rules – is psychologically real. Similarly, many philosophers hold that the theory of meaning for a language is "tacitly known" by speakers of the language. Why suppose that speakers know any more about their language than the little they learned at school (8.4–8.7)?

4) Further, some syntactic rules – those described by "universal grammar", allegedly common to all natural languages – are said to be *innately* known. In psychology, theories which emphasize the role of innate knowledge or innate structure in their explanations of our capacities are known as "nativist" theories. The Chomskyan view of linguistic competence is a paradigm of these nativist views, but what is the evidence for this nativism (8.10)?

5) The linguists, like most philosophers of language, subscribe to the Cartesian assumption. So they think that the competent speaker has "privileged access" to facts about syntax which she expresses in her intuitive

judgments. Indeed, they think that these judgments are derived by some sort of inferential process from the speaker's representation of the syntactic rules. Is this Cartesianism appropriate (8.6)?

As a result of such puzzles as these, controversy has raged at the foundations of generative grammar. This controversy has led to a considerable literature but little of this has centered on the puzzle that we shall start with: the failure to distinguish sharply between the competence of speakers and the symbols they are competent with.

8.2   The Conflation of Symbols and Competence

In chapter 6 we made some introductory remarks about sentence structure, some of them derived from Chomsky. We saw a generative grammar as giving a syntactic description of all the possible sentences of a language. Chomsky agrees. Thus, in the opening pages of *Syntactic Structures*, the work which began generative grammar, we find:

> The fundamental aim in the linguistic analysis of a language L is to separate the *grammatical* sequences which are sentences of L from the *ungrammatical* sequences which are not sentences of L and to study the structure of the grammatical sequences. (1957: 13)

The concern is with sentences, *a human product.*

However, often in the same breath, Chomsky says something very different: the concern is with linguistic competence, *a characteristic of the human mind.* Thus, in another classic work, *Aspects of the Theory of Syntax*, after some remarks like the above, Chomsky says:

> The problem for the linguist . . . is to determine . . . the underlying system of rules that has been mastered by the speaker-hearer . . . Hence, in a technical sense, linguistic theory is mentalistic, since it is concerned with discovering a mental reality underlying actual behavior. (1965: 4)

There are very many such claims in the works of the generative linguists. For them, a grammar is not just a description of the structure of sentences; even more it is an account of the speaker's linguistic competence: it is an account of the mental reality underlying linguistic behavior. A grammar is part of psychology.

The conflation of a theory of symbols with a theory of competence did not start with Chomsky. Indeed, it seems to have a long history (see, for example, Saussure 1966: 77, 90). Not surprisingly, the conflation is also to be found in theories of meaning inspired partly by Chomsky (see, for example, Larson and Segal 1995; their inspiration is also partly Donald

Davidson). And the same conflation has frequently been made quite independently by philosophers; thus, Michael Dummett urges the slogan, "a theory of meaning is a theory of understanding" (1975: 99). Nevertheless, the conflation is bewildering. To bring this out, let us start with some further explanation of the distinction between these two sorts of theory.

To help to make this distinction sharp we shall attend only to symbols in a public language, ones written, spoken and so on. Also we will assume that the grammar the linguists construct is a good account of the structure of these symbols. We shall set aside symbols in "Mentalese", the language of thought (7.2–7.3). However, the distinction between syntax and competence applies equally to Mentalese, as we shall see (8.9). We shall also set aside for a moment a person's competence at linguistic *understanding*, focusing on her competence at linguistic *production*.

Linguistic competence is a mental state of a person, posited to explain his linguistic behavior; it plays a key role – although not, of course, the only role – in *the production of* that behavior. Linguistic symbols are the result of that behavior; they are *the products of* the competence, its *outputs*. They are datable placeable parts of the physical world: sounds in the air, marks on the page, and so on. They are not mental entities at all. A theory of a part of the production of linguistic symbols is not a theory of the products, the symbols themselves. Of course, given the causal relation between competence and symbol we can expect a theory of the one to bear on a theory of the other. But that does not make the two theories identical.

In Part II, we were interested in the properties of symbols that enable them to play certain roles in explaining behavior and informing us about the world. In brief, we were interested in meanings (1.2). Syntactic properties are an important part of meaning. We discovered that properties like being a name, being a verb phrase and being a passive are part of the explanation of meaning. Analogously, we might be interested in what makes a certain movement of a ball a good tennis shot. The answer would be in terms of such properties as speed, direction and height. Or we might be interested in what makes a certain action a chess move. The answer would appeal to the rules of chess. In all of these cases we are concerned with objects or events in the physical world "outside the head".

However, in each case we might have another concern which is very much with something "inside the head" (or, at least, "inside the body"). What is the explanation of the behavior -certain movements of hand and arm, perhaps – producing sentences, tennis shots or chess moves? To answer this, we need a psychological (perhaps, physiological) theory, a theory of competence; we need a theory that explains, for example, how a player knew that a particular action was a chess move. Such a theory is different from a theory of the objects produced by the competence: different from a theory of linguistic symbols, tennis shots or chess moves.

In sum, linguistic competence, together with various other aspects of the speaker's psychology, produce linguistic symbols. A theory of symbols is not a theory of competence.

To distinguish the theory of symbols from psychology is not to make it mysterious. Consider, for example, the balance of payments of some country; say, Canada. There is nothing metaphysically weird about the Canadian balance of payments, however economically or politically questionable it might be. As with other social phenomena, this financial feature of Canada obviously depends on facts about the Canadian environment, togther with those about Canadian behavior and psychology. But it does so in such a complex way that we rightly theorize about such phenomena in a way relatively independent of, or autonomous from, our theory of the psychology and behavior of individual Canadians. Similarly linguistics as a social science has this limited form of autonomy from other theories, including psychology, despite the fact that linguistic phenomena in some way depend on psychological phenomena.

Our theorizing about linguistic objects has, in fact, been very much concerned to explain their properties in terms of psychological states and relations to the environment. The zenith of this concern was in the last chapter. While respecting the relative autonomy of linguistics, we have sought to explain it in other terms. So, the independence of linguistics is a partial independence.

8.3 Two Proposals on the Psychological Reality of Syntactic Rules

In Part II, particularly in chapter 6, we have taken a grammar to be a theory of the syntactic properties of symbols in a language and hence a major contribution to the task of explaining meaning. That, on the face of it, is what a grammar is about. That is what work on phrase structure, case theory, anaphora, and so on, seems to concern. That is what a great deal of the evidence adduced for a grammar seems to bear directly upon: evidence about which strings of words are grammatical; about the ambiguity of certain sentences; about the statement forms and question forms; about the synonymy of sentences that are superficially different; about the difference betweeen sentences that are superficially similar; about coreference; and so on.

So we shall assume that a grammar is indeed a theory of the syntactic properties of symbols. This does not show, of course, that a grammar throws no light on competence. It simply shows that *further argument* is needed to show what light it throws. In particular, further argument is needed to show that the rules (or principles) described by the grammar are psychologically real: *the psychological reality of the rules is not something you "get for nothing" with the truth of the grammar.*

In one respect, we think that it should be uncontroversial that the grammar throws light on competence. Our first proposal about psychological reality concerns this.

We start with a distinction between two sorts of rules, the "structure-rules" governing the products of a competence, and the "processing-rules" governing the production of those products, rules governing the *exercise* of the competence.

In characterizing the products of a competence, we sometimes appeal to rules: the products have rule-governed natures constituted by their place in a structure defined by a system of rules. Thus, consider the product of a chess player: chess moves. The characterization of chess moves must appeal to a rather elaborate system of rules: a bishop may only move diagonally; the king may only move one square; no piece except a knight may move through an occupied square; and so on. Chess moves are rule-governed in that something counts as a chess move at all only if it has a place in the "structure" defined by the rules of chess. Something counts as a particular chess move in virtue of the particular rules that govern it, in virtue of its particular place in the structure. A theory of chess describes these structure-rules. In doing so it describes constraints on the appropriate output of a chess player. Ideally, a chess player should only make moves that have a place in the system the structure-rules describe. That is, a chess player should make only legal moves. The structure-rules *may* also be among the rules governing the psychological process by which she produces chess moves. They may be among the processing-rules active in the exercise of her chess competence. However, this is not necessary and may be unlikely. The rules describing the structure of chess as a game may not be suitable for the task of figuring out a particular move. In any case, the key point is that *being a structure-rule* – a rule governing outputs – is a very different property from *being a processing-rule*, a rule governing the psychological production of outputs.

Bees provide a good example of the distinction. A bee returning from a distant food source dances a message. The positioning of the dance and its pattern indicate the direction and distance of the food source. These dances form a very effective symbol system governed by a fairly simple set of structure-rules. It is the task of a theory of the dance to describe these structure-rules. The processing-rules by which the bee performs this rather remarkable feat remain largely a mystery but doubtless none of the structure-rules are among them.

Language provides another example of the distinction. The products of a linguistic competence, physical sentence tokens, are governed by a system of structure-rules, just like the products of the chess player and bee. From the very beginning of this book (1.2), we have emphasized the systematicity of language. The systematic relations between linguistic expressions reflect the structure-rules that govern them. Something counts as a sentence only if it has a place in the linguistic structure defined by these rules. Something counts as a particular sentence, has its particular syntactic structure, in virtue of the particular structure-rules that govern it, in virtue of its particular place in the linguistic structure. It is the task of a syntactic theory, a grammar, to describe these structure-rules. We distinguish these structure-rules from processing-rules involved in the exercise of linguistic competence. These two sorts of rules have very different roles. The processing-rules produce sentences of the language in the exercise of linguistic competence. It is because those sentences are governed by the structure-rules that they are indeed sentences of the language. It may be possible that a structure-rule will also be a processing-rule, but it is not necessary that it be; for example, the transformations rules that govern structure and capture systematic relations between sentences may not govern any process that a speaker actually goes through in making an utterance.

The words used in talking about the structure-rules of a language – words like "generate", "derive" and "transform" – can mislead. We can take these as helpful metaphorical ways of capturing the systematic relations between sentences. We do not have to take them as literally descriptions of a process taking place somewhere.

We shall use this distinction between the two sorts of rules to bring out the way in which it should be uncontroversial that a theory of syntax, a theory of the structure-rules of symbols, throws light on syntactic competence.

We have emphasized that there is a causal relation between a competence and its product. A "logical" relation should also be emphasized. This arises from the fact that the *very nature* of the competence is to produce its outputs: producing them is what makes it the competence it is. Thus, a chess competence is the ability to produce chess moves, things governed by the structure-rules of chess. And a competence in a language is the ability to produce sentences of that language, things governed by the structure-rules of the language. So a theory of such structure-rules is automatically, to an extent, a contribution to the theory of the competence: it tells us about the outputs the production of which is definitive of the competence. And we can say that these structure-rules must be "respected" by the competence and the processing-rules that govern its exercise in that, performance errors aside, the processing-rules must produce outputs that are governed by those structure-rules.

The proposal that the structure-rules of a language must be thus respected is the minimal one on the psychological reality issue. It is surely not appropriate to say, *solely* on the strength of this minimal proposal, that those rules are psychologically real in the speaker. The respecting might, of course, be the *result* of the rules being psychologically real; for example, they might also be processing-rules. But the respecting alone does not require that the rules be actually realized in the speaker; for example, it does not require that they be processing-rules. For there may be many other possible ways that a speaker might respect the rules. The minimal proposal tells us very little about the competence; in particular, it tells us nothing about the way in which the mind respects the rules of the language.

Our second proposal has in fact been made already: we argued that people think in a Mentalese that is likely to be syntactically similar to their public language (7.3, 7.5). Mentalese is as psychologically real as could be. So, the structure-rules of the public language are, to the extent of that similarity, psychologically real because they are, to that extent, the structure-rules of thought.

This proposal cannot pretend to be uncontroversial. It rests on the folk idea that language expresses thought (7.1) and the language-of-thought hypothesis (7.2). The folk idea may be relatively uncontroversial but the hypothesis is not. In any case, this proposal does not capture the way in which Chomsky and his followers think that the syntactic rules are psychologically real and it seems likely that they would reject it.

8.4   Knowledge-how versus Knowledge-that

Chomskyan linguists mostly seem to have in mind the very controversial view that a speaker's competence involves a *representation* of the rules of the language which is applied in producing and understanding (parsing) the language. Chomsky puts the point with characteristic firmness: "there can be little doubt that knowing a language involves internal representation of a generative procedure" (1991a: 9). On this view, the structure-rules are respected *because the speaker applies the representation of them in language processing.* This is the way in which linguists mostly think that the rules of the language are psychologically real.

We shall look critically at this representational view in this section and the following three. Then, in section 8.8, we shall consider a less popular view among linguists. On this view the rules of the language govern linguistic processing, and so are psychologically real processing-rules, without being represented in the speaker.

The linguists' representational view goes with their assumption that speakers have tacit *knowledge* of the rules of the language. This assumption may seem to be supported by the folk truism that speakers "know the language".

The linguists are concerned with syntactic competence. Many philosophers make a similar assumption about full linguistic competence, as we have noted in our frequent mention of the Cartesian assumption. They assume that competence with an expression consists in tacit knowledge of its meaning; for example, competence with a sentence is knowledge that it is true if and only if certain circumstances hold. Dummett (e.g., 1976: 69–71) is an example. (This view plays a role in his argument against realism to be considered later; 11.3–11.4.) This assumption may also seem to be supported by the truism that speakers know the language.

It is wise to be wary of this truism because it involves the term 'know' and this term is ordinarily used so loosely and widely. Consider the following:

Ralph knows Don Bradman
Ralph knows who Little Caesar is
Ralph knows how to add up by rule R
Ralph knows that R is an algorithm for addition.

These sentences illustrate quite different uses of 'know'. We are particularly concerned with the difference between the last two: *knowing-how* and *knowing-that*. Knowing-how is in the same family as skills, abilities and capacities. Although it can be cognitive, it need not be. In contrast, knowing-that is essentially cognitive: it requires belief and hence mental *representation* (7.1–7.2); it is "propositional" knowledge.

Consider a vast range of human skills. We know how to swim, ride a bicycle, catch a ball, touch type, and so on. These activities are governed by processing-rules that have been built into us largely by learning. But it is not plausible to suppose that our knowing-how, our competence, requires that any of these embodied rules be represented, nor to suppose that many of them are, as a matter of fact, usually represented by the competent. (Even the dimmest fish can swim.) This is even true of some "intellectual" tasks. Ralph *may* know how to add up by R because he knows *that* R is an algorithm for addition and can apply it. If so then this piece of knowing-how is largely knowing-that. But Ralph is more likely to be simply governed by R without representing it to himself: R is psychologically real in him without being represented. Finally, consider the most cognitive skill of all, the skill of thinking, of inferring one thought from another. Most of us know hardly anything about "the rules of thought". And we surely do not think by applying representations of these rules, representations in a meta-Mentalese

In the light of this, much more than the truism that the competent speaker knows the language is needed to support the linguists' view that she represents its rules. The knowledge may be mere knowing-how.

Stephen Stich (1971, 1978b) brings out nicely the implausibility of the view that knowledge of language is knowledge-that by contrasting it with unproblematic cases of propositional knowledge. If a person knows that p, we expect him to be aware of p, or at least to be able to become aware of it when given a suitable prompt; and we expect him to understand expressions of p. The ordinary speaker quite clearly lacks this awareness and understanding for most of the grammar. If a person knows that p, his knowledge should join up with other knowledge and beliefs to generate more beliefs. If a speaker has knowledge of the grammar it is clearly not inferentially integrated in this way. Consider an example. Without tuition, a speaker is unlikely to have the conceptual recourses to understand even the relatively simple claim that '$NP \rightarrow Det + Adj + N$' is a rule of English. If she knows that this is a rule, her knowledge is largely inferentially isolated from her other beliefs.

Of course, Chomsky's view is that speakers' knowledge of the rules of the language is only "tacit". But this is no help to the representational view because our knowledge of the language is very different also from ordinary tacit propositional knowledge. For, such knowledge is knowledge that a person has not entertained but which he would acknowledge in suitable circumstances. Thus, Ron tacitly knows that rabbits don't lay eggs, even though the thought has never crossed his mind, because he would acknowledge that they don't lay eggs if the question were ever to arise. Clearly, the typical speaker does not have this relation to the rules of the language. She would not acknowledge the rules of her language were the question to arise. The rules are often too complicated for her to understand, let alone accept.

In the last section, we noted that the language processing-rules must at least respect the structure-rules of the language (this respecting is compatible with performance errors). This minimal proposal alone does not warrant the claim that the structure-rules are psychologically real. Still, it leaves open the possibility that these rules might also be processing-rules and hence be psychologically real. The moral of this section is that even if they were, our ordinary talk of knowing the language gives no support to the linguists' view that those rules are internally represented in speakers. No more does it give support to the philosophers' view that facts about meaning are known or internally represented. Support for the representational view must be found elsewhere.

8.5   Built-in versus Represented Rules

The site of a person's thoughts, or propositional attitudes, is often called "the central processor". That is where a person's knowledge of a language would be located if it were like ordinary knowledge-that. Stich shows that it is not plausible to think that it is so located. In fact, Chomskyan linguists have a very different location in mind by their talk of "tacit knowledge" of linguistic rules. In their view, the rules are represented in a *module* of the mind. Chomsky thinks of this module as a distinct mental "organ", the "language faculty" (1980: 40–7), that is largely inaccessible to the central processor. So, the linguists' talk of a speaker having tacit knowledge of – or, more recently, "cognizing" – the rules of her language, should not be taken as attributing a normal propositional attitude to her. She is said to have a representation of the rules but not in the central processor.

In this section, we want to cast doubt on the idea that the structure-rules of the language are represented in the speaker *at all*, whether in the central processor or a module, by developing a line of thought from our discussion in the last section. We shall emphasize that processing-rules that govern the exercise of a competence need not be represented. So, even if structure-rules of the language are processing-rules, they need not be represented.

The first point to be made is that any system *has* to have some rules that govern it without being represented and applied. For, if there is a rule that governs by being represented and applied, there has to be another rule that governs the *application*. That rule might also govern by being represented and applied but then *its* application has to be governed by a further rule; and so on. If this regress is to end and any rule is to govern by being represented, there must be some rules that govern without being represented. Given any system that is governed by a rule, it is *an empirical question* whether the system represents and applies the rule or the rule is simply built in to the system without being represented.

Computers demonstrate this point nicely. Software rules represented in RAM can govern the operations of a computer only because there are rules built into the hardware that enable them to do so.

We shall now consider some systems governed by processing-rules that are not plausibly seen as represented in the system (let alone propositionally known by the system).

i) Think of a really simple calculator, perhaps even a mechanical one. The operations of this calculator are governed by rules, the rules of algorithms for solving arithmetical problems. These rules have been built into the machine so that in adding, subtracting, and so on, it goes through mechanical processes that accord with the rules. But the calculator does not represent these rules. It represents *numbers* like 28 and perhaps *functions* like addition, and operates on these representations according to the hardwired rules that govern it.

ii) Consider the cartoon, figure 8.1. The kingfisher catches fish by div-

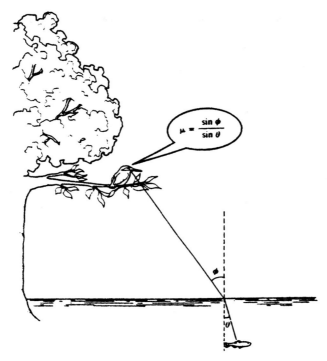

Figure 8.1 After Boden 1984: 153

ing into water. It does not dive vertically, nor does it pursue fish underwater. So, in diving, it must make suitable allowance for the refraction of light: the light deflects as it leaves water for the less dense medium of air. The point of the cartoon is that it would be absurd to suggest that the kingfisher does this as follows: it represents (tacitly knows) that μ for water-to-air refraction is such and such; it represents that the angle ϕ is so and so; it represents that $\mu = \sin \phi / \sin \theta$; it uses this information to calculate the angle θ. Applying this new representation it dives into the water at that angle. It is not plausible to suppose that the kingfisher represents any of these facts about refraction and angles. No more does it represent whatever rules do govern its fishing. Those rules are simply built into it "by nature" just as the rules for the calculator are simply built into it by an engineer.

iii) Think next of insect behavior; for example, the bee's dance. While there may be some plausibility to the idea that the bee represents its food source, there is little to the idea that it represents the rules that govern its dancing.

iv) We have already remarked on a range of human skills like swimming, riding a bicycle, catching a ball, touch typing, adding up, and thinking. It is not plausible to think that the rules that govern these activities are represented. Indeed, applying representations of the rules would be a very inefficient way of performing these tasks. It is more plausible to think that the rules are simply built in.

v) Finally, consider the contrast between a computer loaded up with a word-processing program and a dedicated word-processor. The computer is governed by the rules of that program because the rules are represented in its RAM and it operates by applying them. In contrast, the rules that govern the operations of the dedicated word-processor – perhaps the very same rules – are largely hardwired, not represented. The computer is analogous to a human who knows that certain rules are an algorithm for addition and applies them to add. The dedicated word-processor is analogous to a human who knows how to add by those rules without having any propositional knowledge of them.

This example points to an important generalization. Any processing-rule that governs the behavior of one object by being represented and applied could govern that of another by being built in without being represented. If rules are rules for processing information, then either way of embodying them in an object enables the object's behavior to be explained in terms of the flow of information. So whenever such an explanation applies there is a further empirical question about the way of embodiment.

In sum, the behavior of a machine, an animal or a human can be governed by a hardwired rule that it does not represent. So, even if structure-rules of the language are processing-rules, they may not be represented. Perhaps they are like the rules governing the calculator, the kingfisher, the bee, and various human skills, which are not plausibly seen as represented.

There is a reason for thinking, *a priori*, that the language processing-rules are indeed not represented. In general, representing rules is a good way to get *flexibility* in their use whereas building-in rules is a good way to get *speed* in their use. Language processing is a paradigm of speed without flexibility.

The literature sometimes seems to suggest that the representational view of competence is implied by the rejection of behaviorism. One simple consequence of our discussion is that there is no such implication. Behaviorists deny anything to the mind beyond dispositions to respond in certain ways to certain stimuli. For them the mind, linguistic competence included, is just a set of input/output functions. This reflects the crude empiricist dislike of things unseen; an unwillingness to posit theoretical entities that explain the observed phenomena. Chomsky, in contrast, is enthusiastically theoretical and was an important figure in the rejection of behaviorism. He thinks that the only way to explain human behavior is to ascribe complicated inner states *interacting with each other*, as well as with various stimuli, to produce our responses. We very much agree with him. But a moral of this section is that a lot of the inner complication may involve rules that are built in but not represented. So justifying the representational view needs much more than the the rejection of behaviorism.

None of this shows, of course, that the structure-rules of the language *are not* represented in speakers. But it does show that a lot of work has to be done to establish that they are represented. Even if it can be established that they play a role in language processing at all, a big "if" which does not come for nothing (8.3), it still has to be established that they play this role by being represented.

Trading on considerations like those in this section, Gilbert Harman (1967) has raised the following problem for *any* view that takes competence in a language to require representing its rules. That representation must itself be in a language. What is it to be competent in that more basic language? If we suppose the more basic language is the same as the original language then we are caught in a vicious circle. If we suppose that it is some other language (Mentalese perhaps), then its rules also has to be represented. This requires a still more basic language. And so on. The only way to avoid a vicious circle or an infinite regress is to allow that we can be competent in at least one language without representing its rules. Why not then allow this of the original language, the one spoken?

Some linguists, particularly Fodor (1975; see also Chomsky 1969a: 87–9; 1969b: 155–6), have an answer to this question. They think that there are good reasons for supposing that *learning* a language requires representing its rules and hence competence in another language. However, we can be competent in that other one without representing its rules because it is not learned; it is *innate*.

We shall take a brief critical look at the assumption that learning a language requires representing its rules in section 8.7. We have mentioned the thesis of an innate Mentalese before (7.3). We shall look critically at it in section 8.10.

8.6   Cartesian Intuitions

Often in this work we have expressed skepticism about the Cartesian assumption. This is the assumption that a person's linguistic competence gives her some sort of privileged access to facts about meaning, access that she exemplifies in her intuitive judgments. This intuitive knowledge does not depend on the empirical investigation of the world, the way her other knowledge does. It is available to her simply by introspecting the contents of her own mind.

Why be skeptical of this very popular assumption? We have already argued that the assumption should at least be restricted in its application. Our discussion of Twin Earth and the incompleteness of description theories (3.5, 5.1) suggested that assumption could not cover meanings constituted by relations "outside the head"; meanings explained by our historical-causal theories are examples (5.6). It is hard to see how reflection on what competence with a term makes available "inside the head" could establish such "external" and highly theoretical facts as that certain causal relations determine reference.

Still, the Cartesian assumption might hold for meanings constituted by relations "inside the head"; for example, the meanings of terms covered by description theories, involving inferential relations among terms. But what reason is there to believe that the assumption *does* hold for these meanings? Suppose for example that an internal relation to 'writing instrument' really is part of the meaning of 'pencil'. So if Susan, who understands 'pencil', thinks 'this is a pencil', she is apt to infer 'this is a writing instrument'. The first problem for Cartesianism is that it surely does not follow that Susan thereby notices this. She may not be a keen student of her own inferential dispositions. Suppose, however, that she does notice. The second problem for Cartesianism is that it is still another step for Susan to believe that this inferential relation is *part of the meaning* of 'pencil'. Why should we suppose that her competence alone enables her to make this apparently large *theoretical* step? Suppose, however, that she does make it. The third and most serious problem for Cartesianism is that we seem to have no basis for thinking that, simply in virtue of her competence, Susan's belief is *justified*. We have no basis for giving her belief about meaning any special epistemic authority, and thus turning it into *knowledge*.

Linguists may seem to have some sort of solution to these problems. And it is a solution that may seem to support not only the Cartesian view of intuitions but also the representational view of competence. We have earlier dismissed the ideas that the representational view gets support from the folk truism that a speaker knows her language (8.4) and from the rejection of behaviorism (8.5). In this section we shall consider whether it gets support from the role of the speaker's intuitive judgments in linguistic theorizing.

Linguists claim that the main items of evidence used in constructing grammars are intuitive judgments of the competent speaker, judgments about grammaticality, ambiguity, coreference, and the like. This is thought to be appropriate because those judgments are *inferred* in some way from a representation of the rules of the language in the language faculty; they are derived from the representation by a causal and rational process (though not a perfect process: there is a possibility of performance error). "We can use intuitions to confirm grammars because grammars are internally represented and actually contribute to the etiology of the speaker/hearer's intuitive judgments" (Fodor 1981: 200–1). On this view, we might say, the intuitive judgments are "the voice of competence". Speakers have a Cartesian privileged access to facts about the language in virtue of embodying representations of its rules. So, although the language faculty is largely inaccessible to the central processor, it is not entirely so.

We can see in this story an *argument* for the view that the rules are really represented. Surely the linguists are *right* to put such store by linguistic intuitions. But, the argument runs, how could they be right unless these intuitions really were the voice of competence? How could the intuitions have this evidential status unless they are the result of Cartesian access to the grammar and hence to a representations of the rules? We would like the details of this explanation spelt out, of course. We would like to know about the causal-rational route from an unconscious representation in a module to a conscious judgment in the central processor. Still, the idea of one sort of representation leading to another is familiar and so the Cartesian explanation seems promising.

So the evidential role of intuitions requires that they be derived from an underlying representation of the rules, thus supporting, in one blow, both the Cartesian view of intuitions and the representational view of competence.

The argument is an *inference to the best explanation*. Linguistic intuitions are reliable evidence, and the best explanation of their evidential reliability is that they are infered from rules of grammar represented in the mind of the language user. This is neat, but we have our doubts. They arise from alternative, more modest, views of linguistic competence and linguistic intuitions. We have already suggested the alternative view of competence: it is an ability or skill, a piece of mere knowledge-how not knowledge-that. This view seems to fit the facts. We shall have more to say about it in section 8.9.

What about linguistic intuitions? Questions about the status of intuitions do not arise only in linguistics, of course; intuitions play a role throughout science and seem to dominate philosophy. Consider, for example a paleontologist in the field, searching for fossils. She sees a bit of white stone sticking through grey rock, and thinks "a pig's jawbone". This intuitive judgment is quick, unreflective. She may be quite sure, but unable to explain just how she knows. The paleontologist's intuitions, like intuitions in general, *are empirical, theory-laden, and almost always incomplete responses to worldly phenomena.* She may be sure, but her judgment is still open for checking and revision (1.3).

We should trust a person's intuitions to the degree that we have confidence in her expertise about the phenomena under investigation. Sometimes the folk may be as expert as anyone: intuitions laden with folk "theory" are the best we have to go on. This is probably the case for a range of psychological phenomena. Mostly, it clearly is not: we should trust intuitions laden with established scientific theories. Even where we are right to trust an intuition in the short run, nothing rests on it in the long run because it can be subject to scientific test.

This alternative view of the limited and theory-laden role of intuitions does not need to be modified because of the special situation in the philosophy of language and linguistics: a situation where what we are investigating are the products of a human skill or competence. This situation arises elsewhere; for example, if we are investigating the nature of tennis shots, chess moves, or touch typing. Someone who has the relevant competence has ready access to a great deal of data that are to be explained. Thus, the person who is competent in a language produces tokens that may, as a matter of fact, refer to *x*, be true in certain circumstances, be grammatical, be passives and so on. She does not have to go out and look for data because her competence produces them. Not only that, she is surrounded by similarly competent people who also produce them. As Chomsky says, competent speakers "can easily construct masses of relevant data and in fact are immersed in such data" (1988: 46). As a result, a speaker is in a very good position to become an expert about the data: She simply has to reflect upon the performance of herself and her associates. But this is not to say that she *will* become an expert. A person can be competent and yet reflect little on the output of that competence; consider a bicycle rider, for example. It is a truism in sport that great players do not always make great coaches. The fact that they possess a competence to a superlative degree does not imply that they can articulate and communicate the elements of that competence. Knowledge-how is not knowledge-that. Even if a competent person does become an expert, there is no reason to believe that her opinions carry special authority simply because she is competent; there is no reason to believe that competence gives her Cartesian access to *the truth*. She is privileged in *her ready access to data*, not in *the conclusions she draws from* the data; for example, that they *do* refer to *x*, *are* true in those circumstances, *are* grammatical, or *are* passives. These conclusions of the competent, just like those of the incompetent, are empirical responses to the phenomena and open to question.

Touch typing provides a nice example of reflecting on the output of one's own competence. Ask a touch typist which finger should be used to type, say, a 'k' and very likely she will have no immediate answer: she is an expert typist but not an expert on the "theory" of typing. Still, she will think to herself, "How would I type a 'k'". She will attend as she goes through the actual or mental motions of doing so. Then she will report what she observes: 'k' is typed by the right middle finger in the "rest" position. The only privilege this opinion enjoys is the privilege of being based on what is surely a good datum: on how she, a good touch typist, types a 'k'.

This discussion does not disprove the Chomskyan hypothesis that there is a rational causal relation between linguistic competence and speaker intuition. It does, however, provide an alternative hypothesis: those intuitions are empirical theory-laden responses to linguistic data to which the speaker, in virtue of her competence, has ready access. And this alternative is sufficient to explain both the fact that speakers generally have linguistic intuitions and that the intuitions are rightly regarded as useful data.

If this alternative view is right, linguistic intuitions are indeed good evidence for linguistic theory. However the intuitions that we should rely on most are not those of the folk but of the linguists themselves. Their skill at identifying items with a syntactic property, like the biologist's skill at identifying items with a biological property, is likely to be better than the folk's because their theories are better. As a result of their incessant theory-driven observation of language, linguists are somewhat reliable indicators of syntactic reality; analogously, biologists are somewhat reliable indicators of biological reality. But the intuitions of the linguists are only indirect evidence. The direct evidence is provided by the reality itself, the sentences people produce and understand. Are their natures in fact partly constituted by the syntactic properties we posit? This is a theoretical matter to be settled, like any other, by an indefinitely wide range of evidence.

The linguistic intuitions of the educated about the gross features of sentences are very robust: they do not vary much from person to person, nor do they vary much over time. This is not surprising on the Cartesian view. It is not surprising on our alternative view either. Language is a very striking and important part of the human environment. It is not surprising that humans should be fairly reliable detectors of the most obvious facts about it. We are probably similarly reliable about other striking and important parts of the environment.

Our alternative view of linguistic intuitions is modest in two ways. It treats these intuitions, like intuitions in general, as theory-laden opinions resulting from ordinary empirical investigation. And it treats them naturalistically. The view accommodates the evidential role that intuitions play in linguistics and yet does not require that the intuitions be derived from an underlying representation of linguistic rules. So that evidential role does not support the representational view of competence.

Although the official view is that linguistic intuitions are derived from an underlying representation of the grammar, linguists often show signs of being attracted by something like the alternative view; by the thought that linguistic concepts are highly theoretical, have their place in hard-won empirical theories, and are not plausibly attributed to all ordinary speakers.

In this respect, it is interesting to note Chomsky's skepticism about "contemporary philosophy of language" and its practice of "exploring intuitions about the technical notions 'denote', 'refer', 'true of', etc." He claims that "there can be no intuitions about these notions, just as there can be none about 'angular velocity' or 'protein'. These are technical terms of philosophical discourse with a stipulated sense that has no counterpart in ordinary language" (1995b: 24). Surely just the same skepticism is appropriate in linguistics, and for just the same reason. All the terms in linguistic theory are, in the relevant sense, technical and theory-laden. A few like 'grammatical' and 'sentence' may have counterparts in ordinary language but this need not give intuitions deploying those counterparts the privileged status that would arise from their being the voice of competence. Those intuitions could simply be the result of years of empirical folk linguistics.

We think that our alternative modest proposals about competence and intuitions are plausible but this does not, of course, show that they are right. Perhaps, speakers really do represent the rules of the language in a language module and derive their intuitions from these representations. But we know of no evidence to support this.

8.7   "The Only Theory in Town"

So far, then, we have found no evidence for the representational view of competence in the folk truism that the competent speaker knows her language, in the rejection of behaviorism, nor in the evidential role of linguistic intuitions. It seems that many linguists are influenced toward the representational view by a couple of inferences to the best explanation, one about language parsing and one about language acquisition: the representational view is thought to be "the only theory in town".

These linguists think that we can explain language parsing if we see it as a rational process of testing hypotheses about a person's speech input. *And there is no other way to explain it.* On this view, if the psycholinguistic evidence mentioned in the next section showed that a certain linguistic rule was playing a role in this process (and so was psychologically real), it would have to be represented. For hypothesis testing *is* a process of testing one representation against others.

Similarly, the linguists think that we can explain language learning if we see it as a rational process of hypothesis testing or, recently, of parameter setting, for the language of the child's community. *And there is no other way to explain it.* On this view, any linguistic rule that plays a role in language learning has to be represented, for that is what the rational process demands. So, if the acquisition evidence to be considered in section 8.10 showed that a certain linguistic rule was innate, the rule would have to be innately represented. Fodor (1975), who has hardly ever met an "only theory in town" argument he didn't like, has been most explicit: "*no* account of language learning which does not thus involve propositional attitudes and mental processes has ever been proposed by anyone, barring only behaviorists" (1981: 194; see also 1983: 5).

This is not the place for a detailed discussion of these tricky empirical matters. But our view briefly is that these arguments are too swift. On the one hand, we doubt that the representational explanations of language parsing and acquisition so far provided are sufficiently precise, complete, and successful to be appropriate candidates for such an inference to the best explanation. On the other hand, we think that the possibility of explanations that are more "brute-causal" than rational has been barely explored. Consider language parsing. This is a skill at processing certain inputs. So is catching a ball, bicycle riding, touch typing and, most pertinently, thinking. We know very little about how these processes work but it is surely plausible to think that the rules that govern them are simply built in without being represented. The processes all have the mark of "hardwired" processes: speed and inflexibility (8.5). If we knew more about know how such processes worked without representing rules perhaps we could explain how language parsing worked similarly. Consider language acquisition next. Surely innate but unrepresented rules enable us to acquire the other skills mentioned, for example, bicycle riding and thinking. Yet we do not know how they do so. If we did then perhaps we could figure out how to explain our acquisition of language similarly.

It would be rational to accept that theories of language parsing and acquisition must be representational if we had good representational theories of them and little prospect of good nonrepresentational theories. This is surely not our present situation. We really know very little about parsing and acquisition.

8.8   Are Syntactic Rules Built-in Processing-rules?

So much for the representational view. Are the structure-rules of a language – its syntactic rules – psychologically real in any other way? We have already made two proposals on this score (8.3). First, we pointed out that it should be uncontroversial that the rules must be respected by the competence and its processing-rules. But this minimal proposal alone does not warrant any claim that the syntactic rules are psychologically real. Second, we have argued that these rules are probably similar to the syntactic rules of thought and so are to that extent psychologically real. Linguists have in mind that the rules are psychologically real in another way: they play a role in language processing. Although the most popular version of this is the representational view, we have emphasized the possibility of another version: rather than being represented, the syntactic rules could be built-in processing-rules. We shall briefly consider the support for that view.

First, the evidential role of intuitions, discussed in section 8.6, does not support this view any more than it supported the representational view. A competent speaker has ready access to the outputs of her competence, and hence is in a good position to form opinions about them, *whatever* rules produce that output.

Second, the standard evidence used in constructing a grammar – about grammaticality, ambiguity, coreference, and the like – does not support the view. For this evidence bears on the syntactic rules of the language and does nothing to show that these structure-rules are also processing-rules.

Third, what is really needed to support the view is evidence of what is actually going on in the head during language processing. This is just the sort of evidence that psycholinguistics provides. So, in principle, this evidence could support the view that certain structure-rules of the language really are processing-rules; for example, that transformations from the active form to the passive, from the statement form to the question form, and the like, really take place during processing. In practice, however, it has proved very difficult to find the needed evidence.

The most popular way to pose this problem – it was our way in the first edition, for example – points to the lack of evidence about *which* set of syntactic rules are psychologically real. If we can come up with one grammar for a language, we can come up with many which, though they posit different syntactics rules, are, in some sense, equivalent. We need psycholinguistic evidence to show which syntactic rules are in fact playing a role in linguistic processing, evidence we do not have. But the problem is really more serious than this: we need evidence that *any* syntactic rules are processing-rules, that the rules of *any* grammar are psychologically real in this way.

We think this need is particularly pressing because we suspect that the syntactic rules are simply the wrong sort of rules to be language processing-rules. If we are right about the relation between thought and language, this processing is a matter of "translation". In language production, a thought in Mentalese is translated into, say, English; in language parsing, the reverse. Syntactic rules – for example, the transformation rule for yes–no questions (6.2) – which govern *the structure of the outputs* of these processes seem unsuited to govern *the process of producing them*. It seems very unlikely that the mental process from the thought IS CHESS

GENERALLY PLAYED BY OBSESSIVES? to the utterance 'Is chess generally played by obsessives' takes a detour through 'Chess is generally played by obsessives'.

What, in fact, does the psycholinguistic evidence show? We suggest, although we shall not argue, that the evidence shows which syntactic rules the processing-rules *respect*. So it provides evidence that syntactic rules hypothesized by the grammar are indeed rules of the speaker's language: it provides evidence of the truth of the grammar. But it does not provide any evidence for a position on the psychological reality issue stronger than the uncontroversial minimal one.

Finally, what about the evidence from language acquisition (to be considered in 8.10)? This evidence may show that our processing-rules are innately constrained to respect the universal syntactic rules of human languages. But it is hard to see how the evidence could show that those syntactic rules are processing-rules.

Chomsky has a standard response to doubts about the psychological reality of the langage. He points out that the grammar is a typical scientific hypothesis: it is an inference to the best explanation of the evidence. So we should take it as descriptive of reality just as we would any other such scientific hypothesis. And so we should and, indeed, have (8.3). But what is at issue is: What reality is it descriptive of? Our main claim is that it is descriptive of the rules of the language. It is also in a minimal way descriptive of competence in the language and, we have argued, may be largely descriptive of the structure of Mentalese, the language of thought. We doubt that there is any reason to think that it is otherwise descriptive of psychological reality.

In the next section, we shall develop our alternative non-Cartesian view of competence.

8.9   Linguistic Competence as a Translation Ability

On this modest view, competence in a language does not consist in the speaker's semantic propositional knowledge of or representation of rules. It is a set of skills or abilities, some of them grounded in the external world. It consists in the speaker being able to do things with a language, not in his having thoughts about it. Understanding a language no more involves having propositional knowledge of a semantic sort about the language, or representing its rules, than being able to ride a bicycle involves having propositional knowledge of a mechanical sort about riding, or representing the mechanics of riding.

Our development of this modest view will be guided by our chapter 7 discussion of the priority of thought over language. The development will incorporate the findings of our recent discussion of syntactic competence and our Part II discussions of word competence. The development does not go very far.

The most theory-neutral view of competence in a spoken language is that it is the ability to produce and understand sentences with the sounds and meanings of that language (analogously, of course, competence in a language in another medium, but, for convenience, we will talk only of a spoken language). Our acceptance of the folk idea that speakers have meaningful thoughts which their language expresses (7.1) leads us to a more theory-laden view: the competence is an ability to use sounds of the language to express thoughts with the meanings (contents) that the sounds have in that language; and an ability to assign to sounds thoughts with the meanings (contents) that the sounds have in the language. So competence in the language *requires* a certain conceptual competence, the competence to have thoughts with the meanings expressible in the language. Our acceptance of the language-of-thought hypothesis (7.2–7.3) leads us to an even more theory-laden view: the competence is the ability to translate sentences back and forth between Mentalese and the sounds of the language. So competence in the language *requires* the competence to think Mentalese sentences with meanings expressible in the language. We will offer, then, a view of competence that depends on the language-of-thought hypothesis. Since that hypothesis is conjectural, the picture of competence which depends on it must be conjectural.

On this view, a competence in Mentalese is the essential core of linguistic competence. Just as the theory of linguistic competence should not be conflated with the theory of linguistic sentences, the theory of Mentalese competence should not be conflated with the theory of Mentalese sentences (8.2). The theory of Mentalese sentences is the theory of their meanings, of the properties in virtue of which those sentences, as parts of thoughts, play a role in explaining behavior and informing us about reality. The theory of the competence is the theory of the ability to produce such sentences, the ability to think.

Linguistic competence and its Mentalese core are complex. One part is syntactic competence. Syntactic competence in Mentalese is the ability to combine Mentalese words of the various syntactic categories into the sentences of Mentalese. Whatever this ability may be, it surely does not involve any representation of the rules of Mentalese in a meta-Mentalese. Syntactic competence in the spoken language is the ability to translate back and forth between sounds with the syntactic structures of sentences of the language and Mentalese sentences with structures similar enough to count as translations. This ability must respect the syntactic rules of the language (8.3) but we have doubted that the processing-rules of this ability include any of those syntactic rules (8.8). We doubt even more that the ability involves any representation of those syntactic rules (8.4–8.7).

Another part of our linguistic competence and its Mentalese core is our lexical competence, our competence with words. Consider first our abilities with the most basic words, ones covered by pure-causal theories of reference borrowing and fixing (4.1, 5.2, 7.5). Assume for the sake of argument that the theory of reference fixing is historical-causal rather than indicator or teleological (7.7). Finally, suppose that the natural kind term 'echidna' and its Mentalese correlate ECHIDNA are examples of words covered by this theory. Competence with ECHIDNA consists in having thoughts that are appropriately linked, directly or indirectly, to echidnas. (So a Twin Earthian will not have our competence, even if he is in other ways similar, if his thoughts are linked to different animals.) The direct links are groundings in echidnas, perceptual confrontations with the animals. But most links for most people are indirect, arising from being appropriately linked to the network of causal chains for 'echidna' (or the equivalent in another language), a network involving other people's abilities as well as reference borrowings and groundings in echidnas. Competence with 'echidna' is the ability to translate back and forth between 'echidna' and ECHIDNA, a competence a person has in virtue of being part of the causal network for 'echidna'.

Consider next our abilities with the least basic words, ones that cannot be borrowed and are covered by a description theory of reference fixing (5.4, 7.5). Suppose that 'bachelor' and its Mentalese correlate BACHELOR are examples. Competence with BACHELOR consists in associating it with, say, ADULT, UNMARRIED, and MALE, a functional-role matter consisting in a disposition to infer X IS ADULT, X IS UNMARRIED, and X IS MALE from X IS A BACHELOR. Competence with 'bachelor' is the ability to translate back and forth between 'bachelor' and BACHELOR.

Words may be of other sorts, covered by combinations of various theories of reference fixing and borrowing (5.5, 7.5). Our theories of competence with them and their mental correlates will be obvious combinations of the above ideas.

**Finally, competence in such pragmatic aspects of language as enter into meaning (2.3) is the ability to have thoughts with various illocutionary forces and to translate to and from sounds in the language with the same illocutionary forces.

It is worth noting that competence in using a language can be mediated by skills that are not specifically linguistic. We have, in effect, alluded to this earlier in indicating the way that the context of a remark helps the audience to remove ambiguity (4.2). Consider now, for example, our success at detecting what Grice (1989) calls conversational implicatures.

Effortlessly and accurately we determine that something is implied by an utterance in addition to what is said. To do this we must identify the speaker's intentions. That sort of task comes up also in umpteen non-linguistic contexts. There is no reason to suppose that the identification of intentions in the linguistic context involves any specifically linguistic skills. There is no reason to suppose that the mechanisms by which, say, a wife can recognize *threat* from the way her husband washes his hands differ from those that allow her to pick up what he conversationally implies. Part of the evidence on which her inferential machinery operates differs, that is all.**

The view of competence we have presented raises a radical possibility: there may not be a language faculty. We shall explore this briefly in next section.

8.10   Chomskyan Nativism

Questions of innateness have arisen on several occasions. We have mentioned Chomsky's claim that there are grammatical rules common to all languages – rules described by "universal grammar" ("UG") – which are innately known by speakers. This nativism requires, of course, an innate language in which to represent those rules: innate Mentalese (7.3). Next, considering Harman's objection to the representational view of competence, we mentioned the claim, made by Fodor at least, that the innate language can represent *all* the rules of any public language (8.5). Fodor goes even further: the innate language is rich enough to represent not merely grammatical rules but *anything* that a public language can represent (7.3). (Fodor describes himself rightly, and with characteristic seriousness, as a "mad-dog nativist".)

We shall discuss Chomsky's very famous claims about innateness, claims that are thought by him and others to force a reassessment of the traditional debate between empiricists and rationalists over "innate ideas". Rationalists thought that many concepts were innate. Empiricists rejected this. It is thought that Chomsky's nativism strongly supports the rationalist side. In considering this nativism, it is important to distinguish a range of different theses that are not adequately distinguished in the literature.

First, there is a *boring* thesis. This is the thesis that human beings are innately predisposed to learn languages; it is because of some innate "initial state" that, given linguistic data, almost every human learns a language. The thesis is boring because every informed person, even the crudest empiricist, should believe it and, so far as we know, does believe it. How else could one explain the fact that dogs, for example, cannot learn languages? One needs to go further to make an innateness claim interesting, saying something about the innate initial state. Chomsky does go further. Second, there is a set of four *interesting* theses:

1. Humans are innately predisposed to learn languages *that conform to UG*. Let us describe this as the initial state "respecting" the rules described by UG – the "UG-rules" – on analogy with our earlier talk of the final state of competence respecting the rules described by the grammar of the language learned. We pointed out earlier that the claim about the final state should be uncontroversial (8.3). Not so the claim about the initial state. For, if it is right, the universality of UG-rules is not a mere accident of human history but is determined by our biological heritage: it is "in our genes". This is the minimal interesting nativist thesis.

Note that thesis 1 does not say *what* innate language-constraining rules make us respect UG-rules, nor *where* they reside in the mind. Thesis 2 says the former, thesis 3, the latter.

2. The initial state respects UG-rules *because it embodies UG-rules*. Not merely do we inherit *some* language-constraining rules that makes us respect the UG-rules, which is all that thesis 1 requires, we inherit the UG-rules themselves. This addresses the "what" issue and so is a *more* interesting thesis than 1.

We suspect that linguists find the move from 1 to 2 easy because of their conflation of a theory of syntax – a grammar – with a theory of competence. We pointed out earlier that the conflation encourages the view that the psychological reality of grammatical rules "comes for nothing" with the grammar (8.2–8.3). Similarly it encourages the view that the psychological reality of universal grammatical rules, UG-rules, "comes for nothing" with universal grammar, UG. Suppose that this reality did come for nothing. Then the idea that the initial state respects the UG-rules because the UG-rules are innate would be very inviting, even if not compelling. But the psychological reality does not come for nothing: the conflation is a mistake. The psychological reality of UG-rules is not a "free lunch" but something that requires psychological evidence.

3. The initial state that respects UG-rules is *a language-specific learning device, a language faculty*. The innate state that makes language learning possible is not simply a general learning device that makes all learning possible, as theses 1 and 2 allow: it is a special module of the mind. This addresses the "where" issue and so is another *more* interesting thesis than 1.

4. This thesis combines 2 and 3: the language-constraining rules are UG-rules and they are in a language faculty. This addresses both the "what" and the "where" issue and so is *even more* interesting.

None of these theses entail any innate *knowledge* or *representation* of the linguistic rules: the innate rules might be simply built in (8.5). As a result, the relation of these theses to the traditional debate over innate ideas is unclear. In any case, interesting as these theses undoubtedly are, they are not at the center of the debate. For Chomsky and his followers mostly go significantly beyond them by requiring that linguistic rules are innately known and represented in the mind.

Third, this move to knowledge and representation turns the interesting theses 2, 3, and 4, into *very exciting* theses that clearly involve a commitment to innate ideas. These are theses that no empiricist, traditional or contemporary, could allow:

2R. The UG-rules that are innately embodied according to 2 are so because they are innately represented in Mentalese: UG itself, the theory of those rules, is innately known.

3R. The innate language-constraining rules that are embodied in a language faculty according to 3 are so because they are innately represented in that faculty.

4R. This thesis combines 2R and 3R: the language-constraining rules represented in the language faculty in Mentalese are UG-rules: UG itself is innately known and in the language faculty.

Thesis 4R, the most exciting one of all, seems to be Chomsky's:

> what Chomsky thinks is innate is primarily a certain *body of information*: the child is, so to speak, "born knowing" certain facts about universal constraints on possible human languages. (Fodor 1983: 4)

A great deal of the attention given to Chomsky's claims about innateness comes from construing them in this very exciting way.

We shall now summarize the case for the nativist theses. The case is a series of inferences to the best explanation. It is claimed that nativism can offer a good explanation of various phenomena and there is no plausible empiricist explanation of them.

Universality: The first part of the case is simple. Suppose, as we are prepared to, that the linguists are right in thinking that all human language are governed by UG-rules. Then this is a very striking fact. UG-rules are quite unobvious and it is not hard to invent a language that is not governed by them; for example, one that does not observe the structure-dependency principle (6.2). How come no human language is like this? The most plausible explanation is that humans are innately constrained to speak only UG languages.

Poverty of Stimulus: The part of the case that receives the most emphasis concerns the poverty of stimulus received by the language learner. The grammatical rules picked up by the child are abstract, subtle, and unobvious. Yet, Chomsky claims, the child learns these rules from data of degenerate quality and limited range (1965: 58). The problem with the quality is that the data include many ungrammatical strings: false starts, slips of tongue, 'um's and 'ah's, and so on. The problem with the range is that the data seem to provide no evidence bearing on many of the rules that the child masters; in particular, they contain little explicit instruction and almost no negative evidence, evidence that something is *not* grammatical. It is hard to see how the child could derive the linguistic rules from these impoverished data available to her. She must have a head start, being tightly constrained to favor certain rules.

This thought can be made to look very plausible. Consider our earlier example (6.2). The child must learn that

Chess players who get to be grandmasters are generally obsessive

can be turned into the question

Are chess players who get to be grandmasters generally obsessive?

but not into

*Get chess players who to be grandmasters are generally obsessive?

And the child must learn that the subject can be moved out of structures like

Egbert believed that who was a parricide?

to

Egbert believed whom to be a parricide?

Who did Egbert believe to be a parricide?

Yet it cannot be moved out of apparently similar structures like

Egbert believed the slander that who was a parricide?
Egbert believed that Esme and who were parricides?

For, none of the following are grammatical:

*Egbert believed whom the slander to be a parricide?
*Egbert believed whom Esme and to be parricides?
*Who did Egbert believe the slander to be a parricide?
*Who did Egbert believe Esme and to be parricides?

It is claimed that children never make the error of producing these *strings even though they are unlikely to have had any evidence that they are errors and in the absence of significant evidence for the very subtle rules that make them errors. So surely the rules must be innate.

Sui Generis: Finally, it is pointed out that language learning is *sui generis*: it is quite unlike the acquisition of other cognitive skills. (i) It is done very young and has to be done before about age twelve. (ii) The level of achievement is quite uniform by comparison to other intellectual skills. (iii) All children, whatever their language, acquire elements of linguistic capacity in the same order. Acquisition is developmentally uniform across individuals and cultures. (iv) There is striking evidence, discussed recently by Pinker (1994: 32–9), that children brought up speaking Pidgin – a simple makeshift language with little grammar – "creolize" that language *in one generation* into a language with the complex grammar of any normal human language. The best explanation of these facts is that language learning is constrained by an innate, richly structured, language-specific faculty of the mind.

We shall now briefly see how this case bears on the various nativist theses.

Suppose, for a moment, that the case supports the interesting nativist theses 1 to 4. The first important point is that the case would still not support moving to the very exciting theses 2R to 4R, committed to innate knowledge and representation in Mentalese. Thus, suppose thesis 4 is correct and the innate initial state is a language faculty with built-in UG-rules. That seems a likely basis for explaining the evidence. Of course, we don't know the details of this explanation. But we are no better off for details if we add the further assumption that the UG-rules are innately known rather than simply built in. The addition seems explanatorily gratuitous.

We have already mentioned a response to this (8.7). It is that the only possible way to explain language learning is as a rational process of hypothesis testing or parameter setting, which must involve representation of the innate rules in Mentalese. This is "the only theory in town". We were unconvinced, pointing to the possibility of a more "brute-causal" explanation. Indeed, we now add, the process of setting parameters invites such an explanation.

So our first conclusion is that the case does not support Chomsky's 4R, nor either of the lesser representational theses. Hence it is not obvious, at least, that it supports anything like the traditional doctrine of innate ideas.

Although attention has mostly focused on these representational theses, the more modest theses 1 to 4 are natural fallbacks for the linguistic nativist. Does the nativist case support them? Consider Universality, the explanation of the conformity of human languages to UG. This seems to be a nice argument for thesis 1: the languages conform to UG because humans are innately predisposed to learn languages that conform. Putnam

(1967) offered another explanation: human languages share rules because they are all, as Stephen Stich puts it, "descended from a single common ur-language whose details have been lost in pre-history" (Stich 1978a: 283). But this explanation runs foul of the apparent facts about creolization mentioned in *Sui Generis*: the capacity of children to create a language that conforms to UG almost from nothing. So an inference to the best explanation to thesis 1 is promising. However, we need to look beyond Universality to establish 2, that the initial state respects UG-rules because it embodies them, and 3 that the state is a language-specific faculty.

At first sight, the Poverty of the Stimulus seems to supply that support nicely. It seems to support 2 because the child exhibits a mastery of UG-rules without having received any evidence for them. It seems to support 3 because the UG-rules are so unlike the rules governing other cognitive skills.

However, we think that this case is far less convincing than it appears. First of all, Fiona Cowie (1998: chs. 8 and 9) has persuaded us that the linguists' claims about the data available to the child are dubious at best. Plausible as these claims may be, they are largely based on the intuitions of linguists rather than on empirical investigation. And where attempts have been made to gather the evidence they suggest that the data available to the child is much richer than Chomsky and his followers suppose; for example, that it includes evidence for the Structure-Dependency Principle; and that it includes lots of negative evidence.

Next, we think that the possibility of an alternative empiricist explanation of learning from impoverished data has been dismissed too quickly. Chomsky tends to restrict his opponents to crude empiricist methods of learning. Those who are skeptical of an innate language acquisition device are allowed only simple induction and association of ideas. But these methods are hopelessly inadequate to explain learning *in general*. So one possible response to Chomsky is to posit a richer and more sophisticated innate *general* learning device. In effect, Putnam made a response of this sort (1967: 297–8). Cowie has several interesting further suggestions along these lines. These responses seek empiricist accounts of a process of *rational* learning. But our skepticism about the representational view of competence makes us emphasize another possibility: "brute-causal" learning of the sort that very likely occurs when we gain a skill like bicycle riding and surely occurs when we learn to think.

Until there is much more empirical evidence about the linguistic data available to the child, and until possible empiricist explanations of learning from that data have been more thoroughly explored, we think caution is called for in drawing nativist conclusions from the Poverty of the Stimulus.

What does *Sui Generis*, the very special nature of language learning, show? Perhaps it lends gentle support to thesis 1, the view that the initial state respects UG-rules, but it does nothing for thesis 2: it provides no evidence about which innate rules are responsible for any such respect. And it seems to support thesis 3. The fact that language learning is so different from the learning of other cognitive skills suggests that it is handled by a language-specific module, a language faculty.

The view that there is such a language faculty, distinct from the central processor but nonetheless central, is a received view in linguistics, as we have noted. In its initial state the faculty contains the innate language-constraining rules. In its final state, the state of competence in a language, it contains the rules of that language. We have a suggestion that is radically at odds with this received view.

Set aside the innate initial state for a moment and consider the state of competence. In the last section we proposed a view of competence reflecting the close relation between language and thought. This view suggests that *there may not be a language faculty at all*. For, according to that view, the core of linguistic competence is a conceptual competence, the ability to think Mentalese sentences with the appropriate meanings. This competence must be in the central processor that does the thinking. So, at least, an important "part" of linguistic competence is in the central processor. Of course, the conceptual competence is not sufficient for the linguistic competence: the thoughts that are the products of the conceptual competence have to be matched for meaning with sentences in the language. So, "the rest" of linguistic competence might be in a distinct language faculty. But, given that Mentalese has a syntax very like the speaker's natural language, this may not be so. There may not be much to the rest and what there is may consist in a few relatively peripheral systems. In order to understand English the Mentalese competence has to be linked up to one system (the parser), to speak spoken English, to another (presumably related) system; similarly to read English, write English, read Braille English, send Morse English, and so on. The only competence underlying all of these particular competences, the competence that all of these exemplify, may be the Mentalese competence that resides in the central processor. There may be nothing for a *distinct but central* language-specific faculty to do.

The suggestion has radical implications for the innate initial state as well. Suppose that, despite our caution with the Poverty of Stimulus, we nonetheless conclude that certain rules of UG are indeed innate. The suggestion is that they are innate structure-rules for Mentalese, hence in the "thinking faculty", the central processor, not in a language faculty. Languages are constrained by those rules because languages express thoughts that are so constrained. And language learning is *sui generis* because the development of thought under the stimulus of language (7.6) is *sui generis*.

Of course, the suggestion is speculative and stands in need of empirical support. In particular, it needs to address the evidence that linguistic impairment and cognitive impairment often do not go hand and in hand.

Still we think it attractive enough to be worth investigating as a serious rival to the received view.

In sum, we doubt that there is any evidence for the representational theses of Chomskyan nativism, 2R to 4R, hence any evidence for an innate Mentalese. Our view of the close relation of language and thought makes us wonder whether there is a language faculty and hence doubt thesis 3. We find it quite plausible that there are innate syntactic constraints on Mentalese which restrict human languages to UG-languages – thesis 1 – and a bit plausible that these innate constraints are the UG-rules themselves – thesis 2 – but think that the jury should be still out on these matters: more evidence needs to be found and alternative hypotheses need to be considered.

Suggested Reading

8.2

The conflation is to be found in almost any generativist account of the aim of a grammar. Chomsky 1965, *Aspects of the Theory of Syntax*, ch. 1 is a classic example. Block 1981, Part III, "The Subject Matter of Grammar", contains a number of papers which give a good idea of the controversy over grammar. It starts with a helpful (and witty) survey by Fodor, "Introduction: Some Notes on What Linguistics is Talking About" (1981b), reprinted in Katz 1985, *The Philosophy of Linguistics*.

Our own earlier views are in "What's Wrong with 'the Right View'" (1989), modified and developed in Devitt forthcoming, *Ignorance of Language*. A somewhat similar view is urged in Soames 1984a, "Linguistics and Psychology"; see also his "Semantics and Psychology" in Katz 1985. Katz is also critical of the received Chomskyan view, urging a Platonist view of linguistics; see "An Outline of Platonist Grammar" (1984), reprinted in Katz 1985, and "The Unfinished Chomskyan Revolution" (1996). See also Hornstein 1989, "Meaning and the Mental", and George 1989b, "How Not to Become Confused About Linguistics", in George 1989a.

For Dummett's views see "What is a Theory of Meaning?" (1975), pp. 105–9, 121–5, reprinted in Ludlow 1997, and "What is a Theory of Meaning? (II)" (1976), pp. 68–71. Both of these are reprinted in *The Seas of Language* (1993) which also contains a helpful preface and the 1979 essay, "What Do I Know When I Know a Language". **Davidson is another influential philosopher who seems to conflate competence with meaning and to have a propositional view of the former, but his views are difficult to pin down: see several of his papers in *Inquiries into Truth and Interpretation* (1984), particularly, his classic 1967 paper "Truth and

Meaning", reprinted in Martinich 1996, Geirsson and Losonsky 1996, and Ludlow 1997.**

McGinn 1982, "The Structure of Content", criticizes Dummett and Davidson for conflating the theory of competence with truth-conditional semantics.

A popular approach taking semantics to be about competence has arisen from ideas of Chomsky and Davidson. Larson and Segal 1995, *Knowledge of Meaning*, a short excerpt from which is in Ludlow 1997, is the text. Higginbotham has been influential; see, for example, "Knowledge of Reference" in George 1989a.

8.4–8.7

Chomsky's most thorough discussion of the issue of the psychological reality of language is to be found in his *Knowledge of Language* (1986), chs. 1, 2, and 4. Helpful earlier discussions are "Knowledge of Language" (1975) and *Rules and Representations* (1980), chs. 3, 5, and 6. (In the latter work, Chomsky talks of the speaker "cognizing" the grammar rather than tacitly knowing it. This is to meet the objection that the speaker might not have the justification for her beliefs that knowledge requires.) See also *Language and Problems of Knowledge* (1988) and a paper of the same name in Martinich 1996. Chomsky 1995b, "Language and Nature", is a relevant work of a more philosophical sort.

Harman 1967, "Psychological Aspects of the Theory of Syntax" (reprinted in Stich 1975, *Innate Ideas*), Part I, criticized Chomsky's doctrine of tacit knowledge. This led to a revealing exchange in Hook 1969, *Language and Philosophy*: Chomsky 1969a: 86–9; Harman 1969: 143–8; Chomsky 1969b: 152-6. See also Nagel 1969 (reprinted in Harman 1974) and Schwartz 1969 in the same volume.

Stich 1971, "What Every Speaker Knows", argues clearly and persuasively for the view that the speaker need know nothing. Graves *et al.* 1973, "Tacit Knowledge", is a reply. Stich 1978b, "Beliefs and Subdoxastic States", objects to the way the distinction between beliefs and other states that causally underpin beliefs has been ignored. Stabler 1983, "How Are Grammars Represented?", draws attention (in effect) to the possibility that represented structure-rules might play a role in processing by being *data* for processing-rules. Evans 1985, *Collected Papers*, ch. 11, Dennett 1987, *The Intentional Stance*, ch. 6, and Davies 1989, "Tacit Knowledge and Subdoxastic States", are helpful discussions.

Fodor 1983, *The Modularity of Mind*, is a detailed argument for the view that the language faculty is one among many modules in the mind. Fodor 1985a, "Precis of *The Modularity of Mind*", is a nice summary of this argument, followed by criticisms and Fodor's response.

For Chomsky's opposition to behaviorism, see his famous 1959 review of Skinner's classic *Verbal Behavior* (1957), reprinted in Fodor and Katz 1964 and Geirsson and Losonsky 1996. Fodor 1981a, *Representations*, pp. 1–16, gives a nice account of behaviorism and of its relation to its successor, functionalism. See also, Rey 1997, *Contemporary Philosophy of Mind*, ch. 4. **Quine's skepticism about meaning (see suggested reading for 1.3) seems based on a behaviorism like Skinner's.**

Fodor's 1968 paper, "The Appeal to Tacit Knowledge in Psychological Explanations", reprinted in Fodor 1981a, argues the extreme position that psychological explanations in general should posit representations of rules.

Harman 1975, "Language, Thought, and Communication", helpfully relates views on speakers' knowledge to general views about language.

For doubts about the psychological reality of grammars, see Stich 1972, "Grammar, Psychology, and Indeterminacy", reprinted in Katz 1985, and Katz 1977, "The Real Status of Semantic Representations", in Block 1981. For an interesting discussion, see Matthews 1991, "Psychological Reality of Grammars".

8.10

For Chomsky's views on innateness, see 1965: 47–59; 1980: chs. 4 and 6; "On the Nature, Use and Acquisition of Language" in Lycan 1990. See also his contributions to the following collections: Searle 1971; Hook 1969; Stich 1975; Piattelli-Palmarini, *Language and Learning* 1980; Block 1981; Beakley and Ludlow 1992, Part V.

Many papers by others in these collections are also helpful on innateness. See particularly: those by Putnam and Goodman in Searle; those by Quine, Goodman, and Harman in Hook; those in Part III of Stich; all papers in Piattelli-Palmarini; those in Part IV of Block; those in Part V of Beakley and Ludlow. Stich 1978a, "Empiricism, Innateness, and Linguistic Universals", takes a skeptical view of the thesis that all human languages must conform to a universal grammar.

Two excellent, and very readable, recent works are Pinker 1994, *The Language Instinct*, which is pro-nativism, and Cowie 1998, *What's Within*, which takes a critical look at the nativism of both Fodor and Chomsky.

Fodor's early views are set out at length in *The Language of Thought* (1975) and more succinctly in his contribution to Piattelli-Palmarini 1980. He tries to show that their consequences are not *quite* as implausible as they seem at first sight in "The Present Status of the Innateness Controversy" (1981a). He has recently changed his mind in *Concepts* (1998).

We have accepted the terms of debate here; that the distinction between learned and innate information is a good one. That distinction is itself questionable; see Oyama 1999, *The Ontogeny of Information*.

＊＊9

Defending
Representationalism

9.1 Introduction

In the preceding chapters we have developed a theory of meaning for linguistic and mental tokens. Our starting hypothesis was that the core of a token's meaning is its property of representing something (2.1, 7.1). If the token is a sentence, the property is that of having a certain truth condition; if the token is a word, that of having a certain reference. We soon found a need to enrich this core: the meaning of a token is its property of representing something *in a certain way*, its *mode* of representing it (2.6). We have attempted to support this view by showing what representational meanings can explain and how they themselves might be explained by theories of reference and syntax. Still, many philosophers reject this sort of representationalism. A radical rival we will not consider is eliminativism: the view that there are no thoughts and hence no mental sentences to have representational meanings (contents). We shall consider two rivals that share our realism about thoughts. One holds that our sort of representationalism is only part of the story of thought meaning: it is right about one factor of meaning but there is also another factor. This is a "two-factor" theory. Another holds that representationalism is totally wrong and that thought meaning must be explained in other ways altogether. This is a "one-factor" rival to our "one-factor" representationalism. We shall conclude by considering a famous skeptical argument against our sort of representationalism that Saul Kripke finds in Ludwig Wittgenstein.

These matters are too intricate and difficult to be discussed in any detail in this chapter. Our aim is simply to introduce some of the more important reasons for favoring these rivals and briefly to indicate our responses. It will be convenient to write as if the language-of-thought hypothesis is true – as indeed we think it is (7.2) – but so far as we can see our argument does not depend on this: the argument applies whether the vehicle of thought meaning is a mental sentence or something else.

One reason for favoring a rival to representationalism is apparent already: it has proved disturbingly hard to find convincing theories of reference. There is a range of ideas for the ultimate explanation of reference appealing to historical, reliable, and teleological, causal links (4.1, 5.2, 7.8), but it has to be admitted that there is more promise than fulfillment to these ideas. Some think that the difficulties here indicate that reference cannot be explained naturalistically and hence, of course, that truth cannot be. If they cannot, we agree that explanatory notions of truth and reference must be abandoned and with them the representational view of meaning that depends on them. However, we are not so pessimistic about theories of reference.

It may be thought that pessimism here is *obvously* uncalled for. Talk of truth and reference is so useful and so ubiquitous that it surely will be accommodated within a naturalistic world view if anything is. Who could deny that sentences have truth conditions and words have reference? And if they do, surely this has something to do with their meanings.

This complacency about truth and reference should not survive the discovery that truth and reference might be *deflationary*. For truth and reference to play the roles we have described in a theory of meaning, they must be *robust* "causal-explanatory" properties. Only if they are thus robust could they play a role in a scientific explanation of meaning. Yet, according to the deflationist, we should not take 'true' and 'refer' as specifying explanatory properties but rather as being logical devices like those for disjunction and quantification. Taking them in this way, we can account for all the roles of 'true' and 'refer' that make them seem so generally useful, all the roles apart from their alleged role in the theory of meaning. So the ubiquitous use of 'true' and 'refer' in our ordinary language does not establish that they specify robust properties, properties that can explain meaning and that require substantive theories. Of course, the fact that the terms have these purely logical roles does not rule out the possibility of their *also* having an explanatory role. However, it opens up the possibility that the deflationary view is right: these terms may have only these logical roles. Truth and reference do not *explain* meaning or anything else. Hence we do not need any more than the deflationary theory to explain them. We consider these ideas in the next section.

Of course, if meaning is not to be explained in terms of truth and reference, it has to be explained in some other way. And there are reasons for being interested in other ways quite apart from the attractions of deflationism. We shall consider some one-factor rivals in section 9.3, some two-factor, in 9.4. We shall consider Kripke's skeptical argument in 9.5.

9.2   Deflationism

We shall focus on truth. Those who think that 'true' is simply a logical device place a central emphasis on the *disquotation principle* (or *equivalence principle*). This principle notes that the following two sentences are equivalent:

'The Rolling Stones are the world's greatest rock band' is true
The Rolling Stones are the world's greatest rock band.

The two sentences have the same epistemic load; if we can justifiably assert one, we can justifiably assert the other. Intuitively, they say the same thing. The first exhibits what Quine calls *semantic ascent*: when we are in a position to assert a sentence, we can instead put quotation marks around it and add 'is true'. Disquotation is just coming down again.

In essence, deflationists believe that this disquotational property of 'true' is *all there is* to truth. Truth is not an explanatory property with a "hidden" nature that needs a scientific explanation. The truth term is simply a device with an *expressive* role. There are many examples that persuasively illustrate this expressive role:

(a) Instead of saying

Max said that Hitler was mad, but if that's true, then he was cunningly mad

we could say

Max said that Hitler was mad, but if Hitler was mad, then he was cunningly mad.

Or, in conversation, instead of

Max: Hitler was mad.
Justine: That's true.

we could have

Max: Hitler was mad.
Justine: Hitler was mad.

The role of 'true' in these examples does not seem important. Indeed, 'true' seems rather redundant. (Hence, some deflationary theories of truth have been called "redundancy theories".) However, other examples show that 'true' is much more useful. It, or some other device playing the same role, is indispensible. It enables us to assert briefly something that may otherwise be very tedious, if not impossible, to assert.

(b) Suppose that Imogen wishes to express general but qualified agreement with a certain article. She can say simply,

Most of what that article says is true.

Consider what would be required to say this without using 'true'. Her claim entails that at least half the claims in the article are true, but is not specific about which half. So her claim is equivalent to a long disjunction of conjuncts, each conjunct consisting of a different set of more than half the claims in the article. If she could remember all the claims, she could, of course, manage to express this disjunction. But it would certainly be tiresome to try unless the article was *very* short!

Frequently, people cannot identify all the sentences that they want to assent to. In such cases, their beliefs are beyond assertion altogether without 'true'.

(c) Someone may have heard Goldbach's Conjecture ("Every even number is the sum of two primes") and believed it true even though he has forgotten exactly what it was. With the help of 'true', he can say,

Goldbach's Conjecture is true.

Without it, he must remain silent.

(d) The political beliefs of a once numerous, though fast dwindling, group could be expressed thus:

Everything Chairman Mao said was true.

Anyone who has not kept track of all the Great Helmsman's utterances – which, surely, is everyone – is faced with an impossible task in attempting to assert this without semantic ascent. She must resort to something along the lines:

If Chairman Mao said that the East is red, then the East is red, and if he said that the East is orange, then the East is orange, and so on.

The problem is that to complete the assertion she needs to replace the 'and so on' and that is an *infinite* task.

(e) In the latter case, ignorance makes the alternative to semantic ascent infinite. In others, particularly in logic, the alternative is inevitably infinite. We can assert each instance of a schema that has an infinite number of instances, thus:

Each instance of that schema is true.

Without 'true' our assertion would be literally endless.

Two things emerge from this. First, 'true' does indeed have an expressive role. Second, all it needs to play that role is the disquotational property: all it needs is that the disquotation principle holds of it. This is thought provoking *whatever one thinks of deflationism*. Of course, the deflationist goes further: this expressive role and disquotational nature is all there is to truth. This further step needs more argument.

Our focus has been on truth but much the same goes for reference. Here the deflationist emphasizes the disquotational property of 'refers' illustrated in the equivalence of

'Reagan' refers to that man
Reagan is that man.

And, in essence, the claim is that there is no more to reference than this disquotational property.

If the deflationist is right truth and reference cannot be explanatory notions in any theory. And it is striking that the deflationist can account for so much of the familiar uses of 'true' and 'refers'. To meet the challenge posed by the deflationary theory we must find phenomena that we can explain only with the aid of robust notions of truth and reference. One proposal is that we need truth (hence reference) to explain the success of a creature in achieving its goals. This idea leads to complex argument beyond the scope of this book. Our response to this challenge, one that has guided us so far, is that we need truth and reference to explain meaning.

Meaning, in turn, poses a challenge to the deflationist. She cannot, of course, accept our theory of meaning based on truth and reference. Yet a sentence, whether linguistic or mental, clearly has *some* critical properties that give it its pivotal role in our life. What account can the deflationist offer?

In the next section we consider one proposal open to the deflationist, though, as we shall see, it is a proposal that some have found plausible for other reasons too. Our view is a one-factor theory of meaning: the meaning of an expression is the way it represents something. The view we shall consider is a one-factor theory too, though one taking a very different view of the nature of meaning. The existence of these two contrasting single factor theories of meaning has suggested to some that they are both half-right. The correct theory of meaning is a two-factor theory. We very briefly consider this in section 9.4.

9.3   Functional-role Semantics and "Narrow" Meanings

The guiding idea of the one-factor alternative to our representationalism is that *meaning is functional (or conceptual) role*. A thought's functional role is a feature of its potential causal relations. A given thought is disposed to interact in cognition with other thoughts, with perceptions, and with motor programs as the agent acts in the world. The guiding idea of functional-role theories is that the meaning of a thought – the meaning of a mental sentence – derives from these potential interactions. Thus Alex's thought, 'That is tall even for a giraffe', is causally *distinctive*. It is uniquely related to Alex's perceptual and pattern recognition capacities; to his ability to spot giraffes. It has a distinct complex of relations to other thoughts, in forming the judgment of comparative size. At least potentially, it has a unique role to play in guiding behavior. Most likely this will be verbal behavior. But Alex may have other designs on giraffes – photographic, culinary, sporting – in which their tallness may be relevant. It is these functional roles of thoughts – their places in these networks of causal relations – which makes thoughts (and the linguistic sentences that express them) so important in our lives. Hence these functional roles are their meanings.

This guiding idea can yield a variety of theories depending on which of a thought's functional roles is taken to constitute its meaning. A thought is functionally related to (i) perceptions of the world which cause thoughts; (ii) other thoughts; (iii) to the behaviors which thoughts cause. So is the meaning of a thought (on the functional-role conception) determined by all three elements, all three relations? Perhaps only relations to perceptions and other thoughts matter. Once it has been decided, say, that the relations between a thought and its perceptual causes are relevant to that thought's meaning, the question then arises: *Which relations* between thought and perceptions? A particular thought – say, the belief that tuataras are rare – is potentially linked to a wide variety of perceptions. Consider how many different perceptual experiences could be failures to find a tuatara, thus contributing to the belief in its rarity. Which of these links help form the meaning of the belief? The question is especially pressing with the links between thoughts, for every thought is potentially inferentially related to every other thought. Any two thoughts can figure as premises in the one inference. How are we to choose among this plethora? One response is not to choose: the meaning of a mental sentence is constituted by its functional relations to *all* perceptions, behaviors, and other sentences. So the meaning of every sentence, indeed every word, involves the meaning of every other one! This "meaning holism" has been surprisingly popular. (We will discuss it briefly in 13.2.)

One appealing idea is to choose the relations that play a role in *verifying or confirming* a thought, the relations that count as *evidence* for a thought. So, for example, the meaning of 'That is Sally' is tied closely to perceptions of Sally. However, this idea does not avoid meaning holism if Quine is right ("Two Dogmas", in 1961), as we think he is, in claiming that confirmation is holistic. As we saw above in the tuatara example, almost any perception or other thought can play some role in providing evidence for a sentence. The problem of avoiding meaning holism still dogs functional-role semantics. What is the "principled basis" for taking some functional roles but not others as constituting meaning?

So functional-role theories can vary from one another in their choices of the key functional relations that go into meaning. Some theories, for example, seem mostly concerned with inferential role: the relations between thoughts. Theories can also vary in their attitude towards holism. Given, say, that the focus is on thought–thought relations, are all of these relations relevant to meaning or only some of them?

One final variation has been very important. It is over the *characterization* of these functional roles. One characterization, definitive of "narrow" meaning, takes these roles to be relations only to things inside the head or, at least, inside the skin of the agent. The other, definitive of "wide" (or "broad") meaning, allows in relations to things in the outside world. Consider perceptions, for example. Are the perceptions that constitute the meaning of 'That is Sally' the proximal sensory inputs that help cause the thought or do they also involve Sally, the distal cause of those inputs? Similarly, should we characterise the behavior that the thought (potentially) causes as a sequence of immediate bodily movement or as *actions* impacting on the external world? Defenders of narrow meaning or narrow functional roles urge that we should specify the perceptual links in terms of proximal stimuli, and the behaviors as bodily motions. Defenders of wide meaning or wide functional roles, think that the perceptual links are with Sally, not proximal stimulations, and the behaviors are actions on the world.

A functional-role one-factor theory, whether wide or narrow, is not representational. It explains meaning without any appeal to truth conditions or reference and so allows a person to be deflationist about them.

Thoughts explain behavior. A thought is a relation or attitude to a meaningful mental sentence (7.1). One thing that draws philosophers to functional-role semantics is the intuition that it is the functional role of the sentence that explains its role in causing behavior. Attention to the explanation of behavior has made the narrow version of functional-role semantics particularly popular. The source of the popularity has been the argument from *methodological solipsism.*

Putnam's slogan, "meanings just ain't in the head", has appeared often in this book (3.5, 5.1, 7.5). The point of it is that nothing in the head can be sufficient to determine reference; reference depends in part on causal links to external reality. This point has been exploited to claim that reference and hence truth conditions, which are explained in terms of reference, are causally irrelevant to behavior. What is relevant is narrow functional role.

Consider the Twin-Earth fantasy (5.1). When Oscar thinks and talks about water (= H_2O), Twin Oscar thinks and talks about Twin water (= XYZ). The truth conditions of their thoughts and utterances using 'water' differ. As a result, truth values may differ. Suppose that Oscar and Twin Oscar both token, "Water contains hydrogen". What Oscar says is true but, unless XYZ contains hydrogen, what Twin Oscar says is false. Yet these differences in truth-referential properties make no difference to the internal psychologies of Oscar and Twin Oscar. Indeed, those psychologies are identical, according to the fantasy. Yet, it is claimed, those psychologies determine the behaviors of Oscar and Twin Oscar, which are also identical. So, the truth-referential differences are irrelevant to explaining behavior.

The argument from methodological solipsism suggests that only the narrow meaning of a mental sentence is relevant to behavior. For the narrow meaning is determined by what is in the head. Truth-referential meanings are wide and so are irrelevant to behavior.

We can sum up the suggestion in a simple argument.

P1. Reference and truth condition are irrelevant to the internal psychology of speakers.
P2. The internal psychology of speakers explains their behavior.
C. Reference and truth condition are irrelevant to the explanation of behavior.

So narrow meanings explain behavior. What is the narrow meaning of a sentence? It is its internally constituted functional role: its disposition to causally interact with proximal stimuli and behavior and with other sentences.

So, what are we to say about the one-factor functional-role theory? Let us start by noting its *prima facie* implausiblity. For, it rejects the basic representationalist idea that meaning is to be explained in terms of truth and reference. The history of semantics demonstrates just how plausible this idea is. Indeed, has it ever been doubted before this century? Its appeal is reflected in the very words we use to pick out the objects that have meanings: We call them "symbols" or "representations".

Here is another consideration that adds to the case for representationalism and against functional-role semantics. No other approach offers a ghost of an explanation of why humans and other animals think and talk at all. Humans, and to a lesser extent other animals, have invested at great expense in a large brain. We use a significant chunk of that brain to make and listen to noises. Why have such capacities evolved? The only explanation available is a representational one. In Godfrey-Smith's felicitous phrase, accurately representing one's world, as it is and as it could be, is a "fuel for success" (1996: 172). Creatures whose representations map the world are advantaged in satisfying their needs. This explanation is not without problems. But it is without rivals. In particular, no narrow or internalist theory of thought can explain why the capacity for thinking is adaptive, for that explanation must exhibit systematic relations between creatures so endowed and their environments. But narrow theories look only inside the mind. In sum, representationalism solves an overarching evolutionary problem.

So far we have criticized functional-role semantics by defending representationalism. We turn now to criticizing it directly. First, despite the promises, these meanings are left almost entirely unexplained and mysterious. We have drawn attention to the fact that a sentence has indefinitely many functional relations to three different sorts of things, perceptions, other sentences, and behaviors. We need to know which of these many relations constitute its meaning and we need a principled basis for our decision. This we do not have. Second, even if we had, we have been given no clear idea how such meanings *could* explain behaviors and it seems very unlikely that they could. This is particularly striking with the more popular narrow functional-role meanings. Consider an example: Jim sees Mary looking tired and sweaty and gives her a drink of water. The folk have a view about how Jim's beliefs about Mary and his desire to help explain his behavior. We have no idea how the narrow meanings of these states – meanings Jim shares with Twin Jim – explain Jim's behavior. After all, Jim and Twin Jim do quite different things. Jim gives water to Mary; Twin Jim gives Twin Water to Twin Mary. So how do the narrow meanings explain the fact that Mary is on the receiving end of Jim's action and that water is what she receives? The solipsism argument trades on the idea that Oscar and Twin Oscar behave the same because their behaviors consist in the same brute-physical motor patterns. But we define behavior that way neither in folk psychology nor in scientific psychology: we treat behaviors as intentional actions not as mere bodily movements.

So we doubt that functional-role meanings can explain behavior. It seems even less likely that they can perform the other main role of meanings, informing us about reality (1.2). If a person's thought represents the world, then we can see how knowledge of the thought can tell us about what it represents. But how could knowledge of a thought's functional role tell us about the world? Even if Alex knows the functional role of Jim's thought that Mary is sweaty, how does that tell Alex anything about the sweaty Mary? Again the point is particularly striking with narrow functional roles. How could Alex's knowledge of proximal stimulations, internal inferential connections and Jim's consequent muscle twitches tell Alex about Mary?

9.4   The Two-factor Theory

It is time to turn to the two-factor theory. According to this theory, one factor of meaning is a narrow functional-role and the other is a representational factor explained in terms of truth and reference. Because it has the latter factor it can go along with the representationalist solution to the evolutionary problem. And it has a ready solution to the problem that concluded the last section: the truth-referential factor plays the role of informing us about reality. However, it does not escape the other criticisms we have leveled at the one-factor theory: its functional-role factor is mysterious and unexplained; and it is quite unclear how this factor could explain the sort of behavior – action – that needs to be explained.

The main motivation for two-factor theories is the argument from methodological solipsism. But there is another. We pointed out that there are various traditional problems in taking the referential role of a name, or any other word, to exhaust its meaning (2.5). To solve these problems, we need a finer-grained meaning: we must enrich the meaning with a sense. In effect, two-factor theories do this by positing a functional-role factor to meaning as well as the referential one.

This motivation for the two-factor theory is inadequate. We agree that the meaning of a word has to be more than its referential role. But where the two-factor theorist enriches the meaning by positing a functional-role factor that is independent of reference, we enrich the meaning by enriching the referential factor. On our view, the meaning of a word is its property of referring to something in a certain way; the meaning is its mode of reference. That is how we get the finer grain. So the extra we put into meaning is something we needed anyway: the mechanisms that explain reference. Where the two-factor theory's solution to the traditional problems requires a distinct semantic theory for each independent factor of meaning, one for the functional-role factor and one for the referential factor, our solution requires only one theory, the theory of the one and only referential factor. In brief, our theory has the advantage of being simpler.

Note that our theory does not deny a functional-role element to meaning. For, a word's mode of reference involves a functional role. This is most obvious with a word covered by a description theory. Its reference is determined by its association with a few other words. This association is a functional-role matter, as we have emphasized (7.5). Where then do we differ from two-factor theorists? The only functional roles that go into our meanings are *ones that determine reference*. The functional roles that constitute one of their factors are *non-reference-determining*: they are independent of reference.

(Rather confusingly, some theorists – including us in the first edition! – apply the term "two-factor theory" to any theory that allows a functional-role element into word meaning. On this usage, we come out as two-factor theorists. We think that the term is best reserved for theories that take a word's meaning to have two distinct factors requiring two distinct theories, one for the non-reference-determining functional-role factor and one for the referential factor.)

We shall close this discussion with a central argument for representationalism and against any theory, whether one- or two-factor, that puts a non-reference-determining functional role into meaning. Day in and day out the folk use ordinary thought ascriptions to explain behavior. For example, they say "Jim believed that Mary was thirsty" to explain his giving water to Mary. Furthermore, these folk ascriptions appear to be, by and large, *successful*; the ascription to Jim really does seem to explain his behavior. This is evidence that thoughts really do have whatever properties the folk ascribe to them. Part of what is ascribed is a meaning (the rest is an attitude to that meaning). We would argue that the meanings that the folk ascribe are always, *as a matter of fact*, representational: the (purported) references of the thought always matter to the truth of the ascription and no functional role that does not determine that reference ever matters. Thus, for "Jim believed that Mary was thirsty" to be true, Jim must have a thought that is about Mary and thirst. A thought about Alice and hunger will not do, whatever its functional role. And the functional roles of the words in Jim's thought never matter to the truth except insofar as the roles determine reference. If this is right, representationalism is the semantic *status quo*. Given the explanatory success of this *status quo*, overthrowing it needs both a powerful argument and a plausible alternative semantics. In our view, the argument from methodological solipsism is not the former and functional-role semantics is not the latter.

Finally, we should add a point about the verificationist approach to meaning. We have mentioned this approach in presenting an anti-representational functional-role theory: it is one way to choose the functional roles that constitute meanings. However, verificationism does not *have* to be anti-representational. It can accept that truth and reference are explanatory in a theory of meaning but hold that they themselves must ultimately be explained in epistemic terms. This is to have an epistemic theory of truth and reference, a theory that is like the correspondence theory in being robust not deflationary. Where the earlier verificationism combines an epistemic theory of meaning with a deflationary theory of truth, this one has epistemic theories of both. We shall discuss this alternative much later (11.4). It has a terrible cost: it leads to anti-realism about the external world.

9.5   Kripke's Skeptical Argument

Kripke (1982) has presented a famous argument for skepticism about representational meanings. He finds the argument in the work of Wittgenstein (1953) but does not endorse it himself. He goes on to construct what he takes to be Wittgenstein's solution to this skeptical problem, a solution that involves a very different "use" theory of meanings. There is room for argument about the nature of this different view, let alone about its truth. And, it goes without saying, there is room for argument about the interpretation of Wittgenstein. We shall set these matters aside, concerning ourselves simply with the skeptical argument that Kripke presents (but does not endorse). And we shall focus on the version of the argument that is aimed at our sort of naturalistic representationalism.

The argument concerns the English word 'plus' (or '+'). We have encountered only a finite number of arithmetical problems involving this word. Let us suppose that none of these was about a number bigger than 56. Now suppose we are faced with 'What is 68 plus 57?'. We confidently answer '125'. Kripke's skeptic raises the question: What makes that the right answer? We reply impatiently that 125 is what you get when you add 68 to 57; that's the way it is in arithmetic. But arithmetic is not what the skeptic is worried about. He agrees that if 'plus' meant *plus* then the answer is right. But suppose it meant a different mathematical function which he calls "quus" and defines as follows:

$$x \text{ quus } y = x \text{ plus } y, \text{ if } x, y < 57$$
$$= 5 \text{ otherwise}$$

If 'plus' meant quus then the right answer would be '5'. So, the skeptic wants to know: In virtue of what did we mean plus not quus? He argues that there is no answer, at least none available to a representationalist: "no fact about my past history – nothing that was ever in my mind, or in my external behavior – establishes that I meant plus rather than quus" (1982: 13). And the same goes for any other word: there is no fact of the matter about our meaning *tuatara* rather than *tiger* by 'tuatara'. Nobody ever means anything by anything!

Clearly none of our previous answers to 'plus' problems shows that we meant plus and not quus, for we have never encountered a problem about any number greater than 56. So our answers are compatible with either meaning. Similarly, suppose that you have never encountered a table at the base of the Eiffel Tower. Nothing in your previous application of the term 'table' shows that you mean *table* by it rather than *tabair*, anything that is a table not found at the base of the Eiffel Tower (p. 19).

Perhaps what settles the meaning is not actual past behavior but a *disposition* to behave. So we mean plus by 'plus' because we are disposed to respond to 'plus' problems with answers appropriate to that meaning: had we been asked, say, 'What is 71 plus 63?', we would have responded '134'; and so on. The skeptic has a series of objections to the dispositional view. The one that most impresses him, the famous "normativity" objection, we shall consider last.

The first objection is surprisingly weak. It is that not only is our actual behavior finite, but so also is our disposition. If we make the numbers large enough we will have no disposition to add them; indeed we might die before the 'plus' problem was posed. So far, the objection reflects a crude view of dispositions, overlooking the importance of *ceteris paribus*: the dispositionalist view is that we would give the "right" answer to 'plus' problems, *in ideal conditions*. The skeptic responds:

> But how can we have any confidence of this? How in the world can I tell what would happen if my brain were stuffed with extra brain matter or if my life were prolonged by some magic elixar? Surely such speculation should be left to science fiction writers and futurologists. (p. 27)

This is unconvincing, as many have pointed out. If it were a good objection, it would count count quite generally against idealizations in science; against those involve in Boyle's Law, for example.

The next objection is more serious: "Most of us have dispositions to make mistakes. For example, when asked to add certain numbers, some people forget to 'carry'" (pp. 28–9). What, according to the dispositionalist, makes this a mistake? Why do we not take this disposition into account in determining what we mean by 'plus' with the unhappy result that we mean some function other than plus?

At this point the bearing of the skeptic's argument on discussions in this book becomes very apparent. One of the theories of reference we considered, the *indicator* theory (7.7), is in fact a dispositional theory. The skeptic's present objection raises what we called the "error" problem for the indicator theory. Thus consider our earlier example, the mental word HORSE. We might have put the problem as follows. Most of us are disposed to make mistakes in picking out horses, sometimes identifying muddy zebras, the odd cow, and so on. What makes these mistakes? Why do we not take this disposition into account in determining what we mean by HORSE, with the unhappy result that it means horses, muddy zebras, the odd cow, and so on?

So the skeptic has certainly hit on a real problem for dispositional accounts. We think that there is another, worse, problem, that of harmless "false positives". What is the right response to these problems? Not, it seems to us, the skeptic's despair about meaning. We might try to patch up the dispositional account. If that seems unpromising we should look around for alternative theories of reference. Perhaps the teleological theory will do the job. Perhaps the view that we favor will: a combination of teleology at the lowest level, historical-cause at the next, and description at the highest. The skeptic does not contemplate any of these naturalistic alternatives. We do not claim that any of them is clearly correct. Still, there are some promising ideas here, and reference is too important a notion to give up on easily. Certainly, nothing the skeptic has produced so far gives us good reason to give up.

So the skeptical case comes down to the final objection, normativity. The objection is that the dispositional fact underlying our use of 'plus' fails to determine meaning because it is not a "fact that *justifies* my present response . . . it should *tell* me what I ought to do in each instance" (p. 24). The dispositional fact is simply a matter of how we *do* apply the term whereas what we need is some fact about how we *ought to* apply the term. This is the skeptic's main objection: "Ultimately, almost all objections to the dispositional account boil down to this one" (p. 24).

Commentators have been much exercised by this curious objection. What are we to make of it? What norms are involved in meanings? Here is one: since a term refers to xs and not ys we *ought* (in some sense) to apply it xs and not ys: it is *right* to call horses 'horse' but *wrong* to call muddy zebras and the odd cow 'horse'. This is true enough, but hardly noteworthy. More important, it does not pose any *further* requirement on the *theory of* reference. The theory's job is to explain reference. Since reference has the normative feature just described, what the theory explains will of course have it (for what the theory explains *is* reference). But there is nothing further that the theory has to do. As Fodor says:

requiring that normativity be grounded suggests that there is more to demand of a naturalized semantics than that it provide a reduction of such notions as, say, *extension*. But what could this "more' amount to? To apply a term to a thing in its extension *is* to apply the term correctly; once you've said what it is that makes the tables the extension of 'table's, there is surely no *further* question about why it's *correct* to apply a 'table' to a table. (1990a: 135–6n.)

Perhaps the skeptic's idea is that reference's normative feature alone shows that it cannot be naturalized, for *ought* can never be derived from *is*. Some influential commentators seem to endorse this idea (Wright 1984: 771–2; Blackburn 1984: 291). Yet it is really just a dogma. How could we know in advance that no norm can be naturalized?

It often looks as if the following demand underlies the skeptic's position. Suppose that a certain fact, perhaps a dispositional one, explained the reference of a term. Then that fact must "wear the norm on its face". Knowing the fact has to be sufficient for knowing how the term should be applied: that knowledge alone should "tell me what I ought to do"; it should "justify" my actions. The knowledge must leave no "open question" about the norms. But this demand is simply mistaken. If we knew that the fact explained reference then of course knowing the fact would tell us how the term should be applied. So if the fact "wore on its face" that it explained reference then it would also "wear the norm on its face". But, of course, the antecedent is false. Worldly facts do not come with some sign telling us what they explain. Finding out what they explain is a matter of hard empirical work. So, what could underly the skeptics demand? It seems as if the skeptic is insisting that theories of meaning be knowable *a priori* (the Cartesian assumption once again?). If he is, it will come as no surprise to many that such an unnaturalistic demand can be found in Wittgenstein.

We accept that the representational theory of meaning is a large and uncompleted task. We have argued that Kripke's skeptic has provided no good reason to suppose that it cannot be completed.

Suggested Reading

9.2

For a typically elegant exposition of semantic ascent and its uses, see Quine 1970, *Philosophy of Logic*, ch. 1. For developments of deflationary views of truth and/or reference see Leeds 1978, "Theories of Reference and Truth"; Soames 1984b, "What is a Theory of Truth?"; Horwich 1990, *Truth*; Grover 1992, *A Prosentential Theory of Truth*; Brandom 1994,

Making It Explicit; Field 1994, "Deflationist Views of Meaning and Content". Devitt 1991 is a critical notice of Horwich 1990. See also, Gupta 1993, "A Critique of Deflationism".

9.3–9.4

Brandom 1994 and Harman 1987, "(Nonsolipsistic) Conceptual Role Semantics", are one-factor functional-role theories. For two-factor theories, see Field 1978, "Mental Representation", reprinted in Block 1981; Loar 1981, *Mind and Meaning*, and 1982, "Conceptual Role and Truth Conditions"; Schiffer 1981, "Truth and the Theory of Content"; McGinn 1982, "The Structure of Content" in Woodfield 1982, *Thought and Object*; Block 1986, "Advertisement for a Semantics for Psychology"; Lycan 1988, *Judgement and Justification*, ch. 4.

The argument that psychology should be narrow is to be found in many of these works. See also Stich 1978c, "Autonomous Psychology and the Belief–Desire Thesis", reprinted in Lycan 1990, and 1983, *From Folk Psychology to Cognitive Science*, excerpts of which are in Lycan 1990; Fodor's "Methodological Solipsism", in his *Representations* (1981a). Kitcher 1985, "Narrow Taxonomy and Wide Functionalism", and Burge 1986, "Individualism and Psychology", are excellent criticisms of the idea that the explanation of behavior should be narrow. They, along with Fodor's paper, are reprinted in Boyd, Gasper, and Trout 1991, *The Philosophy of Science*. See also, Horgan and Woodward 1985, "Folk Psychology is Here to Stay", reprinted in Lycan 1990. For a nice discussion, see Lycan 1984, *Logical Form in Natural Language*: 235–48; Fodor 1985b, "Fodor's Guide to Mental Representations". For criticisms of two-factor theories, see Pettit and McDowell 1986, *Subject, Thought and Content*.

Fodor has recently cooled on narrow meaning: see *The Elm and the Expert* (1994). His earlier view was complicated, involving both the idea that psychology should be narrow and an enthusiasm for the wide explanations of folk psychology; see, for example, his 1987, *Psychosemantics* and 1991b, "A Modal Argument for Narrow Content". For a fairly similar view, see Pylyshyn 1980, "Computation and Cognition", later expanded into Pylyshyn 1984.

See Godfrey-Smith 1996, *Complexity and the Function of Mind in Nature*, ch. 6 for the evolutionary case for representationalism.

For our views on these matters, see Sterelny 1990, *The Representational Theory of Mind*, ch. 5; Devitt 1996, *Coming to Our Senses*, chs. 4 and 5. (The latter argues that the representational meaning that the present work assigns to a token expression is one of *several* such meanings that the token has.)

9.5

Kripke's discussion is in *Wittgenstein on Rules and Private Language* (1982). Boghossian 1989, "The Rule-Following Considerations", is a very helpful "state of the art" paper surveying many responses to Kripke up to that point, including Blackburn 1984, "The Individual Strikes Back", Wright 1984, "Kripke's Account of the Argument against Private Language", and McGinn 1984, *Wittgenstein on Meaning*. Wilson 1994, "Kripke on Wittgenstein and Normativity", is a careful account of the difference between the negative position of Kripke's skeptic and the positive position of Kripke's Wittgenstein.

Fodor 1990a, *A Theory of Content*, and Rey 1997, *Contemporary Philosophy of Mind*, contain scattered discussions that have influenced our view. For a teleological response, see Millikan's "Truth Rules, Hoverflies, and the Kripke–Wittgenstein Paradox" in her 1993. Soames 1998a, "Skepticism about Meaning: Indeterminacy, Normativity, and the Rule-Following Paradox", nicely demonstrates the skeptic's implicit demand for *apriority*. His 1998b, "Facts, Truth Conditions, and the Skeptical Solution to the Rule-Following Paradox", is a helpful discussion of much of the key literature. Zalabardo 1997, "Kripke's Normativity Argument", is a helpful recent article.**

10

Linguistic Relativity

10.1 Introduction

Our Part II interest in the meanings of linguistic tokens led to an interest in truth conditions. Our explanation of truth conditions is in terms of structure and reference. Our explanation of those has led, particularly in this Part (ch. 7), to an interest in thoughts. For thoughts play crucial roles in the causal history of sentence tokens.

Thought is linguistic in form. This thesis opens up various relativistic possibilities. If your thought is tied to the *specific* language you speak, and if languages differ in important ways then your thought might be deeply mysterious to the speaker of another language. There are many who argue in this way. Where Chomsky is impressed with similarities between languages (8.10), they are struck by differences. For them, a language is not a neutral medium of communication and thought; it is not a form into which any content might be poured. Rather, they suppose that to speak a particular language is to adopt a parochial conception of reality.

This sort of relativism has been very popular in recent years. We shall consider it in this chapter. We leave until later (chs. 12–13) a consideration of the related, but much more radical, sort of relativism which holds that *reality itself*, not just thought about it, is relative to language. We start with the ur-spokesman of linguistic relativity, Benjamin Lee Whorf, with occasional references to his teacher, Edward Sapir.

We can summarize Whorf's thesis as the conjunction of the following claims:

1. All thinking is "in a language – in English, in Sanskrit, in Chinese" (1956: 252).
2. Each language structures a view of reality.
3. The views of reality structured by languages, or at least by families of languages, differ.

There is certainly *something* to be said for these claims, but nothing to warrant the air of excitement and significance, even mystery, with which Whorf surrounds them. We have already discoursed at length on item 1. We set aside the question of whether a person's language of thought is (largely) her public language but argued that the two languages are surely closely related (7.3, 7.5). Items 2 and 3 are vague. In general, the more excitingly they are interpreted, the less plausible they become. There is no interpretation of Whorf that is both plausible and exciting.

Sometimes Whorf writes as if language simply *influences* the views we come to have. Language is "the shaper of ideas, the program and guide for the individual's mental activity" (p. 212); it *imposes* on experience (Sapir 1931: 128). As a result of this influence or imposition, differences between languages lead to "incommensurable" (p. 128) world views: views that are "widely divergent" (Whorf 1956: 247) or "mutually unintelligible" (p. 246). At other times he suggests the stronger claim that a language *forces* people to think in certain ways and *constrains* their world view; it has "unbreakable bonds" (p. 256), a "tyrannical hold" (Sapir 1931: 128), which prevent them from having certain thoughts (Whorf 1956: 213–14). Differences between languages lead to *insurmountable* incommensurability. What is to be said for these views?

The question divides in two. The first concerns the influence/constraint of *vocabulary*; the second, that of *syntax*. The first is easier to discuss, but the second seems to be what Whorf has chiefly in mind. We shall consider the first in the next section, the second in 10.3.

10.2   The Tyranny of Vocabulary

Clearly the *vocabulary* a language provides does influence thought. It is much more difficult to coin concepts than to use ones already available. And language makes many concepts available. Consider thoughts about unobservables; for example, about genes. It is very hard to have thoughts about genes unless one has been introduced to the word 'gene' (or a translation of that word). Darwin's own writing on evolution and inheritance is confused in places precisely because he lacked this concept. But it is not impossible to have the thoughts without the word. If Mendel had not had thoughts about genes without benefit of the word 'gene', the convention of using that word to refer to genes would never have been created. So the absence of a word does not prevent or constrain, in any strong sense, thought about unobservables. Even less does it constrain thought about observables. Captain Cook had thoughts about kangaroos without having any word for them simply on the strength of observing them. So also, perhaps, does a dog have thoughts about bones.

In effect, this issue of the relation between word and concept has already been discussed in our consideration of Grice (7.5–7.6). There was a respect in which the existence of a public word with a certain conventional meaning was dependent on the existence of a *mental* word with that meaning and a respect in which the reverse was the case. And a mental word is a concept. We could sum up these dependencies as follows: in certain circumstances, the existence of a concept in some people creates the convention for a word; this convention explains the existence of the concept in many others.

This view acknowledges the influence of language on thought while giving ultimate priority to thought. And language does not prevent thought at all.

Whorf does write sometimes as if language constrains and prevents thought. If it did it would lead to an incommensurability between linguistic communities that was insurmountable. How *could* language be that influential? It seems that it would have to be *prior* to thought. But if it were, there could be no plausible explanation of the origin of language. How could the Chinese have come to have their particular linguistic conventions? It would be as if their language sprang miraculously out of nothing. The plausible view is that our distant ancestors were, like other higher animals, thinkers but not talkers; talking evolved from thinking.

So we reject prevention or constraint but accept lesser forms of linguistic influence. Let us explore the extent of that influence.

It helps to avoid exaggerating the influence to note how different are the views that can be expressed in the one language. Language provides us with conceptual resources, but it does not determine how those resources are to be used. The word 'Earth' helps us to think about the Earth but it does not tell us whether it is flat. Once we have words like 'god' and 'sacred' we can think religious thoughts, but we can still end up atheists. The radically different philosophies of Descartes and Derrida were both written in French.

Consider next the effect on thought of the differences between languages. The number of Eskimo words for snow is legendary, and the legend suggests that the contemporary Eskimo thinks thoughts about snow that the typical English speaker does not. Sadly for this example, the legend is apparently merely a legend (Pinker 1994: 64–5). But even if the Eskimo are less vocabulary-enriched with respect to snow than legend has it, the point surely survives. Every specialist group with their own technical vocabulary illustrates both the point and its limitations. Wine tasters, chess and bridge masters can all think certain thoughts more easily than the rest of us. But while this is a sign of the influence of language it does not show prevention or constraint. And very often there will not even be any incommensurability. Thus, very likely, all Eskimo words for snow can be translated into English. Of course, each Eskimo word is likely to require a complex English phrase, thus discouraging thought. But discouragement is one thing, prevention another.

The ultimate explanation of this difference in thought between the Eskimoes and the English is obvious enough and has nothing to do with language: they live in different natural environments. It is that difference that accounts for *both* the difference in language and the difference in thought. In some other cases the key difference is in socio-economic conditions or religious beliefs; a popular example of such a difference is in the kinship relation. As we move from community to community, natural and social conditions change and so does thought and language. There is nothing surprising nor mysterious about this and certainly no basis for imbuing language with any deep power over thought.

Even where there are differences between languages that defy translation, there may not be differences in thought. Consider the difference between the English and the Dani, a New Guinea people, over color words. The English have eleven basic color words whereas the Dani have only two, 'mili' for dark, cold hues and 'mola' for bright, warm hues. Yet various experiments have failed to produce any evidence that the Dani think about or perceive colors differently from the English.

Despite this, there are surely some differences between languages that defy translation and do accompany radical differences in thought. These are cases of genuine incommensurability. The language of Plato could not express the ideas of quantum physics and nobody who spoke it had any such ideas. These absences from Classical Greek strongly influenced the thought of Plato and his contemporaries. However, the case also provides striking evidence of the influence of thought on language. We have the language of quantum physics because some scientists thought up quantum physics and passed on the benefits to others. Plato did not have the language because those scientists did not have their thoughts until two millennia after his death.

We have mentioned one way for a community to gain a concept and a word that expresses it: some people think up the concept and establish the convention of using the word for it. Another way is common and easier:

borrow the concept and word from another community. A person comes across aliens using a word he cannot translate. He masters the use of the word and adopts it, thus introducing the concept into his community. The English-speaking community has always been very receptive to adoptions; think of 'kosher' and 'kowtow', for example.

In sum, we reject entirely the idea that vocabulary forces or prevents thought. Hence we reject the idea of linguistic differences leading to an insurmountable incommensurability. Ultimately, thought is prior to vocabulary. However, vocabulary does influence, perhaps even impose on, thought. Weak influence, involving no incommensurability (as in the Eskimo case), is doubtless quite common. Even where the influence does involve incommensurability, and so is strong (as in the Plato case), the conceptual differences can be readily removed by modifying the vocabulary.

10.3   The Tyranny of Syntax

It seems that Whorf is more impressed with the way syntax structures a view of reality than with the way vocabulary does. The role of syntax is much more difficult to discuss than that of vocabulary. The problem is that we lack clear and convincing examples of significant syntactic differences between languages.

To avoid exaggerating the influence of vocabulary, we indicated the range of views expressible within the one vocabulary. The same point applies to syntax. It is possible to express fundamentally different conceptions of reality in the one syntax. Our picture of the world, and of our place in it, has changed enormously in the last few thousand years. We have gone from the primeval animist conception, regarding the forces of nature as agents, to the Aristotelian purpose-governed picture; from there to Newton's mechanical picture; finally, to contemporary physics. These fundamentally different views can all be expressed in English. The syntax of English pushes us neither towards seeing the wind as an agent, as a being with desires or plans, nor as a vast cloud of particles whose aggregate movement is a vector of many physical forces. Qua English speakers, we could believe any of these alternatives, or many others. Of course, it is possible that these world views are brothers under the skin compared to some radical alternative inexpressible in English, but we need powerful reasons for thinking so.

It is going to be impossible to produce such reasons if all languages are, at bottom, syntactically similar, as Chomsky thinks (8.10). For if they are similar, we must lack any way of *expressing* that radical alternative! What we need in the first place, therefore, is evidence that languages are syntactically different in a way that influences or constrains world views.

Whorf has several suggestions about the syntactic differences between "Standard Average European" (SAE) languages like English and American Indian languages like Hopi. These are mostly brief and obscure. We shall consider his main suggestion, which concerns *time*

Whorf argues that SAE languages thrust a certain conception of time on us. We see it

> as a smooth flowing continuum in which everything in the universe proceeds at an equal rate, out of a future, through a present, into a past; or, in which, to reverse the picture, the observer is being carried in the stream of duration continuously away from a past and into a future. (1956: 57)

Whorf's key point is that SAE languages make us see time as an objective quantifiable kind of stuff like space. We *reify* time. How does language work this trick?

(i) We quantify time in exactly the same way that we quantify physical aggregates: 'ten days' has exactly the same linguistic form as 'ten men'.

(ii) Most crucially, our tense/aspect system has a tripartite distinction of past/present/future which encourages this view of time.

(iii) Metaphor is spatialized and reified. Thus Whorf writes:

> all languages need to express durations, intensities, and tendencies. It is characteristic of SAE . . . to express them metaphorically. The metaphors are those of spatial extension, i.e. of size, number (plurality), position, shape, and motion. We express duration by 'long, short, great, much, quick, slow', etc.; intensity by 'large, great, much, heavy, light, high, low, sharp, faint', etc.; tendency by 'more, increase, grow . . . '; and so on through an almost inexhaustible list of metaphors that we hardly recognize as such, since they are virtually the only linguistic media available.
> It is clear how this condition "fits in". It is part of our whole scheme of OBJECTIFYING – imaginatively spatializing qualities and potentials that are quite nonspatial . . . (1956: 145)

According to Whorf, things are different in Hopi. In that language, physical and temporal aggregates have distinct linguistic structures. Metaphors for duration, intensity, and tendency are not spatial. Most importantly, their tense/aspect system does not map onto our past/present/future dichotomy. Whorf claims that their "tense" markers are validity forms; they have *epistemic* interpretations. One form indicates *direct report*: it applies roughly to occasions in which we use simple past or present. Another indicates *expectation*: it is roughly equivalent to our future, though it can be used to describe an event distant from but simultaneous with the utterance. Finally, there is a *nomic* form: it is roughly equivalent to the English generic present, as in 'A man lives and dies in sin'. In addition, there are temporal conjunctions. These link clauses and translate approximately as 'earlier than' and 'later than'.

Whorf is suggesting that SAE influences/constrains us to one conception of time, Hopi influences/constrains the Hopi to another. It is "gratuitous" (p. 57) to attribute our concept of time to them.

There are serious problems with this line of thought. First, his gloss on the Hopi language is controversial (Lenneberg 1953). However, let us suppose, for the sake of argument, that he is near enough right about the differences between SAE and Hopi.

Second, it is not obvious from these differences in language whether we do differ from the Hopi in our conception of time. Indeed, it is not obvious what our conception of time is, let alone what the Hopi's is. These are not matters that can be simply read off language, particularly since most talk that is directly about time seems straightforwardly metaphorical (How *could* time flow?). Whorf's own accounts of the metaphysics of the Hopi (pp. 57–64) cast more darkness than light. Further, his claim that the Hopi conception of time is operationally equivalent to ours (p. 58) – so that it is just as useful for daily life – is evidence *against* the conceptions being different. However, let us suppose again that Whorf is right and that the two conceptions are different.

Third, the supposition that we differ from the Hopi in language and thought is quite compatible with the view we have urged: that thought is ultimately prior to language. On this view the linguistic difference between Hopi and English has arisen from the conceptual difference, not vice versa. Of course once the linguistic difference exists it will influence the thought of those that come after. That is the full extent of the influence of language. There is no constraint. Indeed, the supposition that there is constraint seems absurd because it would make the origins of language miraculous.

Granting the differences between us and the Hopi, we have allowed some influence to language. How extensive might it be?

We have already seen in discussing vocabulary that the extent of influence depends on translatability. If Hopi syntax could be translated into SAE, albeit clumsily, then the influence would be slight. SAE could express the Hopi conception of time, but would not encourage its adoption. There would be no incommensurability between SAE and Hopi. The situation would be analogous to the Eskimo case.

Whorf does seem to think that Hopi cannot be translated into SAE, but his evidence for this is weak, and his own glosses on Hopi (for the most part) give it the lie. Indeed, it seems doubtful that the *syntax* of any known language prevents its translation into any other.

It is only if the Hopi syntax did defy translation into SAE that we would have incommensurability. We would be in a situation analogous to the

Plato case: a situation of strong linguistic influence (but still no constraint). However, the incommensurability might be more serious in our situation. It seems likely that it would be more difficult for us to learn the Hopi's conception of time than it would be for Plato to learn our quantum conceptions. But, as we have said, we lack any persuasive reason for supposing that Hopi syntax is untranslatable.

We have been supposing, for the sake of argument, that languages do differ significantly in their syntax. Yet that is just what Chomsky and his followers deny. They think that there is a rich set of "linguistic universals" common to all languages (8.10). Further, they argue that the tense-aspect system – the syntactic feature most emphasized by Whorf – is part of the surface structure. The tense markings on verbs are determined by relatively superficial transformation rules, together with the morphology of the language. The tense-aspect system is not, therefore, one of the structural fixtures of the language. If this is right, the underlying form of the auxiliary verb system will be similar across languages. So, linguistic influences on conceptions of time are likely to be fairly trivial.

In sum, syntax no more forces or prevents thought than did vocabulary. Hence syntax gives rise to no insurmountable incommensurability. Indeed it is doubtful that it gives rise to any incommensurability at all. If Chomsky is right there are unlikely to be metaphysically significant syntactic differences between languages; the influence of syntax on thought is trivial. Even if there are significant differences between languages, the determining influence is from world view to syntax, not vice versa.

Whorf's remarks are interesting and suggestive, but the argument for an important linguistic relativity evaporates under scrutiny. The only respect in which language clearly and obviously does influence thought turns out to be rather banal: language provides each of us with most of our concepts.

In their exaggeration of the influence of language over thought, and their consequent relativism, Sapir and Whorf exemplify important parts of structuralist thinking, as we shall see (13.3–13.4).

10.4   The Scientific Whorfians

Whorf argued that linguistic communities can be opaque to each other. In the last 30 years or so some philosophers of science, led by Thomas Kuhn and Paul Feyerabend, have argued that scientific communities can be so also. They claim that the languages of different theories in the one area are not inter-translatable and hence the theories are "incommensurable". This claim is part of a radical critique of orthodox views about science.

Twentieth-century orthodoxy has two sources: the logical positivists, and Karl Popper and his followers. As a result it is not homogeneous. The positivists hold an accumulationist and evolutionary view of science. Science consists in a steady accumulation of data punctuated at intervals by its theoretical reorganization as theories become more general and precise. Thus, Newton made Kepler's laws of planetary motion more general (Newton's applied to other celestial and all terrestrial objects) and more precise. Popper disputes this picture: theory change is not an elaboration but a replacement; it is a revolution rather than a reform.

Nonetheless, underlying this disagreement are many common threads. In particular, both groups took science to have a common language. That language is the language of *observation*. However much theories may differ from one another, they share a language in which reports of experiment and observation can be given. This common language has great epistemic and semantic significance for the orthodox.

This language is epistemically prior to theoretical language in that statements in it – observation statements – settle the fate of theories. Popper emphasized the role of these statements in falsifying theories. The positivists emphasized their role in confirming theories. In both cases, observation rules.

This language is also semantically prior, for the positivists at least. It was held that ultimately the meaning of the special theoretical language of a science depends on the meaning of the observation language shared by all science. Much ink was spilt attempting to explain this dependence.

Kuhn and Feyerabend and the other radicals reject the whole orthodox picture. We shall be concerned only with their Whorfian rejection of the commensurability of theories.

First, they deny the existence of any common scientific language that is neutral between all competing theories. When the theories are comprehensive ones within an area – what Kuhn calls *paradigms* – there is no way of translating the language of one theory into the language of another. This failure of translation stretches even to the observational consequences of the theories; the theories do not share a neutral observation language.

Many of the most important episodes in the history of science are clashes between relatively comprehensive theories: Ptolemaic versus Copernican astronomy; Newtonian versus relativistic physics; special creation versus Darwinian views of life. In such situations, according to the radicals, the competitors cannot be compared. Each theory is a complex intellectual structure which creates its own language; the meaning of a term is determined by its place in that structure. Consider, for example, the term 'species'. In Darwinian biology, species are conceived of as changing and evolving, with characteristics that are the relatively accidental product of selection and chance. In creationism, species are fixed and immutable, created for some purpose from a template in the mind of God. These different conceptions result in different meanings for 'species'. Even when a term in one theory is of the same physical type as one in another, it is of a different semantic type (4.2); it expresses a different "concept".

Second, as a result of this lack of shared concepts, the radicals think that comprehensive theories cannot be compared in the ways dear to the heart of the orthodox. Because there are no shared concepts there can be no logical relations between the theories. So the idea of one theory being reduced to, or included in, another must go: it requires that the statements of one theory entail the statements of another. That requires a common language, which is precisely what is lacking here. Worse still, there can be no question of one theory refuting another. That requires that statements be inconsistent, which again requires a common language. Theories become as different as chalk and cheese.

This incommensurability thesis has drastic consequences for the picture of science. Science is not a steady accumulation of knowledge. It is not the replacement of one theory by another that refutes it, but nevertheless takes over many of its findings. Rather, science is a succession of incommensurable theories. The whole idea of progress in science becomes problematic.

10.5   The Rejection of Scientific Whorfianism

The incommensurability thesis talks of meaning, a very broad notion. The first point to make in assessing the thesis is that the comparison of theories does not require that terms share meanings; it is sufficient that they share *referents*. Thus, to take a simple example, we can compare the "theories", 'the evening star is closer than the Earth to the Sun' and 'the morning star is not closer than the Earth to the Sun', even though the terms, 'the evening star' and 'the morning star', differ in meaning. We can do so because the terms are coreferential. Given this fact, we can see that the two theories cannot both be true; one refutes the other. So we can set aside talk of meaning and concentrate on reference.

It is clear that Kuhn and Feyerabend think that incommensurability survives this point. For, they think that theory change involves reference change, not just meaning change. Indeed, they seem to think that *reality itself* changes when theories change. We are setting that sort of view aside until the next Part of the book (12.3, particularly). Meanwhile, we shall adopt a robust realism and assume that view of reality false. In so doing, it is only fair to add, we are seriously undermining the plausibility of the incommensurability thesis. With reality "fixed", it turns out that there is only a little to be said for a radical view of reference change; for a view that undermines theory comparison.

1) Some terms in discarded theories that were once thought to refer are now thought to be empty. 'Witch', 'phlogiston', and the 'humours' of the blood are cases in point. Yet these are not cases of reference change. There never were witches, phlogiston and humours and so the terms in question never did refer. What has changed is not their reference but our view of their reference. And this change poses no problem for theory comparison. From our theoretical perspective, these discarded theories are thoroughly misguided. Statements in such a theory implying the existence of, say, witches, are perfectly intelligible – we still have the word 'witch'; they are just plain false.

2) Sometimes there really are cases of reference change. A theory takes over a term from an old theory and uses it in a new way. We are told that this happened to the term 'atom' in the nineteenth century. However, the reference change need not be problematic for theory comparison. Suppose, first, that from the perspective of the new theory, the term in its old use referred (which was the case with 'atom'); from the new perspective, the entities referred to by the old use are still thought to exist. So there is no problem comparing what the two theories say about those entities. Suppose, next, that from the new perspective the term in its old use does not refer; there has been a change in view about what exists. Provided the past theory is dismissed as thoroughly misguided, there is again no trouble with theory comparison. It would be as if physicists called some newly discovered fundamental particles "witches".

3) There is one genuinely problematic sort of reference change. It is one where, from the new perspective, a term in its old use does not refer *and yet the old theory is not dismissed as thoroughly misguided*. Consider the change from classical physics to relativistic physics. Terms like 'mass', 'force', and 'gravitation' were taken over by Einstein from Newton and given a new reference. Further, from the relativistic perspective, those terms in their classical use lack reference altogether. The problem is that we do not dismiss classical physics the way we dismiss the theory of witches. We see that physics as more or less true, within certain limits, and give or take an error or two. Though Einstein made a major advance, we think of him as having retained much of Newton. This is seen as a typical example of accumulation in science. But how can it be, since the crucial terms in Newton's theory fail to refer?

So Kuhn and Feyerabend have raised a problem. We think that the problem is not beyond solution, though the solution is technical. The key idea is to replace reference and truth in our semantic theory with *partial reference* and *partial truth* (4.3, 5.2). The contrast between classical physics and the theory of witches can then be brought out as follows: the terms in the former, unlike those in the latter, partially refer; as a result the former theory, unlike the latter, is partially true.

We agree that there is a problem of reference change but think it arises rarely. Kuhn and Feyerabend, in contrast, think it utterly pervasive. In a really revolutionary change like that to relativistic physics, *all* terms are affected. Not even terms like 'flask', 'ruler', and 'pointer', referring to the paraphernalia of the laboratory, are exempt. Why do they exaggerate in this way?

The answer is that they subscribe to versions of the description theory of reference. On that theory, if we change the descriptions associated with a term we are likely (barring accidental coreference) to change its reference, for the term applies to whatever is picked out by those associated descriptions. In a radical theory change, our whole view of the world changes. Different descriptions are associated with all the terms taken over from the old theory. This is true even of the observational terms. The result is wholesale reference change.

We have, in effect, already given our response to this. The description theories of reference that Kuhn and Feyerabend rely on are false. Indeed, the implausibility of the view that references of words like 'pointer' change with the move from Newton to Einstein, is an extra reason for rejecting those theories of reference. We allow that there may be a place for description theories of some sort for some terms (5.4–5.5). But reference is ultimately determined by causal links to reality that are, unlike associated descriptions, importantly independent of theory. As a result, the terms of a false theory can still refer. Without a description theory there is no plausibility to the view that theory change leads to wholesale reference change.

There is a deeper reason for the exaggeration by Kuhn and Feyerabend. They do not approach the problem of reference change with a firm view of the reality to which reference is to be made. Rather they allow their preconceptions about reference to form their views of reality. We shall have much to say about this mistake, and about the realism that underlies our response to the incommensurability thesis, in the next Part.

Suggested Reading

10.1–10.3

For Whorf's views see *Language, Thought, and Reality* (1956), particularly, "An American Indian Model of the Universe", "The Relation of Habitual Thought and Behaviour to Language", and "Science and Linguistics". His most famous paper is "Language, Mind, and Reality", but it bears more on the concerns of chapter 12.

McCormack and Wurm 1977, *Language and Thought*, Part II, is a useful anthology of some of the Sapir–Whorf material. Hook 1969, *Language annd Philosophy*, Part I, consists of essays on Whorf.

See Fishman 1960, "A Systematization of the Whorfian Analysis", for a sympathetic overview of Whorf. See Black's paper, "Linguistic Relativity: The Views of Benjamin Lee Whorf", in *Models and Metaphors* (1962), for a less sympathetic one.

Rosch 1977, "Linguistic Relativity", in Johnson and Laird 1977, *Thinking*, argues that the strong form of the Whorfian hypothesis is empirically untestable, and that even the weaker form lacks much empirical support. Lenneberg 1953, "Cognition in Ethnolinguistics", criticizes Whorf's handling of Hopi. Anderson 1980, *Cognitive Psychology and its Implications*, has a brief discussion of the evidence, including that about the Dani (pp. 385–6).

It turns out that the terms for plants and animals that indigenous groups coin correlate very well (though not perfectly, of course) with the terminology independently introduced by biologists. The language of indigenous Papuans does not structure, constrain, or influence the way they think about plants and animals in ways that result in an ethnobiology that is incommensurable with standard western biology. To the contrary, they agree remarkable well: Atran 1990, *Cognitive Foundations of Natural History*; Berlin 1992, *Ethnobiological Classification*. Recently, Sperber has extended this result, arguing that there is a stock of basic concepts that is expressed in similar ways in all languages: *Explaining Culture* (1996), ch. 3.

10.4

See Nagel 1961, *The Structure of Science*, for a detailed discussion of the positivist viewpoint. Suppe's introduction to *The Structure of Scientific Theories* (1977) is a good overview of positivist philosophy of science. Popper's famous work is *The Logic of Scientific Discovery* (1959), first published in German in 1934.

Kuhn's views were first set out in his very influential *The Structure of Scientific Revolutions* (1962); see particularly, chs. 10 and 12. Feyerabend's views appeared in a series of articles from 1962 on. Perhaps the most helpful is "Against Method" (1970b), later expanded into a book (1975). See also Kuhn 1970, "Reflections on my Critics", and Feyerabend 1970a, "Consolations for the Specialist", both in Lakatos and Musgrave 1970, *Criticism and the Growth of Knowledge*.

10.5

Scheffler 1967, *Science and Subjectivity*, particularly ch. 3, makes the point that reference not meaning is the crucial notion for theory comparison.

Incommensurability has generated a storm of responses. See Newton-Smith 1981, *The Rationality of Science*, chs. 5–8 for a nice survey of Kuhn, Feyerabend, and the incommensurability debate. Bishop 1991, "Why the Incommensurability Thesis is Self-Defeating", Hoyningen-Huene 1993, *Reconstructing Scientific Revolutions*, and Sankey 1994, *The Incommensurability Thesis* are more recent responses. Horwich 1993, *World Changes*, is an interesting collection of papers inspired by Kuhn with "Afterwords" by Kuhn.

Devitt 1979, "Against Incommensurability", criticizes the incommensurability thesis. Devitt 1997, *Realism and Truth*, ch. 9, includes these criticisms within a critique that is relevant to chapter 12 below.

Part IV

Language and Realism

11

Verificationism

11.1 Realism

It is hard to talk about language without talking about the world. We have made no such attempt: this book is replete with claims about sentient life and its place in an impersonal world. A theory of language is bound to be influenced by a theory of the extra-linguistic world. Should a theory of that world be influenced by a theory of language? One would think not. Language, after all, is a local phenomenon, probably confined to humans. It is hard to see why our ideas of the stars, of biochemistry and geology, should be influenced by our ideas of language.

Surprisingly, current orthodoxy goes against this obvious thought. The literature is full of arguments seeking to illuminate the structure of the world on the basis of considerations about language. We think that these arguments are wrong-headed. In this Part of the book we aim to analyze and rebut some representative samples.

The main target of these arguments has been *realism* about the external world. This is a metaphysical doctrine with two dimensions. First it is a doctrine about what exists, and second it is doctrine about the nature of that existence. Concerning the first, it holds that such physical entities as stones, trees and cats – exist ("are real"). Concerning the second, these entities do not depend for their existence or nature on our minds, nor on our awareness, perception or thought about them. Realists thus speak of these entities as being "independent" of and "external" to the mind. They say that an entity exists "objectively" in that its existence does not depend on anyone's opinion; nor does it arise from the imposition of our concepts or theories. Universal disbelief in the existence of stones does not lead to stonelessness. Neither do theories that make no mention of stones. Nor would stones cease to exist if we had no word or concept for stones. The world would not be stoneless if, say, in our thoughts and language we made no distinction between naturally occurring hard middle-size accretions of minerals (stones) and artificial ones; bricks, concrete slabs, and the like.

It is important to note that realism's independence dimension does not deny certain familiar causal relations between our minds and the physical world: we sometimes throw stones, plant trees, kick cats, and so on. But what realism does deny is that thinking or saying that the physical world is so makes it so.

Realism has traditionally been opposed by idealism. Idealists typically did not reject the first dimension of realism; they did not deny the existence of the ordinary furniture of our environment (Hume was one notable exception). What they typically rejected was the second dimension: mind independence. An example of this is captured in Berkeley's famous slogan: "*esse est percipi*", "to be is to be perceived".

The realism we are interested in should be distinguished from another called "scientific realism". That doctrine is concerned with the *unobservable* entities posited by science – such entities as electrons, muons, and curved space-time. Our realism is concerned with *observable* entities, particularly those of common sense, but also those of science (e.g. the moons of Jupiter). So, perhaps our doctrine would be more aptly called "commonsense realism". The two doctrines have obvious affinities, but they are independent: it is possible to hold either without the other. One might accept commonsense realism but reject scientific realism on the ground that unless we can observe an entity we can have no strong reason for supposing that it exists. A scientific realist might reject commonsense realism on the ground that science shows that our folk view of the world is hopelessly wrong and that nothing exists but swarms of quarks and gluons. In general, however, the two doctrines tend to go together.

Realism about the ordinary observable physical world is a compelling doctrine. It is almost universally held outside intellectual circles. Indeed, it is regarded as too obvious to be worth stating. Yet within philosophy the doctrine has enjoyed little popularity. Anti-realism is an occupational hazard of philosophy.

Traditional philosophical arguments against realism start from a thesis in epistemology: from an assumption about the nature of knowledge. In one way or another it was then argued that we could have knowledge only if we gave up realism. For knowledge to be possible, "the gap" between the object known and the knowing mind must be closed; the object must, in some way, be made dependent on our way of knowing. In the twentieth century, in contrast, arguments against realism typically start from a thesis in the philosophy of language. For reference to be possible, "the gap" between the object referred to and the referring mind must be closed; the object must, in some way, be made dependent on our way of referring, dependent on our language. With this recent change has gone another which is decidedly unwelcome: the anti-realist nature of conclusions is often only implicit and is nearly always shrouded in mystery. Attention has centered so heavily on language that the metaphysical issue has tended to disappear; or to be redefined in linguistic terms; or, worst of all, to be confused with linguistic issues. In general, the philosophy of language has become too big for its boots (1.1).

In this chapter we shall discuss two examples of anti-realist positions stemming from *verificationist* views of language.

11.2 Logical Positivism and the Elimination of the Realism Dispute

Logical positivism began in central Europe in the early twenties with the forming of a group known as "the Vienna Circle". Membership was not limited to philosophers, but included scientists and mathematicians. The members were all scientifically minded people who were shocked by what was happening in philosophy, particularly in German philosophy of that period. An example they were fond of disparaging was the following from Heidegger's *What is Metaphysics*.

> What is to be investigated is being only and – *nothing* else; being alone and further – *nothing*; solely being, and beyond being – *nothing*. *What about this Nothing?* . . . *Does the Nothing exist only because the Not, i.e. the Negation, exists?* Or is it the other way around? *Does Negation and the Not exist only because the Nothing exists?* . . . We assert: *the Nothing is prior to the Not and Negation*. . . . Where do we seek the Nothing? How do we find the Nothing . . . We know the Nothing . . . *Anxiety reveals the Nothing.* . . . That for which and because of which we were anxious, was "really" – nothing. Indeed: the Nothing itself – as such – was present . . . *What about this Nothing? – The Nothing itself nothings.* (quoted in Carnap 1932: 69)

The positivists felt that such philosophical talk was literally meaningless and they sought a way to show this.

They found their way in the *Verifiability Principle*: at its simplest, "Meaning is method of verification". A corollary is that if a sentence has no method of verification – if it does not have associated with it a *way of telling* whether it is true or not – then it is meaningless. With this weapon, the positivists hoped to *eliminate* metaphysics.

One metaphysical dispute that had to go, according to the positivists, was that between realists and idealists. Whether there was a reality external to the mind, as the realists claim, or whether all reality is made up of "ideas", "sense data", or "appearances", as idealists claim, is a "meaningless pseudo-problem" (Schlick 1932–3: 86). For, both parties to the dispute agree on the "empirical evidence" (Ayer 1940: 16) – the "given" (Schlick: 83). The given is what verifies statements and hence is all that can provide meanings. Agreement on the given leaves nothing substantive to disagree on. All there is to the dispute between realists and idealists is a pragmatic dispute "about the choice of two different languages" (Ayer: 18): whether to choose a material-thing language defined in terms of the given or a sense-datum language defined in terms of the given. There is no fact of the matter about one choice or other being right.

The positivists dismissed metaphysical issues and replaced them with linguistic ones. The philosophical task was to analyze what statements mean, in terms of the given, and thus prepare them for testing. The move from metaphysics to language was known as the "linguistic turn" in philosophy.

The Verifiability Principle ran into massive problems and has long since been abandoned. In particular, it proved impossible to frame it in a moderate enough form to save much of our cherished knowledge; the weapon eliminated not only German metaphysics, but just about everything else as well. Further, it cast doubt on its own status. How was *it* to be verified?

Our whole approach to language is at odds with the Principle, as we shall bring out later (11.4). In this section, we shall consider another matter. Suppose the Principle were true. Would the positivists then have succeeded in eliminating metaphysics? They would not.

On the basis of the Principle, the positivists claim that there is no substantive question about whether there are material things, sense data, and so on. It is all just a matter of choosing a convention for language. This choice does not concern a matter of fact; it is simply pragmatic. What then are the matters of fact that the realists and idealists agree on? The answer is clear: those that concern the given. For it is the given alone that verifies any true statement. The given is what stops us saying *absolutely anything* in our theories: it is the reality we must accurately describe. In fact, all statements, insofar as they have meaning, are translatable into statements about the given. When the chips are down, the positivist must talk only of the given.

So, at the same time that the positivists are rejecting the metaphysical dispute about the nature of reality, they are making a strong metaphysical assumption about reality: it consists only of the given. What exactly *is* the given? The positivists find it very hard to say. However, a certain view of it always comes through in their writings: it is *the indubitable content of experience.* In other words, the given is indistinguishable from the ideas and sense data of traditional idealists. The positivists are closet anti-realists. Despite their disavowals, they are committed to a powerful and, we claim, thoroughly false metaphysics.

One cannot theorize about anything, least of all language, without implicit commitment to a view of the world. As a result, attempts to eliminate metaphysics lead not to its elimination but to its mystification; the philosopher has to hide or deny his own metaphysical assumptions. The problem is not metaphysics but bad metaphysics: claims about the nature of the world that are obscurantists, at odds with science, that are defended *a priori.*

11.3   Dummett and the Misidentification of the Realism Dispute

Though the Verifiability Principle of the positivists has been abandoned, verificationism has recently been reborn under the influence of the Oxford philosopher, Michael Dummett. We have seen that the positivists used verificationism in an attempt to *replace* the metaphysical issue of realism with an issue about language. Dummett attempts to *identify* realism with such an issue and then use verificationism to show that realism is false.

Dummett's discussion of realism is voluminous, repetitive, and difficult. It is aimed not only at the realism that concerns us – realism about commonsense physical entities like stones, trees, and cats – but also at realism about scientific entities, about mathematical entities, about the past, and so on. He identifies each realism dispute with a dispute about the *truth conditions* of the relevant set of statements. In the present case, these would be commonsense physical statements containing words like 'stone', 'tree' and 'cat'. So his argument begins with the following premise:

(I) The commonsense realism dispute is the dispute about whether these statements have realist or only verificationist truth conditions.

Dummett goes on to argue that the statements have only verificationist truth conditions, and so realism is false.

"Realist" truth conditions involve a "realist" notion of truth. A notion of truth is realist, for Dummett, if it does not make the truth of a statement dependent on the *evidence* we have or might have for the statement. So a statement could be true even though we had no effective way of *telling* whether it was. Truth can "transcend the evidence" for it. Clearly the notion of truth that we have been using to explain meaning is a realist one: it is explained in terms of reference and structure without any mention of the evidence for truth. In contrast, a notion of truth is verificationist if it takes a statement to be true only if it is, or could be, *established* to be true.

The distinction is brought out nicely by one of Dummett's favorite examples: the person who died without ever having been put in danger. Consider the following statement about that person:

The person was brave.

Is it true or false? If the statement has only verificationist truth conditions, this question amounts to: Can we discover whether it is true or false? Very likely we cannot discover any information about this person that is relevant to the statement. In which case, the statement is neither true nor false. On the other hand, if the statement has realist truth conditions, its truth or falsity transcends this evidential matter. There was something about that person, whether we can discover it or not, that makes the statement true or false.

The idea that truth conditions are verificationist is clearly a relative of the discarded Verifiability Principle. Oversimplifying, if meaning is truth conditions and truth conditions are verificationist, then meaning is method of verification.

Set aside the rest of Dummett's argument until the next section and consider premise (I). Dummett identifies the realism dispute with one in semantics. Moreover, that identification is neither covert nor abashed: Dummett thinks it is his main contribution.

> The whole point of my approach to [the various disputes concerning realism] has been to show that the theory of meaning underlies metaphysics. If I have made any worthwhile contribution to philosophy, I think it must lie in having raised this issue in these terms. (1978: xl)

Dummett is an enthusiast for the linguistic turn (11.2).

We could summarize our description of realism in section 11.1 as follows:

Commonsense physical entities objectively exist independently of the mental.

This says nothing about language at all: it contains no semantic or grammatical term like 'mean', 'true', or 'noun'; it says nothing about linguistic items like sentences or words. It is a doctrine about what there is and what it is like. It is about the largely impersonal and inanimate world. In contrast, a theory of language has its place within a theory of people. (Of course realism is stated *in* language. *How else* could it be stated?! But it is not *about* language. Using language is one thing, mentioning it another; 2.7.)

Given that the doctrine we have called "realism" seems to have nothing to do with language, it is appropriate to wonder whether Dummett is using the term 'realism' in some other way. If so, our disagreement with him would be only verbal. However, it is clear that Dummett sees himself as reinterpreting and rejecting the traditional metaphysical doctrine of realism.

What licenses this reinterpretation? On Dummett's view, a metaphysical thesis by itself is only a metaphor or picture. Such a thesis is only "a picture which has in itself no substance otherwise than as a representation of the given conception of meaning" (1977: 383).

A metaphor has to be made literal if it is to be more than suggestive. Dummett's view, very much in the spirit of positivism, is that a metaphysical metaphor can be cashed only by a theory of meaning. Central to his identification of realism with a semantic thesis is his view that *without* that identification, realism has no genuine content, however irresistible an image it might present.

We think that this "metaphor thesis" should be rejected and that premise (I) is false.

To start with, note that the metaphor thesis could only seem plausible if one *already* thought that metaphysical views were special in some way. Doubtless this thought is encouraged by the allegedly a priori nature of metaphysics, and by Heideggerian excesses. From our naturalistic perspective (1.3), metaphysics is empirical and not special.

Nobody should think that the theory that there are stones is just a metaphor; nor the theory that there are trees; nor the theory that there are cats. The existence dimension of realism is just a generalization of such theories and so is not the least bit metaphorical. It is harder to keep a metaphorical element out of the independence dimension. Anti-realist characterizations of the alleged dependence of objects on the knowing mind – the attempts to close "the gap" – often strike us as metaphorical, as will become apparent in the next two chapters. However, removing these metaphorical elements does not reduce the realism dispute to one about meaning; it remains a metaphysical dispute about the nature of reality.

Nor are Dummett's reasons for the metaphor thesis compelling. They rest on an analogy with a dispute in the philosophy of mathematics. In that discipline there has been disagreement over mathematical entities. Some philosophers have denied that there are any such entities; this is the mathematical analogue of denying the existence dimension of our realism about the external world. However, if the existence of mathematical entities is accepted, then the dispute becomes analogous to one over our independence dimension. Given that there are numbers, what are they like? Do they exist independently of us? Do mathematicians *discover* their properties and relations, just as a biochemist discovers the structure of a virus? Or are numbers rather our own creations? Do we construct the number system and so invent the properties of numbers rather more than discover them?

These are deeply puzzling questions. Suppose that numbers are real and independent of us. No naturalistic account of their nature has so far been successful, so the result is *platonism*: numbers are real but not physical nor even spatiotemporal at all. Thus their nature is deeply mysterious. And how could we come to know about these strange and causally isolated objects?

The alternative, known as *constructionism* or *intuitionism*, is no more appealing. If we have invented mathematics in somewhat the same way that we have invented the game of chess, it is very odd that it is so useful, indeed indispensable, in our investigation of the world.

In the face of these puzzles, Dummett proposes that we should treat the platonism/intuitionism dispute over entities as a metaphorical version of a dispute over the conditions on mathematical proofs. This turns quickly into an issue about the truth conditions of mathematical statements.

Dummett's proposal has some plausibility, but the extension of this approach beyond the mathematical dispute to commonsense realism does not. For the plausibility of Dummett's proposal in mathematics comes precisely from the *contrast* between mathematical entities and familiar physical entities. Numbers (if there are any) contrast with stones, trees, and cats in their strange non-spatiotemporal properties, their causal isolation, and their inaccessibility to experimental investigation. That is what makes the mathematical dispute seem so metaphorical.

In sum, we think that Dummett's premise (I) is false. *Prima facie*, realism is a metaphysical dispute – a dispute about the nature of reality. Dummett needs a strong argument to show that, despite appearances, it is about language. His attempt to show this by establishing the metaphorical nature of the realism dispute fails. It rests on a mistaken analogy with mathematics. It is precisely the *dis*analogy between numbers and ordinary things that makes a metaphor thesis seem plausible for the mathematical dispute.

It follows from this that whatever the strengths of the rest of Dummett's argument, that argument alone does not establish anything about realism.

11.4   Verificationism

We have argued that verificationism does not eliminate metaphysics as the positivists claim, nor does it establish anti-realism as Dummett claims. In this section we shall assess verificationism itself, and consider what relation it does have to realism.

Let us start by considering the rest of Dummett's argument. This seeks to establish that statements have only verificationist truth conditions. In its most prominent form it attempts this by arguing that these are the only sort of truth conditions that the competent speaker could *know*. Suppose that the truth conditions of a statement are: it is true if and only if certain circumstances hold. Dummett claims that the speaker could not know these truth conditions if those circumstances transcend those in which the statement could be verified. The main problem with this argument is that it presupposes that the competent speaker must know about the meanings and truth conditions of the sentences of her language, at least "implicitly" or "tacitly". We have argued against this Cartesian assumption (8.4–8.7). If we are right then Dummett's claim that the speaker could not know realist truth conditions is irrelevant to realist truth. We shall therefore say no more of this prominent form of the argument.

Despite this prominence, various factors, including the unclarity of his talk of "implicit" or "tacit" knowledge, suggest that this is not the form of argument that Dummett intends. Rather, he seems to have in mind one that takes competence as simply a practical ability not really requiring any propositional knowledge about the language. According to this form of the argument, statements can have only verificationist truth conditions because a statement that had truth conditions that transcended its conditions of verification could not be understood. For, a speaker must be able to manifest her understanding in behavior, and all she can manifest is her ability to associate the statement with the conditions that verify it. Most simply, she can show that she *recognizes* a certain situation as conclusively justifying the assertion of the statement.

The details of this argument are complicated and will not concern us. But, in summary, Dummett argues that understanding must be verificationist and so truth conditions must be also.

We indicated earlier (11.2) that verificationism is at odds with our whole approach to language. We can bring this out by moving from sentences to words. According to verificationism the competent speaker must be able verify the sentences she uses, to tell that they are true if they are true. To do this she must be able to identify what its words refer to. Consider the name 'Reagan', for example. To be able to verify a sentence like 'Reagan is wrinkled' that contains this name a person must be able to identify Reagan. How might she do that? By describing him or recognizing him in a crowd. So verificationism requires what we called "the identification theory", a broader Fregean theory of names than the description theory (3.5). So, it is no surprise that Dummett does subscribe to the identification theory. Causal theories of names were born out of the rejection of description and identification theories and are essentially anti-verificationist. *If the arguments from ignorance and error offered against description and identification theories (3.3–3.5) are correct, then verificationism is false.* A person can use a term to refer though almost entirely wrong or ignorant about its referent.

So we think that verificationism is basically implausible. However, we think that there are deeper considerations against it. These emerge from a consideration of its relation to realism.

Dummett identifies realism with realist truth. We must avoid this mistake. The issues are quite distinct. Nevertheless, they are related. We need to consider how they are related. What conclusions about truth and understanding can we draw from a position on realism? And what conclusions about realism can we draw from a position on truth and understanding? These questions give rise to another. Where should we start? Should we start with a position on realism and see what follows from that about truth and understanding, or vice versa? Those, like Dummett, who are part of the linguistic turn in philosophy, think that we should start with truth and understanding.

Suppose that Dummett were right that we should be verificationist about truth and understanding. Then this starting place might well seem to establish anti-realism (even without Dummett's mistaken identification). The verificationist position is that a statement is true if and only if it is verifiable. (By "verifiable" we mean verifiably true, not, as the positivists usually meant, verifiably true or false.) For example:

'Caesar had five moles' is true if and only if 'Caesar had five moles' is verifiable.

Now it is a relatively trivial fact about truth, captured in the *disquotation principle* (9.2), that a sentence in the form of

'Caesar had five moles' is true

is equivalent to another in the form of

Caesar had five moles.

If we are entitled to assert one of these two sentences then we are entitled to assert the other. So we can substitute the latter for the former in the earlier sentence to get:

Caesar had five moles if and only if 'Caesar had five moles' is verifiable.

This claim relates a state of the world – Caesar having five moles – very closely to our abilities. The world can *be* a certain way only if we can *verify* a certain statement. In contrast, realists think that there are indefinitely many facts about the world that could never be discovered. It is not essential to the nature of the world that we can know about it. Unless our minds are so powerful that everything we can think and talk about (and that is just about everything) we can find out about, the world could be related to our verifying abilities in the way illustrated only if it were somehow dependent on us for its existence or nature; it must be, in some way, our creation. Such a world is not the objective independent one that the realist believes in. Thus:

Verificationism → anti-realism.

The '→' here does not represent an entailment. Rather it represents an inference to the best explanation. So there is no *inconsistency* in being a verificationist and a realist. The point is that once verificationism has been accepted, the most plausible view of the world seems to be an anti-realist one.

We think that this procedure of arguing from a view of language to a view of the world is all wrong. We have garnered a theory of the extralinguistic world through arduous years of living. We think that there are stones, trees, cats, and so on: a huge impersonal universe that does not depend on us for its existence or nature; indeed, a universe often singularly impervious to us. That is, we are committed to realism. It is not a mysterious doctrine. It causes no mystical glow. It is dull and familiar. But that is not to its discredit. On the contrary, it indicates that realism is as firm a starting point as we can expect to find. Certainly it is a much firmer one than speculations in the largely unknown areas of truth and understanding. This is not to say that realism is unquestionable; perhaps our commonsense ontology is largely false. However, what is scarcely conceivable is that realism could be shown to be false by discoveries about language and understanding.

Our attitude here reflects our naturalism (1.3, 14.1). For us, a theory of language is just one empirical theory among many others of the world we live in. As such it does not compare in strength to realism, which is an overarching ontological doctrine abstracted from our most secure

244 Language and Realism

commonsense and scientific theories of physical reality. To think otherwise is to take an *a priori* view of the theory of language. Speculating
from the comfort of our armchairs, we are supposed to be able to decide
what truth and understanding *must* be like, and hence what the world
must be like, without concerning ourselves with empirically established
theories of extra-linguistic reality. In our view, such speculations are base-
less.

We started this section by indicating the clash between verificationism
and the arguments from ignorance and error used against description theories. The case against verificationism is deeper. If we start thinking about
language from a firmly realist perspective, as we have just urged we should,
then we think it most unlikely that we will end up with a verificationist
theory of truth and understanding. Rather, we are likely to end up with
something along the lines of the realist theory that we *have* ended up with
in Parts II and III; with a theory that relates a speaker's words to the
world in a way that does not require her to have any capacity to verify
that they are so related. (However, it must be admitted that indicator
theories – discussed in section 7.7 – have a somewhat verificationist appearance.) So, the inference to the best explanation that we favor is:

realism → anti-verificationism.

In conclusion, the realism dispute cannot be eliminated in favor of an
issue about language, nor can it be identified with such an issue. Further,
it is not appropriate to base an argument against realism on largely uncertain and *a priori* speculations about language. Rather, we should speculate about language from a firm realist base. From that base, we think
that verificationism must be rejected.

Suggested Reading

11.1

See Devitt 1997, *Realism and Truth*, ch. 2 for a more detailed account of
realism, and ch. 5 for a defense. "A Naturalistic Defense of Realism"
(1998a) presents the main arguments of the book.

11.2

The most persuasive defense of the classical logical positivist position on
realism is in Schlick 1932-3, "Positivism and Realism", reprinted in Ayer
1959, *Logical Positivism* and Boyd, Gasper, and Trout 1991. The former
is a very helpful collection of articles from the heyday of positivism.

Ayer 1940, *The Foundations of Empirical Knowledge*, particularly chs. 1, 2, and 6, is a nice example of the positivist approach to realism. Ayer 1946, *Language, Truth and Logic*, was the very successful introduction of positivism to the English-speaking world.

Carnap 1950, "Empiricism, Semantics and Ontology", and Hempel, "Problems and Changes in the Empiricist Criterion of Meaning", both reprinted in Linsky 1952, *Semantics and the Philosophy of Language*, are more recent statements of the positivist position.

Ashby 1967, "Verifiability Principle", in Edwards 1967, *Encyclopedia*, is a helpful discussion.

11.3–11.4

The great quantity and difficulty of Dummett's writing on realism make suggestions difficult. However, we think that a fairly good idea of his views can be obtained from "Realism" and "Preface" in *Truth and Other Enigmas* (1978). **For more details of his verificationist views of language, see the first few essays in *The Seas of Language* (1993). Wright 1993, *Realism, Meaning and Truth*, is an impressive work reflecting Dummett's influence.** McGuinness and Oliveri 1994, *The Philosophy of Michael Dummett*, is a collection of papers with responses by Dummett.

For a more detailed criticism of Dummett see Devitt 1997, ch. 14 (also chs. 3 and 4), which contains many references to appropriate parts of Dummett's work.

Musgrave 1997, "The T-Schema Plus Epistemic Truth Equals Idealism", has a view of the relation between verificationism and realism that is similar to ours.

Quine's skepticism about meaning involves a holistic verificationism; see the suggested readings for 1.3.

12

Worldmaking

12.1 Kant

The approach of this book has been uniformly naturalistic. Philosophy is just part of the empirical attempt to understand nature. Neither philosophy in general, nor philosophy of language in particular, has any special status. Such a view has been unappealing to the philosophically inclined. Overtly or covertly, most have practiced "first philosophy": philosophy thought of as anterior to science in particular, and empirically based knowledge in general. The *a priori* armchair approach to the philosophy of language criticized in the last chapter (11.4) is an example of first philosophy.

Traditional epistemology is another example. It tried to show how skepticism could be refuted and knowledge claims justified. Since these claims include science, it would be circular to place epistemology within science. Science itself needs justification. That justification can only be given by a discipline that is conceptually and epistemically prior to science. Thus epistemology got its traditional role.

In this chapter and the next we shall be concerned with various first philosophers who draw metaphysical conclusions about the nature of reality from reflections on language. To understand these conclusions, which are usually inchoate and obscure, it is important to have some acquaintance with the views of the great German philosopher, Immanuel Kant. Acquaintance is not easy because Kant is deep, dark, and difficult. His concern is not with language but with knowledge. Kant's views on realism are a result of his struggles with the traditional epistemological problem of skepticism.

Prior to Kant there was a view of the mind and of perception that makes the skeptical worry acute. It is sometimes called, anachronistically, "the movie-show model" of the mind. The mind, the conscious self, does not have direct access to the external world: its access is via the sense organs. That much is obvious. So what is immediately presented to the mind, the model concludes, is not the world but perceptual impressions ("ideas", "sense data"): images, sounds, tastes, touches, and smells, channeled to the mind from the appropriate organs. The mind is like a person sitting in a movie theater watching these perceptual impressions play on a screen. However, there is one crucial difference. The person can leave the theater and look outside, but the mind cannot; it is forever confined to the action on the inner screen.

If we are guided by this model, it is no wonder that skeptical worries obtrude. What grounds has the person who never leaves the theater for thinking that he is watching a documentary? If he never compares the external reality with the images on the screen, then he can never know if any of the images are accurate. No more can the mind know if its images are accurate. The perceptual impressions cohere, of course, but so do most movies, however fictional. Perhaps the mind is entitled to think that *something* must be causing the inner show, but what? There is no warrant for assuming that what causes the picture is *like* the picture. The world is forever shrouded behind the "veil of ideas".

We have mentioned earlier "the gap" between the object known and the knowing mind (11.1). The movie-show model makes that gap seem unbridgeable. At least, it seems unbridgeable if the object is independent of the mind, as the second dimension of realism requires.

Kant closed the gap with his view that the object known is in part constituted by the knowing mind. Objects as we know them – stones, trees, cats, and so on – are not to be confused with objects as they are independent of our knowledge. Kant calls the former "appearances" and the latter "things-in-themselves". Appearances inhabit the "phenomenal" world; things-in-themselves, the "noumenal" world. Appearances are obtained by our *imposition* of *a priori* concepts; for example, causality, time, and the Euclidian principles of spatial relation. Only things-in-themselves have the objectivity and independence required by realism. Appearances do not, as they are partly our construction. And, it must be emphasized, the familiar furniture of the world are appearances not things-in-themselves.

Kant's metaphysics is often explained with the help of the cookie-cutter metaphor. The dough (things-in-themselves) is independent of the cook (us). The cook imposes cookie-cutters (concepts) on the dough to create cookies (appearances).

This deeply mysterious metaphysics has fascinated philosophers for two centuries. Reality as it is in itself is mysterious in being forever inaccessible. Reality as we know it is mysterious in being somehow the result of our own handiwork. How could the cookie-cutters in our head reach out, literally, and make the stars?

Many contemporary anti-realisms combine Kantianism with relativism. Kant was no relativist: the concepts imposed to constitute the known world were common to all mankind. Contemporary anti-realisms tend to retain Kant's ideas of things-in-themselves and of imposition, but drop the universality of what is imposed. Instead, different languages, theories, and world views are imposed to create different known worlds. Such "worldmaking" is extraordinarily popular. It is often known as "constructivism". We shall now consider some examples.

12.2 Whorfian Constructivism

The contemporary route to Kantian metaphysics starts not with the theory of knowledge but with the theory of language (which is why we are concerned with it in this book). Passage along the route is aided and abetted by a persistent vacillation between talk of theory and talk of the world. This vacillation is of enormous help to the anti-realist because, of course, *theories really are mind-dependent*. So, if the distinction between theories and the world is blurred, an anti-realist position will seem much more plausible.

It is obvious that people construct their theories of the world, and that they do so partly on the basis of their innate inheritance but largely on the basis of the experiential stimuli that they receive. And we accept Whorf's point that the theories they construct are influenced (but not constrained) by the language of their community (10.2–10.3). So we can go along with Whorf's claim that a language

> is a classification and arrangement of the stream of sensory experience; (1956: 55)

and that

> the world is presented in a kaleidoscopic flux of impressions which has to be organized by our minds – and this means largely by the linguistic systems in our minds. (p. 213)

For the sake of argument, let us also go along with the following exaggeration by Sapir:

No two languages are ever sufficiently similar to be considered as representing the same social reality. (1949: 162)

However, none of this has anything directly to do with the world. It is *experience* of the world that we are organizing, not the world itself; it is a *theory* of the world that language helps us construct, not the world itself. Yet Whorf and Sapir slip quickly from talking of experiences and theories to talk of the world. Whorf's "classification and arrangement" of experience "results in a certain world-order". The worlds in which Sapir's linguistically different societies live "are distinct worlds". How could anything a person does to his experience – how could any of his modes of representation – affect stones, trees, cats, and stars? In one breath, Whorf runs together the ideas of imposition on the world and imposition on experience:

different languages differently "segment" the same situation or experience. (p. 162)

We are frequently told of our handiwork on reality: "we dissect nature"; "we cut nature up" (Whorf 1956: 213); "the 'real world' is to a large extent built up on the language habits of the group" (Sapir 1949: 162).

It is plausible to claim that our minds, concepts, and languages construct theories out of experience. It is wildly implausible to claim that our minds, concepts, and languages construct the world out of experience. Imposition on experience is one thing, imposition on the world is another. Are Sapir and Whorf simply conflating the two (cf. Dummett's identification: 11.3)? If so they are seriously confused. If not, they must think that their claims about world construction *follow from* their claims about theory construction. Yet this is an inference of such startling badness that only its apparent popularity excuses anyone bothering to reject it.

In the passages quoted, and many others, we find two central Kantian ideas: first, the idea of the known world being partly created by an act of human imposition; second, the idea of there also being a noumenal world independent of us and beyond our ken. Whorf describes the latter with mystical fervor:

the unknown, vaster world – that world of which the physical is but a surface or skin, and yet which we ARE IN, and BELONG TO. (p. 248)

The writings of Sapir and Whorf add a third idea to these two: relativism. Studies of different linguistic communities lead Sapir and Whorf to conclude that the communities have different world views (10.1). These different views are imposed to yield different realities; the world that each community lives in is relative to its language and theory. This is constructivism.

Are we being uncharitable in attributing these ideas to Sapir and Whorf? We shall consider that possibility in a moment. Meanwhile, let us see what is wrong with the ideas.

To start with, the idea of noumenal things-in-themselves is explanatorily useless and probably incoherent. Constructivists are attracted to things-in-themselves to provide an external constraint on theorizing. The plausibility of the view that there is *some* external constraint is, of course, overwhelming: there must be something outside us determining that some theories are better than others. However, things-in-themselves provide the appearance of constraint without the reality. Since we can, *ex hypothesis*, know nothing about things-in-themselves, we can know nothing about the mechanisms by which they exercise their constraint, nor can we explain or predict any particular constraint. For Kant himself, the very idea of *causal* constraint by the noumenal world is incoherent because CAUSALITY is one of the concepts imposed by us. So causality is part of the phenomenal world and cannot hold between the noumenal and phenomenal worlds. If this is not the position of constructivists, it surely ought to be. Why should causality be the exception to the rule of creation by imposition? If it is not an exception, the constructivists face the same problem that has baffled Kant scholars for years: the nature of the noncausal constraint exercised by things-in-themselves.

Worse still, if that is possible, is the idea that we make the known world of stones, trees, cats, and the like with our concepts. We have already indicated the main mystery (12.1). How could cookie-cutters in the head literally carve out cookies in dough that is outside the head? How could dinosaurs and stars be dependent on the activities of our minds? It would be crazy to claim that there were no dinosaurs or stars before there were people to think about them. Constructivists do not seem to claim this. But it is hardly any less crazy to claim that there *would not have been* dinosaurs or stars if there *had been not been* people (or similar thinkers). And this claim seems essential to constructivism: unless it were so, dinosaurs and stars could not be dependent on us and our minds.

Finally, consider relativism. We concluded earlier that Whorf exaggerates the differences in world views (10.2–10.3). Nonetheless, there are real and important differences. What is the proper response to these differences? Not to come to the conclusion that each community "lives in its own world". There is only one world. Rather, we should examine these differences and see what we can learn from them. Sometimes we will discover a people that has learned about things we know nothing of. Their theories of the world will be complementary with ours, and we can borrow from them. Sometimes, though, their views and ours will be inconsistent. Then we must decide who is right. Perhaps the aliens are right; in which case we should change our own theory. Perhaps we are right and the aliens wrong. To grant this possibility is not cultural chauvinism; it is taking the aliens seriously. It would be condescension to refuse to apply to their views the same critical standards that we apply to our own. The people that believe that they gain the strength of their enemy by eating his liver and drinking his blood are simply mistaken. Similarly, the people that think that every Sunday they eat the body, and drink the blood, of God.

We do not suggest that claims about language and mind have *no* implications for metaphysics. We have already allowed that some do (11.4). What we insist is that Whorf's particular claim *has no metaphysical implications at all.* Furthermore, we think that the procedure of arguing from theories of language or mind to metaphysics is generally wrongheaded: it puts the cart before the horse (11.4).

Is it uncharitable to take Sapir and Whorf to be constructivists? Perhaps we should not take their talk so literally. Indeed, our discussion immediately suggests some metaphorical interpretations. (i) Our *theories* of the world really are our constructions. So we can take talk of world construction as a colorful way of talking of theory construction. (ii) It is plausible to think of the mind as imposing theories on our *experiences* of the world. So we can take talk of imposition on the world as a colorful way of talking of imposition on experience. (iii) Finally, talk of x existing relative to a language can be taken as a colorful way of saying that there is a *concept* of x within the language.

We think that charity is misplaced here. First, it would then be hard to accommodate the claims of Sapir and Whorf about the incommensurability of different world views, for reasons to be brought out in the next section. Second, we suspect that only by taking their views literally can we explain the breathless excitement – *the aura of significance* – with which they are presented and received.

12.3 Scientific Constructivism

Radical philosophers of science like Kuhn and Feyerabend are also, we think, constructivists. Once again, it is hard to be certain of an interpretation. Like their arch-rivals, the positivists, the radicals are ontologically coy.

The vacillation we have complained of between talk of theory and talk of the world is to be found in the writings of the radicals. Thus, following a discussion of duck–rabbit gestalt switches, Kuhn has this to say about the discovery of the planet Uranus:

a number of astronomers . . . had seen a star in positions that we now suppose must have been occupied at the time by Uranus . . . [Herschel's] scrutiny disclosed Uranus' motion among the stars, and Herschel therefore
announced that he had seen a new comet! Only several months later, after
fruitless attempts to fit the observed motion to a cometary orbit, did Lexell
suggest that the orbit was probably planetary. When that suggestion was
accepted, there were several fewer stars and one more planet in the world of
the professional astronomer. (1962: 114)

The change from seeing something as a star to seeing it as a planet is
striking, just as is the change from seeing a figure as a duck and seeing it
as a rabbit. One does often say of such changes that 'it's as though the
world changes', or of people on different sides of such changes that 'they
live in different worlds'. But it would be absurd to take such dramatic and
essentially metaphorical statements literally. So surely, one is inclined to
think, we should not take Kuhn as claiming that the acceptance of a suggestion by a few astronomers literally destroyed stars and created a planet.

However, consider the following from Kuhn's account of the discovery
of oxygen:

At the very least, as a result of discovering oxygen, Lavoisier saw nature
differently. And in the absence of some recourse to that hypothetical fixed
nature that he "saw differently", the principle of economy will urge us
to say that after discovering oxygen Lavoisier worked in a different world.
(p. 117)

Here the difference between claiming that things *look* different as a result
of a theory change and claiming that they *are* different as a result of the
change is acknowledged, and still the latter claim is made. And it is made
for a very Kantian reason: "fixed nature" is beyond our ken; it is the other
side of "the gap"; it is a mere thing-in-itself. There is little room for charity here.

Many such passages in Kuhn and others – passages that talk of the
different worlds of different thinkers – seem to combine the three ideas of
constructivism: our creation of the known world by imposition; the existence of an unknowable noumenal world; and relativism. But quite apart
from these passages, there are good reasons to abandon charity and take
the radicals to be deeply anti-realist.

First, there is their forthright rejection of a correspondence view of truth.
By itself, this is not decisive evidence of anti-realism. It is possible to be a
realist and accept any theory of truth (except perhaps an epistemic one;
11.4), or none. But, as we have attempted to show in this book, a correspondence theory of truth is the natural semantic side salad to a realist
metaphysics. The sharpness with which the radicals reject it is certainly
some evidence for their anti-realism.

Much more decisive evidence comes from the radicals' enthusiasm for the incommensurability of theories (10.4). This incommensurability requires that theory change be accompanied by extensive reference change. But if the world remains the same through theory change, it is not plausible to think that there is extensive reference change; most terms will continue to refer to entities in that unchanging world. Indeed, we have earlier found it easy to argue against incommensurability by presupposing, in effect, that theories referred to a theory-independent world (10.5).

To accommodate the incommensurability thesis, and what goes with it, we must take literally the idea that theories do create their own worlds: the Kantian idea, once again, of human imposition on reality. However, these worlds do not exist "absolutely" but only "relative-to-theory". All that exists "absolutely" is a "nature" beyond reach of knowledge or reference: a Kantian Thing-In-Itself. Throughout the writings of the radicals, there are references to this independent reality which, in some ineffable way, theories are constrained by and must conform to. It is dough awaiting the cookie-cutter of theory.

It would be nice to find a clear statement of this unappealing metaphysics in the writings of the radicals. Understandably, we do not; for their metaphysics, no news is good news.

We have made general objections to constructivism in the last section. Constructivism in science has further problems. Despite much labor by Kuhn, Feyerabend, and others, it has not yielded a satisfactory account of the confirmation of scientific theories, of their conflict, or of scientific progress.

We have noted that constructivists blur the crucial distinction between theories of the world and the world itself. This is no accident: such plausibility as constructivism has depends on the blurring. If constructivist talk that is apparently about the world is metaphorical talk about theories, it is true. But then it will not be able to sustain the incommensurability thesis. To sustain this, the talk has to be taken literally. But then it is false. By blurring the distinction the truth about theories can appear to do the job of the falsehood about the world.

What drives the radicals to constructivism? First, they start with a theory of language, in particular a theory of reference. Second, the theory they subscribe to is a description theory, as we have already indicated (10.5). Applying this theory, they conclude that, from our present perspective, none of the terms of past theories refer. For, from that perspective, the descriptions associated with those terms do not pick anything out. So, still from that perspective, the purported referents do not exist. This applies across the board to observables and unobservables alike: even the flasks, rulers, pointers, stones, trees, and cats talked of in Newtonian times do not exist from our perspective. To sugar this bitter pill, we are told that those entities all do exist-relative-to-the-Newtonian-perspective.

We have urged an opposite procedure. We start with metaphysics. As theories have changed, have we abandoned our belief in entities that we previously thought to exist? First, consider observables. Theoretical progress certainly results in the addition of new observables, terrestrial and celestial, to our catalogue. But there have been very few deletions. Cases like witches, Piltdown Man, and Vulcan (it was once thought that there was a planet, Vulcan, between Mercury and the sun) are relatively rare. There have been some mistakes, but there is nothing in our intellectual history to shake our confidence that we have steadily *accumulated* knowledge of the make-up of the observable world. We have been wrong often enough about the *nature* of those entities, but it is *their* nature we have been wrong about. We have not been wrong about the fact of their existence. In brief, theory change is no threat to commonsense realism.

Furthermore, we should be sufficiently confident of this metaphysics to reject any theory of language that fails to fit it. It is not that the historical facts of theory change, together with a description theory of reference, show realism to be false. Rather, those facts, together with realism, show description theories to be false, for many terms at least. The main significance of the radicals' argument at the observable level is to put another nail in the coffin of description theories of reference.

It is less easy to rebut Kuhn and Feyerabend on unobservables. It is plausible to suppose that we have often been wrong in supposing that an unobservable exists. Even there, the radicals' commitment to the description theory leads them to exaggerate our degree of error. Without these exaggerations, scientific realism is not in much trouble: while our views of, say, the subatomic particles have changed and evolved, we still believe in the entities posited by Bohr and Rutherford. *At most*, the history of science should make us cautious in our commitment to unobservables. It should not lead us into constructivism.

Constructivism is to be found way beyond the influence of Whorf, Kuhn, and company. It is endemic to the structuralist movement, to be discussed in the next chapter. Indeed, it has some claim to being the dominant metaphysics of our time, at least among intellectuals.

12.4   The Renegade Putnam

We will finish this chapter with a surprising example of a philosopher led into Kantian idealism by considerations of language. Hilary Putnam was a founder of causal theories of reference and was, at that time, a staunch realist. He now finds his former position, which he calls "metaphysical realism", incoherent. Putnam's route to his present position is complex and difficult; part of it depends on one of the paradoxes of modern logic. We shall deal briefly with what we take to be the two main elements.

1) We have mentioned "the gap" between the object known and the knowing mind, and the skeptical problem that this gives rise to (11.1, 12.1). Given the gap, how do we know that our senses are not deceiving us? Descartes made this problem vivid by raising the possibility that there was a Deceitful Demon interfering with our senses; from the point of view of our senses, it was exactly *as if* there were the familiar external world, but there wasn't really. This worry has been translated into modern idiom. Perhaps you are a brain in a vat, nourished and deceived by Superscientist. The realist makes a sharp distinction between what could *be* the case and what we could *discover* to be the case (11.4). So the realist is committed to the view that you could be a brain in a vat even though you could never discover you were (because Superscientist was too clever to let you discover). That is an admission that worries many. How, then, do you know you are not a brain in a vat?

The skeptical problem is not the concern of this book. What is our concern is Putnam's argument to show, *contra* realism, that you could *not* be a brain in the vat. For the realist thinks that you could be; it's just that you aren't. The argument is as follows:

If you were a brain in a vat, you could not think that you were.
So, you could not be a brain in a vat.

The premise is an application of the historical-causal theory of reference. Ultimately, reference is determined not by what is in the head but by appropriate causal links to objects. Vatbrain is not appropriately linked to any object; it lacks the perceptual links that are necessary for reference. None of its thoughts are *about* anything. So, though Vatbrain could think the sentence 'I am a brain in a vat', that would not amount to thinking that it was a brain in a vat. We, who are not brains in vats, can think that thought only because we are appropriately linked to brains and vats. It is not enough to be a brain to think about brains, nor to be in a vat to think about vats.

One might try to resist Putnam's premise by rejecting his causal theory. If an indicator or teleological theory of reference (7.7) turns out to be correct, it is much less obvious that the premise is true. For example, according to indicator theory, a thought refers to features of the thinker's world that it is reliably correlated with in normal conditions. It may be that Vatbrain's VAT-thoughts actually would be correlated with vats in normal conditions. It is just that conditions never are normal for poor Vatbrain. So Vatbrain can think about vats, but never veridically. As it happens, we think that neither indication nor teleosematic theories give the right account of reference for concepts like VAT, whatever their other successes. So we think Putnam's premise is probably true.

However, the argument is fallacious: the conclusion does not follow from the premise. Putnam wants to show that a certain kind of illusion is impossible. But all that his argument actually shows is that, were we suffering from that illusion, we could not even conjecture that we were. This the realist can, and we do, grant. But from such reflections about what we can and cannot think in various circumstances, reflections about our minds and language, nothing follows at all about the essential nature of the world. To suppose otherwise is to *already accept* that nature itself (in this case, human nature) is not independent of our thoughts. There is nothing in Putnam's argument to threaten realism.

The following analogous argument may help to make this clear:

> If everything were red, you could not think that it was.
> So, everything could not be red.

The premise is plausible. You cannot have thoughts about redness without the concept RED; and people need to be struck by the difference between red things and non-red things to introduce and sustain that concept. Yet the conclusion obviously does not follow from the premise.

2) We think that we have the bones of a satisfactory theory of language consonant with realism. That confidence is largely based on a causal theory of reference. Putnam thinks that the confidence is misplaced and offers the earlier-mentioned argument from logic to prove it. Underlying this argument is a certain picture of our referential situation. We start from scratch, locked in our minds, wondering how a thought can fasten onto objects outside the mind. Can the causal theory provide an answer? According to Putnam, all that theory does is add further thoughts *in the mind*; for example, the thought that *a* refers to *x* in virtue of causal link L. What makes *that* thought reach outside the mind to "grasp" *x* and the causal link L? To suppose it does is to have a "magical theory of reference" (1981: 51). It is to suppose that we can get outside our minds and have a "God's Eye View" of the correspondence between mental signs and mind-independent things (pp. 73–4).

Putnam's solution is a Kantian one that makes the world we wish to refer to immediately accessible to our minds. He offers the following as "the metaphor" for his position: "the mind and the world jointly make up the mind and the world" (p. xi). He cashes the metaphor as follows:

> "objects" do not exist independently of our conceptual schemes. We cut up the world into objects when we introduce one or another scheme of description. (p. 52)

This is, once again, the Kantian idea of imposition on reality, which we have already dismissed (12.3). Putnam talks in a Kantian way also of things-in-themselves, but ultimately seems to regard such talk as "nonsense", even if psychologically irresistible (pp. 61–2, 83). So far, then, his metaphysics is like those discussed earlier in this chapter. However, his differs from those by avoiding any interesting relativism. He avoids this with the aid of the "principle of charity", which we shall criticize later (15.4).

The picture that leads Putnam to this desperate metaphysics is wrong-headed. We are not hermetically sealed in the prison of our minds, trying to push our thoughts through the bars of perception. The causal theorist does not think that it is our *thought*, "*a* refers to *x* in virtue of causal link L", that makes *a* refer to *x*. What makes it do this is the fact that *a is* so causally linked to *x*. It is not our thoughts about causal links, but our having of those links, that welds our thoughts onto the world.

Putnam proceeds in the wrong direction. In theorizing about language, we do not start with the mind locked up and innocent; we start with what we already know. Reflection on our best science has committed us to many entities of the largely inanimate and impersonal world. We go on, naturalistically, to seek an explanation of that small part of the world which exhibits the phenomenon of reference: people and their words. The result is a theory of no special status. It is, of course, *possible* that the formulation of theory might lead us to revise our views of what exists in other areas. But great changes are unlikely: the theory is narrow in scope and, for the foreseeable future, tentative. It is particularly unlikely to change our view of the independence of what exists from theorists and theories. Finally, semantic relations are no more inaccessible than other relations. Theorizing about the relation between a thought or expression and an object no more requires a God's Eye View than does theorizing about the relation between, say, Margaret Thatcher and Ronald Reagan.

In sum, we reject the views of the various worldmakers considered in this chapter. Their talk of imposition should be just a metaphor: the idea that we literally make stars and dinosaurs with our languages or theories is preposterous. Their talk of things-in-themselves gives the illusion of some external constraint on worldmaking without the reality. Their relativism arises from exaggerating the differences between languages and between theories. Finally, their metaphysics all exemplify a deep mistake: that of inferring what the world is like from a theory of language. Any theory of language is less secure than most others from common sense and science. If an implausible world view is a consequence of a theory of language, then we should unhesitatingly reject that theory not accept the consequence. The philosophy of language is exactly the wrong place to start metaphysics.

Suggested Reading

12.1

The most accessible of Kant's accounts of his metaphysics is *Prolegomena to Any Future Metaphysics* (1953; first published, 1783). **His great work is *Critique of Pure Reason* (1929; first published, 1781), but this is very long and very difficult. Strawson 1966, *The Bounds of Sense*, is about as readable an account of the *Critique* as can be had.**

12.2

The most helpful papers in Whorf 1956, *Language, Thought, and Reality*, for the concerns of this section are: "Science and Linguistics", "Languages and Logic", and his most famous paper, "Language, Mind, and Reality". For general reading on Sapir and Whorf, see suggestions for sections 10.1–10.3.

12.3

See the readings concerned with Kuhn and Feyerabend suggested for 10.4 and 10.5. See also, Laudan 1990, *Science and Relativism*.

12.4

The best place to find Putnam's views is *Reason, Truth and History* (1981), particularly chs. 1–3. His views have generated a storm of responses. Lewis 1984, "Putnam's Paradox", and Sosa 1993, "Putnam's Pragmatic Realism", are particularly helpful ones. See also many articles in French, Uehling, and Wettstein 1988, *Midwest Studies in Philosophy, Volume XII*, and Clark and Hale 1994, *Reading Putnam*; also, Ludwig 1992, "Brains in a Vat, Subjectivity, and the Causal Theory of Reference", Ebbs 1992, "Skepticism, Objectivity, and Brains in Vats", and Steinitz 1994, "Brains in a Vat".

For a wonderfully entertaining discussion of the history of worldmaking, see Stove 1991, *The Plato Cult and Other Philosophical Follies*. For a more detailed criticism along the lines of the text, see Devitt 1997, chs. 12 and 13 and afterword part IV.

13

Structuralism

"To be human . . . is to be a structuralist." (Hawkes 1977: 15)

13.1 Introduction

A book on language should not fail to discuss the extremely influential movement known as *structuralism*, an approach to the theories known sometimes as *semiotics* and sometimes as *semiology*. Parts of that discussion would have been appropriate enough in each of the previous two parts as well as in this part. However, we have preferred to gather the discussion together in one chapter. And we have put that chapter here because most of the excitement generated by structuralism has come not from its views of language but from what it is thought to show about the world in general.

The term 'structuralism' refers to a certain theoretical approach; briefly, it is an approach that sees the object of study as defined relationally. 'Semiology' and 'semiotics' both have their roots in the Greek word for a sign and refer to the "science of signs". The first term was invented by the Swiss linguist, Ferdinand de Saussure, and is preferred in Europe. The second was invented by the American philosopher, C. S. Peirce, and is preferred by English speakers. For most purposes, the three terms can be treated as equivalent: the science of signs has been the major home of the structuralist approach; and everything done under the banner of semiotics or semiology has been structuralist, or deeply influenced by structuralism.

It is usual to see structuralism as beginning with Saussure's *Course in*

General Linguistics (1966), published posthumously in 1916. It is the movement arising out of that work, particularly in France where it has dominated intellectual life, that we shall be considering in this chapter. However, it should be noted that a different but related movement known also as structuralism arose independently in America. This started with Edward Sapir and was made prominent by Leonard Bloomfield's *Language* (1933), a landmark in American linguistics. The structuralist influence remains in generative grammar. Structuralist ideas are also to be found in the movement known as "Russian Formalism", which began in Moscow and St Petersburg during the First World War.

Saussure saw linguistics as only part of his concerns, for he thought that there were many signs other than linguistic ones. The structuralist approach he found appropriate in linguistics was to be projected into human culture in general. Structuralism has been taken to span anthropology, social theory (particularly Marxian), psychology (particularly Freudian), literary criticism, philosophy, the history of ideas, and much else besides: the structuralizing of everything. Key figures in this movement have been Claude Lévi-Strauss, Louis Althusser, Jacques Lacan, Roland Barthes, and, perhaps, Michel Foucault.

Structuralism's relational view of the world is plausible in linguistics and the social sciences. It is reasonable to think, for example, that in economic explanations we focus on the relations between agents and on the constraints on their activities imposed by the economic system in which they operate. But what about the world of the natural sciences, the natural world? Relations matter in the natural sciences but so do the objects themselves. These natural objects – particularly people and their output – stand in the relations that concern the social sciences and, as a result, constrain those sciences. To take a banal example, though economics can, perhaps, afford to ignore the differences between different employees and between different employers it cannot afford to ignore the fact that people need to eat. The economics of a society of agents who could obtain their food by photosynthesis while sunbathing would, we conjecture, be rather different from the economics of our societies. So while we think there is some partial and limited validity on the structuralists' focus on relations in the social sciences, even there it is overdone. And we see no reason to export this idea to the natural sciences.

"Post-structuralism", the philosophical arm of "post-modernism", grew out of structuralism. Its most famous proponent is Jacques Derrida, who introduced the very influential idea of "deconstructing" a text. Post-structuralism is a radical movement that denies the possibility of objective meaning and truth, the distinction between rational inquiry and political action, the distinction between literal and metaphorical meaning, and much else beside. It is seen by many, rightly in our view, as "rejecting most of the fundamental intellectual pillars of modern Western civilization" (Cahoone 1996: 2). We shall not discuss it but think that its central failings arise from what it takes from structuralism: the rejections of reference and realism.

13.2   Saussure's Linguistics

1) Saussure's linguistics is the way into structuralism. We shall begin our characterization of that linguistics with its most important thesis: that a language is constituted by its *internal relations*.

A language can be decomposed into a number of elementary units that appear and reappear. Thus the sound type /t/ would be tokened four times in any pronunciation of the immediately preceding sentence; the letter type 't' is tokened five times. In virtue of what are such sounds or letters tokens of the one type? We shall concentrate on the case of sound types, since the primary form of language is speech not writing. Sound types are called *phonemes*. So our question becomes: when are different sounds tokens of the same phoneme?

The natural answer is: when the tokens of share *acoustic* properties, the physical properties of the sound wave. Saussure and the linguists following him think that phonemes cannot be defined in this way. For one thing, the phonetic environment of a sound affects the way it is pronounced and hence its acoustic properties: /t/ pronounced in the middle of a word is acoustically different from /t/ pronounced at the end. For another, speech is a continuous stream; it does not break into discrete units. Finally, differences between speakers are also considerable. For instance, the pitch – the frequency of sound waves – is typically higher for women than for men. There must be some limits, but the degree of variation of the physical signal is considerable.

What determines the amount of allowable variation? According to Saussure, it is the linguistic system itself. Some differences are *marked*: they correspond to a difference in sign. Others are not. In English, consonants may be *voiced*: their pronunciation involves the rapid vibration of the vocal chords as air is expelled past them. The phonemes /d/ and /t/ differ only in that /d/ but not /t/ is voiced. Thus English distinguishes /bed/ from /bet/. Not every language marks every distinction English does, and English does not mark distinctions other languages do. It is notorious, for example, that some Asian languages do not mark the distinction between /l/ and /r/. So, it is the linguistic system itself that defines phonemes, for the linguistic system determines which physical similarities and differences between sounds count as important.

This approach to phonology developed into "binary feature analysis".

The essential idea was to define phonemes as clusters of articulatory features: features like voice (vibrating versus nonvibrating vocal chords); nasality (open versus closed nasal passages); front versus back tongue position; upper versus lower tongue position; and so on. These features are binary: they are present or not present. This involves ignoring some aspects of the pronunciation process (for example, there are many different tongue positions that are classified as front), while highlighting others. The linguistic system plays its role in determining which features are to be highlighted. Thus round *versus* non-round lips is a difference that makes a difference in standard English (between /cot/ and /caught/, for example), but not in a number of American regional accents. The contrasts marked by the linguistic system determines which articulatory features are relevant to the definition of phonemes.

A central idea of structuralism has been to extend this approach to defining phonemes to *all* the categories of linguistic theory; to extend it from the phonetic and phonological to the morphological, syntactic, and semantic. The linguistic contribution of each item is given by its *differences from other items* in the language; "each linguistic term derives its value from its opposition to all the other terms" (Saussure 1966: 88). This exemplifies the structuralist approach. An item is defined not by what it is in itself – not by its intrinsic properties – but by its relations in a *structure*:

> that the world is made up of relationships rather than things, constitutes the first principle of that way of thinking which can properly be called "structuralist". (Hawkes 1977: 17–18)

In applying the approach to words, Saussure distinguishes two sorts of relations that words have to each other: *syntagmatic*, and *associative* or *paradigmatic*. Syntagmatic relations are those a word holds to other words, typically of other syntactic categories, with which it can be conjoined in well-formed strings called *syntagms*. Thus the relation between 'Zanzibar' and 'explodes' is syntagmatic; the two can be conjoined to form a syntagm, in this case the sentence, 'Zanzibar explodes'. Paradigmatic relations are those a word holds to other words which are possible alternatives to it in the well-formed string; i.e., to words that could be substituted for it. Thus the relation between 'explodes' and 'approves' is paradigmatic; the latter could replace the former in the above sentence.

It is a central tenet of structuralism that syntagmatic and paradigmatic relations constitute, and *exhaust*, the meaning of a word. Meaning is determined wholly by the role of a term within a language. So, Culler claims, there is nothing more to the meaning of 'brown' than these relations; our concepts of color "are nothing but a product or result of a system of distinctions" (1976: 25).

Language is a system of interdependent terms in which the value of each
term results solely from the simultaneous presence of the others . . . (Saussure
1966: 114)

From our perspective, this is the most surprising and objectionable feature of structuralism, for it *omits reference*. It is central to the meaning of
'brown' that it refers to brown things. A word's relations to others in the
language – *internal* relations – may often be important to its meaning;
for example, the relation of 'pediatrician' to 'doctor'. But a language's
relations to the nonlinguistic world – its *external* relations – are always
important. We shall return to this criticism in the next section.

2) The next important feature of Saussure's linguistics is its *holistic*
view of language. *All* of a word's syntagmatic and paradigmatic relations
go into its meaning. The meaning of each word is defined not simply by
its relations to a few other words but by its place in the entire structure.
Make the least change in that structure and the term's meaning changes.
Thus Philip Pettit, in his commentary on structuralism, writes of the paradigmatic ones:

if a word lost some such relationships or gained others it would lose its old
formal identity: . . . [it] would become a . . . different word. (1977: 9)

It follows that the introduction of one new term into a language changes
all terms. And there is no question of the new term "bringing a meaning
with it". We cannot coin a term, giving it a meaning, and simply add it
with its meaning to the language. We cannot borrow a foreign word with
its meaning; once borrowed, its old meaning is irrelevant:

it exists only through its relation with, and opposition to, words associated
with it, just like any other genuine sign. (Saussure 1966: 22)

This extreme holism is a direct consequence of ignoring reference. This
is most striking on our Fregean assumption that a word's property of
referring to something in a certain way – its mode of reference – exhausts
its meaning. For, on that assumption, the meaning of a word covered by a
description theory will be dependent on its relations to *only a few* others;
and the meaning of one covered by a causal theory will be dependent on
no others (chs. 4 and 5). Either way, there is no holism. If we abandon the
Fregean assumption but still keep a place for reference in a word's meaning, we get a two-factor theory (9.4). What we have just said will still
apply to the referential factor of a word's meaning. Only its non-reference-determining functional-role factor could be holist. So, the holism
could infect only one factor of the meaning.

3) With the view that a language is constituted by its internal relations

goes the view that a language is an *autonomous* system, to be explained entirely in its own terms without any reference to anything outside its structure:

> the structure is *self-regulating* in the sense that it makes no appeals beyond itself . . . The transformations act to . . . "seal off" the system from reference to other systems. A language . . . does not construct its formations of words by reference to the patterns of "reality", but on the basis of its own internal and self-sufficient rules. (Hawkes 1977: 16–17)

It is "self-defining" and "self-contained" (p. 26).

In this regard, Saussure's often-used analogy with chess is instructive:

> In chess, what is external can be separated relatively easily from what is internal . . . everything having to do with its system and rules is internal. (Saussure 1966: 20)
>   But just as the game of chess is entirely in the combination of the different chesspieces, language is characterized as a system based entirely on the opposition of its concrete units. (p. 107)

Saussure is clearly right about the autonomy of chess. The notion of check is defined only *within* the rules of chess; it has no content independent of that rule system. Change the relevant rules – as for example in "blitz" chess, which allows the king to be taken – and you change or eliminate check.

Chess is indeed a good model for Saussure's view of language, but it is a poor one for language itself, as we shall emphasize (13.3).

4) If the elements of a language depend on the linguistic system, it is plain that linguistics must be concerned with that system itself. The structuralist is therefore not interested in particular linguistic acts. No set of acts can be more than a partial and inexact reflection of the system. Saussure distinguishes the linguistic system he is studying, *langue*, from its manifestations in the behavior of speakers, *parole*. This distinction is an ancestor of Chomsky's much-discussed one between competence and performance (6.1).

5) If the study is of a self-contained system then it is ahistorical. How the system originated is beside the point. Thus Saussure distinguished himself from his predecessors in arguing for the importance of a *synchronic* approach in linguistics. Prior to that, linguistics had been entirely concerned with the historical and causal development of languages: it had been *diachronic*. Saussure did not deny a place for diachronic linguistics, but he did want to keep it sharply distinct from the synchronic. Moreover, he thought that "the synchronic viewpoint predominates" (p. 90). History creates the interrelations and structures that constitute the sys-

tem. However, the story of this creation is irrelevant to our understanding of that system. Thus it is of no consequence to synchronic linguistics how English came to mark the distinction between /t/ and /d/ as significant, but not that between mid-word and word-final /l/. What matters is just that the one difference is part of the structure and the other is not.

13.3 The Rejection of Reference

The rejection of reference is central to the relational, holistic, and autonomous view of language that is definitive of structuralism. We shall now consider that rejection.

At first sight it may seem that the structuralist does take some note of reference. For, he sees a sign as a composite entity made up of the *signifier*, that which signifies, and the *signified*, that which is signified. However, the signified is not a language-independent referent. Rather, it is a *concept*, the nature of which is entirely determined by relations internal to the language, syntagmatic and paradigmatic relations of the language. In this way the linguistic system imposes on thought:

> our thought – apart from its expression in words – is only a shapeless and indistinct mass . . . without the help of signs we would be unable to make a clear-cut, consistent distinction between two ideas. Without language, thought is a vague, uncharted nebula. There are no pre-existing ideas, and nothing is distinct before the appearance of language. (Saussure 1966: 111–12)

We have, in effect, already rejected this structuralist idea in discussing Whorf (10.2–10.3).

Talk of concepts need not involve denying reference, of course, if a concept is thought of as something that *determines* reference. This would be to treat it like our notion (following Frege) of *sense* (2.6). However, there is no suggestion in Saussure of this role for the signified. Indeed his rejection of reference is clear, even if rather more implicit than explicit. As Fredric Jameson points out in his critical survey:

> The emphasis [in Saussurean linguistics on the relationship between the signifier and the signified] tended . . . to exclude any consideration of the thing itself, of the object of reference in the "real world". (1972: 105–6)

And one structuralist has been quite explicit.

> The word 'dog' exists, and functions within the structure of the English Language, without reference to any four-legged barking creature's real existence. (Hawkes 1977: 17)

From our perspective, this rejection of reference makes structuralism fundamentally implausible. For reference has been a central notion in our theory of language. With its rejection must go the rejection also of a place for a notion of truth in linguistics.

We can bring out the main basis for this charge of implausibility by considering the structuralists' favorite analogy: chess. For chess is like language *as the structuralists view it*, but it is importantly difference from language *as it really is*.

(i) Chess is a game. It is something we indulge in "just for fun". It is "valuable in itself". None of these things are true of language. Language has a lot to do with life in general: it expresses thoughts that explain behavior and inform us about the world (1.2). The point of language is not simply to have fun, but to further nonlinguistic purposes; a word game is not communication. The theoretical notion that is crucial to capturing this difference between chess and language is reference, the very notion that the structuralists ignore. Chess pieces and chess moves do not refer to the world. No consideration from outside the game can validate or undermine anything within the game. In contrast, linguistic symbols do refer to the world and are open to external assessment; most notably, they can be true or false.

(ii) The rejection of reference and consequent holism make it difficult to give a natural account of developmental facts about language. Linguistic items cannot be identified across systems. How then are we to explain language acquisition? We want to say that a child begins by learning a minimal vocabulary and a few rudimentary syntactic rules. The child continues by expanding its vocabulary and revising and extending these rules. On a structuralist picture of language, we cannot say this. Vocabulary does not remain constant across changes in the system. Each time the child changes the system, *everything changes*. Language learning cannot be represented as a cumulative process.

(iii) What goes for development goes also for linguistic change. Consider the simplest change, lexical borrowing. It is natural to claim that the word is borrowed because its meaning fills a gap in the language. Not infrequently that gap will be referential: the borrowed term will name a natural kind or artifact only recently encountered by the speakers of the borrowing language. The structuralists can make sense of neither element of this claim. Talk of "gaps" is subversive of the idea that a language system is autonomous, complete in itself. Plugging a gap with a borrowing implies that meaning can be constant over systems.

(iv) Translation is surely mysterious from the structuralist perspective. If meanings are determined wholly be relations within a language system, how can the elements of one structure be equivalent to the elements of another? What could make one translation – one matching of the elements of one with the elements of another – better than another? (Structuralists tend to accept that translation is often difficult but not that it is impossible: Saussure 1966: 116; Culler 1976: 21–2).

What drives structuralists into this implausible rejection of reference? They are not very explicit on this matter but we have unearthed two possible reasons.

First, they seem to think that the *arbitrariness* of linguistic signs tells against reference. Thus Jameson points out that the construction of the sign (= signifier + signified)

> strikes down . . . the apprehension of language as names and naming. There can no longer be any question of such an intrinsic relationship once the utterly arbitrary character of language has been made clear. (1972: 30)

Consider also the way structuralists typically move directly from arbitrariness to their relational view:

> The fact that the sign is arbitrary . . . means that [it] require[s] an ahistorical analysis . . . Since the sign has no necessary core which must persist, it must be defined as a relational entity, in its relations to other signs. (Culler 1976: 36)

This move could seem appropriate only if arbitrariness undermined reference. If reference remains, the sign need not be defined solely by its internal relations.

What has arbitrariness got to do with reference? Jameson's use of 'intrinsic' is a clue. The structuralists seem to think that the only possible theory of reference is a naive picture theory. If signs were "pictures" of things then, the thinking goes, they would not be arbitrary: they would be constrained by what the things were like. Yet signs are arbitrary. So, they are not "pictures". So, reference must be rejected. Some such line of thought seems necessary to make sense of the structuralists' remarks about reference. And consider this revealing passage:

> The overall characteristic of this relationship is... arbitrary. There exists no necessary "fitness" in the link between the sound-image, or signifier 'tree', the concept, or signified that it involves, and the actual physical tree growing in the earth. The word 'tree', in short, has no "natural" or "tree-like" qualities . . . (Hawkes 1977: 25)

The mistake here is obvious. Reference does not depend on picturing, as any causal theory shows. Arbitrariness and reference are perfectly compatible.

Second, there is a suggestion of an argument against reference in some curious and overstated remarks by Culler about teaching someone the meaning of 'brown' (1976: 24–6). It is alleged that the person cannot be taught this by the presentation of brown objects.

> It is only when he has grasped the relation between brown and other colors that he will begin to understand what brown is. (p. 25)

A little later Culler claims that

> the signifieds of color terms are nothing but the product or result of a system of distinctions. (p. 25)

So, the signified of those terms does not include their references.

Everything goes wrong with this argument. First, the premise about learning needs to be taken with caution. The concept of brown, and hence a word for it, would probably not be acquired by an organism that could not discriminate between brown and other colors (11.4). But reference borrowing at least opens up the possibility that 'brown' could be learned without the ability to make those discriminations. Second, even if it is necessary to discriminate brown from other colors to learn 'brown', it does not follow 'brown' has no reference. Indeed, even if it is necessary to learn other color terms to learn 'brown', it does not follow 'brown' lacks reference. Nor would it follow that this referential link was dependent on the other color terms featured in the learning process. What is required to learn reference is one thing; what reference is, is another.

In sum, structuralism's rejection of reference is not well-based and is thoroughly implausible.

13.4   The Rejection of Realism

The rejection of reference not only leads to an implausible theory of language, it has very serious consequences for metaphysics. It encourages anti-realism.

Reference is the link between language and independent reality. Deny reference, and reality is likely to seem problematic. Indeed how can reality be made relevant at all to an *autonomous* system? Jameson brings out nicely this "contradiction within Structuralism":

> its concept of the sign forbids any research into the reality beyond it, at the same time that it keeps alive the notion of such a reality by considering the signified as a concept *of* something. (1972: 106)

The structuralist solution is to take the language system as creating its own reality, an example of what we have called "worldmaking".

> Language . . . allows no single, unitary appeals to a "reality" beyond itself. In the end, it constitutes its own reality. (Hawkes 1977: 26)

> Writing . . . can be seen to *cause a new reality to come into being.* (p. 149)

If taken literally, this talk of language's power over the world is mysterious and inexplicable, if not absurd. Taken metaphorically, it seems to leave us without a world at all (cf. 12.3). Certainly, a world created in this way cannot be the realist's world of "independently existing objects" (Hawkes 1977: 17).

Structuralist discussions of reality contain several unappealing features of a sort already criticized in the last two chapters.

First, anti-realism is made easy by a swift move from talk of the language-dependence of theories to talk of the language-dependence of reality (12.2-12.3):

> since [language] . . . constitutes our characteristic means of encountering and of coping with the world beyond ourselves, then perhaps we can say that it constitutes the characteristic human structure. From there, it is only a small step to the argument that perhaps it also constitutes the characteristic structure of human reality. (Hawkes 1977: 28)

A small step indeed! Constituting theories of the world is one thing, constituting the world, a very different thing.

Second, the structuralists' metaphysics is a form of Kantianism. One aspect of this is apparent already: the world we know is one created, constructed, etc. by our language. This world is like Kant's world of appearances. Do the structuralists also believe in a world independent of our knowledge, a world of things-in-themselves (12.1)? It has been claimed so:

> all the Structuralists: Lévi-Strauss with his idea of nature, Barthes with his feeling for social and ideological materials, Althusser with his sense of history, *do* tend to presuppose, beyond the sign-system itself, some kind of ultimate reality which, unknowable or not, serves as its most distant object of reference. (Jameson 1972: 109–10)

Thus independent reality becomes mysterious and inaccessible, scarcely to be mentioned without scare quotes; "a formless chaos of which one cannot even speak in the first place" (p. 33). This is completely unacceptable (12.3–12.4).

Third, the metaphysics of the structuralists is like that of Whorf and Kuhn in being relativistic (12.2–12.3). This is an inevitable result of the view that a system of signs is both autonomous and the creator of its own reality. As we change cultures and hence systems, we change worlds.

> all societies construct their *own* realities in accordance with mental or psy-
> chological principles that determine form and function...they then covertly
> project these upon whatever the real world may in fact be . . . this is what
> *all* societies do, not just "primitive" or "savage" ones. (Hawkes 1977: 56)

By adding relativism to the two Kantian theses, the structuralists provide another example of constructivism.

Finally, the structuralists exemplify the mistake that we have been emphasizing throughout this Part of the book: the mistake of attempting to derive a world view from a theory of language (11.4, 12.1). This is the deep cause of their obscure and implausible metaphysics. The right procedure, we have argued, is to start with a world view and attempt to derive a theory of language. And the plausible world view to start with is realism.

Suggested Reading

Saussure 1966, *Course in General Linguistics* (first published in 1916), is the *locus classicus* of stucturalist linguistics and is quite readable. Barthes 1967, *Elements of Semiology*, is a more recent classic. Aarsleff 1982, *From Locke to Saussure*, is a good survey of the ideas leading up to structuralism. Lyons 1981, *Language and Linguistics*, pp. 219–23, is a neat summary of the main ideas. See also Culler 1976, *Saussure*, Holdcroft 1991, *Saussure*, and Thibault 1997, *Re-Reading Saussure*. Akmajian, Demers, and Harnish 1979, *Linguistics*, has a good introduction to the basic ideas of phonology.

Nearly all the works of the key figures in contemporary structuralism are very difficult. Eco 1984, *Semiotics and the Philosophy of Language*, is widely taken to be a classic. Amongst commentaries, Hawkes 1977, *Structuralism and Semiotics*, particularly chs. 1–2, is the best to start with. It contains an excellent annotated bibliography. See also Jameson 1972, *The Prison-House of Language*, and Pettit 1977, *The Concept of Structuralism*.

The writings of Derrida are voluminous and obscure. *The Archeology of the Frivolous* (1980) is an example, treating philosophy in a typically tantalizing way. Norris 1982, *Deconstruction*, is a relatively clear introduction to the subject. See also Wood 1992, *Derrida: A Critical Reader*.

Searle is a trenchant critic of post-structuralism. See particularly the debate on deconstruction: Derrida 1977a, "Signature Event Context"; Searle 1977, "Reiterating the Differences: A Reply to Derrida"; Derrida 1977b, "Limited Inc abc..."; Searle 1983b, "The Word Turned Upside Down"; Searle and Mackey 1984 "An Exchange on Deconstruction".

Sturrock 1979, *Structuralism and Since*, is a useful introduction to significant structuralist and post-structuralist figures. Kearney 1994, *Modern Movements in European Philosophy*, is a brief, relatively clear, and relentlessly flattering synopsis. Eagleton 1983, *Literary Theory*, contains excellent material on the place of semiotics in literary theory. Cahoone 1996, *From Modernism to Post-Modernism*, is a large collection of readings. Sarup 1993, *An Introduction to Poststructrualism and Postmodernism* is a relatively clear introduction to this movement, but embraces uncritically its profoundly anti-realist and anti-scientific character.

Part V

Language and Philosophy

14

First Philosophy

14.1 Philosophy Naturalized

In Part IV we were concerned with the relation between the study of language and the realism issue. In this part, we are concerned with the relation between that study and philosophy.

Philosophers ask many difficult questions. Amongst the most difficult are questions about philosophy itself. What is it? Our answer must reflect a major theme of this book: naturalism. We advocate *philosophy naturalized*.

Philosophy, we say, is not an *a priori* discipline. It is not a subject that can be developed apart from other areas of human knowledge. Its results form no body of knowledge against which the lesser breeds are to be tested. It is not an intellectual police force. It is empirical and fallible. Philosophy is continuous with science. But it is mostly less secure than common sense and mature science.

Briefly, and roughly, we can divide philosophy's role in three.

(1) Philosophy's most basic task is to reflect upon, and integrate, the results of investigations in the particular sciences to form a coherent overall view of the universe and our place in it.
(2) Philosophy is concerned with certain problems in particular sciences, for example, in physics, biology, psychology, and mathematics. These problems arise in the most speculative and conceptually difficult parts of the sciences.

(3) Some sciences, or areas of sciences, are traditionally done in philosophy, in some cases, but certainly not all, because they are not mature enough to go out on their own: epistemology, logic, morals, politics, and aesthetics. (We confess to having only the dimmest of ideas about how to accommodate some of these within our naturalistic viewpoint.)

Our Part II discussion of word meaning and reference comes very much under (3). Our discussion of syntax, and Part III as a whole, falls mostly under (2). However, Part III also exemplifies the integrative concerns of (1). Those concerns dominate Part IV.

Our naturalistic view of philosophy underlies all these discussions. The view is controversial. This book is not the place to attempt a detailed defense of it, but we can say something in its favor.

To a degree, the book itself is a defense. A theory of philosophy, like any other theory, should be judged on its results. We have outlined some of the results of naturalism in this book. We hope to have provided the beginnings of a coherent and plausible account of language. If we have, that is a positive argument for philosophy naturalized.

A central aspect of defending a theory is criticizing its rivals. That will be the concern of the rest of the book. Our choice of rival philosophies to discuss, and our discussion of them, are influenced by the dominant concern of this book: language. So we shall be particularly concerned with rivals that tie philosophy, in one way or another, to the study of language. And we shall continue theorizing about language and its relations to other matters even while considering the general question of the nature of philosophy.

In this chapter we will consider some forms of first philosophy, a philosophy that is thought to be conceptually and evidentially independent of empirical scientific thinking (12.1). Much of the history of philosophy is the history of first philosophy. We shall start with the traditional form of this, particularly as it is exemplified in a problem that we think stems from one in language: the "one-over-many" problem. We shall then consider some recent manifestations of first philosophy, all of them part of the linguistic turn in philosophy. In the next chapter we shall consider some philosophers who reject naturalized philosophy less directly. They claim that important parts of human knowledge – parts concerned with humans themselves – are ascientific. This knowledge is not worse than scientific knowledge; it is just irreducibly different. Folk psychology and folk linguistics are given a special status outside science.

14.2   Traditional First Philosophy; The One-over-Many Problem

A first philosophy stance was natural for the rationalist tradition. For, according to that tradition, knowledge in general was *a priori*: rationalists thought that important truths about people and the universe were discoverable through reflection and reason. However, interestingly enough, the same stance was taken by the rival tradition, that of empiricism. Empiricists thought that all knowledge of the world was derived ultimately from perceptual experience. There is therefore a tension between their philosophical stance and their view of knowledge. How can the *a priori* method that they practiced in philosophy yield knowledge if all knowledge is empirical? This tension was never satisfactorily removed. The favored response was to see philosophy as yielding *analytic* truths. Sometimes these were thought to be sentences true solely in virtue of meaning, sometimes sentences reducible by definition to logical truths. Either way, the response has the problem that it seems to make philosophy trivial. Yet philosophy does not seem trivial, particularly not to those who practice it. And, in relation to one of these ideas of analyticity, we have argued that no sentence is in fact true solely in virtue of meaning (5.6).

We have already mentioned one of the major concerns of traditional first philosophy: skepticism (12.1, 12.4). *A priori* reflections about what is required for knowledge – epistemological reflections – make all ordinary knowledge seem open to doubt. How, Descartes asked, could he be certain even that he was sitting by the fire? Perhaps his senses were deceiving him. Perhaps he was dreaming. Perhaps there was an Deceitful Demon misleading him into thinking that he was by the fire. Attempts to solve this problem have typically led to implausible and mysterious antirealist metaphysics; Kant's metaphysics is a famous example (12.1, 12.3). Such implausible consequences of first philosophy's treatment of skepticism alone count against that approach. However, worst of all, despite the aid of metaphysical systems designed to provide a solution to the skeptical problem, first philosophy has never produced a convincing solution. We would argue that the approach should be abandoned in favor of the naturalistic one. This does not so much solve the skeptical problem as set it aside as uninteresting; it is a problem so framed as to be insoluble.

What we will discuss is another central problem of traditional first philosophy: the one-over-many problem. It is obvious that the world is full of individual things; stones, trees, cats and so on. But in addition to these "particulars", are there "universals" shared by many particulars?

Recently, a number of philosophers have argued that there are theoretical advantages in positing the existence of universals. But historically they were posited because of the one-over-many problem. That leads to universals as follows. Here is a red rose. There is a red house. That is a red sunset. Now surely, it is claimed, there must be something that all these things have in common that makes them red. That something is the "attribute" redness. So argued Quine's adversary, McX, in Quine's classic paper "On What There is" (1953: 9–10). Each thing must partake of the "form" redness. So argued Plato two millennia ago. These things have the same nature, the "property" redness. So argues David Armstrong to this very day (1978). This attribute, or form, or property, is "the one" that spreads itself over, or runs through, "the many". It is a universal shared by many particulars. In this way first philosophers through the ages have convinced themselves of the existence of universals.

The conviction has generated a host of bizarre metaphysical problems. What is a universal? Where does it exist? Is there a universal for every predicate, even empty ones? What is a particular? How is a universal related to particulars? Universals are said to "inhere in" particulars and the particulars to "partake of" the universals, but how is that achieved? By metaphysical glue ("Plato's grip")? Even particulars begin to look mysterious, for what are they when stripped of their clothing of universals? Philosophers have been driven to think of them as "bare particulars", "mere thisnesses", or propertyless "substrata". Struggles with these problems have led some to say that there are, instead of, or as well as, properties, property-instances: "abstract particulars" or "tropes".

Controversy has raged over these problems for centuries. If we can dissolve them, we should. In particular, we should not believe in the existence of universals unless we really have to. We should favor here, as in science, simple and economical theories. In ontology, the less the better.

Does the one-over-many argument really require us to posit universals? We think not. Certainly there are red roses, houses and sunsets. We are tempted to say that there is something, redness, that they all share, but we need not say that. We do just as well saying that they are all red. What we are tempted to say is a mere manner of speaking, to be avoided when the ontological chips are down. There is nothing about the situation that requires us to talk of redness. To suppose that there is redness as well as red things clutters the landscape without explanatory or descriptive gain.

The friend of universals will object. "You have failed to say in virtue of what all these things are red." Our failure here could be a scientific one: we have not said what it is, physically, about a thing that makes it red. However, this is not the failure the friend of universals has in mind. Suppose we removed the failure, pointing out that it is in virtue of being P that things are red, where 'P' is the appropriate physical predicate. The friend would still not be satisfied. "In virtue of what are the things P?" He does not want a scientific explanation, he wants a metaphysical explanation.

At this point, the naturalistic philosopher demurs: there is nothing further to explain. "Things just are P. What more could you want to know?" The first philosopher will insist that a metaphysical explanation is needed. We seem to be at an impasse. However, the naturalistic philosopher has one more card to play. If there really were something requiring a metaphysical explanation here, we would expect to find some sign of progress in the two thousand years that philosophers have struggled to provide that explanation. Yet there is no sign of progress: Armstrong is no closer to a solution than Plato. This is strong evidence that there is no problem: the one-over-many is a pseudo problem; the explanations prompted by it are pseudo explanations.

We have chosen to discuss the one-over-many not only because it is a major example of first philosophy, and one of its most conspicuous failures, but also because we suspect that the reason philosophers are beguiled by this pseudo problem is to be found in their theory of language. We suspect that underlying their response to the one-over-many is an implicit commitment to the "'Fido'-Fido" theory of meaning.

This theory has had a persistent hold over the minds of philosophers and many others. According to the theory, the meaning of a term is its role of naming something. It will be remembered that on the Millian view (2.5) the meaning of the name, 'Fido', is its role of naming Fido. The 'Fido'-Fido theory generalizes this view of meaning to all terms.

Consider:

That rose is red.

This sentence, like all others, has a certain complexity. It has two terms, the singular term 'that rose' and the general term 'red', of different grammatical categories and playing quite different roles (2.2, 2.4). How can the 'Fido'-Fido theory cope with this complexity? It has to see the two types of term naming two types of entities: the different roles of the terms require different types of entities. The entity named by 'that rose' is a particular rose; that named by 'red' is the universal, redness, which can be shared by many particulars. The one-over-many begins to look like a real problem.

The 'Fido'-Fido theory is false. Our Part II discussion exemplifies a quite different way of coping with the complexity of sentences. It is not that each term stands in the one semantic relation of naming to different kinds of entities. Rather, the terms stand in different semantic relations to the same kinds of entities, neither "particulars" nor "universals" but just plain objects. Thus 'that rose' *designates* a certain object, a rose, while 'red' *applies to* many objects, including many roses. Where the 'Fido'-Fido theory catches the complexity with different sorts of entity, we catch it with different sorts of relation. The only entities we need are objects of the familiar sort.

If we are right in these speculations, the one-over-many is not only an example of the failure of traditional first philosophy, but also another example of a bad theory of language leading to a bad theory of the world (Part IV).

14.3   The Linguistic Turn: Ordinary Language Philosophy

When the naturalistic philosopher points his finger at reality, the linguistic philosopher discusses the finger.

The linguistic turn has dominated Anglo-American philosophy in the twentieth century (much to the astonishment of many laymen). According to this movement, briefly, philosophers should approach all issues by attending to language. It is characteristic of the movement, therefore, to be concerned not with morals, but with the language of morals; not with science, but with the language of science; and so on. Philosophy of language becomes the center, if not all, of philosophy.

What is the explanation of this turn? One factor has already emerged (11.2): a dissatisfaction with the metaphysical excesses of much nineteenth-century philosophy, particularly that emanating from Germany. Such dissatisfaction became common in Britain and America. The dissatisfaction encouraged the turn because philosophers thought that a close attention to language would prevent the excesses. This certainly seems to be true of G. E. Moore, who was very influential in determining the path of philosophy in Britain. Beyond this dissatisfaction, it is hard to account for the turn. We conjecture that it is partly a response to the earlier mentioned tension between first philosophy and empiricism (14.2). If philosophy is prior to science it cannot be part of science. Yet empiricism seems to rule out any role for philosophy outside science. The favored response, as we mentioned, is to see philosophy as yielding analytic truths, truths holding "in virtue of the meanings" of words. So meanings, and hence language, become the concern of philosophy.

Within the linguistic movement, philosophers can be distinguished by the degree to which their focus on language makes them negative about philosophy. The various positions tend to shade into each other because most philosophers in the movement – positivists excepted – were not explicit about their metaphilosophy.

The very influential philosopher, Ludwig Wittgenstein, who was certainly explicit enough, was probably the most negative of all about philosophy. He thought that the study of language would *dissolve* all philosophical problems: he saw philosophy as grammatical therapy and encouraged those for whom the therapy was successful to give it up. We shall call this negative wing *ordinary language philosophy*. (This name is reasonably in accord with history, though it is often used more broadly.) We shall consider it in this section.

The logical positivists, whom we have already discussed in connection with realism (11.2), were less negative. Though urging the elimination of metaphysics, they thought that it should be replaced by significant philosophical problems about language. For example, many saw one of their tasks as the construction of an ideal language of and for science: one purged of the ambiguity and vagueness of ordinary language, a language in which the logical structure of sentences was wholly explicit. Less negative still is Michael Dummett, whom we have also discussed in connection with realism (11.3–11.4). He identifies philosophical issues with problems about language, and has a very positive view of the role of philosophy in solving them. In this he is typical of the most common version of the linguistic turn in recent years: philosophy as *conceptual analysis*. We shall consider this positive wing of the movement in the next section.

Wittgenstein's concern with language in his famous *Philosophical Investigations* (1953) is explicit: "our investigation is . . . a grammatical one" (no. 90). However, he does not see the investigation as concerned with genuine intellectual problems. The problems arise from "misunderstandings concerning the use of words" (no. 90); we are entangled in our own rules (no. 125); we are in the grip of "confusions" (no. 132) and "plain nonsense" (no. 119). "Philosophy is a battle against the bewitchment of our intelligence by means of language" (no. 109). "A philosophical problem has the form: 'I don't know my way about'" (no. 123).

What we should attempt to do is free ourselves of these problems by close attention to how language is actually used. The problems arise "when language is like an engine idling, not when it is doing work" (no. 132). We need a rich diet of examples to help free us from the bewitchment (no. 593). The result we hope for is not "any kind of theory" or "explanation" (no. 109). Philosophy "leaves everything as it is" (no. 124); its problems should completely disappear (no. 133). What we look for is a cure of the philosopher not a piece of philosophical knowledge. Philosophy "is like the treatment of an illness" (no. 255). In a characteristically vivid metaphor, he describes the aim of philosophy as: "to shew the fly the way out of the fly bottle" (no. 309). Interestingly enough, one of the main targets of his therapy was the 'Fido'-Fido theory of meaning (14.2).

In sum, philosophical problems are pseudo problems, arising from the misuse of language. Philosophers should study language not to come up with theories, even ones about language, but to dissolve problems.

If this book is close to being right then ordinary language philosophy is mistaken. We have been urging solutions to genuine problems in the philosophy of language and the philosophy of mind. And we have alluded to others in metaphysics and epistemology. Nevertheless, we do think that there is *some* truth in this view of philosophy. It is likely that some philosophical problems are pseudo problems, and we have nominated one that we think is: the one-over-many problem. And we have suggested, in a Wittgensteinian way, that this problem arises from the bewitchment of language. In general, however, philosophy's task is constructive.

Wittgenstein taught at Cambridge until 1947, but it was at Oxford in the 1950s that ordinary language philosophy had its heyday. Two Oxford philosophers, to a degree independently of Wittgenstein, were very influential: Gilbert Ryle and J. L. Austin. Wittgenstein set out the ideology of ordinary language philosophy in its starkest form and, to a considerable degree, conformed to that ideology in his philosophical practice. Ryle and Austin were less explicitly negative in ideology and in practice. Thus they were closer than Wittgenstein to the conceptual analysis wing of the linguistic movement.

14.4   The Linguistic Turn: Conceptual Analysis

The conceptual analysis view of philosophy is ordinary language philosophy gone positive. The conceptual analysts come not to bury philosophy but to do it. They take philosophy to consist in the investigation of the structure of our concepts, especially the important ones for our understanding of the world. G. J. Warnock characterizes their view as follows.

> Political philosophy involves the study of political concepts, but says nothing of the rights or wrongs of political issues. The moral philosopher examines the "language of morals", but does not as such express moral judgements. The philosopher of religion may be, but by no means need be, a religious believer . . . philosophy is the study of the concepts that we employ, and not of the facts, phenomena, cases, or events to which those concepts might be or are applied. (1958: 167)

Since all the concepts that the analysts are interested in are ones for which we have words (on the language-of-thought hypothesis, the concepts are mental words synonymous with the public words that express them), their method is hardly distinguishable from the ordinary language philosophers' investigation of the use and misuse of words.

An analysis is necessary and knowable by a non-empirical method, it is knowable *a priori*. It is not, of course, always known by all who have the requisite concepts; it is implicit rather than explicit in the structure of concepts. Conceptual analysis is characterized not only by the kind of truths sought but even more by its method. It proceeds by "armchair" thought experiment. The analyst considers a range of imagined situations, both actual and possible (in the widest sense) and asks, "What would we say?". Our intuitions about these situations are generalized to construct an analysis, which is then tested against further cases.

Consider a famous example of analysis, that of the concept of knowledge. Is knowledge true belief? No: we imagine a situation where someone has a true belief accidentally and so we would not say that he *knew*. Is knowledge true belief for which the believer has good reasons? This won't do either: we imagine situations in which the believer has the reasons, but they are psychologically inert. Someone who correctly guesses the answer to a mathematical problem does not know the answer even if she has the information from which the answer can be deduced. And so on, until we come up with an analysis of knowledge that resists these imagined counter-examples.

What sort of "fact" makes an analysis true? It must be something implicit in the concept being analyzed. How can we come to know this fact *a priori*? It must be inside the mind, for if it were outside the mind, we would have to look outside to know of it. We would have to depend on experience to know of it and hence our knowledge could not be *a priori*. What could there be in the mind that we come to know in analysis? The popular answer is the only plausible one: facts about meanings. Our ordinary understanding of a word is thought to be in the mind. *Analysis probes the associations between words implicit in the very understanding of those words*, associations established in learning them. These associations are the facts implicit in our concepts. A likely example of the fruits of such an investigation would be the discovery that all bachelors are adult unmarried males, a fact alleged to hold in virtue of the fact that the meaning of 'bachelor' is constituted by its association with 'adult unmarried male'. Clearly, the links must be more subtle, and about more philosophically significant topics than these, if conceptual analysis is to have a central role in philosophy.

We doubt that there is *any* conceptual analysis, hence that conceptual analysis plays any role in philosophy. Our reasons are implicit in our earlier rejection of the view that analytic truths can be known *a priori* (5.6). The first reason is that conceptual analysis rests on the Cartesian assumption. It rests on the view that *simply* in virtue of understanding words, and having concepts, we can know about their natures; that by introspecting our concepts we can form *justified* beliefs about them without the benefit of any empirical investigation. We have argued against the

Cartesian assumption at some length (8.6). Insofar as meanings are "outside the head" – the sorts of meanings historical-causal, indicator, and teleological theories attempt to explain – the assumption seems hopeless. How could reflection on what competence with a term makes available "inside the head" establish such "external" and highly theoretical facts as that certain causal relations determine reference? But even with meanings covered by description theories and "inside the head" the Cartesian assumption is badly in need of an argument it never gets. Finally, we have urged a more modest alternative view of competence: it is an ability or skill, a piece of mere knowledge-how not knowledge-that (8.9).

There is a second reason for doubting that there is any conceptual analysis. Suppose that the Cartesian assumption really were true and that reflection on concepts did indeed yield the alleged knowledge about the meaning of 'bachelor'. Then we would know *a priori* that the meaning of 'unmarried' is part of the meaning of 'bachelor'. So we would know a priori that 'All bachelors are unmarried' is true provided 'All unmarrieds are unmarried' is true. But how do we know that the latter is true *a priori*? No satisfactory account of the *a priori* knowledge of such logical truths has ever been given. If we do not know the logical truth *a priori*, then we do not know 'All bachelors are unmarried' *a priori*.

So our favored position on conceptual analysis is that there isn't any. But we have a fall-back position. We can see no hope for Cartesianism about meanings that are "outside the head" but suppose that, contrary to our argument, we do have Cartesian access to meanings that are "inside the head", *covered by description theories*. Suppose further that, contrary to our doubts, logic is somehow known *a priori*. So, there would, after all, be some conceptual analysis. We would then allow that conceptual analysis *might* have a role in philosophy, that it *might* yield philosophical knowledge. However, we would still reject the conceptual analysis view of philosophy, the view that *all* philosophy was conceptual analysis. We think that there would still be good reason to think that little if any was.

We think this because the knowledge yielded by conceptual analysis would probably all be *boring*. Consider the circumstances in which it would arise. It would be expressed by a sentence of the form, 'All Fs are G'. But what would be required for conceptual analysis to yield *knowledge* of what this sentence expresses? First, 'F' must be covered by a description theory. Second, 'G' must be among the descriptions that determine the meaning of 'F' so that the meaning of 'G' is part of the meaning of 'F'. Perhaps the knowledge that all bachelors are unmarried, and the like, would meet these requirements. But such knowledge is uninteresting. *Interesting* knowledge will often involve an 'F' that is covered by a causal theory of some sort; consider natural kind terms (5.2), for example. And where the knowledge does not, it is likely to involve a 'G' whose meaning is *not* part of the meaning of '*F*'. Interesting knowledge is simply unlikely to meet the requirements. So even if we did have *a priori* knowledge, interesting knowledge (outside mathematics and logic) is likely to be *empirical*.

Conceptual analysis is supposed to yield knowledge about such areas as the mind, semantics, morals and epistemology. But compare these areas of knowledge with others, for example, biology. It would be absurd to say that any interesting parts of biology were knowable *a priori*. Why suppose that the situation is any different with the areas that concern conceptual analysis? Why suppose that an interesting theory of the mind is any more to be discovered by examining our ordinary mental concepts than an interesting theory of biology is to be discovered by examining our ordinary biological concepts?

Our favored view is that there is no conceptual analysis. Our fall-back view is that little if any conceptual analysis is philosophically interesting. So what are to say of the large amount of interesting work produced by philosophers claiming to be conceptual analysts? Despite what these philosophers claim, they are not doing conceptual analysis. What then are they doing?

Our answer starts by returning to the matter of intuitions (8.6). We are all full of intuitions, quick unreflective judgments about the world. The most basic of these identify instances and non-instances of some kind with which we are familiar: the folk will say, "This is a cat but that is not"; the zoologist will say, "This is an echidna but that is not"; the paleontologist will say, "This is a pig's jawbone but that is not". We should trust a person's intuitions to the degree that they are expert in the area in question. But, however expert they are, their intuitions are empirical, theory-laden, revisable, responses to worldly phenomena.

When starting pretty much from scratch in investigating the nature of some kind we need to consult the basic intuitions of the experts in the area. We can then examine the instances and non-instances that the experts identify in the hope of discovering the nature of the kind: we hope to see what is common and peculiar to instances of the kind.

The would-be conceptual analysts are starting pretty much from scratch with the kinds that concern them in areas such as the mind, semantics, morals and epistemology. These kinds are ones which the folk are as expert at identifying as anyone: they are good at telling whether someone is in pain, whether a word refers to a certain object, whether a certain act is right, whether a certain belief is knowledge, and so on. So, one way to begin investigating these kinds would be to discover the basic intuitions of the folk by conducting "identification experiments": "Is this person in pain?"; "Is that knowledge?"; and so on. But two shortcuts are available for philosophers. First they are surely entitled to count themselves as members of the folk and so they can use their own basic intuitions. Second, instead of conducting "real" experiments that confront people with phenomena and ask whether these are instances of the kind or not, the philosophers can conduct "thought experiments" that confront them with *descriptions* of phenomena and ask whether they *would say* that these were instances of the kind or not. The intuitions elicited in these thought experiments depend rather on precisely how the phenomena are described and so may not be as evidentially valuable as those in the real experiments. Still they are evidence. But they have just the same empirical theory-laden status as the ones expressed in the real experiments. On the basis of these empirical judgments about instances of the kind, the philosopher constructs a theory of the nature of the kind, a theory that is then tested by more thought experiments. Since this theory is built on what are in effect folk intuitions, we might call it the "tacit folk theory".

This is our picture of what philosophers who claim to be doing conceptual analysis are really doing: they are constructing empirical theories about the nature of kinds on the bases of empirical judgments about instances and non-instances of the kind. What philosophers probe from their armchairs is not their tacit *a priori* knowledge about meanings or concepts but their tacit empirical knowledge about kinds, knowledge acquired through a lifetime of acquaintance with the kinds. We do not deny a role for thought experiments; we simply deny that this role is *a priori*.

We conclude that the conceptual analysis view of philosophy is wrong. The study of language, and the concepts it expresses, is important but it should not be identified with philosophy or even made central to it. The linguistic turn is a mistake and does not re-establish first philosophy.

Some further remarks are appropriate about the consequences of subscribing to the conceptual analysis view. We have seen that the practitioners of this view make explicit the tacit folk theory reflected in empirical folk intuitions about kinds. This is a result worth seeking. In the areas in question – areas like mind and meaning – tacit folk theory is often just about all we have got to start with. However, discovering folk theory can be only the beginning of the theoretical task. That theory then needs to be critically examined against the phenomena.

How right is the folk theory? It reflects the wisdom of the ages and so is likely to be not bad so far as it goes. But some folk theories in the past have been spectacularly wrong (1.3). So it should always remain an open question how correct the folk theory is.

How adequate is the theory? It is likely to be inadequate in at least two ways. First, its account of the kinds is unlikely to go far enough. Further empirical investigation will be needed to fill it out. Second, and more serious, the kinds in question may not be the *right* kinds and are unlikely to be *all* the right kinds. The right kinds are the ones that really do play explanatorily significant roles in the mind, semantics, morals, epistemology, and so on. The right kinds are the ones that our best theories will advert to. Perhaps our best epistemology will not advert to knowledge. Perhaps our best psychology will not advert to pains. If not, the folk theories of knowledge and of pains, theories that philosophers labor to make explicit, would be rather beside the point. Even where the folk have identified explanatory kinds, our best theories will surely identify others. We will need to give an account of these others, an account of kinds undreamt of by the folk.

Unfortunately, the conceptual analysis view works against the critical examination of folk theory. For, if a person holds the view, he takes his results to be known *a priori*, and he takes the task to be complete once the mining of ordinary concepts is exhausted. So, though the conceptual analysis view can lead to useful results, it also leads to a complacency about those results. It discourages attention to the phenomena which led to the folk opinions in the first place and which it is the task of the theory to explain.

In this chapter, we have defended our naturalistic view of philosophy by criticizing various versions of *a priori* first philosophy. Our criticism of traditional first philosophy focused on one of its central and perennial problems: the one-over-many. This is a pseudo problem, arising, we suspect, from an implicit commitment to the false 'Fido'-Fido theory of meaning. The linguistic turn has dominated Anglo-American first philosophy in this century. At its most negative, this turn sees all philosophical problems as pseudo problems, arising from linguistic confusions. Mostly, it has the more positive view that the problems are soluble by linguistic or conceptual analysis. Philosophical problems are not, in general, pseudo problems, and analysis has little if anything to do with solving them.

Suggested Reading

14.1

The focus of arguments for naturalism in philosophy has been on epistemology. The major figure has been Quine: see "The Scope and Language of Science" in *Ways of Paradox* (1966), "Epistemology Naturalized" in *Ontological Relativity* (1969), and "The Nature of Natural Knowledge" in Guttenplan 1975, *Mind and Language*. The second of these essays is reprinted in Kornblith 1994, *Naturalizing Epistemology*, which is a good collection of essays with a helpful introduction and a massive bibliography. See also Devitt 1997 for a detailed defense of the naturalistic approach to philosophy. Millikan 1984, *Language, Thought, and Other*

Biological Categories, is an extended defense of a naturalist approach to the philosophy of language and epistemology.

14.2

Quine's "On What There Is" in *From a Logical Point of View* (1961) is the classic rejection of the one-over-many problem. Armstrong 1978, *Nominalism and Realism*, takes the problem seriously and critically examines all known attempts to solve it; see also his 1989, *Universals: An Opinionated Introduction*. Campbell 1991, *Abstract Particulars*, argues for tropes. Mellor and Oliver 1997, *Properties*, is a helpful collection including, *inter alia*, Quine's paper, some earlier classics, an exchange between Devitt and Armstrong, and a paper by Campbell.

14.3–14.4

Wittgenstein's views are expounded in his classic *Philosophical Investigations* (1953). Useful introductions are Pears 1971, *Wittgenstein*; Kenny 1973, *Wittgenstein*. Baker and Hacker 1988, *Wittgenstein, Rules, Grammar, and Necessity*, is a sympathetic commentary.

Two classics of ordinary language philosophy/conceptual analysis are Ryle 1949, *The Concept of Mind*; Austin 1962b, *Sense and Sensibilia*. The former is much more positive in its view of philosophy and has been very influential. It founded philosophical behaviorism.

Warnock 1958, *English Philosophy Since 1900*, is a very sympathetic survey. Gellner 1959, *Words and Things*, is a biting and unsympathetic assault. Passmore 1966, *A Hundred Years of Philosophy*, ch. 18, is short readable survey. Rorty 1967, *The Linguistic Turn*, is a collection of classic papers with a useful but difficult introduction.

Stich 1982, "On the Ascription of Content", in Woodfield 1982, *Thought and Object;* and Dennett 1991a, *Consciousness Explained* (1991), ch. 4, have similar views to ours of what is really going on in "conceptual analysis". Lewis 1994, "Reduction of Mind", and Jackson 1994, "Armchair Metaphysics", give clear defenses of a more traditional view.

See also the suggested readings for 5.6.

** 15

Rational Psychology

15.1   Rational Psychology versus Protoscience

In this chapter, we shall consider a view of people that challenges both our naturalistic approach to philosophy and the theory of language that we have urged in this book.

We all gain an apparatus for thinking about people, if not with our mother's milk at least with our play lunch. Early in life we gain folk psychology. This psychology ranges over sensations (e.g. pain), emotions (e.g. envy), character (e.g. bravery), and thought (e.g. belief). The folk psychology that will concern us is the last, folk cognitive psychology.

We use this folk psychology to explain behavior. Why is Otto eating candied ants? We take Otto to have a certain desire: he craves something sweet and crunchy. We take him to have a certain belief: that candied ants are sweet and crunchy. So we can explain Otto's behavior.

We use folk psychology to explain noncognitive mental states. Why does Otto hate Felix? We know that Otto believes Felix deliberately humiliated him. We know that people frequently hate those they believe humiliated them. So we can explain Otto's mental state.

We use folk psychology to explain cognitive mental states. Why does Otto believe that Felix humiliated him? Otto believes that Felix snickered and giggled when beating him at chess and told others that he, Otto, was an idiot. Further, Otto believes that anyone who does such things humiliates those to whom they are done. So we can explain Otto's mental state.

What is the status of folk psychology? There are two very different answers to this question.

The answer dictated by our naturalism is that folk psychology, like all folk theories, is a *protoscience*. It differs from a science proper in being immature: it is imprecise, inexplicit and unsystematic; it is held uncritically; it is not associated with a methodology for its development (1.3). Nonetheless, it has the same general characteristics as a science. It contains, or yields, empirical lawlike generalizations that enable explanation and prediction. It is open to scientific revision.

The alternative answer rejects this naturalistic view. It does not take folk psychology to be inferior science, but rather takes it not to be science at all. It is a different category of knowledge that is incommensurable with science. Two prominent defenders of this view are Daniel Dennett and Donald Davidson. They argue for what we shall call the *rational psychology* approach to folk psychology. Or, so it seems.

It is important to distinguish the rational psychology approach from two other views. One is the view that the subject matter of folk cognitive psychology – beliefs and other thoughts – do not really exist; the behaviorism that dominated psychology for so many years is an example of such a view. On this anti-realist or eliminativist view, folk psychology is a totally *false* protoscience. We do not agree with this view (for reasons briefly indicated in section 7.1), but there is nothing unnaturalistic about it. Rejecting the subject matter of a science is always a possibility for the naturalist.

Anti-realism can be combined with *instrumentalism*, the view that a theory is not properly thought of as descriptive of some underlying reality but rather as a useful instrument for predicting observations on the basis of past observations.

Rational psychology also needs to be distinguished from "philosophical" behaviorism, which is realist about thoughts but takes them to be nothing but dispositions to behavior; Gilbert Ryle's *The Concept of Mind* (1949) is the *locus classicus*. The facts that constitute an agent's intentional profile – the agent's stock of beliefs and preferences – are not facts about the inner causes of behavior. They are patterns in behavior. What makes it true, say, that an agent really wants to smoke are facts about their past and future behavioral dispositions. The patterns of an agent's behavior are not just evidence of their intentional states, or symptoms of those states. Intentional concepts like belief and preference are *about* behavior. Again, while we do not accept behaviorism, it is not in and of itself an anti-naturalist position.

It is hard to be confident about the position of Dennett and Davidson on this important matter. They often write about folk psychology in an instrumentalist anti-realist vein. And Dennett often writes about it in the realist vein of philosophical behaviorism. Still, at bottom, we think that they are urging the rational psychology approach. The anti-realism we have just described denies that there are *any* mental facts: adapting our earlier terminology (11.1), we might say that it rejects "the existence dimension" of mental realism. In contrast, rational psychology denies "the independence dimension": there are mental facts but they are of a special sort *imposed by us* and not open to scientific explanation. In this way, rational psychology conflicts with the metaphysical respect of our naturalism (1.3), which requires that all facts be not only scientifically explicable but, ultimately, physically explicable. Rational psychology conflicts also with the epistemological respect of our naturalism in claiming that our way of knowing about these mental facts is outside empirical science. We find rational psychology in the following four related theses of Dennett and Davidson.

1) *The no-replacement thesis.* Folk psychology is not replaceable by science, in particular by scientific psychology. There are two ideas here. First, science could not show folk psychology to be wrong, to be making deeply mistaken claims about human nature. Second, a scientific theory could not serve the same functions in our lives as the folk theory. It is, Dennett suggests (1987: ch. 3), a different tool for a different job. The task of folk psychology is to *rationalize* people; it is to *understand* people in a special nonscientific way; it is to *impose an interpretation.*

2) *The no-reform thesis.* Folk psychology is not open to scientific reform; it cannot become science-like. Folk explanations are necessarily loose, imprecise, and laced with escape clauses and hence are different from those in science (Davidson 1980: 221–3; though Dennett does seem to think it can made like mathematics by reforming it into decision theory; 1987: ch. 3).

3) *The no-integration thesis.* Folk psychology cannot be integrated with science; the two cannot be joined to form a single seamless theory of people. Davidson seems to leave no room for a scientific psychology at all, and rejects the possibility of a reduction of folk psychology to physics. Dennett, too, at one stage seemed to hold no hope for an integration of folk with scientific psychology. For he drew a sharp distinction between "the intentional stance", the domain of folk psychology, and "the design stance", the province of scientific psychology. In recent years his position seems to have shifted. In his 1995 the distinction between "the design stance" and the "intentional stance" is less sharp than in his earlier work. Even so, folk psychology, in his view, is still very different from, say, a theory of the neurophysiology of vision.

4) *Principles of charity.* Finally, folk psychology involves principles that have no place in science. In ascribing beliefs and desires, we have to be charitable: we have to see people as rational and believers of the truth.

These surprising principles are central to rational psychology and are thought to underpin the other ways in which folk psychology is marked off. It is because we must apply them that folk psychology is thought to be ascientific; in applying them we impose an interpretation. The principles will be the concern of sections 15.4 and 15.5.

Rational psychology's challenge to naturalism (and hence to naturalistic philosophy) is clear: it takes us to have ascientific knowledge of facts that are not open to physical explanation.

What are the consequences of rational psychology for the theory of language? Dennett draws no conclusions about language. Indeed his work does not include a systematic discussion of language. Davidson's certainly does, but the bearing of his rational psychology on that discussion is not clear, as we shall see (15.3). On almost any plausible view, the theory of language will have close links with cognitive psychology (chs. 7, 9). Certainly, on our Gricean view, the speaker meaning of a linguistic symbol is to be identified with the content of a thought (7.4). Rational psychology places the folk view of content outside science and so should place folk semantics outside it also. Explanations of symbols in terms of meaning, truth and reference should also be ascientific. There would still be a place, presumably, for scientific linguistics, but it would not include the truth-referential semantics that we have placed in center stage.

The rational psychology of Davidson and Dennett is reminiscent of a tradition that has been well established in continental Europe since the turn of the century through the work of Wilhelm Dilthey (1976) and Max Weber (1949). The tradition takes a "humanist" view of the social sciences, insisting that they differ from the natural ones in requiring *Verstehen*, a sort of empathetic understanding. Indeed, Graham McDonald and Philip Pettit (1981) have derived a *Verstehen* view from an explicitly Davidsonian perspective. They also claim that this is the only good route to *Verstehen*. If they are right about this, our arguments against rational psychology will count also against the continental tradition.

Dennett and Davidson are not philosophical twins. We shall briefly characterize their rather different philosophies of mind before turning to the principles of charity.

15.2   Dennett

Dennett is not a mystery-monger. In general he seems to have a thoroughly naturalist world view, taking humans to be evolved biological machines. In his work on consciousness (1991a), for example, he has campaigned relentlessly against the idea, still widespread, that consciousness is an ineffable mystery beyond scientific explanation. Given all this, the fact that he does not see folk psychology as a protoscience is puzzling. Our best estimate of his underlying view is that while he does not think folk psychology is good enough to qualify as even a protoscience, it is still too valuable to be discarded. But his work is difficult to understand, apparently weaving together three inconsistent strands of thought: instrumentalism, philosophical behaviorism, and rational psychology.

Dennett distinguishes two stances: the *intentional stance*, which is the one of folk cognitive psychology; and the *design stance*, which is the one of scientific cognitive psychology.

One standard way of explaining the intentional stance, one often used by Dennett, brings out the instrumentalist strand in his thought. Suppose that we are confronted by a chess player – a person or a computer – and wish to predict its next move. We adopt the intentional stance when we attribute to it certain desires, including that to win, and certain true beliefs, and then try to work out the *best* move. What, given those thoughts, would it be most rational to do? Something whose behavior can be predicted like this – or approximately predicted, because some slippage is allowed – is called an intentional system. In treating something as an intentional system, we are not supposing that it really embodies thoughts which cause it to behave as it does. It is just that it is convenient for prediction to treat the object *as if* it embodied them. In other words, the intentional stance is not realist but instrumentalist about beliefs and desires: they are mere instruments for prediction. It is not literally true that a low grade chess playing computer has beliefs and preferences about chess or anything else. But it is convenient to pretend that it does.

> *all there is* to being a true believer is being a system whose behavior is reliably predictable via the intentional strategy, and hence *all there is* to really and truly believing that p (for any proposition p) is being an intentional system for which p occurs as a belief in the best (most predictive) interpretation. (Dennett 1987: 29)

The design stance, in contrast, is thoroughly realist. It is concerned with what is really going on in the object that causes it to behave as it does. What are its internal states, and what sort of structure do they operate in? These are the concerns of scientific psychology. Like any science it will introduce a range of theoretical entities, but none of these will be beliefs and desires. If the intentional stance is rightly seen as instrumentalist (as the quote above suggests) it is not about anything at all, and certainly not the theoretical entities that cause behavior.

However, there is another way of interpreting the intentional stance. On this alternative, organisms really have beliefs and desires, and sentences ascribing them are literally true. But those sentences are not about the causes of behavior, they are about patterns in behavior. This is the philosophical behaviorist strand in Dennett's thinking. There are signs of it in the above quote. And consider:

> Suppose . . . some beings of vastly superior intelligence . . . were to descend upon us and suppose we were to them as simple thermostats are to engineers. Suppose that is that they did not *need* the intentional stance – or even the design stance – to predict our behavior in all its detail. . . . would we be right then to say that from *their* point of view we really were not believers at all (any more than a simple thermostat is). If so, our status as believers is nothing objective, but something in the eye of the beholder . . . our imagined Martians might be able to predict the future . . . But if they did not see us as intentional systems, they would be missing something perfectly objective: the *patterns* in human behavior that are describable from the intentional stance, and only from that stance, and that support generalizations and predictions. (Dennett 1987: p. 25)

It looks here as if intentional folk psychology is giving objectively true descriptions of patterns in behavior. That is philosophical behaviorism.

So far, then, we have two strands in Dennett's thinking. The behaviorist strand is realist about folk psychology, the instrumentalist strand is anti-realist. Right or wrong, there is nothing anti-naturalist about either view. The anti-naturalist strand of rational psychology enters with the principles of charity. These principles cannot be combined with a realist position like philosophical behaviorism.

The problem emerges when we ask which organisms and artifacts have patterns in their behavior that make belief/desire psychological theories true of them? In answering this question the principles of charity play a central role. For the pattern in behavior described by an intentional profile is the behavior an agent would exhibit if (i) it were fully informed about its environment; (ii) it had an appropriate set of preferences given its needs; (iii) it acted rationally given its preferences and information. Intentional agents are *ex officio* rational. This idea seems to abandon naturalism. For on this picture it is not an empirical fact to be discovered that intentional agents in ordinary circumstances are well informed and prudent. It is a conceptual truth about what it means to be a believer/ desirer. Moreover, from the perspective of the consistent philosophical behaviorist, the observer-relativity that Dennett often insists upon seems to have no place. In places, Dennett argues that there is a most important difference between deploying the intentional stance towards humans (and many animals) and deploying it towards, say, automatic door-openers. We can use other strategies with the door opener but not the person. People and perhaps some other animals are highly complex in their internal structure. So we can successfully interact with them only by taking the intentional stance towards them. But for the consistent philosophical behaviorist, we should adopt the intentional stance if and only if the object really has, independent of us and what we can do, the patterns in behavior that constitute having particular beliefs and preferences.

Philosophical behaviorism accepts that there are thoughts. That is the existence dimension of mental realism. But it also accepts the independence dimension and so must reject principles of charity. Thoughts are not imposed by us, they are there for us to discover. To suppose otherwise is to adopt rational psychology: thoughts depend for their existence on our charitable decision. To the extent that the intentional stance is a version of rational psychology it is inconsistent with naturalism. Claims about the rationality and complexity of agents which, if facts at all, are empirical facts turn into *a priori* ones.

We have argued that principles of charity can have no place in the behaviorist strand of Dennett's thinking. But we must acknowledge that they may have a place in the instrumentalist strand. For with instrumentalism, no issue about the truth or falsehood of intentional ascriptions arises. On this view, the sentence "Dennett believes that creationists are crackpots" is strictly speaking neither true nor false. Rather, it is or is not part of an intentional profile we can usefully attribute to Dennett to predict his behavior. So no issues of nonphysical facts in the world or nonempirical ways of finding out about the world arise. In this context, principles of charity might have a role because they were *useful*. A reasonable case can be made that the principles are indeed useful: they help us to formulate predictively useful intentional profiles. For though no real agents behave as an epistemically optimal agent would, well-designed agents acting in their normal environment approximate the behavior of a rational agent. If we consider any well designed organism or artifact operating in its normal environment, we can predict its behavior fairly well by asking "What should it believe, given its circumstances? What should it want given its purposes? What should it do, given those beliefs and wants?". We then predict that it *will* do what it should do. We can predict what a tree, a person, an automatic door opener should do fairly well using this strategy.

However wrong it may be, this sort of instrumentalism is thoroughly naturalistic. So if Dennett were consistently an instrumentalist in his view of intentional psychology, his use of principles of charity would be no departure from naturalism. For on a consistently instrumentalist view, there are no facts of any kind, natural or not, about belief and desire. Nor are there discoveries to make about them, by empirical means or any other. The use of principles of charity would raise only pragmatic issues. Is it the best way of formulating a predictively useful intentional stance? (There would, of course, be a question of why a philosopher of generally naturalistic inclinations would take that view of intentional psychology.) But

Dennett is not consistently instrumentalist: he often seems to be a philosophical behaviorist. Yet this realist strand in his thinking cannot be combined with principles of charity. There seems to be a third strand, rational psychology: there *are* thoughts, contrary to instrumentalism, but they are dependent on our charitable decisions, contrary to philosophical behaviorism. This strand does pose a problem for Dennett's naturalism. For it generates *a priori* and observer dependent claims about intentional agents.

15.3   Davidson

Davidson's view of the mind is obscure. He has much to say about what psychological states are not, but is rather coy about what they are. He calls his position *Anomalous Monism*. His monism is clear enough: each token mental state or event is simply a physical state or event; in humans, it is a brain state or event. The difficulty comes with the alleged anomalousness of the mental.

Anomalousness is the denial that there can be any psychological laws, and hence that beliefs and desires are scientific kinds:

> there are no strict deterministic laws on the basis of which mental events can be predicted and explained. (Davidson 1980: 208)

This view depends in some way on the denial that there are psychophysical laws (pp. 209, 224): there are no laws linking the psychological to the physical. These two denials are not accompanied by any clear statement of what, as a result, mental states are. What are psychological explanations and what are they for? How do mental facts relate to physical facts?

If there are no psychological laws, if psychological kinds are not natural kinds, then folk psychology cannot be protoscience. What then is it? It is rational psychology. For Davidson takes the use of principles of charity to be central to psychology.

There is another important strand in Davidson's thought: his views on the nature of science are deeply conditioned by the model of physics. He argues that intentional explanation is irredeemably loose. Any psychological explanation must be "holistic" (p. 217), in the sense that it involves implicit reference to the agent's entire belief–desire system. Furthermore, psychological phenomena do not constitute a closed system. Both militate against there being genuine psychological laws.

Consider some piece of behavior: Tommygun Marsala's voting for Reagan in 1984. Why did Tommygun so vote? It will obviously be very difficult to have a complete and accurate story here. We may cite various desires of Tommygun: his opposition to gun control, his dissatisfaction with street crime, and the like. We may cite some of his beliefs: that Reagan too is opposed to gun control and mugging. However, this explanation remains somewhat loose. If Tommygun had had various additional beliefs and desires, he would have voted for Carter or stayed home. These interfering factors must be guarded against in the explanation; it is implicitly holistic. Yet, according to Davidson, it is impossible to specify all these factors so that anyone who had that complex of thoughts would have voted for Reagan. The best we can expect are generalizations that embody "practical wisdom", and that "are insulated from counterexample by generous escape clauses" (1980: 219).

To qualify as a scientific law, Davidson thinks, generalizations must be tight, precise, quantifiable, and near enough deterministic. These conditions are satisfied only by "comprehensive closed systems" (p. 219). The psychological realm is not a closed system. Psychological processes are constituted out of, and hence depend on, neural and other biological processes. Psychological prediction and explanation assume the normal functioning of our internal machinery. Hence, an explanation can fail, not because of a psychological error, but because the machinery is not functioning normally. "Too much happens to affect the mental that is not itself a systematic part of the mental" (p. 224).

We can grant Davidson's premises, yet deny his conclusions. Such a paradigm science as biology manifests the same characteristics as folk psychology. Consider, for example, the processes involved in meiosis, fertilization, and development; the processes by which genotype is translated into phenotype. There is no closed system here either. The nonbiological affects the biological: radiation induces mutations; chemicals induce developmental abnormalities. Thalidomide is a tragic example of the latter. Few deny that genetics and embryology discover laws, or, at least, generalizations importantly like laws. These generalizations are "loose" in the same way as are psychological laws. Consider the phenotypical consequences of the presence of some gene. (i) The specification of consequences is holistic: the effect of a given gene depends on which others are present (this is called "epigenesis"). (ii) We assume the process is normal: there is no interference from trauma, unusual chemicals, radiation, and so on. "Generous escape clauses" are allowed.

On Davidson's view of laws, the only laws would be those of physics and physical chemistry.

Davidson has written extensively on semantics. What has anomalous monism to do with his semantic views? Strangely enough, Davidson does not say. Yet the two views are obviously intimately related because principles of charity are central to them both.

At first sight, Davidson's semantics is a curious combination. His theory is truth-conditional, based on Tarski's theory of truth. We agree with this, of course, and have been influenced by this aspect of his view. Yet he differs from us in denying the need for, and possibility of, theories of reference. His attitude to reference seems to be instrumentalist. So truth is not *explained* in terms of reference. Indeed, Davidson seems to treat truth as an unexplained primitive. This would go against physicalism. Yet there are physicalist overtones, including many approving references to the arch-physicalist Quine, in Davidson's presentation. What are we to make of this combination?

The answer is too complicated to be attempted here, but we think that it is clear where it is to be found: in the "interpretative" perspective demanded by anomolous monism. Davidson takes the semantic task to be that of saying how to construct a theory of "radical interpretation" for a language. From our perspective this task is worthwhile but not fundamental enough: it rests on semantic notions of meaning, truth, and reference that need independent explanation. Davidson would disagree, for he thinks that there is no more to these notions than would be revealed by accomplishing his task. This reflects his anomolous monism. He does not take thoughts to be objective states posited independently of language that can be used in the explanation of the language that expresses them. Rather, influenced by Quine, he starts the explanation of language from a behaviorist assumption: "Meaning is entirely determined by observable behavior, even readily observable behavior" (Davidson 1990: 314; cf. Quine 1991: 272). This slender basis seems to demand semantic eliminativism. But Davidson has another sort of anti-realism in mind. Meanings are not for the most part objective properties with natures awaiting our discovery. The only independent reality captured by meaning talk is a set of verbal dispositions. Beyond that there is nothing but our *practice of interpreting* each other using principles of charity, a practice that should be seen more as *imposing* a semantic reality than as discovering one (Davidson 1984, 1990).

We shall look at these principles in the next two sections. But, first, let us note how Davidson's approach looks from our realist perspective. We think that no good reason has been produced to treat theories of mind and meaning differently from theories in any other science. The folk ascribe meanings to thoughts and utterances. For the most part these ascriptions appear to be successful in explaining behavior and guiding us to reality. So we have good reason to suppose that the thoughts and utterances really have those meanings, independently of our ascribing them. Davidson (like Quine) gives no argument for the behaviorism that underlies his anti-realist perspective.

15.4   Principles of Charity

It needs emphasizing that any principle of charity strong enough to mark off folk psychology from science must be a *constitutive* one: one that must apply to an object if it is to be a believer-desirer. Constitutive principles are very different from epistemic or heuristic ones. A good epistemic principle may be: we are justified in assuming that a person is, for the most part, rational or a believer of the truth. A good heuristic principle may be: start your explanation of a person with the assumption that she is rational and a believer of the truth. But such principles would not distinguish folk psychology from science. Being the object of charity must be of the very essence of an intentional system.

We have noted the problems of interpreting Dennett (15.2). But in thinking that the rationality of intentional agents is not something we need to discover or demonstrate, Dennett does seem to hold a constitutive principle of charity. Moreover, he explicitly takes the principle to be *normative* and *idealizing* rather than descriptive. Intentional psychological explanation then inherits this characteristic. This may help explain why Dennett sees intentional psychology as more like the formal mathematical theories of game and decision theory than natural science. For these formal theories are theories of how perfectly rational agents would behave.

We believe that the fact/value gap is not a chasm, and that values are a kind of fact. The formal sciences may be ultimately empirical too. On this the jury is still out. But even if they are, if belief–desire psychology is rather like decision theory, and ought eventually to become more like it, then folk psychology is not protoscience in the relevant sense. However, we shall argue (15.5) that folk psychology does not deploy any principle of charity that is nearly strong enough to warrant separating it from science.

It is still less clear why Davidson thinks that a principle of charity demarcates the mental from the physical. It is clear that he endorses a constitutive principle:

> in inferring this system [of beliefs and desires] from the evidence, we necessarily impose conditions of coherence, rationality, and consistency. These conditions have no echo in physical theory, which is why we can look for no more than rough correlations between psychological and physical phenomena. (1980: 231)

There is a *prima facie* puzzle here. Davidson goes straight from the claim that the mental has a different nature or essence from the physical, to the denial of psycho-physical laws. But from the fact that what, constitutively, makes something food "has no echo" in physical theory, it hardly follows that digestion is not a lawlike process.

We will see that there is no single principle of charity, but rather a cluster of related ones varying on two dimensions. Some of these principles sustain the demarcation in that, were they true, folk psychology could not be protoscience. But that is not the case for all the principles. Some of them can be seen plausibly as capturing part of the *scientific* essence of an intentional system. As such they are part of empirical science.

The *first dimension* of principles of charity concerns *topic*: principles may be of true belief, rational belief, or rational action. Those, like Dennett and Davidson, who urge a principle of charity tend to run these together. Yet they are very different, with very different degrees of plausibility.

1) *Charity-as-true-belief*. Charity sometimes appears as the thesis that most of the beliefs of an intentional system must be true. False beliefs are comparatively rare and require a special explanation. Thus Davidson writes:

> it cannot be assumed that speakers never have false beliefs. Error is what gives belief its point. We can, however, take it as given that *most* beliefs are correct. (1984: 168)

In a similar vein, Dennett writes:

> A species might "experiment" by mutation in any number of inefficacious systems, but none of these systems would deserve to be called belief systems precisely because of their defects, their nonrationality, and hence a false belief system is a conceptual impossibility. (1978: 17)

Assigning beliefs to a system so that they come out true amounts to assigning ones that agree with ours, for our beliefs represent our best view of what is true. So, "a good theory of interpretation maximizes agreement". (Davidson 1984: 169)

Charity, as they say, begins at home. A striking consequence of the principle of charity-as-true-belief is that most of our own beliefs must be true.

It is this version of the principle which most clearly threatens the naturalistic view of folk psychology. There is no scientific basis for linking beliefs to truth in this way.

2) *Charity-as-rational-belief*. Charity sometimes requires the rationality of beliefs given other beliefs; the inferential connections among beliefs must be rational. There are signs of this in the above passage from Dennett. Consider also:

> The assumption that something is an intentional system is the assumption

that it is rational . . . the animal . . . must be supposed to *follow* the *rules* of logic. (1978: 10–11)

Davidson talks of the rationality and consistency of the system (see above and 1984: 159). The intentional system must apply good rules of deduction. If Igor believes that one million volts kills any vampire, and if Igor believes that Yorga is a vampire, then Igor must believe that one million volts will kill Yorga. The system must also apply good rules of induction. It must not, for example, argue counter-inductively. If Igor believes that all previous vampires were stake-proof, he will not infer that Vorga will perish from stake insertion.

It is not obvious that commitment to this principle would show that folk psychology is ascientific. It is an open scientific question what sort of structure a system must have to have beliefs and desires. Perhaps the system has to operate according to certain rules. Perhaps those are the rules of logic that we think exemplify rational inference. Whether or not this is so is a matter for scientific investigation and no threat to naturalism.

3) *Charity-as-rational-action.* Finally, charity sometimes requires that the connection between an intentional system's beliefs and desires and its actions be rational. Davidson puts it as follows:

The belief and desire that explain an action must be such that anyone who had that belief and desire would have a reason to act in that way. (1984: 159)

Dennett has a similar view (1978: 59). If a piece of behavior is to be treated as something the agent *does* – as *intentional* behavior, as an action – and not as a mere bodily movement, then it must be rational given the agent's beliefs and desires. The basic pattern of belief–desire explanation is: an agent desires that p, believes that doing A will bring it about that p, and so does A. Igor desires that Yorga be dead, believes that this can be achieved by electrocuting him, and so electrocutes him.

This principle is surely right in one sense: to explain an agent's action by appeal to an agent's beliefs and desires is for it to be rational in just this way. Still, we should note, that in another "normative" sense the action might be irrational. Although it was caused by certain beliefs and desires and so is rational in a "descriptive" sense, it might be irrational in a "normative" sense: the agent may have other beliefs and desires that played no causal role but would give her decisive reason not to perform the action. In any case, commitment to the descriptive principle does not make folk psychology in the least bit nonscientific. The principle simply captures the nature of an action, what distinguishes it from mere bodily movement.

The *second dimension* of principles of charity concerns *strength*. Some qualifications are already apparent; charity-as-true-belief, for Davidson, requires only that *most* beliefs be correct. Dennett has a similar view (1978: 18). Both philosophers also accept lapses from perfect rationality (Dennett 1978: 11; Davidson 1984: 159). These qualifications increase plausibility at the cost of introducing vagueness.

Davidson sometimes suggests a further qualification: that we can be uncharitable provided that the error we attribute is *explicable* (1984: 196). If this were simply the requirement that we should minimize the inexplicable, then it would not distinguish folk psychology from science. It would just be an instance of a general principle of scientific methodology. The general principle of minimizing the inexplicable applies, of course, as much to the attribution of true beliefs as to the attribution of false ones. A rational reader does not interpret the ramblings of Nostradamus as expressing advance knowledge of our times, because there could be no explanation of Nostradamus's acquisition of that knowledge. So it is an important feature of this further qualification that it applies only to error: falsity and irrationality require explanation, but truth and rationality do not. This asymmetry is necessary if the principle of charity is to distinguish folk psychology from science.

15.5   Against Charity

We think that there is no truth in the principle of charity-as-true-belief, some truth in that of charity-as-rational-belief, and a good deal of truth in that of charity-as-rational-action. Since it is only-charity-as-true-belief that really threatens naturalism, we shall concentrate on it.

From our naturalistic perspective, the task in ascribing beliefs and desires to a person and truth values to his utterances is the usual one of explanation. The canons of good explanation we use here are just the same as those (largely unknown) ones we use elsewhere. A good explanation is likely to see the person as often agreeing with us, but it is likely also to see him as often disagreeing. And there is no asymmetry: falsehoods we ascribe should be explicable, but so too should truths. We do not interpret a five-year-old's finger painting as a derivation of Planck's constant because we are confident that such a derivation is beyond her. Our best explanation of many of our fellows may take an uncharitable view of their opinions on religion, semantics, politics, the weather, etc. It remains an entirely empirical question how true a person's beliefs are.

We reject, therefore, Davidson's frequently stated claim (e.g. 1984: 199–200) that the possibility of error and disagreement depends on general correctness and agreement. Davidson thinks that some error is possible. Why does disaster suddenly strike our explanation if we suppose that error goes beyond the Davidsonian limit? We have heard the suggestion that though we can ascribe error in a few areas we cannot in most. But what difference does it make to our attempt to explain a person uncharitably in, say, semantics that we have already explained him uncharitably in, say, religion and politics? Why does accumulation of error make a difference?

Prima facie it is implausible to commit folk psychology to any principle that demarcates it from the rest of our knowledge. There is only one world, so our knowledge of it should be unified. It ought to be possible to construct a single, integrated picture of nature, including our place in it. Furthermore, Davidson and Dennett do not offer any persuasive reason for thinking otherwise. We shall now consider their reasons.

1) Talk of "the principle of charity" was begun by N. L. Wilson in the process of urging a description theory of names (1959: 532). The description theory does indeed require charity. At one point, Davidson appeals implicitly to that theory as support for charity:

> how clear are we that the ancients – some ancients – believed that the earth was flat? *This* earth? Well, this earth of ours is part of the solar system, a system partly identified by the fact that it is a gaggle of large, cool, solid bodies circling around a very large, hot star. If someone believes *none* of this about the earth, is it certain that it is the earth that he is thinking about? ... It isn't that any one false belief necessarily destroys our ability to identify further beliefs, but that the intelligibility of such identifications must depend on a background of largely unmentioned and unquestioned true beliefs. (1984: 168)

We think that the answer to Davidson's rhetorical question is clear. The ancients believed that *this* earth was flat. What other earth is there? Indeed, the fact that the description theory leads to the paradoxical view that the ancients did not have that belief gives us a very good reason for rejecting it (3.3, 10.4, 12.3).

2) Dennett has argued that natural selection underwrites charity (1978: ch. 1). A creature that is irrational or largely in error will not survive to reproduce. We have three comments.

i) The argument might show that it is reasonable to be charitable about any creature we confront simply because it has survived to be confronted. But that is an epistemic principle. To establish the constitutive principle, it needs to be established that we should be charitable also about the creatures we do not confront because they have not survived. Evolutionary considerations do not establish this. Indeed, they suggest exactly the opposite: *the best explanation of nonsurvival may be error and irrationality.* Abandoning charity may be central to explaining evolutionary failure.

ii) We can imagine environments that systematically mislead creatures with a certain perceptual equipment. On some accounts of perceptual properties (like colors), *our* environment is one such. There is nothing incoherent in the claim that our commonsense picture of the world is radically mistaken. So, not only is the constitutive principle false, but the epistemic one has to be taken with caution.

iii) Natural selection does not favor true beliefs but rather ones that work in the creature's limited environment. Thus, it will not matter to the survival of a mouse that it is mostly wrong when it thinks, "Look out, a predator". What matters is that it is always right when it thinks, "All clear" (7.8).

In sum, evolution gives some support, but very far from conclusive support, to the epistemic principle that creatures that survive are likely to be believers of the truth and rational. It helps to refute the constitutive principle that concerns us here.

3) Both Dennett and Davidson advocate a *holistic* theory of belief and desire. A belief is identified relationally, in virtue of its role in the intellectual system of the believer. This requires that the belief have some systematic connections with other beliefs. These connections, the suggestion runs, yield charity-as-rational-belief.

First, this holism is too extreme: beliefs are partly identified by their reference-determining causal links to the external world. This is similar to a point we made earlier against structuralism (13.2–13.3). Second, this holism alone does not require that the connections be rational, only that they be systematic. Perhaps an intentional system could be systematically overconfident in its inductions (as a result of living in a very uniform environment). Or perhaps one could be systematically underconfident. There is no reason to suppose, as Dennett does (1978: 21), that lapses from optimal rationality are arbitrary, accidental, and unsystematic. It is an empirical question how well people infer. The answer emerging from cognitive psychology is that they often infer rather badly. Finally, as we have pointed out, even if some degree of rationality is required in an intentional system, that alone does not place folk psychology outside science.

In sum, charity needs to be split into various distinct principles. One of these is near enough true, one false, and one probably half and half. Such truth as there is in charity is no threat to naturalism. Folk psychology is rough and unsystematic, but there is no reason to suppose that it cannot be suitably modified and developed into a scientific theory.

Finally, there is a puzzle about principles of charity. Why bother to use them? It seems as if Davidson adopts them simply because without them no interpretation would be possible: "What makes interpretation possible . . . is the fact that we can dismiss *a priori* the chance of massive error"

(1984: 168–9). But, if the principles were necessary for interpretation, why should we bother with interpretation? What is the point of attaching a meaning to a person's words if they don't have that meaning independently of our charity? Of course, it may seem obvious that they do really have an independent meaning. If so, so much the worse for charity in semantics.

Suggested Reading

15.1

For Dilthey's views, see a recent collection, *Selected Writings* (1976). For Weber's, see *The Methodology of the Social Sciences* (1949).

  See McDonald and Pettit 1981, *Semantics and Social Science*, ch. 2, for a nice discussion of the *Verstehen* tradition and of its relationship to Davidson's view.

15.2

Dennett's view of folk psychology is to be found in *Brainstorms* (1978), Part I, and *The Intentional Stance* (1987), particularly chs. 1–4. See also *Consciousness Explained* (1991a). For his philosophical behaviorist strand, see particularly "Real Patterns" (1991b). Dennett thinks the intentional stance is a special case of "adaptive thinking" in evolutionary biology, a technique, very controversial within biology itself, of inferring an organism's functional organization from the problems its environment poses: *Darwin's Dangerous Idea* (1995), chs. 13–14. Dennett's views are discussed in Dahlbom 1993, *Dennett and His Critics* and in Hill 1994, a special issue of *Philosophical Topics* (1994).

15.3

For Davidson's theory of mind, see *Essays on Actions and Events* (1980), pp. 207–60. This is discussed in Lepore and McLaughlin 1985, *Actions and Events*. For Davidson's theory of language, see *Inquiries into Truth and Interpretation* (1984). This is discussed in Lepore 1986, *Truth and Interpretation*. Stalker 1993, *Reflecting Davidson*, is a collection with a terrific bibliography. Platts 1997, *The Ways of Meaning*, is a Davidsonian introduction to the philosophy of language.

  Lycan 1981, "Psychological Laws", is a good critical discussion of Anomalous Monism.

  For a discussion of the Davidsonian position on reference, see the suggested reading for section 2.2.

15.4–15.5

The best place to find Dennett's principle of charity, though not under that name, is 1978, ch. 1. Davidson discusses charity in many places in the two collections of his essays cited above; see references in their indexes.

McGinn 1977, "Charity, Interpretation, and Belief", is a critical treatment of Davidson on charity.

For a discussion of the extent to which natural selection will, and will not, build truth-finding minds, see Godfrey-Smith 1992, "Indication and Adaptation", and 1996, *Complexity and the Function of Mind in Nature*; and Stich 1990, *Fragmentation of Reason*, ch. 3.

Cohen 1981, "Can Human Irrationality be Experimentally Demonstrated", argues for charity-as-rational-belief in a different way. Stich 1985, "Could Man be an Irrational Animal?", in Kornblith 1994, *Naturalizing Epistemology*, argues against Cohen and also Dennett. The paper has a nice summary of some of the psychological literature allegedly demonstrating human irrationality.

For discussions with a similar perspective to that in the text, see Devitt 1981a, section 4.8, and 1997, ch. 10.**

Glossary

***A posteriori* or Empirical**   Primarily applied to knowledge. *A Posteriori* or empirical knowledge depends for its justification on our experience of the world. Empirical methods are those of observation and experiment. Cf. *A priori.*

A priori   Primarily applied to knowledge. *A priori* knowledge does not depend for its justification on our experience of the world. Logical and mathematical knowledge provides favorite examples. *A priori* methods are those of armchair reflection. Cf. *A posteriori or Empirical.*

Analytic   Primarily applied to sentences. An analytic sentence depends for its truth value only on the meaning of its elements, not on meaning together with extra-linguistic reality. 'Bachelors are unmarried' is a standard example. In a weaker sense, an analytic sentence is either a logical truth (cf. *Logical truth*) or a sentence that can be turned into a logical truth by substituting synonyms for synonyms. Cf. *Synthetic.*

Anaphoric   An expression is anaphoric if it depends for its interpretation on some other expression in the discourse. Pronouns are typical examples. Thus, 'he' and 'himself' in 'Max is he who hates himself' are anaphoric, depending for their interpretation on 'Max'. 'Max' is said to be their *antecedent*. Antecedents typically, but not always, precede the expression that is anaphorically linked to them. In 'That he lost the election upset Peacock greatly', ''Peacock' may be the antecedent of 'he'. Cf. *Deictic.*

Application   In this work, a species or mode of reference. The relationship between a predicate and the objects it refers to.

Attributive   In this work, the use of a singular term, or a token of that use, to refer (without any particular object in mind) to whatever is alone in having a certain property. An attributive term depends for identifying reference on denotation. Cf. *Designational*.

Cartesian Assumption   In this work, the view that for a person to be competence with an expression is for her to tacitly know about its meaning; that competence alone provides knowledge about the meaning.

Compositionality   A constraint placed on semantic theories. It is the requirement that the semantic properties of complex expressions (phrases, clauses, sentences) be a function of the semantic properties of the elements composing those complexes.

Constituent   An element of a sentence. Elements may be words or larger groupings like phrases or clauses, but not every sequence of words within a sentence is a constituent. 'Every dog chases' is not a constituent of 'Every dog chases some man'. The grammar of a language reveals the constituent structure of each sentence in the language.

Constructivism   A metaphysical doctrine that combines two Kantian ideas with relativism. The Kantian ideas are that the known world is partly made by our imposition of concepts (and the like); and that there is an unknowable world that exists prior to our imposition of concepts. The addition of relativism yields the view that different groups impose different concepts making different worlds.

Content   A synonym of "meaning", used particularly for the meaning of a thought.

Contingent truth   A true sentence that might not have been true. It is not true "in all possible worlds". Cf. *Necessary truth*.

Conventional meaning   The meaning of an expression determined by the established linguistic conventions of the speaker's language. Cf. *Speaker meaning*.

D-chain   Short for "designating chain". A causal chain between an object and person consisting of groundings, reference borrowings, and abilities to designate. A singular term can designate an object only if there is a d-chain connecting the user of the term to the object.

D-Structure (deep structure)   A level of structure distinguished from S-structure by transformational generative grammar. It displays the fundamental organization of a sentence: its organization into main and subordinate sentences; the subject and object; the application of modifying words and phrases, and the like. Cf. *S-structure (surface structure)*.

Definite description   A species of singular term whose basic form is 'the *F*', where '*F*' stands in for a general term. However, superlatives like 'the tallest mountain', and expressions like 'her father' (= 'the father of her') are also definite descriptions.

Deictic A use of a pronoun, demonstrative, or description that is not anaphoric. A use that is out of the blue and directly indicates an object. Cf. *Anaphoric*.

Denotation A species or mode of reference. It has a general use as the relation between a singular term and its referent. In this work, it is used more narrowly: the mode of reference of an attributive term. So it is the relationship between an attributive term and the unique object the term's associated description applies to. Cf. *Designation*.

Designation A species or mode of reference. It has a general use as the relation between a singular term and its referent. In this work, it is used more narrowly: the mode of reference of a designational term. So it is the relationship between a designational term and the object in which the d-chains underlying it are grounded. Cf. *Denotation*.

Designational In this work, the use of a singular term to refer to a particular object the speaker has in mind. A designational term depends for identifying reference on designation. Cf. *Attributive*.

Direct Reference A term refers directly if it refers without the mediation of a Fregean descriptive sense and is a rigid designator. The direct-reference view of proper names is that a name has no meaning beyond its role of referring to its bearer.

Eliminativism To be eliminativist about a theory is to believe that the objects posited by it simply do not exist; thus atheists are eliminativists about religion.

Empirical Cf. *A posteriori*.

Epistemology The theory of knowledge, of our way of knowing.

First Philosophy The branch of, or view concerning, philosophy in which philosophy is seen as prior to any empirical or scientific enterprise. Philosophy's role is to discover important truths *a priori*. Sometimes used to cover that part of philosophy which determines what there is (cf. *Ontology*) prior to finding out *about* what there is. Cf. *Naturalism*.

Functional- (Conceptual-) role semantics A family of theories of meaning that apply most obviously to thoughts. The meaning of a thought is determined by the pattern of its causal interactions in the mind of an agent: its causal relations to perceptions; its inferential relations to other thoughts; its role in the generation of behavior. Also sometimes known as "inferential-role semantics".

General term (Count noun) A term that can apply to each severally of any number of objects; e.g. 'cat'. Cf. *Mass term* and *Singular term*.

Generative (Transformational) grammar A generative grammar for a language provides an *explicit* statement of the rules for generating all and only the possible sentences of the language from the words (or morphemes) of the language. It thus provides a syntactic description of the sentence. Generative grammars recognize two kinds of rules. Base rules assemble the primitive elements into D-structures. These structures are mapped onto S-structures by transformation rules.

Grounding   In this work, a perception (or quasi-perception) of an object that begins a reference determining causal chain for a term.

Idealism   A metaphysical doctrine: the entities that make up the world are dependent for their existence or nature on minds, or are themselves mental. Cf. *Realism*.

Idiolect   The variety of language spoken by a single speaker.

Indicator semantics   A theory of meaning developed for the meaning of thoughts, especially perceptual thoughts. The meaning of a particular thought type is determined by the feature of the world with which it is reliably correlated. Thus, if some agent does or would produce tokens of the type FIRE only in the presence of fire, FIRE refers to fires.

Innate   Applied to knowledge or to concepts that an agent does not have to learn; information that is "wired into" the agent. Cf. *Nativism*.

Logical truth   A sentence that remains true under all reinterpretations of its terms (other than the logical particles like 'all' and 'not'); for example, 'All unmarrieds are unmarried'.

Mass term   A term that refers cumulatively: thus 'gin' refers to any sum of parts which are gin. Cf. *General term* and *Singular term*.

Meaning holism   The view that a word's meaning is determined by a large proportion – perhaps even all – of its relations with all other words in the language.

Meaning localism   The view that a word's meaning is determined by few if any of its relations with other words.

Metaphysics   The area of philosophy concerned with the ultimate nature of the world, with what there is and with what it is like.

Nativism   A psychological theory of the human mind, or an important aspect of the human mind, that holds that human minds have a rich stock of innate concepts and/or innate knowledge. Cf. *Innate*.

Natural kinds   The kinds required for the explanation of the natural universe.

Natural language   A language is one that has developed naturally and has, or has had, native speakers (speakers who acquired it as their first language).

Naturalism   Epistemologically, it is the view that philosophical knowledge, indeed all knowledge except perhaps mathematics and logic, is empirical; philosophy is continuous with science and not *a priori*. Metaphysically, it is the doctrine of physicalism (cf. *Physicalism*). Cf. *First Philosophy*.

Necessary truth   A sentence that must be true. It is true "in all possible worlds". Favorite examples are the truths of logic and mathematics; more recently and controversially, identity statements like 'water is H_2O'.

Cf. *Contingent truth*.

Ontology   The theory of what there is; i.e. of the basic kinds of entities that comprise the universe, and of their general nature. Derivatively, the ontology of a theory is the set of entities posited by the theory.

Opaque, or intensional, context   A place within a sentence where the substitution of a singular term for a coreferential term may change the truth value of the sentence. Cf. *Transparent, or extensional, context.*

Ostension (ostensive definition)   The act of pointing out an object or property. Hence, an ostensive definition is an explanation of the meaning of a term by pointing out (examples of) its referent. Cf. *Grounding*.

Phrase-structure trees or phrase-markers   Displays of syntactic structure. The trees show how a unit (typically a sentence) is organized into its immediate sub-units; how the sub-units in turn decompose into smaller units, and so on down to the primitive elements, words or morphemes. Both D- and S- structures are typically displayed as phrase-structure trees. Cf. *Generative (transformational) grammar.*

Physical type   In this work, a type of entity identified by overt physical characteristics and used as a medium of language; for example, a certain type of sound. Cf. *Semantic type.*

Physicalism   The doctrine that the only entities are physical entities and that, ultimately, physical laws explain everything (in some sense).

Qua-problem   A problem for the theory of reference fixing by grounding, particularly of names and natural kind terms. When a speaker grounds a term through perceptual experience, in virtue of what is the term grounded in the cause of that experience *qua*-one-kind and not *qua*-another? For that cause will always be an instance of many kinds; e.g. the one object may be an echidna, a monotreme, a mammal, a vertebrate, and so on.

Quantifier   An expression like 'all', 'some', 'most', and 'a few' that determines the interpretation of what are called "variables" in logic. Thus a variable is anaphoric. The variables of natural language are typically pronouns or other proforms. These are often bound by their quantifiers; for example, in 'Every gunman who says he wants to die with his boots on hopes he will die in bed', the quantifier 'every gunman' binds the two tokens of the pronoun 'he' and the relative clause proform 'who'. However, sometimes variables are unbound, most obviously in a dialogue when one speaker's variable gets its interpretation from an earlier speaker's quantifier.

Realism   A metaphysical doctrine. In this work, commonsense realism is the doctrine that most of the observable entities posited by common sense objectively exist independently of the mental. Scientific realism is the parallel doctrine about the unobservables posited by science. Cf. *Idealism*.

Reference   In this work, the genus of which all referential relationships – for example, application, designation, denotation – are species. Often used more narrowly for the relationship between a singular term and its referent.

Reference borrowing   A person's acquisition or reinforcement of an ability to use a term as a result of the exercise of such an ability by another person in an act of communication.

Rigid applier   If a rigid general (mass) term applies to an object (a stuff) in the actual world, and that object (stuff) exists in another possible world, then it applies to that object (stuff) in that world. Natural kind terms are widely held to be rigid.

Rigid designator   A singular term that designates the same object in each possible world in which that object exists. Proper names are widely held to be rigid.

Semantics   The theory of meaning. Sometimes contrasted with syntax: semantics is seen as the study of the relations between symbols and the world, whereas syntax is the study of the relations between symbols. The contrast is overdrawn: the semantic properties of complex expressions depend in part on their structure, i.e. on their syntactic properties. Cf. *Syntax*.

Semantic type   A type of entity identified by semantic characteristics; thus, a sound token and an inscription token can be of the same semantic type. Cf. *Physical type*.

Sense   In this work, a word's property of referring to something in a certain way, its mode of reference. More is usually required of a sense; for example, that it is "grasped" by competent speakers.

Singular term   An expression purporting to refer to just one object; examples are names, definite descriptions and demonstratives. Cf. *General term* and *Mass term*.

Speaker meaning   What the speaker means by an expression on a particular occasion of its use. This meaning is determined by the content (meaning) of the thought that the speaker is expressing. Cf. *Conventional meaning*.

Structuralism   An approach to language and other systems that holds them to be autonomous, and hence to be explained by appeal to the relations within the systems and not by relations to realities external to the systems. There are two, somewhat similar, structuralist movements: one which began in France early in the century; and one which begun in the USA somewhat later.

S-structure (surface structure)   A level of structure distinguished from D-structure by transformational generative grammar. It determines how the sentence is pronounced or written by displaying the superficial organization of the elements of the sentence into words, phrases and clauses. Cf. *D-structure (deep structure)*.

Syntax The theory of the principles determining the formation of complex symbols from simple ones; in particular, of the formation of sentences from words and phrases. Cf. *Semantics*.

Synthetic Primarily applied to sentences. A synthetic sentence depends for its truth value not only on the meaning of its elements, but also on extra-linguistic reality. Cf. *Analytic*.

Teleological semantics A semantic theory, usually of thoughts, that hold that the meaning of an expression type is determined by the selective history of that type. If in an agent the thought type FIRE exists because of selection on that agent's ancestors to recognize and avoid fires, FIRE is about fire.

Thoughts or propositional attitudes Mental states that differ in two dimensions. One is in the kind of attitude: belief, hope, desire, fear, etc. The other is in content: that Reagan is wrinkled, that Thatcher is tough, that Andropov is dead, etc.

Transparent, or extensional, context A place within a sentence where the substitution of a singular term for a coreferential term never changes the truth value of the sentence. Cf. *Opaque, or intensional, context*.

Truth conditions That property of a sentence in virtue of which it is true if a certain situation in the world obtains and not true if that situation does not obtain.

Variable Cf. *Quantifier*.

Verificationism A theory of meaning that identifies the meaning of a sentence with our method of determining whether it is to be accepted or rejected.

Bibliography

Aarsleff, H. 1982. *From Locke to Saussure: Essays in the Study of Language and Intellectual History*. Minneapolis: Minnesota University Press.

Aizawa, Kenneth L. 1997. "Explaining Systematicity". *Mind and Language* 12: 115–36.

Akins, Kathleen. 1996. "Of Sensory Systems and the 'Aboutness' of Mental States". *Journal of Philosophy* 93: 337–72.

Akmajian, A., R. A. Demers, and R. M. Harnish. 1979. *Linguistics: An Introduction to Language and Communication*. Cambridge, Mass.: MIT Press.

Almog, J. 1985. "Form and Content" *Nous* 19: 603–16.

Anderson, John. 1980. *Cognitive Psychology and its Implications*. San Francisco: W. H. Freeman and Co.

Antony, Louise. 1987. "Naturalized Epistemology and the Study of Language". In Abner Shimony and Debra Nails (eds.), *Naturalistic Epistemology*. Dordrecht: D. Reidel: 235–57.

———, and Joseph Levine. 1991. "The Nomic and the Robust". In Loewer and Rey 1991: 1–16.

Aqvist, L. 1965. *A New Approach to the Logical Theory of Interrogatives*. Uppsala: Filosofiska Institutionen, Uppsala University.

Armstrong, D. M. 1971. "Meaning and Communication". *Philosophical Review* 80: 427-47.

———. 1978. *Nominalism and Realism: Universals and Scientific Realism, Volume 1*. Cambridge: Cambridge University Press.

———. 1989, *Universals: An Opinionated Introduction*. Boulder: Westview Press.

Ashby, R. W. 1967. "The Verifiability Principle". In Edwards 1967, vol. 8: 240–7.

Atran, S. 1990. *Cognitive Foundations of Natural History: Towards an Anthropology of Science*. Cambridge: Cambridge University Press.

Austin, J. L. 1962a. *How to do Things with Words*. Oxford: Clarendon Press.
——. 1962b. *Sense and Sensibilia*. Oxford: Clarendon Press.
Ayer, A. J. 1940. *The Foundations of Empirical Knowledge*. London: Macmillan and Company.
——. 1946. *Language, Truth and Logic*. 2nd ed. with a new introduction: London: Victor Gollancz. First ed., 1936.
——, ed. 1959. *Logical Positivism*. New York: The Free Press.
Bach, Kent. 1987. *Thought and Reference*. Oxford: Clarendon Press.
——. 1992, "Paving the Road to Reference". *Philosophical Studies* 67: 295–300.
Baker, C. L. 1995. *English Syntax*, 2nd ed. Cambridge,Mass.: MIT Press. First edn 1989.
Baker, G. P. and P. M. S. Hacker. 1988. *Wittgenstein, Rules, Grammar, and Necessity*. Oxford: Blackwell.
Baker, Lynne Rudder. 1991. "Has Content Been Naturalized?". In Loewer and Rey 1991: 17-32.
Barwise, Jon and Robin Cooper. 1981. "Generalized Quantifiers and Natural Language". *Linguistics and Philosophy* 4: 159–219.
Barthes, Roland. 1967. *Elements of Semiology*, tr. Annette Lavers and Colin Smith. (French ed. 1964). New York: Hill and Wang.
Beakley, Brian and Peter Ludlow. 1992. *The Philosophy of Mind: Classical Problems/Contemporary Issues*. Cambridge, Mass.: MIT Press.
Belnap, Nuel D. , and Thomas B. Steel, Jr. 1976. *The Logic of Questions and Answers*. New Haven: Yale University Press.
Bennett, J. 1976. *Linguistic Behaviour*. Cambridge: Cambridge University Press.
Berlin, B. 1992. *Ethnobiological Classification: Principles of Categorization of Plants and Animals in Traditional Societies*. Princeton: Princeton University Press.
Bertolet, Rod. 1979. "McKinsey, Causes and Intentions". *Philosophical Review* 88: 619-32.
——. 1980. "The Semantic Significance of Donnellan's Distinction". *Philosophical Studies* 37: 281-8.
Bickerton, D. 1991. *Language and Species*. Chicago: Chicago University Press.
Bishop, Michael A. 1991. "Why the Semantic Incommensurability Thesis is Self-Defeating". *Philosophical Studies* 69: 343–56.
Black, Max. 1962. *Models and Metaphors*. Ithaca, NY: Cornell University Press.
Blackburn, Simon. 1984. "The Individual Strikes Back". *Synthese* 58: 281–302.
Block, Ned, ed. 1981. *Readings in Philosophy of Psychology, Volume 2*. Cambridge, Mass.: Harvard University Press.
——. 1985. "Advertisement fo a Semantics for Psychology". *Midwest Studies in Philosophy, Volume X: Studies in the Philosophy of Mind*, eds. Peter A. French, Theodore E. Uehling Jr., and Howard K. Wettstein, in press.
Bloomfield, L. 1933. *Language*. New York: Holt, Rinehart & Winston.
Boden, M. A. 1984. "Animal Perception from an Artificial Intelligence Viewpoint". In C. Hookway (ed.), *Minds, Machines and Evolution*, Cambridge: Cambridge University Press.
Boghossian, Paul. 1989. "The Rule-Following Considerations". *Mind* 98: 507–49.
——. 1991. "Naturalizing Content". In Loewer and Rey 1991: 65–86.
Boolos, George. 1990. *Meaning and Method: Essays in Honor of Hilary Putnam*. New York: Cambridge University Press.

Boyd, Richard, Philip Gasper, and J. D. Trout (eds.). 1991. *The Philosophy of Science*. Cambridge, Mass.: MIT Press.

Braddon-Mitchell, David, and John Fitzpatrick. 1990. "Explanation and the Language of Thought", *Synthese* 83: 3–29.

Bradley, R. and N. Swartz. 1979. *Possible Worlds*. Oxford: Blackwell.

Brandom, Robert B. 1994. *Making It Explicit: Reasoning, Representing, and Discursive Commitment*. Cambridge, Mass.: Harvard University Press.

Burge, Tyler. 1979. "Individualism and the Mental". *Midwest Studies in Philosophy, Volume IV: Studies in Metaphysics*, eds. Peter A. French, Theodore E. Uehling Jr., and Howard K. Wettstein: 73–121.

———. 1986. "Individualism and Psychology". *Philosophical Review* 95: 3–45. Reprinted in Boyd, Gasper and Trout 1991.

Byrne, Richard. 1995. *The Thinking Ape: The Evolutionary Origins of Intelligence*; Oxford: Oxford University Press.

Cahoone, Lawrence, ed. 1996. *From Modernism to Postmodernism: An Anthology*. Oxford: Blackwell.

Campbell, Keith. 1991. *Abstract Particulars*. Oxford: Blackwell.

Canfield, John V. 1977. "Donnellan's Theory of Names". *Dialogue* 16: 104–27

Carnap, Rudolf. 1932. "The Elimination of Metaphysics Through Logical Analysis of Language". In Ayer 1959: 60–81. First. publ. in German in *Erkenntnis* 2.

———. 1950. "Empiricism, Semantics and Ontology". *Revue Internationale de Philosophie* 4: 20–40. Reprinted in Linsky 1952 and Boyd, Gasper, and Trout 1991.

———. 1956. *Meaning and Necessity: A Study in Semantics and Modal Logic*. Chicago: University of Chicago Press, 2nd ed. First ed., 1947.

Carroll, Lewis. 1962. *Alice's Adventures in Wonderland and Through the Looking Glass*. New York: Collier Books. First ed. of *Through the Looking Glass*, 1872.

Chastain, Charles. 1975. "Reference and Context". In Gunderson 1975: 194–269.

Chomsky, Noam. 1957. *Syntactic Structures*. The Hague: Mouton & Co.

———. 1959. Review of Skinner 1957. *Language* 35: 26–58. Reprinted in Fodor and Katz 1964 and Geirsson and Losonsky 1996.

———. 1965. *Aspects of the Theory of Syntax*. Cambridge, Mass.: MIT Press.

———. 1966. *Topics in the Theory of Generative Grammar*. The Hague: Mouton & Co. Excerpts in Searle 1971.

———. 1969a. "Linguistics and Philosophy". In Hook 1969: 51–94. Excerpts in Stich 1975.

———. 1969b. "Comments on Harman's Reply". In Hook 1969: 152–9.

———. 1975. "Knowledge of Language". In Gunderson 1975: 299–320.

———. 1980. *Rules and Representations*. New York: Columbia University Press.

———. 1981. *Lectures on Government and Binding*. Dordrecht: Foris.

———. 1986. *Knowledge of Language: Its Nature, Origin, and Use*. New York: Praeger Publishers.

———. 1988. *Language and Problems of Knowledge: The Managua Lectures*. Cambridge, Mass.: MIT Press.

———. 1990. "On the Nature, Use and Acquisition of Language". In Lycan 1990: 627–46.

———. 1995a. *The Minimalist Program*. Cambridge, Mass.: MIT Press.

——. 1995b. "Language and Nature". *Mind* 104: 1–61.

Churchland, Paul M. 1979. *Scientific Realism and the Plasticity of Mind.* Cambridge: Cambridge University Press.

——. 1988. *Matter and Consciousness.* Cambridge, Mass.: MIT Press.

——. 1993. "Evaluating Our Self Conception". *Mind and Language* 8: 211-22.

Churchland, Paul M., and Patricia S. Churchland. 1983. "Stalking the Wild Epistemic Engine". *Nous* 17: 5–18. Reprinted in Lycan 1990.

Clark, Andy. 1993. *Associative Engines: Connectionism, Concepts and Representational Change.* Cambridge, Mass.: MIT Press.

——. 1997. *Being There: Putting Brain, Body, and World Together Again.* Cambridge, Mass.: MIT Press.

Clark, Peter, and Bob Hale, eds. 1994. *Reading Putnam.* Oxford: Blackwell.

Cohen, L. J. 1981. "Can Human Irrationality be Experimentally Demonstrated?" *Behavioral and Brain Sciences* 4: 317–70 (includes peer commentaries and response by author).

Corballis, Michael. 1991. *The Lopsided Ape: Evolution of the Generative Mind.* Oxford: Oxford University Press.

Cowie, Fiona. 1998. *What's Within: Nativism Reconsidered.* New York: Oxford University Press.

Crane, Tim. 1991. "All the Difference in the World". *Philosophical Quarterly* 41: 1–25.

Cresswell. Max. 1985. *Structured Meanings: The Semantics of Propositional Attitudes.* Cambridge, Mass.: MIT Press.

——. 1988. *Semantical Essays: Possible Worlds and Their Rivals.* Dordrecht: Kluwer.

——. 1994. *Language in the Worlds: A Philosophical Enquiry.* Cambridge: Cambridge University Press.

——. 1996. *Semantical Indexicality.* Dordrecht: Kluwer.

Culler, Jonathan. 1976. *Saussure.* London: Fontana.

Currie, Gregory. 1982. *Frege, an Introduction to his Philosophy.* Totowa, NJ: Barns and Noble.

Dahlbom, Bo, ed. 1993. *Dennett and His Critics.* Oxford: Blackwell.

Davidson, Donald. 1980. *Essays on Actions and Events.* Oxford: Clarendon Press.

——. 1984. *Inquiries into Truth and Interpretation.* Oxford: Clarendon Press.

——. 1986. "A Nice Derangement of Epitaphs". In Lepore 1986: 433–46.

—— and Gilbert Harman, eds. 1972. *Semantics of Natural Language.* Dordrecht: Reidel.

—— and Jaakko Hintikka, eds. 1969. *Words and Objections: Essays on the Work of W. V. Quine.* Dordrecht: Reidel.

Davies, Martin. 1989. "Tacit Knowledge and Subdoxastic States". In George 1989a: 131–52.

——. 1991. "Individualism and Perceptual Content". *Mind* 100: 461–84.

Davis, Steven, ed. 1991. *Pragmatics: A Reader.* New York: Oxford University Press.

Dennett, Daniel. 1978. *Brainstorms.* Cambridge, Mass.: Bradford Books.

——. 1987. *The Intentional Stance.* Cambridge, Mass.: MIT Press.

——. 1991a. *Consciousness Explained.* Boston: Little, Brown and Company.

——. 1991b. "Real Patterns". *Journal of Philosophy* 87: 27–51.

318   Bibliography

——. 1995. *Darwin's Dangerous Idea*. New York: Simon and Shuster.
Derrida, Jacques. 1977a. "Signature Event Context". *Glyph* 1: 172–97.
——. 1977b. "Limited Inc abc ... " *Glyph* 2: 162–254.
——. 1980. *The Archaelology of the Frivolous*. Pittsburg: Duquesne University Press.
Devitt, Michael. 1979. "Against Incommensurability". *Australasian Journal of Philosophy* 57: 29–50.
——. 1981a. *Designation*. New York: Columbia University Press.
——. 1981b. "Donnellan's Distinction". *Midwest Studies in Philosophy, Volume VI: The Foundations of Analytic Philosophy*, eds. Peter A. French, Theodore E. Uehling Jr., and Howard K. Wettstein: 511–24.
——. 1985. Critical Notice of Evans 1982. *Australasian Journal of Philosophy* 63: 216-32.
——. 1990. "Meanings Just Ain't in the Head". In Boolos 1990: 79–104.
——. 1991. "Minimalist Truth", a critical notice of Horwich 1990. *Mind and Language* 6: 273–83.
——. 1996. *Coming to Our Senses*. Cambridge: Cambridge University Press
——. 1997. *Realism and Truth*. 2nd ed. with new Afterword. Princeton: Princeton University Press.
——. 1998a. "A Naturalistic Defense of Realism". In Stephen D. Hales (ed.), *Metaphysics: Contemporary Readings*. London: Wadsworth.
——. 1998b. "Naturalism and the A Priori". *Philosophical Studies* 92: 45–63.
——. Forthcoming. *Ignorance of Language*.
—— and Kim Sterelny. 1989. "What's Wrong with 'the Right View'". In *Philosophical Perspectives, 3: Philosophy of Mind and Action Theory, 1989*, ed. James E. Tomberlin. Atascadero: Ridgeview Publishing Company, 497–531.
Dilthey, W. 1976. *Selected Writings*, ed. H. P. Rickman. Cambridge: Cambridge University Press.
Donald, M. 1991. *Origins of the Modern Mind: Three Stages in the Evolution of Culture and Cognition*. Cambridge, Mass.: Harvard University Press.
Donnellan, Keith S. 1966. "Reference and Definite Descriptions". *Philosophical Review* 75: 281–304. Reprinted in Schwartz 1977, Davis 1991, Martinich 1996, Ludlow 1997, and Ostertag 1998.
——. 1968. "Putting Humpty Dumpty Together Again". *Philosophical Review* 77: 203–15.
——. 1972. "Proper Names and Identifying Descriptions". In Davidson and Harman 1972: 356–79.
——. 1974. "Speaking of Nothing". *Philosophical Review* 83: 3–31. Reprinted in Schwartz 1977.
——. 1983. "Kripke and Putnam on Natural Kind Terms". In Carl Ginet and Sydney Shoemaker (eds.), *Knowledge and Mind: Philosophical Essays*. Oxford: Oxford University Press.
——. 1993. "There is a Word for That Kind of Thing: An Investigation of Two Thought Experiments". In *Philosophical Perspectives, 7: Language and Logic, 1993*, ed. James E. Tomberlin. Atascadero: Ridgeview Publishing Company: 155–71.
Dowty, D. R., R. E. Wall, and S. Peters. 1981. *Introduction to Montague Semantics*. Dordrecht: Reidel.
Dretske, Fred. 1981. *Knowledge and the Flow of Information*. Cambridge, Mass.:

MIT Press.
——. 1986. "Misrepresentation". In R. Bogdan (ed.), *Belief: Form, Content, and Function*. Oxford: Clarendon Press.
——. 1988. *Explaining Behavior*. Cambridge, Mass.: MIT Press.
Dummett, Michael. 1973. *Frege: Philosophy of Language*. London: Duckworth.
——. 1975. "What is a Theory of Meaning?" In Guttenplan 1975: 97–138.
——. 1976. "What is a Theory of Meaning? (II)" In G. Evans and J. McDowell (eds.), *Truth and Meaning: Essays in Semantics*. Oxford: Clarendon Press: 67–137.
——. 1977. *Elements of Intuitionism*. Oxford: Clarendon Press.
——. 1978. *Truth and Other Enigmas*. Cambridge, Mass.: Harvard University Press.
——. 1993. *The Seas of Language*. Oxford: Clarendon Press.
Dupre, J. 1981. "Natural Kinds and Biological Taxa". *Philosophical Review* 90: 66–90.
Eagleton, Terry. 1983. *Literary Theory: An Introduction*. Oxford: Blackwell.
Ebbs, Gary. 1992. "Skepticism, Objectivity, and Brains in Vats". *Pacific Philosophical Quarterly* 73: 239–66.
Eco, Umberto. 1984. *Semiotics and the Philosophy of Language*. London: Macmillan.
Edwards, Paul, ed. 1967. *The Encyclopedia of Philosophy*. London: Macmillan.
Erwin, E., L Kleinman, and E. Zemach. 1976. "The Historical Theory of Reference". *Australasian Journal of Philosophy* 54: 50–7.
Evans, Gareth. 1973. "The Causal Theory of Names". *Proceedings of the Aristotelian Society*, Suppl. vol. 47:187–208. Reprinted in Schwartz 1977, Martinich 1996, and Ludlow 1997.
——. 1982. *The Varieties of Reference*, ed. John McDowell, Oxford: Clarendon Press.
——. 1985. *Collected Papers*. Oxford: Clarendon Press.
Feyerabend, Paul. 1970a. "Consolations for the Specialist". In Lakatos and Musgrave 1970: 197–230.
——. 1970b. "Against Method: Outline of an Anarchistic Theory of Knowledge". *Minnesota Studies in the Philosophy of Science, Volume IV: Analyses of Theories and Methods of Physics and Psychology*, eds. Michael Radner and Stephen Winokur: 17–130.
——. 1975. *Against Method: An Outline of an Anarchistic Theory of Knowledge*. London: New Left Books.
Field, Hartry. 1972. "Tarski's Theory of Truth". *Journal of Philosophy* 69: 347–75. Reprinted in Platts 1980.
——. 1973. "Theory Change and the Indeterminacy of Reference". *Journal of Philosophy* 70: 462-81.
——. 1978. "Mental Representation". *Erkenntnis* 13: 9–61. Reprinted with Postscript in Block 1981: 78–114.
——. 1994. "Deflationist Views of Meaning and Content". *Mind* 103: 249–85.
Fine, Arthur. 1975. "How to Compare Theories: Reference and Change". *Nous* 9: 17–32.
Fishman, J. A. 1960. "A Systematization of the Whorfian Analysis". *Behavioral Science* 5: 329–39. Reprinted in J. W. Berry and P. R. Dasen (eds.), *Culture and Cognition: Readings in Cross-Cultural Psychology*. London: Methuen, 1974.
Fodor, Jerry A. 1975. *The Language of Thought*. New York: Thomas Y. Crowell.

———. 1981a. *Representations: Philosophical Essays on the Foundations of Cognitive Science*. Cambridge Mass.: Bradford Books/MIT Press.

———. 1981b. "Introduction: Some Notes on What Linguistics is About". In Block 1981: 197–207. Reprinted in Katz 1985.

———. 1983. *The Modularity of Mind: An Essay on Faculty Psychology*. Cambridge, Mass.: Bradford Books/MIT Press.

———. 1985a. "Precis of *The Modularity of Mind*". *Behavioral and Brain Sciences* 8: 1–42 (includes peer commentaries and response by author).

———. 1985b "Fodor's Guide to Mental Representations: The Intelligent Auntie's Vade-Mecum". *Mind* 94: 76–100.

———. 1987. *Psychosemantics: The Problem of Meaning in the Philosophy of Mind*. Cambridge: MIT Press.

———. 1990a. *A Theory of Content and Other Essays*. Cambridge: MIT Press.

———. 1990b. "Psychosemantics or: Where Do Truth Conditions Come From?" In Lycan 1990: *Mind and Cognition*.

———. 1991a. "Replies". In Loewer and Rey 1991: 255–319.

———. 1991b, "A Modal Argument for Narrow Content". *Journal of Philosophy* 88: 5–26.

———. 1994. *The Elm and the Expert*. Cambridge, Mass.: MIT Press.

———. 1998. *Concepts: Where Cognitive Science Went Wrong*. Oxford: Clarendon Press.

——— and Jerrold J. Katz, eds. 1964. *The Structure of Language: Readings in the Philosophy of Language*. Englewood Cliffs, NJ: Prentice-Hall.

——— and Brian McLaughlin. 1991. "Connectionism and the Problem of Systematicity: Why Smolensky's Solution Won't Work". *Cognition* 35: 185–204.

——— and Zenon Pylyshyn. 1988. "Connectionism and Cognitive Architecture: A Critical Analysis". *Cognition* 28: 3–71.

Follesdal, D, and R. Hilpinen. 1981. "Deontic Logic: An Introduction". In Hilpinen 1981: 1–35.

Frege, G. 1918. "The Thought". *Mind* 65 (1956): 289–311. Reprinted in Ludlow 1997. First published in German, 1918–19.

———. 1952. *Translations from the Philosophical Writings of Gottlob Frege*, eds. Peter Geach and Max Black. Oxford: Blackwell. 2nd ed., corr., 1960.

French, Peter A., Theodore E. Uehling, Jr., and Howard K. Wettstein, eds. 1988. *Midwest Studies in Philosophy, Volume XII: Realism and Antirealism*. Minneapolis: University of Minnesota Press.

Geach, Peter. 1962. *Reference and Generality*. Ithaca: Cornell University Press.

Geirsson, H., and M. Losonsky, eds. 1996. *Readings in Language and Mind*. Cambridge, Mass.: Blackwell.

Gellner, E. 1959. *Words and Things*. London: Victor Gollanz.

George, Alexander, ed. 1989a. *Reflections on Chomsky*. Oxford: Blackwell.

———, 1989b. "How Not to Become Confused About Linguistics". In George 1989a: 90–110.

Gibson, Roger F. 1982. *The Philosophy of Willard Van Orman Quine – an Expository Essay*. Gainesville: Gainsville University Press of Florida.

Godfrey-Smith, Peter. 1989. "Misinformation". *Canadian Journal of Philosophy* 19: 533-50.

———. 1991. "Signal, Detection, Action". *Journal of Philosophy* 88: 709–22.

———. 1992. "Indication and Adaptation". *Synthese* 92: 283–312.

——. 1996. *Complexity and the Function of Mind in Nature.* Cambridge: Cambridge University Press.

Graves, Christina, J. J. Katz, Y. Nishiyama, Scott Soames, R. Stecker, and P. Tovey. 1973. "Tacit Knowledge". *Journal of Philosophy* 70: 318–30.

Grice, H. P. 1957. "Meaning". *Philosophical Review* 66: 377–88. Reprinted in Grice 1989, Martinich 1996, Geirsson and Losonsky 1996.

——. 1989. *Studies in the Way of Words.* Cambridge Mass.: Harvard University Press.

Griffin, D. 1992. *Animal Minds.* Chicago: Chicago University Press.

Grover, Dorothy L. 1992, *A Prosentential Theory of Truth.* Princeton: Princeton University Press.

Gunderson, Keith, ed. 1975. *Minnesota Studies in the Philosophy of Science, Volume VII: Language, Mind, and Knowledge.* Minneapolis: University of Minnesota Press.

Gupta, Anil. 1993. "A Critique of Deflationism". *Philosophical Topics* 21: 57–81.

Guttenplan, S., ed. 1975. *Mind and Language.* Oxford: Clarendon Press.

Haegeman, Liliane. 1994. *Introduction to Government and Binding Theory,* 2nd edn. Oxford: Blackwell. First ed. 1991.

Hannan, Barbara. 1993, "Don't Stop Believing: The Case Against Eliminative Materialism" *Mind and Language* 8: 165–179.

Harman, Gilbert. 1967. "Psychological Aspects of the Theory of Syntax". *Journal of Philosophy* 64: 75–87. Reprinted in Stich 1975.

——. 1969. "Linguistic Competence and Empiricism". In Hook 1969: 143–51.

——. 1973. *Thought.* Princeton: Princeton University Press.

——, ed. 1974. *On Noam Chomsky: Critical Essays.* Garden City, NY: Anchor Press/Doubleday.

——. 1975. "Language, Thought, and Communication". In Gunderson 1975: 270–98.

——. 1987. "(Nonsolipsistic) Conceptual Role Semantics". In Ernest Lepore (ed.), *New Directions in Semantics.* London: Academic Press: 55–81.

Hauser, Marc. 1996. *The Evolution of Communication.* Cambridge, Mass.: MIT press.

Hawkes, Terence. 1977. *Structuralism and Semiotics.* London: Methuen & Co.

Hempel, C. G. 1950. "Problems and Changes in the Empiricist Criterion of Meaning". *Revue Internationale de Philosophie* 11: 41–63. Reprinted in Linsky 1952.

——. 1954. "A Logical Appraisal of Operationism". *Scientific Monthly* 1: 215–20.

——. 1966. *Philosophy of Natural Science.* Englewood Cliffs, NJ: Prentice-Hall.

Higginbotham, James. 1989. "Knowledge of Reference". In George 1989a: 153–74.

Hill, Christopher, ed. 1994. *Philosophical Topics* 22, 1–2. Fayetteville: University of Arkansas Press.

Hilpinen, Risto, ed. 1981. *Deontic Logic: Introductory and Systematic Readings.* Dordrecht: Reidel, 2nd ed. First ed., 1971.

Hintikka, Jaakko. 1962. *Knowledge and Belief.* Ithaca, New York: Cornell University Press.

Holdcroft, David. 1991. *Saussure: Signs, System, and Arbitrariness.* New York: Cambridge University Press.

Hook, Sidney, ed. 1969. *Language and Philosophy: A Symposium.* New York:

New York University Press.

Horgan, Terence, and James Woodward. "Folk Psychology is Here to Stay". *Philosophical Review* 94: 197–226. Reprinted in Lycan 1990.

Hornstein, Norbert. 1989. "Meaning and the Mental: The Problem of Semantics after Chomsky". In George 1989a: 23–40

Horwich, Paul. 1990. *Truth*. Oxford: Blackwell.

——, ed. 1993. *World Changes: Thomas Kuhn and the Nature of Science*. Cambridge, Mass.: MIT Press.

Hoyningen-Huene, P. 1993. *Reconstructing Scientific Revolutions: Thomas S. Kuhn's Philosophy of Sciece*. Trans. A. T. Levine. Chicago: University of Chicago Press.

Jackson, Frank. 1994. "Armchair Metaphysics". In John O'Leary-Hawthorne and Michaelis Michael (eds.), *Philosophy in Mind*. Dordrecht: Kluwer: 23–42.

——. 1998. "Reference and Description Revisited". In James E. Tomberlin (ed.), *Philosophical Perspectives 12: Language, Mind, and Ontology, 1998*: Oxford: Blackwell: 201–18.

Jameson, Frederic. 1972. *The Prison-House of Language*. Princeton: Princeton University Press.

Kant, Immanuel. 1929. *Critique of Pure Reason*. Tr. Norman Kemp Smith. London: Macmillan, 1929. First German ed., 1781.

——. 1953. *Prolegomena to Any Future Metaphysics*. Tr. Peter G. Lucas. Manchester: Manchester University Press. First German ed. 1783.

Kaplan, David. 1969. "Quantifying In". In Davidson and Hintikka 1969: 206–42. Reprinted in Linsky 1971 and Davidson and Harman 1976.

——. 1978a. "Dthat". In P. Cole (ed.), *Syntax and Semantics 9: Pragmatics*. New York: Academic Press: 221–43. Reprinted in Yourgau 1990, Martinich 1996 and Ludlow 1997.

——. 1978b. "On the Logic of Demonstratives". *Journal of Philosophical Logic* 8: 81–98. Reprinted in Davis 1991.

——. 1989a. "Demonstratives: An Essay on the Semantics, Logic, Metaphysics, and Epistemology of Demonstratives and Other Indexicals". In J. Almog, J. Perry, and H. Wettstein (eds.), *Themes from Kaplan*. Oxford: Oxford University Press: 481–563.

——. 1989b. "Afterthoughts". In J. Almog, J. Perry, and H. Wettstein (eds.), *Themes from Kaplan*. Oxford: Oxford University Press: 565–614.

Kasher, Asa (ed.). 1991. *The Chomskyan Turn*. Oxford: Blackwell.

Katz, Jerrold J. 1972. *Semantic Theory*. New York: Harper & Row.

——. 1975. "Logic and Language: An Examination of Recent Criticisms of Intensionalism". In Gunderson 1975: 36–130.

——. 1977. "The Real Status of Semantic Representations". *Linguistic Inquiry* 8: 559-84. Reprinted in Block 1981: 253–75.

——. 1984. "An Outline of a Platonist Grammar". In T. G. Bever, J. M. Carrol, and L. A. Miller (eds.), *Talking Minds: The Study of Language in Cognitive Sciences*. Cambridge, Mass.: MIT Press: 17–48. Reprinted in Katz 1985.

——, ed. 1985. *The Philosophy of Linguistics*. Oxford: Oxford University Press.

——. 1990. "Has the Description Theory of Names Been Refuted". In Boolos 1990: 31–62.

——. 1996. "The Unfinished Chomskyan Revolution". *Mind and Language* 11: 270–94.

——— and Jerry A. Fodor. 1963. "The Structure of a Semantic Theory". *Language* 39: 170–210. Reprinted in Fodor and Katz 1964.

Kaye, Lawrence J. 1995. "The Languages of Thought". *Philosophy of Science* 62: 92–110.

Kearney, R. 1994. *Modern Movements in European Philosophy*. 2nd ed. Manchester: Manchester Universty Press.

Kenny, A. 1973. *Wittgenstein*. London: Pelican Books.

Kitcher, Patricia. 1985. "Narrow Taxonomy and Wide Functionalism". *Philosophy of Science* 52: 78–97. Reprinted in Boyd, Gasper, and Trout 1991.

Kornblith, Hilary. 1980. "Referring to Artifacts". *Philosophical Review* 89: 109–14.

———, ed. 1994. *Naturalizing Epistemology*, 2nd ed. (First ed. 1985.) Cambridge, Mass.: MIT Press.

Kripke, Saul A. 1959. "A Completeness Theorem in Modal Logic". *Journal of Symbolic Logic* 24: 1–14.

———. 1962. "Semantical Considerations on Modal Logic". *Acta Philosophica Fennica* 16: 83–94. Reprinted in Linsky 1971.

———. 1971. "Identity and Necessity". In Milton K. Munitz (ed.), *Identity and Individuation*, New York: New York University Press: 135–64. Reprinted in Schwartz 1977.

———. 1979. "Speaker's Reference and Semantic Reference". In Peter A. French, Theodore E. Uehling, Jr., and Howard K. Wettstein (eds.), *Contemporary Perspectives in the Philosophy of Language*, Minneapolis: University of Minnesota Press: 6–27. Reprinted in Davis 1991, Ludlow 1997, and Ostertag 1998.

———. 1980. *Naming and Necessity*. Cambridge, Mass.: Harvard University Press. A corrected version of an article of the same name (plus an appendix) in Davidson and Harman 1972, together with a new preface.

———. 1982. *Wittgenstein on Rules and Private Language: An Elementary Exposition*. Cambridge, Mass.: Harvard University Press.

Kroon, Frederick W. 1982. "The Problem of 'Jonah': How *not* to Argue for the Causal Theory of Reference". *Philosophical Studies* 43: 281–99.

———. 1985. "Theoretical Terms and the Causal View of Reference". *The Australasian Journal of Philosophy* 63: 143–66.

———. 1987. "Causal Descriptivism". *Australasian Journal of Philosophy* 65: 1–17.

———. 1989. "Circles and Fixed Points in Description Theories of Reference". *Nous* 23: 373–92.

Kuhn, Thomas S. 1962. *The Structure of Scientific Revolutions*. Chicago: Chicago University Press. 2nd ed. 1970.

———. 1970. "Reflections on my Critics". In Lakatos and Musgrave 1970: 231–78.

Lakatos, Imre, and Alan Musgrave, eds. 1970. *Criticism and the Growth of Knowledge*. Cambridge: Cambridge University Press.

Larson, Richard, and Gabriel Segal. 1995. *Knowledge of Meaning: An Introduction to Semantic Theory*. Cambridge, Mass.: MIT Press.

Lasnik, Howard, and Juan Uriagereka. *A Course in GB Syntax: Lectures on Binding and Empty Categories*. Cambridge, Mass.: MIT Press.

Laudan, Larry. 1990. *Science and Relativism: Some Key Controversies in the Philosophy of Science*. Chicago: Chicago University Press.

Leeds, Stephen. 1978, "Theories of Reference and Truth". *Erkenntnis* 13: 111–29.

Lenneberg, E. H. 1953. "Cognition in Ethnolinguistics". *Language* 29: 463–71.

Lepore, Ernest, ed. 1986. *Truth and Interpretation: Perspectives on the Philosophy of Donald Davidson*. Oxford: Blackwell.

———, and Brian McLaughlin, eds. 1985. *Actions and Events: Perspectives on the Philosophy of Donald Davidson*. Oxford: Blackwell.

Lewis, David K. 1969. *Convention: A Philosophical Study*. Cambridge, Mass.: Harvard University Press.

———. 1972. "General Semantics". In Davidson and Harman 1972: 169–218. Reprinted in Lewis 1983.

———. 1973. *Counterfactuals*. Oxford: Blackwell.

———. 1974. "Languages, Language, and Grammar". In Harman 1974: 253–66.

———. 1975. "Languages and Language". In Gunderson 1975: 3–35. Reprinted in Lewis 1983, Martinich 1996, and Geirsson and Losonsky 1996.

———. 1983. *Philosophical Papers, Volume I*. Oxford: Oxford University Press.

———. 1984. "Putnam's Paradox". *Australasian Journal of Philosophy*. 62: 221–36.

———. 1985. *On the Plurality of Worlds*. Oxford: Blackwell.

———. 1994. "Lewis, David: Reduction of Mind" in Samuel Guttenplan, ed., *Companion to Philosophy of Mind*. Oxford: Blackwell: 412–31.

Lieberman, P. 1991. *Uniquely Human: The Evolution of Speech, Thought and Selfless Behavior*. Cambridge, Mass.: Harvard University Press.

Linsky, Leonard, ed. 1952. *Semantics and the Philosophy of Language*. Urbana: University of Illinois Press.

———, ed. 1971. *Reference and Modality*. Oxford: Oxford University Press.

———. 1977. *Names and Descriptions*. Chicago: Chicago University Press.

Loar, Brian. 1976. "The Semantics of Singular Terms". *Philosophical Studies* 30: 353–77.

———. 1981. *Mind and Meaning*. Cambridge: Cambridge University Press.

———. 1982. "Conceptual Role and Truth Conditions". *Notre Dame Journal of Formal Logic* 23: 272–83.

———. 1983. "Must Beliefs be Sentences?" in *PSA 1982* Vol 1, eds. P. D. Asquith and T. Nickles. East Lansing, Mich.: Philosophy of Science Association: 627–43.

Loewer, Barry and Georges Rey. 1991. *Meaning in Mind: Fodor and his Critics*. Cambridge, Mass.: Blackwell.

Loux, M. S., ed. 1979. *The Possible and the Actual*. Ithaca: Cornell University Press.

Ludlow, Peter, ed. 1997. *Readings in the Philosophy of Language*. Cambridge, Mass.: MIT Press.

———, and Stephen Neale. 1991. "Indefinite Descriptions: In Defense of Russell". *Linguistics and Philosophy* 14: 171–202. Reprinted in Ludlow 1997.

Ludwig, Kurt. 1992. "Brains in a Vat, Subjectivity, and the Causal Theory of Reference". *Journal of Philosophical Research* 17: 313–45.

Lycan, W. G. 1981. "Psychological Laws". *Philosophical Topics* 12: 9–38.

———. 1984. *Logical Form in Natural Language*. Cambridge, Mass.: Bradford Books/MIT Press.

———. 1985. "The Paradox of Naming" in *Analytical Philosophy in Comparative Perspective* ed. B. K. Matilal and J. L. Shaw. Dordrecht: D. Reidel: 81–102.

———. 1988. *Judgement and Justification*. Cambridge: Cambridge University Press.

——, ed. 1990. *Mind and Cognition*. Cambridge, Mass.: Blackwell.

——. 1994. *Modality and Meaning* Dordrecht: Kluwer Academic Publishers.

Lyons, John. 1981. *Language and Linguistics: An Introduction*. Cambridge: Cambridge University Press.

McCormack, W. C., and S. A. Wurm, eds. 1977. *Language and Thought: Anthropological Issues*. The Hague: Mouton.

McDonald, G., and P. Pettit. 1981. *Semantics and Social Science*. London: Routledge & Kegan Paul.

McDowell, John. 1977. "On the Sense and Reference of Proper Names". *Mind* 86: 159–85. Reprinted in Platts 1980.

——. 1978. "Physicalism and Primitive Denotation: Field on Tarski". *Erkenntnis* 13: 131–52. Reprinted in Platts 1980.

McGinn, Colin. 1977. "Charity, Interpretation and Belief". *Journal of Philosophy* 74: 521–35.

——. 1982. "The Structure of Content". In Woodfield 1982: 207–58.

——. 1984. *Wittgenstein on Meaning*. Oxford: Blackwell.

McGuinness, Brian, and Gianluigi, Oliveri, eds. 1994. *The Philosophy of Michael Dummett*. Dordrecht: Kluwer.

McKay, Thomas. 1984. "Critical Study" of Devitt 1981a. *Nous* 18: 357–67.

——. 1994. "Names, Causal Chains, and De Re Beliefs". In Tomberlin 1994.

McKinsey, Michael. 1976. "Divided Reference in Causal Theories of Names". *Philosophical Studies* 30: 235–42.

——. 1978. "Names and Intentionality". *Philosophical Review* 87: 171–200.

McLaughlin, Brian, ed. 1991. *Dretske and His Critics*. Oxford: Blackwell.

Martinich, A. P. ed. 1996. *The Philosophy of Language*. New York: Oxford University Press.

Matthews, Robert J. 1991. "The Psychological Reality of Grammars". In Kasher 1991: 182–99.

Mellor, D. H. 1977. "Natural Kinds". *British Journal for the Philosophy of Science* 28: 299–312.

Mill, J. S. 1961. *A System of Logic*. London: Longmans, 8th ed., rev. First ed., 1867.

Miller, Richard B. 1991. "Reply of a Mad Dog". *Analysis* 51: 50–4.

——. 1992. "A Purely Causal Solution to One of the Qua Problems". *Australasian Journal of Philosophy* 70: 425–34.

Millikan, R. G. 1984. *Language, Thought, and Other Biological Categories: New Foundations for Realism*. Cambridge: The MIT Press.

——. 1990. "Seismograph Readings for Explaining Behavior". *Philosophy and Phenomenological Research* 50: 807–812.

——. 1991. "Speaking Up for Darwin", in Loewer and Rey 1991: 151–64.

——. 1993. *White Queen Psychology and Other Essays for Alice*. Cambridge: MIT Press.

Montague, R. E. 1974. *Formal Philosophy: Selected Papers of R. E. Montague*, ed. R. H. Thomason. New Haven: Yale University Press.

Musgrove, Alan. 1997. "The T-Schema Plus Epistemic Truth Equals Idealism". *Australasian Journal of Philosophy* 75: 490–7.

Nagel, Ernst. 1961. *The Structure of Science*. London: Routledge & Kegan Paul.

Nagel, Thomas. 1969. "Linguistics and Epistemology". In Hook 1969: 171–82. Reprinted in Harman 1974.

Neale, Stephen. 1989. "Paul Grice and the Philosophy of Language". *Linguistics and Philosophy* 15: 509–59
———. 1990. *Descriptions*. Cambridge, Mass.: MIT Press.
Neander, Karen. 1995. "Misrepresenting and Malfunctioning". *Philosophical Studies* 79: 109–41.
Newson, Mark and V. J. Cook. 1996. *Chomsky's Universal Grammar*. Oxford: Blackwell.
Newton-Smith, W. H. 1981. *The Rationality of Science*. London: Routledge and Kegan Paul.
Noble, William, and Iain Davidson. 1996. *Human Evolution, Language and Mind: a Psychological and Archaeological Inquiry*. Cambridge: Cambridge University Press.
Norris, Christopher. 1982. *Deconstruction: Theory and Practice*. London: Methuen.
Ostertag, Gary, ed. 1998. *Definite Descriptions*. Cambridge, Mass.: MIT Press.
Oyama, S. 1999. *The Ontogeny of Information*. 2nd ed. Durham, NC: Duke University Press. First ed. 1985.
Papineau, David. 1979. *Theory and Meaning*. Oxford: Clarendon Press.
———. 1984. "Representation and Explanation". *Philosophy of Science*. 51: 550–72.
———. 1987. *Reality and Representation*. Oxford: Blackwell.
Passmore, John. 1968. *A Hundred Years of Philosophy*. London: Penguin Books, 2nd ed. First ed. 1957.
Pears, David. 1971. *Wittgenstein*. Fontana Modern Masters.
Perry, John. 1977. "Frege on Demonstratives". *Philosophical Review* 86: 474–97. Reprinted in Yourgau 1990, Davis 1991, and Ludlow 1997.
Pessin, A., and S. Goldberg, eds. 1996. *The Twin Earth Chronicles: Twenty Years of Reflection on Hilary Putnam's "The Meaning of 'Meaning' "*. New York: M. E. Sharpe.
Pettit, Philip. 1977. *The Concept of Structuralism*. Berkeley: University of California Press.
Pettit, Philip and John McDowell, eds. 1986. *Subject, Thought and Context*. Oxford: Oxford University Press.
Piattelli-Palmarini, M., ed. 1980. *Language and Learning: The Debate between Jean Piaget and Noam Chomsky*. Cambridge, Mass.: Harvard University Press.
Pietroski, Paul. 1992. "Intentionality and Teleological Error". *Pacific Philosophical Quarterly* 73(3): 267–82.
Pinker, S. 1994. *The Language Instinct: How the Mind Creates Language*. New York: William Morrow and Co.
Plantinga, Alvin. 1974. *The Nature of Necessity*. Oxford: Oxford University Press.
Platts, Mark. 1997. *The Ways of Meaning*. 2nd ed. Cambridge, Mass.: MIT Press.
———, ed. 1980. *Reference, Truth and Reality: Essays on the Philosophy of Language*. London: Routledge & Kegan Paul.
Popper, Karl. 1959. *The Logic of Scientific Discovery*. London: Hutchinson. First German ed., 1934.
Putnam, Hilary. 1967. "The 'Innateness Hypothesis' and Explanatory Models in Linguistics". *Synthese* 17: 12–22. Reprinted in Searle 1971, in Stich 1975, and in Block 1981: 292–9. (Page reference is to Block.)
———. 1973. "Meaning and Reference". *Journal of Philosophy* 70; 699–711. Re-

printed in Schwartz 1977.
——. 1975. *Mind, Language and Reality: Philosophical Papers, vol. 2.* Cambridge: Cambridge University Press.
——. 1981. *Reason, Truth and History.* Cambridge: Cambridge University Press.
Pylyshyn, Z. 1973. "What the Mind's Eye Tells the Mind's Brain: A Critique of Mental Imagery". *Psychological Bulletin* 80, 1973: 1–24.
——. 1980. "Computation and Cognition: Issues in the Foundations of Cognitive Science". *Behavioral and Brain Sciences* 3: 111–69 (includes peer commentaries and response by author).
——. 1984. *Computation and Cognition.* Cambridge, Mass.: Bradford Books/ MIT Press.
Quine, W. V. O. 1940. *Mathematical Logic.* New York: W. W. Norton.
——. 1960, *Word and Object.* Cambridge, Mass.: MIT Press.
——. 1961. *From a Logical Point of View.* Cambridge, Mass.: Harvard University Press, 2nd ed., rev. First ed., 1953.
——. 1966. *The Ways of Paradox and Other Essays.* New York: Random House.
——. 1969. *Ontological Relativity and Other Essays.* New York: Columbia University Press.
——. 1970. *Philosophy of Logic.* Engelwood Cliffs, NJ: Prentice-Hall.
——. 1975. "The Nature of Natural Knowledge". In Guttenplan 1975: 67–81.
Radford, Andrew. 1988. *Transformational Grammar: A First Course.* Cambridge: Cambridge University Press.
Recanati, Francois. 1993. *Direct Reference: From Language to Thought.* Oxford: Blackwell Publishers.
Reimer, Marga. 1991, "Do Demonstratives Have Semantic Significance". *Analysis* 51: 177–83.
——. 1992. "Incomplete Descriptions". *Erkenntnis* 37: 347–63.
Rey, Georges. 1997. *Contemporary Philosophy of Mind.* Oxford: Blackwell.
Rice, Martin. 1989. "Why Devitt Can't Name His Cat". *Southern Journal of Philosophy* 27: 273–83.
Roitblat, Herbert and Jean-Accady Meyer, eds. 1995. *Comparative Approaches to Cognitive Science.* Cambridge, Mass.: MIT Press.
Romanos, G. D. 1983. *Quine and Analytic Philosophy: The Language of Language.* Cambridge, Mass.: Bradford Books/MIT Press.
Rorty, R., ed. 1967. *The Linguistic Turn.* Chicago: Chicago University Press.
Rosch, Eleanor. 1977. "Linguistic Relativity". In P. N. Johnson-Laird and P. C. Wason (eds.), *Thinking: Readings in Cognitive Science.* Cambridge: Cambridge University Press: 501–19.
Rosenthal, David, ed. 1991. *The Nature of Mind.* Oxford: Oxford University Press.
Russell, Bertrand. 1919. *Introduction to Mathematical Philosophy.* London: George Allen and Unwin.
——. 1956. *Logic and Knowledge,* ed. R. C. Marsh. London: George Allen and Unwin.
——. 1957. *Mysticism and Logic.* New York: Doubleday Anchor. First published 1917.
——. 1967. *The Problems of Philosophy.* London: Oxford Paperbacks, 1967. First published 1912.
Ryle, Gilbert. 1949. *The Concept of Mind.* London: Hutchinson.

Salmon, Nathan U. 1981. *Reference and Essence*. Princeton: Princeton University Press.
——. 1982. "Assertion and Incomplete Descriptions". *Philosophical Studies* 42: 37–45.
——. 1986. *Frege's Puzzle*. Cambridge, Mass.: MIT Press.
Sankey, Howard. 1994. *The Incommensurability Thesis*. Brookfield: Avebury.
Sapir, Edward. 1931. "Conceptual Categories in Primitive Languages". *Science* 74: 578. Reprinted in D. Hymes (ed.), *Language in Culture and Society: a Reader in Linguistics and Anthropology*, New York: Harper & Row, 1964: 128. (Page references are to Hymes.)
——. 1949. *Selected Writings in Language, Culture and Personality*, ed. David G. Mandelbaum. Berkeley: University of California Press.
Sarup, M. 1993. *An Introduction to Poststructrualism and Postmodernism*. 2nd ed. Athens: University of Georgia Press.
Saussure, Ferdinand de. 1966. *Course in General Linguistics*, eds. Charles Bally and Albert Sechehaye, tr. Wade Baskin. New York: McGraw-Hill. First French ed. 1916.
Savage-Rumbaugh, S. 1986. *Ape language: From Conditioned Response to Symbol*. New York: Columbia University Press.
—— and Roger Lewin. 1994. *Kanzi: The Ape at the Brink of the Human Mind*. New York: John Wiley and Sons.
Scheffler, I. 1967. *Science and Subjectivity*. New York: Bobbs Merrill.
Schiffer, Stephen. 1972. *Meaning*. Oxford: Clarendon Press.
——. 1978. "The Basis of Reference". *Erkenntnis* 13: 171–206.
——. 1981. "Truth and the Theory of Content". In Herman Parrett and Jacques Bouveresse (eds.), *Meaning and Understanding*. Berlin: Walter de Gruyter.
Schlick, Moritz. 1932–3. "Positivism and Realism". In Ayer 1959: 82–107. Reprinted in Boyd, Gasper and Trout 1991. First publ. in German in *Erkenntnis* 3.
Schwartz, Robert. 1969. "On Knowing a Grammar". In Hook 1969: 183–90.
Schwartz, Stephen P., ed. 1977. *Naming, Necessity, and Natural Kinds*. Ithaca: Cornell University Press.
——. 1978. "Putnam on Artifacts". *Philosophical Review* 87: 566–74.
——. 1980. "Natural Kinds and Nominal Kinds". *Mind* 89: 182–95.
Searle, J. R. 1958. "Proper Names". *Mind* 67: 166–73. Reprinted in Martinich 1996 and Ludlow 1997.
——. 1969. *Speech Acts: An Essay in the Philosophy of Language*. Cambridge: Cambridge University Press.
——, ed. 1971. *The Philosophy of Language*. London: Oxford University Press.
——. 1972. "Chomsky's Revolution in Linguistics". *New York Review of Books*. Reprinted in Harman 1974: 2–33.
——. 1977. "Reiterating the Differences: A Reply to Derrida". *Glyph* 1: 198–209.
——. 1983a. *Intentionality: An Essay in the Philosophy of Mind*. Cambridge: Cambridge University Press.
——. 1983b. "The Word Turned Upside Down". *New York Review of Books* 30: 74–9.
——, and L. H. Mackey. 1984. "An Exchange on Deconstruction". *New York Review of Books* 31: 47–8.

Skinner, B. F. 1957. *Verbal Behavior*. New York: Appleton-Century-Crofts.

Smart, J. J. C. 1984. *Ethics, Persuasion and Truth*. London: Routledge & Kegan Paul.

Smolensky, Paul. 1988a. "On the Proper Treatment of Connectionism". *Behavioral and Brain Sciences* 11: 1–23.

———. 1988b. "Putting Together Connectionism – Again". *Behavioral and Brain Sciences* 11: 59–74.

Soames, Scott. 1984a. "Linguistics and Psychology". *Linguistics and Philosophy* 7: 155–79.

———. 1984b. "What is a Theory of Truth?". *Journal of Philosophy* 81: 411–29.

———. 1985. "Semantics and Psychology". In Katz 1985: 204–26.

———. 1986. "Incomplete Definite Descriptions". *Notre Dame Journal of Formal Logic* 27: 349–75. Reprinted in Ostertag 1998.

———. 1998a. "Skepticism about Meaning: Indeterminacy, Normativity, and the Rule-Following Paradox". In Ali Kazmi (ed.), *Meaning and Reference: Supplementary Volume 23 of the Canadian Journal of Philosophy*: 211–49.

———. 1998b. "Facts, Truth Conditions, and the Skeptical Solution to the Rule-Following Paradox". In James E. Tomberlin (ed.), *Philosophical Perspectives 12: Language, Mind, and Ontology, 1998*: Oxford: Blackwell: 313–48.

Sosa, Ernest. 1993. "Putnam's Pragmatic Realism". *Journal of Philosophy* 90: 605–26.

Sperber, D. 1996. *Explaining Culture: A Naturalistic Approach*. Oxford: Blackwell.

Stabler, Edward, Jr. 1983. "How Are Grammars Represented?" *Behavioral and Brain Sciences* 6: 391–402.

Stalker, Ralf. 1993. *Reflecting Davidson*. Berlin: Walter de Gruyter.

Stampe, Dennis. 1979. "Toward a Causal Theory of Linguistic Representation". In *Contemporary Perspectives in the Philosophy of Language*, eds. Peter A. French, Theodore E. Uehling Jr., and Howard K. Wettstein. Minneapolis: University of Minnesota Press: 81–102.

Steinitz, Yuval. 1994. "Brains in a Vat: Different Perspectives". *Philosophical Quarterly* 44: 213–22.

Sterelny, Kim. 1983. "Natural Kind Terms". *Pacific Philosophical Quarterly* 64: 110–25. Reprinted in Pessin and Goldberg 1996.

———. 1990. *The Representational Theory of Mind: An Introduction*. Oxford: Blackwell.

———. 1993. "Refuting Eliminitavism on the Cheap?" *Mind and Language* 8: 306–15.

Stich, Stephen P. 1971. "What Every Speaker Knows". *Philosophical Review* 80: 476–96.

———. 1972. "Grammar, Psychology, and Indeterminacy". *Journal of Philosophy* 69: 799–818. Reprinted in Block 1981 and Katz 1985.

———, ed. 1975. *Innate Ideas*. Berkeley: University of California Press.

———. 1978a. "Empiricism, Innateness, and Linguistic Universals". *Philosophical Studies* 33: 273–86.

———. 1978b. "Beliefs and Subdoxastic States". *Philosophy of Science* 45: 499–518.

———. 1978c. "Autonomous Psychology and the Belief–Desire Thesis". *Monist* 61: 573–91. Reprinted in Lycan 1990.

———. 1982. "On the Ascription of Content". In Woodfield 1982: 153–206.

——. 1983. *From Folk Psychology to Cognitive Science.* Cambridge, Mass.: Bradford/MIT Press.

——. 1985. "Could Man be an Irrational Animal? Some Notes on the Epistemology of Rationality". In Kornblith 1994: 337–57.

——. 1990. *Fragmentation of Reason.* Cambridge, Mass.: MIT Press.

—— and Ted Warfield. 1994. *Mental Representation: A Reader.* Oxford: Blackwell.

Strawson, P. F. 1950. "On Referring". *Mind* 59: 320–44. Reprinted in Martinich 1996, Ludlow 1997 and Ostertag 1998.

——. 1959. *Individuals: An Essay in Descriptive Metaphysics.* London: Methuen.

——. 1966. *The Bounds of Sense: An Essay on Kant's Critique of Pure Reason.* London: Methuen and Co.

Stove, D. C. 1991. *The Plato Cult and Other Philosophical Follies.* Oxford: Blackwell.

Sturrock, J. 1979. *Structuralism and Since.* Oxford: Oxford University Press.

Suppe, Fred (ed.). 1977. *The Structure of Scientific Theories*, 2nd ed. Urbana: University of Illinois. First ed. 1973.

Tarski, Alfred. 1944. "The Semantic Conception of Truth and the Foundations of Semantics". *Philosophy and Phenomenological Research* 4: 341–375. Reprinted in Martinich 1996 and Geirsson and Losonsky 1996.

——. 1956. *Logic, Semantics, Metamathematics.* Tr. by J. H. Woodger. Oxford: Clarendon Press.

Thibault, Paul J. 1997. *Re-Reading Saussure: The Dynamics of Signs in Social Life.* London: Routledge.

Tomberlin, James E., ed. 1994. *Philosophical Perspectives, 8: Logic and Language.* Atascadero: Ridgeview.

Unger, Peter. 1983. "The Causal Theory of Reference". *Philosophical Studies* 43: 1–45.

Warnock, G. J. 1958. *English Philosophy Since 1900.* London: Oxford University Press.

Webelhuth, Gert, ed. 1995. *Government and Binding Theory and the Minimalist Program.* Oxford: Blackwell.

Weber, Max. 1949. *The Methodology of the Social Sciences*, tr. and eds. E. A. Shils and H. A. Finch. Chicago: Free Press.

Wettstein, Howard. 1982. "Demonstrative Reference and Definite Descriptions". *Philosophical Studies* 40: 241–57. Reprinted in Ostertag 1998.

——. 1986. "Has Semantics Rested on a Mistake?". *Journal of Philosophy* 83: 185–209.

Whorf, Benjamin Lee. 1956. *Language, Thought, and Reality*, ed. and intro. John B. Carroll. Cambridge, Mass.: MIT Press.

Wilson, George. 1978. "On Definite and Indefinite Descriptions". *Philosophical Review* 86: 48–76.

——. 1984. "Pronouns and Pronominal Descriptions: A New Semantical Category". *Philosophical Studies* 45: 1–30.

——. 1991. "Reference and Pronominal Descriptions". *Journal of Philosophy* 88: 359–87.

——. 1994. "Kripke on Wittgenstein and Normativity". *Midwest Studies in Philosophy, Volume XIX: Philosophical Naturalism*, eds. Peter A. French, Theodore E. Uehling Jr., and Howard K. Wettstein. Notre Dame: University of Notre Dame Press: 366–90.

Wilson, N. L. 1959. "Substances without Substrata". *Review of Metaphysics* 12: 521–39.

Wittgenstein, Ludwig. 1953. *Philosophical Investigations*. Tr. by G. E. M. Anscombe. Oxford: Blackwell.

Wood, David. 1992. *Derrida: A Critical Reader*. Oxford: Blackwell.

Woodfield, A., ed. 1982. *Thought and Object*. Oxford: Clarendon Press.

Wright, Crispin. 1984. "Kripke's Account of the Argument against Private Language". *Journal of Philosophy* 81: 759–77.

——. 1988. "Realism, Antirealism, Irrealism, Quasi-Realism". *Philosophical Quarterly* 31: 47–67.

——. 1993. *Realism, Meaning and Truth*, 2nd edn. Oxford: Blackwell. First ed. 1986.

Yourgau, Palle, ed. 1990. *Demonstratives*. Oxford: Oxford University Press.

Zalabardo, Jose L. 1997. "Kripke's Normativity Argument". *Canadian Journal of Philosophy* 27: 467–88.

Zemach, Eddy. 1976. "Putnam's Theory on the Reference of Substance Terms". *Journal of Philosophy* 73: 116–27.

Index